THE UNITED NATIONS SECURITY COUNCIL AND THE AUTHORISATION OF FORCE

This book examines the United Nations Security Council's authorisation of the use of force, considering the extensive body of UN Security Council resolutions across its now eighty years of existence.

As one of the established exceptions to the Article 2(4) UN Charter prohibition on the use of force, UN Security Council authorisation of force remains a key focus for both States and scholars alike. Despite the apparent consequences of authorisation, authorising resolutions lack prescribed formats or mandatory content. The UN Security Council has over time, however, developed a consistent practice of prior explicit authorisation.

The development of this practice is reflected in a number of essential characteristics within authorising resolutions of the UN Security Council. These include explicit determinations of a threat to international peace and security, the invocation of Chapter VII (or VIII) of the UN Charter, the use of specific authorising language, the inclusion of time or functional limits on authorisation, and the imposition of reporting obligations on those authorised to use force. The book ultimately argues that prior explicit authorisation constitutes a well-established practice, rejecting the legality and admissibility of implicit and retroactive authorisation.

Volume 99 in the series Studies in International Law

Studies in International Law

Recent titles in this series

State Responsibility for Non-State Actors: Past, Present and Prospects for the Future
Richard Mackenzie-Gray Scott

International Agreements between Non-State Actors as a Source of International Law
Melissa Loja

Judicial Decisions in International Law Argumentation: Between Entrapment and Creativity
Letizia Lo Giacco

South-South Migrations and the Law from Below: Case Studies on China and Nigeria
Oreva Olakpe

Territorial Status in International Law
Jure Vidmar

Marine Bioprospecting, Biodiversity and Novel Uses of Ocean Resources: New Approaches in International Law
Edited by Niels Krabbe and David Langlet

The Standard of Review Before the International Court of Justice: Between Principle and Pragmatism
Felix Fouchard

Global Lawmaking and Social Change: The Varieties of Customary International Law
Gregor Novak

The Effectiveness of the Inter-American Court of Human Rights: The Case of Indigenous Territorial Rights
Gabriela CB Navarro

Individuals in International Humanitarian Law: A Historical Analysis
Sarina Landefeld

The Pathology of Plenty: Natural Resources in International Law
Lys Kulamadayil

The United Nations Security Council and the Authorisation of Force: Form, Character and Nature
Marko Svicevic

For a complete list of titles in this series
see www.bloomsbury.com/uk/series/studies-in-international-law/

The United Nations Security Council and the Authorisation of Force

Form, Character and Nature

Marko Svicevic

•HART•

OXFORD • LONDON • NEW YORK • NEW DELHI • SYDNEY

HART PUBLISHING
Bloomsbury Publishing Plc
Kemp House, Chawley Park, Cumnor Hill, Oxford, OX2 9PH, UK
1385 Broadway, New York, NY 10018, USA
Bloomsbury Publishing Ireland Limited, 29 Earlsfort Terrace, Dublin 2, D02 AY28, Ireland

HART PUBLISHING, the Hart/Stag logo, BLOOMSBURY and the Diana logo are trademarks of Bloomsbury Publishing Plc

First published in Great Britain 2025

A catalogue record for this book is available from the British Library.

A catalogue record for this book is available from the Library of Congress

Library of Congress Control Number: 2025936846

ISBN: HB: 978-1-50997-125-1
ePDF: 978-1-50997-127-5
ePub: 978-1-50997-126-8

Typeset by Compuscript Ltd, Shannon
www.bloomsbury.com

For product safety related questions contact productsafety@bloomsbury.com

To find out more about our authors and books visit www.hartpublishing.co.uk. Here you will find extracts, author information, details of forthcoming events and the option to sign up for our newsletters.

Foreword

THE AUTHORISATION OF the use of force by the United Nations Security Council (UNSC) is arguably one of the most studied topics in the field of international law. Nevertheless, it remains a topic of considerable interest and controversy, as well as a source of innovative scholarship, as evidenced by Marko Svicevic's comprehensive analysis of the 'Form, Character and Nature' of UNSC authorisations.

As such authorisations represent a pivotal exception to the prohibition of the use or threat of force enshrined in Article 2(4) of the UN Charter, their consequences are of paramount significance. However, these consequences are frequently complicated by a lack of clarity regarding the existence, purpose and duration of the authorisation. In the case of the UNSC's initial exercise of its Chapter VII powers during the Korean War in 1950, the authorisation for Member States to use force was inferred from the wording and context of the relevant UNSC resolutions. Moreover, the question of whether the authorisation to use force was based on Article 42 or Article 51 of the UN Charter remains unresolved. Similar questions pertaining to the character, form and nature of authorisations have been raised anew in the wake of the resurgence of the authorisation model since the 1990s. This is despite the more structured approach followed by the UNSC when resorting to Chapter VII ever since the end of the Cold War.

For instance, authorising resolutions typically explicitly establish the existence of a threat to international peace and security, which represents the threshold requirement for exercising Chapter VII powers. In addition, they consistently invoke Chapter VII (and occasionally Chapter VIII) explicitly when resorting to coercive measures. Additionally, they tend to employ the phrase 'all necessary measures' or 'all means' when such measures include authorisations to use force. Furthermore, authorising resolutions frequently impose temporal and functional limitations, as well as obligations to report on the execution of the mandate to the UNSC.

Nevertheless, the UNSC has, on occasion, adopted resolutions that are shrouded in ambiguity and have consequently given rise to considerable debate. To illustrate, at the time of their adoption, there was considerable debate as to whether the resolutions pertaining to Liberia (1992–93), Sierra Leone (1997–98), Kosovo (1999) and Iraq (2003) authorised the use of force. In academic discourse (and on occasion in the state practice), arguments in favour of 'implied authorisation', 'implicit authorisation', 'presumed authorisation', 'retroactive authorisation' and even 'revived authorisation' have been put forth.

Concurrently, the UNSC's references to the right of self-defence either in combination with Chapter VII (eg UNSC Res. 678 (1990); UNSC Res. 1373 (2001)) or more recently without reference thereto (eg UNSC Res. 2249 (2015)), could be indicative of the UNSC's implicit endorsement of a collective security model that is based on the right to self-defence in article 51 of the UN Charter. This in turn raises the question whether any role remains for the UNSC in authorising and overseeing the use of force, once it has endorsed the invocation of the right to individual or collective self-defence – which by its very nature relies on the unilateral action of states. Similarly, the incorporation of the right to intervene militarily in member states within the security frameworks of regional organisations, such as the AU or ECOWAS, potentially indicates a further marginalisation of the UNSC as a gatekeeper with regard to authorisations on the use of force.

In his examination of these questions, Marko Svicevic draws upon a vast corpus of UNSC resolutions spanning nearly eight decades of UNSC practice. In doing so, his analysis provides a substantial body of empirical information, while also constituting an intriguing historical journey. The analysis reveals a surprising consistency in the UNSC's framing of the majority of its authorisations to use force, concluding that any such authorisation requires a prior and explicit UNSC resolution to this effect. Furthermore, it displays a tenacious support by states for the primacy of the UNSC in matters of the use of force, despite multiple setbacks and novel challenges brought about by an ever-changing geopolitical landscape.

Erika de Wet
Graz, December 2024

Acknowledgements

This book is a condensed version of my PhD thesis submitted to the University of Pretoria in 2020 under the supervision of Professor Erika de Wet. I am grateful to all those involved in both the PhD journey and the drafting of this book.

The research for this book benefited from various positions held across several institutions. I am grateful to the University of Pretoria, the Faculty of Law, the OR Tambo Library staff and the South African Research Chair in International Constitutional Law, where I undertook my doctoral studies. These studies were generously funded by the South African Research Chairs Initiative under the National Research Foundation. I am grateful to the University of Johannesburg's South African Research Chair in International Law (Grant No 85104) and to Professor Hennie Strydom, where this book's conceptualisation commenced.

I am particularly indebted to Dr Martin Faix and colleagues at the Centre for International Humanitarian and Operational Law at the Faculty of Law, Palacký University in Olomouc, where this book was completed. Research for this book was also supported by funding from the Junior Research Grant (JG_2023_043). I am also grateful to the helpful assistance of the library staff of the Milada Horáková library.

Along the way, numerous discussions with colleagues helped shape this book. I am thankful to Professor Martha Bradley, Dr Ben Murphy, Dr Petr Stejskal, Dr Patrick Butchard,Dr Antal Berkes and František Tóth.

I am profoundly grateful to Professor Erika de Wet, for her mentorship and supervision all these years.

Finally, I am grateful to the Hart Publishing team, to Sinead Moloney and to Sasha Jawed, for their dedication to see this book to fruition.

Contents

Table of UN Security Council Resolutions

1

Introduction

I. UN SECURITY COUNCIL AUTHORISATION OF FORCE: OF FORMS AND CONSEQUENCES

On 29 November 1990, the United Nations Security Council (UNSC) adopted its historic Resolution 678 (1990) in response to the Iraqi invasion of Kuwait. The UNSC's authorisation of force in Resolution 678 (1990) was explicit. It recalled previous resolutions which had determined the situation a 'breach of the peace' under Article 39 of the Charter of the United Nations (UN Charter) and invoked Chapter VII when it 'authorise[d]' Member States to 'use all necessary means' to implement its previous resolutions to 'restore international peace and security'. The UNSC's authorisation of force through delegated enforcement action, the legality thereof once hotly debated, had come of age.

Over a decade later, the UNSC adopted Resolution 1441 (2002). When the United States commenced *Operation Iraqi Freedom* alongside its allies the following year, Australia, the United Kingdom and the United States argued that the authorisation to use force under Resolution 678 (1990) had been *revived*. What followed were extensive debates both in favour of and against the need for prior explicit UNSC authorisation and the legality and permissibility of implicit authorisation. These debates were not new; nor were they entirely surprising. Neither the Charter of the United Nations nor the UNSC's Provisional Rules of Procedure dictate the form and character UNSC decisions should take when it authorises force. Additionally, the prolonged Cold War meant that UNSC practice in authorising force was almost non-existent.

The problem is neither unique to Resolution 1441 (2002) nor isolated to the precise form that authorising resolutions should take. A handful of other situations and corresponding resolutions have raised similar questions on whether force had been authorised: the enforcement of safe-havens and no-fly zones in Iraq in 1991, the situation in Liberia in 1992–93, the situation in Sierra Leone in 1997–98 and NATO's campaign in Yugoslavia in 1999.

Where form and character of authorising resolutions concerns, recurring questions persistently emerge: Is the explicit invocation of Chapter VII necessary for the UNSC to authorise force? Should an authorising resolution include a determination of a threat to international peace and security under Article 39? What language does the UNSC ordinarily use in operative paragraphs when authorising force? Beyond explicitly mentioning 'use of force' and 'all necessary means', is there practice of any additional phrasing the UNSC uses when it authorises force?[1]

Discussions concerning UNSC authorisation of force have not been limited to the mere form authorising resolutions take. The precise legal basis for the UNSC's authorisation model has been the topic of much debate. Occasionally, the relevance of Article 51 self-defence as a basis for UNSC authorisation has arisen. Similarly, UNSC resolutions authorising force to enforce embargoes have been met with arguments on the relevance of Article 41. These considerations have been and continue to be raised (and addressed) in both scholarship and practice.

Eight decades since it was first established, the UNSC is approaching its 3000th resolution. Of these, only a handful are regularly cited as UNSC practice for the authorisation of force.[2] Examining UNSC practice on a case-by-case basis, this book considers some 300 resolutions which can authoritatively be considered as authorising force. In so doing, the book examines three 'forms' of authorisation: prior explicit authorisation, implicit authorisation and retroactive authorisation. Considering both the practice of the UNSC and doctrinal debates, the book ultimately asserts that prior explicit authorisation is both required under the UN Charter and is arguably a well-established practice of the UNSC.

As will be shown in subsequent chapters, prior explicit authorisation entails explicit Article 39 determinations, explicit Chapter VII (or VIII) invocations, explicit authorising language in operative paragraphs, the imposition of time limits on authorisations and mandates and corresponding reporting obligations on those authorised to use force.

II. THE UN CHARTER SYSTEM OF COLLECTIVE SECURITY AND UN SECURITY COUNCIL AUTHORISATION OF FORCE

A. The Article 2(4) Prohibition and its Exceptions

Over the last century, rules governing the use of force have undergone monumental development. The establishment of the League of Nations and the signing of

[1] In 2008, *Security Council Report* published its landmark research report on *Security Council Action Under Chapter VII: Myths and Realities* wherein it tackled numerous questions pertaining to UNSC authorisation. Chief among these included whether a reference to Chapter VII was necessary to authorise Member States to use force. See Security Council Report, 'Security Council Actions under Chapter VII: Myths and Realities' (23 June 2008) (Security Council Report).

[2] Erika de Wet, 'Article 42' in Bruno Simma et al, *The Charter of the United Nations: A Commentary* (4th edn, vol II, Oxford University Press 2024) 1693–706; Olivier Corten, *The Law Against War: The Prohibition on the Use of Force in Contemporary International Law* (2nd edn, Hart Publishing 2021) 317–18; Christine Gray, *International Law and the Use of Force* (4th edn, Oxford University Press 2018) 341–61; Stuart Casey-Maslen, *Jus ad Bellum: The Law on Inter-State Use of Force* (Hart Publishing 2020) 83–87.

the Treaty of Versailles represent one of the first attempts at prohibiting force among States. These attempts were subsequently complimented by the 1928 Kellogg-Briand Pact; the first contemporary initiative at renouncing war as an instrument of national policy. Despite these attempts, they ultimately failed to prevent the outbreak of war.[3]

The position changed significantly with the adoption of the UN Charter in 1945 and the establishment of the UNSC. Considered one of the cornerstones of the Charter system of collective security, Article 2(4) provides that '[a]ll members shall refrain in their international relations from the threat or use of force against the territorial integrity or political independence of any state, or in any other manner inconsistent with the purposes of the United Nations'.[4]

In addition to prohibiting the use of force, the UN Charter also regulates resort to force. Two exceptions to the prohibition are explicit within the UN Charter. These include the right of individual or collective self-defence under Article 51 and cases where the use of force has been authorised by the UNSC.[5] Authorisation of force is provided for under Chapter VII, through which the UNSC may delegate enforcement action to Member States, and Chapter VIII, under which the UNSC may authorise regional enforcement action.[6] In so far as UNSC authorisation of force remains one of the UN Charter exceptions to the prohibition, it is worth recalling its precise nature and character.

B. UN Security Council Action under Chapter VII

UN Charter Article 24(1) confers upon the UNSC the primary responsibility of maintaining international peace and security.[7] In line with this primary responsibility, the UN Charter bestows upon the UNSC a broad range of powers under Chapters VI, VII, VIII and XIII. While the powers of the UNSC range in their nature, those under Chapter VII are most comprehensive.[8] These concern actions with respect to threats to peace, breaches of the peace and acts of

[3] Marc Weller, 'Introduction' in Marc Weller (ed), *The Oxford Handbook of the Use of Force in International Law* (Oxford University Press 2015) 8–11; Erika de Wet and Marko Svicevic, 'The Military Clauses in the Treaty of Versailles and the Birth of a Collective Security System' in *The Versailles Treaty: French and German Perspectives in International Law on the Occasion of the Centenary* (Pedone 2019) 153–55.

[4] Art 2(4), United Nations, Charter of the United Nations (adopted 26 June 1945, entered into force 24 October 1945) UNCIO XV, 335 (UN Charter); *Armed Activities on the Territory of the Congo (Democratic Republic of the Congo v Uganda)*, Judgment, ICJ Reports 2005, p 168, para 148.

[5] Arts 42, 51, UN Charter.

[6] Arts 42, 53(1) UN Charter.

[7] Art 24(1) UN Charter.

[8] On the UNSC's powers under Arts 41 and 42, see Erika de Wet, *The Chapter VII Powers of the United Nations Security Council* (Hart Publishing 2004) 217–50. See also Michael Wood and Eran Sthoeger, *The UN Security Council and International Law* (Cambridge University Press 2022) 59–69.

aggression, within which decisions taken by the UNSC bind all Member States.[9] The UNSC may, under Article 39, consider any situation and subsequently determine whether it constitutes a 'threat to the peace, breach of the peace, or act of aggression'.[10] In order to maintain or restore international peace and security, the UNSC may adopt coercive measures of a military or non-military nature. Article 41 outlines non-military measures the UNSC may take and includes the 'complete or partial interruption of economic relations and of rail, sea, air, postal, telegraphic, radio, and other means of communication, and the severance of diplomatic relations'.[11]

Should Article 41 measures prove insufficient, the UNSC may under Article 42 of the UN Charter authorise military measures.[12] Article 42 states:

> Should the Security Council consider measures provided for in article 41 would be inadequate or have proved to be inadequate, it may take such action by air, sea, or land forces as may be necessary to maintain or restore international peace and security, such action may include demonstrations, blockade, and other operations by air, sea, or land forces of members of the United Nations.

Although the UN Charter drafters initially envisaged that Member States would make available forces to the UNSC under Article 43 agreements, these agreements never materialised in practice.[13] This in itself did not prohibit the UNSC from taking action. Instead, the UNSC developed its now well accepted practice of delegated enforcement action whereby Member States and regional organisations are authorised to use force on its behalf.[14]

It is worth noting that the power of the UNSC to authorise measures under Articles 41 and 42 has been interpreted to be subject to an Article 39 determination.[15] A determination under Article 39 is therefore considered a threshold requirement before the UNSC may employ measures under Articles 41 and 42.[16] In order to cross this threshold, Article 39 specifically refers to the

[9] Art 25, UN Charter. In *Certain Expenses of the United Nations* (Art 17, para 2, of the Charter), Advisory Opinion of 20 July 1962: ICJ Reports 1962, p 151 (*Certain Expenses of the United Nations)* 163, the ICJ concluded that while the UNSC bears primary responsibility over matters of international peace and security, that responsibility is not exclusive.

[10] Art 39, UN Charter.

[11] Art 41, UN Charter.

[12] Art 42 UN Charter (read together with Arts 43–48 of the UN Charter); see also de Wet, 'Article 42' (n 2) 1696–97.

[13] Erika de Wet, 'Article 43' in Simma (n 2) 1716.

[14] See also Nigel D White, *The United Nations System: Towards International Justice* (Lynne Rienner Publishers 2002) 141–45; Thomas M Franck, *Recourse to Force: State Action Against Threats and Armed Attacks* (Cambridge University Press 2002) 24–26.

[15] Erika de Wet, 'Threat to Peace' *Max Planck Encyclopaedia of Public International Law* (online edn, Oxford University Press, last updated Jan 2022), <https://shorturl.at/M5Bjb> para 1; Michael Wood, 'Breach of Peace' *Max Planck Encyclopaedia of Public International Law* (online edn, Oxford University Press, last updated Apr. 2009), <https://shorturl.at/xIL1c> para 3.

[16] Erika de Wet, 'Article 39' in Simma et al (n 2) 1651–52; Terry D Gill and Kinga Tibori-Szabó, *The Use of Force and the International Legal System* (Cambridge University Press 2024) 76; Michael Wood, 'Towards New Circumstances in Which the Use of Force May Be Authorised?' in Niels

UNSC determining a 'threat to the peace', 'breach of the peace' or 'act of aggression'.[17] Acting under Article 39, the UNSC has rarely referred to breaches of the peace or an act of aggression; instead, it prefers to refer to the existence of a 'threat to the peace'.[18]

Since its formulation in the UN Charter, the UNSC has significantly expanded what constitutes a threat to the peace. It has developed the concept to include a broad range of situations, determining, for example, terrorism, the proliferation of nuclear weapons, the overthrow of democratically elected leaders and refugee crises to constitute a threat to the peace.[19] In essence, the UNSC has a wide margin to make such a determination and its authority to authorise force in maintaining or restoring international peace and security today seems undeniable.[20] The UNSC's observance of an Article 39 determination preceding coercive non-military and military enforcement action has been predominantly consistent.[21] In this regard, Chapter VII resolutions typically contain a clause in which the UNSC determines a situation to be a threat to the peace.[22]

Alternatively, Chapter VII resolutions often recall a previous UNSC resolution in which such a determination has been made.[23] When the UNSC authorises the use of force, these authorising resolutions also usually invoke Chapter VII or VIII of the UN Charter, either after the preamble to the resolution, or under a specific paragraph. In addition, they also contain specific language authorising the use of force, most commonly through the 'all necessary means [or] measures' phrasing.

As subsequent chapters will attempt to show, such practice is arguably both consistent and well-established.

C. UN Security Council Authorisation of Regional Enforcement Action

Apart from authorising the use of force by States, the UNSC may also utilise regional organisations to enforce military measures on its behalf.[24] Chapter VIII

Blokker and Nico Schrijver (eds), *The Security Council and the Use of Force: Theory and Reality – A Need for Change?* (Martinus Nijhoff Publishers 2005) 79.

[17] Art 39, UN Charter.

[18] De Wet, 'Article 39' (n 16) 1628; Wood and Sthoeger (n 8) 64–65; De Wet, 'Threat to Peace' (n 15) para 6.

[19] De Wet, 'Article 39' (n 16) 1630–32, 1640–42; see for example UNSC Res 1295 (2000); UNSC Res 1291 (2000); UNSC Res 1333 (2000); and UNSC Res 1474 (2003). See also Inger Österdahl, 'By All Means, Intervene! The Security Council and the Use of Force under Chapter VII of the UN Charter in Iraq (to protect the Kurds), in Bosnia, Somalia, Rwanda and Haiti' (1997) 66 *Nordic Journal of International Law* 246–47, 270–71.

[20] De Wet, 'Article 39' (n 16) 1625.

[21] De Wet, 'Article 39' (n 16) 1652–53.

[22] De Wet, 'Article 39' (n 16) 1653.

[23] De Wet, 'Article 39' (n 16) 1652.

[24] Art 53(1) UN Charter. The terms 'regional organisation' and 'regional arrangements or agencies' are used interchangeably.

of the UN Charter recognises regional arrangements and agencies and their participation in matters of international peace and security.[25] Article 52(1) read together with Article 53(1) raises two important questions. The first is that of the definition of enforcement action, and the second is that of the definition of regional organisations. The latter is not specifically defined, although a working definition of 'enforcement action' was given by the ICJ as being 'coercive' in nature.[26] The term 'action' is further regarded as 'action which is solely in the province of the Security Council', as is indicated by the title of Chapter VII – actions in response to threats to the peace, breaches of the peace and acts of aggression.[27] Therefore, enforcement action may be characterised as coercive military measures against a State.[28]

In addressing the definition of a regional organisation, Article 52(1) provides a starting point in making this determination, namely, that regional organisations have the task of ensuring the peaceful settlement of disputes in their regions.[29] To this end, organisations such as the African Union (AU) and its Regional Economic Communities (RECs), the European Union (EU) and the North Atlantic Treaty Organisation (NATO) may be considered as regional organisations for the purposes of Chapter VIII. Considering the divergent character of these organisations, one question which arises is whether UNSC authorised enforcement action would be taken under Article 42 (Chapter VII) or Article 53 (Chapter VIII). As will be seen in subsequent chapters, UNSC authorisation under Article 53 suggests enforcement action by an organisation either against its own Member States, or within its geographical area in which its Member States are situated. Consequently, the UNSC has consistently invoked Chapter VII when authorising enforcement action by a regional organisation taken against a non-Member State or an out-of-area deployment (such as NATO's intervention in both Yugoslavia and Libya), suggesting it is therefore based on Article 42.[30]

The development of regional organisations (particularly in Africa) as well as collective defence alliances (such as NATO), has led to significant debate on both the decentralisation of the use of force in international law as well as the very need for UNSC authorisation of force. Particularly, the increasing prominence of regional organisations taking responsibility over matters of international peace and security has placed significant strain on the UNSC's primacy in

[25] Arts 52(1), 52(2), 52(3) UN Charter.
[26] *Certain Expenses of the United Nations* (n 9) 164.
[27] *Certain Expenses of the United Nations* (n 9) 165.
[28] *Certain Expenses of the United Nations* (n 9) 164-65.
[29] Art 52(1) UN Charter; Erika de Wet, 'Regional Organisations and Arrangements: Authorisation, Ratification, or Independent Action' in Weller (n 3) 315; see also Suyash Paliwal, 'The Primacy of Regional Organisations in International Peacekeeping: The African Example' (2010) 51(1) *Virginia Journal of International Law* 192–93.
[30] See the conclusions reached in ch 4 at p 128–131; see however White, *The UN System* (n 14) 145.

this regard.[31] Consequently, the need for UNSC authorisation must also be examined against the ever-growing role these organisations play. In the African regional and sub-regional context, the examination is informed by both the increase in military operations by the African Union and its RECs as well as the development of these organisations' security frameworks in a manner which suggests they do not require prior explicit UNSC authorisation.[32] In the NATO context, this examination is informed by the fact that NATO has at least on one occasion taken military measures without explicit UNSC authorisation (Kosovo 1999).[33] In addition, the challenge posed to UNSC authorisation of force is rooted too in reliance on individual and collective self-defence (beyond NATO). As one of the well-established exceptions to the prohibition of force requiring no UNSC authorisation, questions arise whether reliance on self-defence is one way in which the need for UNSC authorisation is bypassed.[34] The situation is complicated further when considering instances in which the UNSC recognises and potentially acknowledges alterative legal basis for resort to force (such as self-defence) but without authorising force itself. These considerations are taken up fully in chapter eight.

D. The Legal Basis for UN Security Council Authorisation of Force

In addition to analysing the form and nature of UNSC resolutions authorising force, the basis on which they have at times been interpreted to authorise force must also be considered. Such an analysis is rooted in the fact that the UNSC usually only references a chapter of the UN Charter under which it is acting (usually Chapter VII). In turn, it does not reference (and has never referenced) a specific article of the UN Charter when authorising force.[35] This has occasionally drawn ambivalence when ascertaining whether a Chapter VII resolution authorising force has been based on Article 42 or Article 51 of the UN Charter. In principle, basing a resolution on either of these articles would allow for the use of force.

However, the scope and extent to which force may be used differ. A resolution based on Article 42 would authorise the use of force to a greater degree. This is because the UN Charter under Article 42 empowers the UNSC to authorise the use of force to 'restore international peace and security' under its regime of collective security. In contrast, Article 51 allows for the use of force based on individual or collective self-defence. Article 51, however, does not create this

[31] See for example De Wet, 'Regional Organisations and Arrangements' (n 29) 318–21; Paliwal (n 29) 190, 219–220.

[32] See ch 8 at p 198–207 concerning decentralised collective security.

[33] See ch 6 at p 162–164 and ch 7 at p 190–193 on the (in)admissibility of implicit and retroactive authorisation.

[34] See ch 8 at p 207–213 concerning self-defence and its invocation in UNSC resolutions.

[35] The exception to this practice remains the limited invocation of Art 41 non-military measures.

right in international law, but merely reflects its existence as an inherent right. Should the basis of an authorising resolution fall under Article 51, the use of force must adhere to the principles of necessity and proportionality. Moreover, such a basis for the use of force may only be invoked 'until the Security Council has taken the measures necessary to maintain international peace and security'.[36]

The ambivalence surrounding this issue was most prominently raised with the adoption of Resolution 83 (1950) on the Korean War and again with Resolution 678 (1990) on the Iraqi invasion of Kuwait.[37] In Resolution 83 (1950), for example, the UNSC referred to North Korea's actions as an 'armed attack' and 'recommend[ed]' Members States furnish 'assistance' to South Korea in order to 'repel the armed attack'. This language is indicative of the substantive right of self-defence under Article 51. However, the resolution also determined that the armed attack constituted a 'breach of the peace' – an Article 39 determination, followed by recommendations for Member States to use force to (also) 'restore international peace and security'.[38] The subsequent authorisation given to Member States was therefore interpreted by some as based on Article 42, and by others as based on Article 51.[39] For these reasons, the precise legal basis behind UNSC authorisation too needs consideration, an assessment primarily undertaken in chapter two.

III. ANALYTICAL FRAMEWORK OF THE STUDY

A. The Need for Prior and Explicit UN Security Council Authorisation

Since the beginning of the twenty-first century, the UNSC has adopted some 1400 resolutions on situations ranging from inter-state conflicts and terrorism to the non-proliferation of nuclear weapons and piracy. No less than 500 of these resolutions have been explicitly adopted under Chapter VII. While its earlier authorisations suggest no explicit format was required when force was authorised, its practice particularly from 1990 onward indicates a consistent trend towards explicit authorisation.[40] As indicated above, resolutions authorising force (authorising resolutions) have consistently followed a systematic approach: They contain an explicit Article 39 determination, invoke the phrase 'acting under Chapter VII' and contain authorising language in their operative paragraphs explicitly authorising force.[41] These paragraphs usually

[36] Art 51 UN Charter. For an in-depth analysis on the limits to self-defence and when such a right ceases to exist, see Terry Gill, 'When Does Self-Defence End?' in Weller (n 3) 737.

[37] See ch 2 at p 19–23 and 33–35.

[38] UNSC Res. 83 (1950) para 6.

[39] Nigel White, 'The Korean War – 1950–53' in Tom Ruys and Olivier Corten (eds), *The Use of Force in International Law: A Case-based Approach* (Oxford University Press 2018) 31–32.

[40] Security Council Report (n 1) 3.

[41] ibid 17. See the analysis in chs 2–5.

include instructive verbs ('decides', 'authorises' or 'calls upon') in combination with authorising language ('all necessary means' or 'all necessary measures').[42] Moreover, UNSC authorisation is usually given prior to the use of force in question and is therefore prospective in nature. As a result, it often includes a mandate, upon completion of which, terminates the enforcement action. Alternatively, the UNSC has stipulated temporal limitations to these mandates.

That having been said, the UNSC has also adopted several ambiguous resolutions with potentially far-reaching implications: arguments in favour of both implicit and retroactive authorisation. These situations most notably concerned Liberia, Sierra Leone and Kosovo. Consequently, they have generated considerable debate among academics both in support of and opposed to the legality of implicit and retroactive authorisation.[43]

B. Objectives of Study

Given the above, the book's central objective is to assess the nature and character of UNSC authorisation of force by considering the extensive practice of the UNSC. This examination is undertaken in two respects. The first part attempts to show that prior explicit UNSC authorisation of force is both a consistent and well-established practice. The examination is therefore focused on previous UNSC resolutions which have clearly authorised force. For feasibility, authorisations of force are considered and largely grouped according to the entity authorised. These include authorisation to Member States, regional organisations and regional peacekeeping initiatives, collective defence alliances (NATO) and UN peacekeeping missions. In so doing, the analysis takes into account the language and form of UNSC resolutions, the context surrounding their adoption and supplementary documents concerning these resolutions. In this way, the subsequent practice of the UNSC as an international organisation authorising the use of force may be established. Moreover, the analysis pays particular attention to the manner in which UNSC resolutions have been implemented by States and regional organisations. Therefore, it takes into account the subsequent practice of States when interpreting and implementing these resolutions.

Thereafter, subsequent chapters consider challenges to this well-established practice. These include either cases alleged to be examples of implicit and retroactive authorisation, or situations where UNSC authorisation is argued to be unnecessary. The latter consideration arises specifically with regard to the practice of regional organisations in the African context, as well as the reliance on individual and collective self-defence (and the UNSC's recognition therefore)

[42] Rarely has the term 'use of force' appeared in UNSC resolutions. See for example UNSC Res 221 (1966) and UNSC Res 836 (1993). See also De Wet, 'Article 42' (n 2) 1706–07; White, *The UN System* (n 14) 146.

[43] See chs 6 and 7 on the permissibility of such forms of authorisation.

suggesting no UNSC authorisation is required. In principle, the book argues both in favour of UNSC authorisation and that such authorisation should be prior and explicit.

In doing so, it outlines the following dominant characteristics of prior explicit authorising resolutions: Authorising resolutions: (a) Explicitly determine a situation a threat to international peace and security or recall such an explicit determination made in a previous resolution on the same situation; (b) invoke Chapter VII (or VIII) either in the preamble or operative paragraphs of a resolution; (c) use specific 'authorising language' in its operative paragraphs; (d) are adopted prior to the use of force in question; (e) usually identify an entity (States, States acting through regional organisations, regional organisations, UN peacekeeping missions) which has been authorised to use force; (f) usually impose specific time limits to mandates; (g) usually impose certain reporting obligations.

C. Methodology

The examinations undertaken herein take a desk-based, doctrinal approach. The research is therefore analytical in nature and consults the traditional sources of international law as stipulated in Article 38(1) of the Statute of the International Court of Justice.[44] Primary consideration is given to international treaties, such as the UN Charter, as well as the relevant security frameworks and founding instruments of the regional organisations in question. Decisions of the UNSC and international organisations are regarded as secondary (derived) treaty law, as they are taken by organisations in accordance with international treaties to which States have consented to.[45] The interpretation of treaties is conducted in accordance with the rules of interpretation laid down in Articles 31 and 32 of the Vienna Convention on the Law of Treaties (VCLT).[46] The principles under the VCLT further serve as a point of departure for the interpretation of UNSC decisions as well as decisions of other international organisations, although the interpretation of UNSC resolutions requires other factors to be considered.[47] Section IV below examines the interpretation of UNSC resolutions.

Further, a fundamental task the study concerns itself with is the identification of those UNSC resolutions that have previously authorised the use of force. This identification takes two forms. The first is determining those UNSC

[44] Art 38(1) Statute of the International Court of Justice (adopted 24 October 1945, entered into force San Francisco) 33 UNTS 993 (ICJ Statute).

[45] See s IV below on the interpretation of UNSC resolutions.

[46] Arts 31, 32 VCLT.

[47] *Accordance with International Law of the Unilateral Declaration of Independence in Respect of Kosovo, Advisory Opinion*, ICJ Reports 2010, p 403 (Kosovo Advisory Opinion), 442, para 94. See s IV on the interpretation of UNSC resolutions.

resolutions that have in the past explicitly authorised the use of force (within the parameters of what this book considers to be explicit authorisation). The second identification concerns those resolutions that States have previously invoked, or that is argued in literature, as constituting authorisation of force. These resolutions predominantly concern cases of implicit or retroactive authorisation. In identifying, collating and distinguishing between these resolutions, it was also necessary to undertake an examination of State reactions and implementation of resolutions. The result of this process collectively is the consolidation of some 300 resolutions which have been identified as authoritatively authorising the use of force.

Finally, it should be mentioned that while the parameters of what constitutes explicit authorisation seem strictly construed, the resolutions identified herein are nonetheless broadly considered, since there may be divergence in interpretation, and what the UNSC undertakes as authorisation in practice. To this end, in identifying and determining explicit authorising resolutions, the analysis directs attention to the resolutions in question, council debates preceding and following their adoption, supplementary documents and subsequent state practice in the implementation of these resolutions. These considerations are also informed by doctrinal debates. When all is said, it must be acknowledged that the criteria used to identify and categorise authorising resolutions cannot be concrete. Some resolutions have established authorisation, while others have extended this authorisation. On occasion, it remains debatable whether established authorisation was at all extended in subsequent resolutions.

IV. THE INTERPRETATION OF UN SECURITY COUNCIL RESOLUTIONS

Although taking broader sources of international law into account, including doctrinal debates, much of the analysis conducted within various chapters of this book engages in interpretation of UNSC resolutions. For this reason, it is important to underline certain aspects of interpretation as it pertains to UNSC resolutions.[48]

A. The Drafting and Content of UNSC Resolutions

The drafting of UNSC resolutions is a complex task, finely balancing consensus among the 15-member UNSC. The drafting process of these resolutions,

[48] UNSC resolutions are interpreted by a number of entities. The UNSC may interpret its own decisions and does so through subsequent resolutions, press statements and presidential statements. See for example UN Doc SC/10878-AFR/2502 interpreting UNSC Res 2985 (2013). In addition, UNSC resolutions are interpreted by UNSC Members, non-UNSC members, international courts and tribunals and international and regional organisations.

therefore, is pivotal in understanding how and upon what basis a final text of a resolution ultimately translates to UNSC authorisation of force. As Michael Wood has well pointed out, the drafting of UNSC resolutions is a complicated process involving haste, issues of translation and sometimes deliberate ambiguity.[49] There are no uniform rules for drafting UNSC resolutions, negotiation and drafting history are often not on public record and political pressure seeks to receive unanimity among UNSC members resulting in resolutions becoming deliberately ambiguous.[50]

Typically, UNSC resolutions are composed of two parts: a preamble and operative paragraphs. It is in the preamble to a resolution that the UNSC usually determines a situation to be a threat to peace and security. The preamble explains the motive behind a resolution and reflects previous decisions the UNSC has taken on a certain situation.[51] The interpretative weight of the preamble of a resolution was highlighted in the ICJ's *Namibia Advisory Opinion.* Interpreting Resolution 276 (1970), the ICJ found that the pronouncement by the UNSC in the resolution's preamble that it was 'mindful of its responsibility to take necessary action to secure strict compliance … [of] member states … under the provision of article 25 of the UN Charter' in effect meant that the UNSC was imposing binding obligations under that resolution.[52]

Once the UNSC has made an Article 39 determination, a resolution then states that the UNSC takes certain decisions 'acting under Chapter VII [or VIII] of the Charter of the United Nations'. The invocation of Chapter VII may refer to all the listed decisions, or it may be invoked under a specific decision. Decisions taken by the UNSC are given in a numbered list. Moreover, where force is authorised, such UNSC decisions usually contain explicit reference to, among others, the term 'by all necessary means [or] measures'.

[49] Michael Wood, 'The Interpretation of Security Council Resolutions, Revisited' (2017) 20(1) *Max Planck Yearbook of United Nations Law* 12–14; see also Michael Wood, 'The Interpretation of Security Council Resolutions' (1998) 2(1) *Max Planck Yearbook of United Nations Law* 80–82. See also Alexander Orakhelashvili, *Collective Security* (Oxford University Press 2011) 42.

[50] Wood 2017 (n 49) 13; Wood 1998 (n 49) 80–82; De Wet, *The Chapter VII Powers* (n 8) 108. As De Wet points out, UNSC debates are usually only a formality, since they merely confirm what Member States have already agreed upon in private. See also Orakhelashvili (n 49) 42. On the general nature of UNSC resolutions, see also Loraine Sievers and Sam Daws, *The Procedure of the UN Security Council* (4th edn, Oxford University Press 2014) 393–95.

[51] Johan Kaufmann, *United Nations Decision Making* (Sijthoff & Noordhoff 1980) 119. As with the UN Charter, the preamble to a resolution forms an integral part of the collective text, specifically highlighting the motives of the drafters of the resolution. See Rüdiger Wolfrum, 'Preamble' in Bruno Simma et al (eds), *The Charter of the United Nations: A Commentary, Volume 1* (3rd edn, Oxford University Press 2012) 105.

[52] *Legal Consequences for States of the Continued Presence of South Africa in Namibia (South West Africa) notwithstanding Security Council Resolution 276* (1970), Advisory Opinion, ICJ Reports 1971, 16 at 52–53, paras 110–16 (*ICJ Namibia Advisory Opinion*). See also Orakhelashvili (n 49) 43.

B. How should UNSC Resolutions be Interpreted?

While the VCLT provides a starting point in interpreting UNSC resolutions, other factors require attention. These include that UNSC resolutions are drafted very differently to that of treaties, the need to take into account the structure of resolutions and UNSC debates preceding and following the adoption of resolutions.[53]

This approach was adopted by the International Criminal Tribunal for Yugoslavia (ICTY) in its *Prosecutor v Dušco Tadić* Appeals Chamber case.[54] In interpreting the jurisdiction clause of the ICTY Statute, which was adopted under UNSC Resolution 827 (1993), the ICTY considered a literal and teleological interpretation in line with Article 31 of the VCLT.[55] Under Article 31, treaty provisions (in this context, the provisions of a resolution) are to be interpreted in good faith, with the ordinary meaning to be given to terms incorporated, within their context and in light of their object and purpose.[56] A special meaning may be given to a term only if it is established that the parties so intended. Although resolutions have no parties to them, such an interpretative provision seems logical when interpreting resolutions.[57]

The terms of the resolution are also of crucial importance as far as interpretation concerns. These include the resolution's preamble, annexes, as well as supplementary documents in connection with parties to a treaty or parties mentioned in a resolution. This is particularly important as UNSC resolutions are not independent or free-standing.[58] They often refer to other international legal documents, referencing treaty provisions, previous UNSC resolutions, and reports of the Secretary-General.[59] These resolutions may, for example, extend or extinguish certain mandates given to organs, by recalling previous resolutions.

Article 32 of the VCLT states that recourse may be had to supplementary means of interpretation including the preparatory work of a treaty and the circumstances of its conclusion.[60] In the context of UNSC resolutions, the drafting history of the resolution, the draft text of the resolution and UNSC debates

[53] *Kosovo Advisory Opinion* (n 47) para 94; Wood 1998 (n 49) 87. See also Efthymios Papastavridis, 'Interpretation of Security Council Resolutions under Chapter VII in the Aftermath of the Iraqi Crisis' (2007) 56(1) *International and Comparative Law Quarterly* 100–11.

[54] *Prosecutor v Dušco Tadić, Decision on the Defense Motion for Interlocutory Appeal on Jurisdiction*, IT-94-1 (2 October 1995) (*Tadić*).

[55] *Tadić* (n 54) paras 10–12, 14–15; De Wet, *The Chapter VII Powers* (n 8) 107.

[56] Art 31(1) VCLT; Wood 1998 (n 49) 89.

[57] Art 31(4) VCLT; Wood 1998 (n 49) 89.

[58] Wood 1998 (n 49) 87.

[59] Wood 1998 (n 49) 87.

[60] Art 32 VCLT.

preceding its adoption serve as critical points of consideration when interpreting the resolution and ascertaining the intentions of the UNSC.[61]

Although the VCLT is a convenient and necessary point of departure for interpretation of UNSC resolutions, regard must be given to the difference between treaty interpretation and the interpretation of UNSC resolutions. Given that treaties are concluded by the parties to it, they differ significantly in comparison to the interpretation of a resolution as a decision of an international organisation. As mentioned, the ICJ in the *Kosovo Advisory Opinion* highlighted that additional factors should be taken into account when interpreting UNSC resolutions.[62] Unlike treaty interpretation, UNSC resolutions are issued by a single, collective body and include a drafting process very different to that of the conclusion of treaties. The final text of a UNSC resolution, the product of a voting process under Article 27 of the UN Charter, represents the views of the UNSC as a body.[63]

Moreover, UNSC resolutions may have a binding effect on all States, irrespective of whether those states played any part in the drafting or conclusion of the resolution in question.[64] Owing to these differences, the interpretation of UNSC resolutions requires an analysis of 'statements by representatives of members of the Security Council made at the time of their adoption, other resolutions of the Security Council on the same issue, as well as the subsequent practice of relevant United Nations organs and of States affected by those given resolutions'.[65] With that said, it is clear that any interpretation of UNSC resolutions, although guided by Articles 31 to 33 of the VCLT, must therefore bear in mind differences between treaty drafting and resulting obligations to that of resolution drafting and adoption, as well as corresponding obligations imposed by the UNSC on Member States.[66]

Equally important in assessing the language, form and context of UNSC resolutions is analysing UNSC practice. The ICJ in its *Nuclear Weapons Advisory Opinion* recognised constitutions of international organisations (the UN Charter included) as particular types of treaties.[67] Specifically referring to Article 31(3)(b) of the VCLT, the ICJ reiterated that one particular means of interpretation concerns 'any subsequent practice' in the application of the treaty which establishes the agreement of the parties regarding its interpretation.[68] To this end, it has been suggested that the interpretation of

[61] Wood 1998 (n 49) 93–94.
[62] *Kosovo Advisory Opinion* (n 47) para 94.
[63] *Kosovo Advisory Opinion* (n 47) para 94.
[64] *Kosovo Advisory Opinion* (n 47) para 94.
[65] *Kosovo Advisory Opinion* (n 47) para 94.
[66] As indicated by Wood 2017 (n 49) 34–35.
[67] *Legality of the Use of Force by a State of Nuclear Weapons in Armed Conflict*, Advisory Opinion, 1996, ICJ Reports 66, para 19 (*Nuclear Weapons Advisory Opinion*); Niels Blokker, 'The Security Council and the Use of Force: On Recent Practice' in Blokker and Schrijver (n 16) 9–10.
[68] Art 31(3)(b) VCLT; *Kasikili/Sedudu Island (Botswana/Namibia), Judgment, I.C.J. Reports 1999*, p. 1045 para 48–50. See also Blokker (n 67) 11 who points out that 'as is clear from the example of

UNSC resolutions as a decision of an international organisation taken under the UN Charter requires ascertaining what has been agreed upon in such a decision. Therefore, effective interpretation requires consideration of the agreement reached by the UNSC as a collective body, rather than interpreting a resolution depending on its effectiveness to, for example, contribute to peace and security.[69]

Finally, it is worth mentioning that the importance of interpretation extends not only to whether a resolution has authorised force, but the extent to which force has been authorised. Resolution 83 (1950) is a classic example which has led to questions about whether force was authorised to end North Korea's armed attack or more broadly to 'restore international peace and security'. A more recent example includes that of Resolution 1973 (2011) which had authorised the subsequent NATO enforcement action in Libya for, among others, the protection of civilians against the Gaddafi regime. NATO's involvement in Libya, despite unambiguously authorised by the UNSC, raised questions as to whether Resolution 1973 (2011), authorising force to protect civilians, also authorised force for purposes of regime change as an element of civilian protection.[70] While some interpreted the resolution strictly, others argued that any interpretation in favour of regime change would be contrary to the principles of the *jus ad bellum*.[71] For these reasons, holistic account must be taken of UNSC practice when interpreting its resolutions.

V. CHAPTER OVERVIEW

This chapter has already laid down the parameters of this study – aiming to provide the framework for this research. The book hereafter is divided into three parts. Part I focuses on the UNSC's longstanding practice of prior explicit authorisation. Chapter two examines prior explicit authorisation to Member States, chapter three examines authorisation to regional organisations and regional peacekeeping initiatives, chapter four examines authorisation to NATO as a collective defence alliance and chapter five examines authorisation of UN peacekeeping missions. Part II then examines the nature and character of implicit and retroactive authorisation. Based on consistent, well-established

the practice of abstention by permanent members – that at a certain point practice will become "established" or "generally agreed" and therefore will gain normative relevance'.

[69] As suggested by Orakhelashvili (n 49) 41.

[70] See broadly Dire Tladi, 'Security Council, the Use of Force and Regime Change: Libya and Côte d'Ivoire' (2012) 37(1) *South African Yearbook of International Law* 1–24; Oliver Corten and Vaios Koutroulis, 'The Illegality of Military Support to Rebels in the Libyan War: Aspects of *Jus Contra Bellum* and *Jus in Bello*' (2013) 18(1) *Journal of Conflict and Security Law* 59–93; Gray (n 2) 378–79.

[71] Corten and Koutroulis (n 70) 64–65, 91. As Corten and Koutroulis warn, '[t] Libyan precedent may teach us that broad interpretations of a Security Council authorization are not to be advanced light-heartedly' in so far as regime change has been argued under Resolution 1973 (2011).

practice to the contrary, these chapters conclude against the legality of such forms of authorisation. Finally, Part III examines well-established practice of UNSC authorisation against the practice of international organisations and contemporary developments, most notably that of African regional and sub-regional organisations and the ever-increasing reliance on self-defence as a possible avenue to bypass the requirement of UNSC authorisation. Chapter nine concludes with some overall findings.

2

Explicit Authorisation to UN Member States

I. INTRODUCTION

ARTICLE 24(1) OF the United Nations Charter (UN Charter) entrusts the UN Security Council (UNSC) with primary responsibility over matters of international peace and security.[1] In so doing, the UNSC is given a broad range of powers under Chapters VI–XI. Most notable of these include the UNSC's power to authorise the use of force under Chapter VII to Member States and under Chapter VIII to regional organisations.[2]

The primary purpose of this part of the book is to examine the form and character of UNSC authorisation of force to Member States; outlining the routine approach consistently employed by the UNSC. Subsequent chapters pertaining to explicit authorisation examine authorisation to regional organisations, NATO as a collective defence alliance and UN peacekeeping missions.[3] The examination is based on an analysis of both the language and form authorising resolutions take, subsequent State practice following the adoption of the resolutions in question, as well as specific legal issues raised under certain resolutions. Thereafter, context, council debates, presidential statements and the subsequent practice of the UNSC, regional organisations and Member States is considered.

As has already been detailed in the introductory chapter, in authorising the use of force, the UNSC routinely employs a uniform regime. It adopts resolutions which determine a threat to the peace under Article 39, invoke Chapter VII (or Chapter VIII) of the UN Charter and contain one or several operative paragraphs explicitly authorising force.[4] Moreover, these explicit authorising resolutions are adopted prior to the enforcement action in question.

[1] Art 24(1), United Nations, Charter of the United Nations (adopted 26 June 1945, entered into force 24 October 1945) UNCIO XV, 335 (UN Charter).

[2] Arts 42, 53, UN Charter.

[3] See chs 3, 4 and 5.

[4] See ch 1 at p 10; Security Council Report, 'Security Council Action Under Chapter VII: Myths and Realities' (23 June 2008) (Security Council Report) 17.

II. EXPLICIT AUTHORISATION DURING THE COLD WAR ERA

Despite the hope ignited with the signing of the UN Charter and the establishment of the UNSC in 1945, the Cold War had emerged as a paralysing force. The UNSC was able to authorise the use of force only on two occasions. Early UNSC practice shows that authorisation of force was not subject to the explicit determination of a threat to international peace and security nor an explicit invocation of Chapter VII.[5] Consequently, the intention of the UNSC only became clear from the context and explicit wording used in its resolutions.[6] This practice was particularly evident with the UNSC's resolutions on the Korean War in 1950 and on the situation in Southern Rhodesia in 1966.

A. Resolutions 83 and 84 (1950) | The Korean War

On 25 June 1950 the Korean peninsula was drawn into war when North Korean forces crossed the north-south border (38th parallel), invading South Korea. The political climate of the Cold War at the time meant that the Communist North Korean regime received support from the Soviet Union and the People's Republic of China, while South Korea was principally supported by the United States. The invasion quickly resulted in the capture of Seoul on 28 June 1950. The UNSC's response came on the same day the invasion started, adopting Resolution 82 (1950). It declared the North Korean invasion constituted an 'armed attack' against South Korea and determined a breach of the peace.[7] On 27 June 1950, for the first time since its creation, the UNSC authorised the use of force under Resolution 83 (1950).[8] Several days later, the UNSC adopted Resolution 84 (1950), designating a unified command to the United States.[9] Given the unparalleled nature of the UNSC's actions within a highly divisive political climate, widespread scrutiny followed. In particular, the legality of the resolutions was challenged given they were adopted in the absence of the Soviet Union and that force was authorised against North Korea (a non-UN Member at the time).[10]

[5] Security Council Report (n 4) 3. The first UNSC resolution to determine a situation a threat to the peace was UNSC Res. 54 (1948) when it addressed the question of Palestine. The first UNSC resolution to have explicitly invoked Chapter VII was UNSC Res. 253 (1968) on the situation in Southern Rhodesia.

[6] Security Council Report (n 4) 3.

[7] UNSC Res 82 (1950).

[8] UNSC Res 83 (1950).

[9] UNSC Res 84 (1950).

[10] Had it not been for the Soviet Union's absence, it is doubtful whether the resolutions would have been adopted at all. See also Anthony Clark Arend and Robert J Beck, *International Law and the Use of Force: Beyond the UN Charter Paradigm* (Routledge 1993) 52–53; Radhika Withana, *Power, Politics, Law: International Law and State Behaviour During International Crises* (Martinus Nijhoff Publishers 2008) 97; Nigel White, 'The Korean War – 1950-53' in Tom Ruys and Olivier Corten (eds), *The Use of Force in International Law: A Case-Based Approach* (Oxford University Press 2018) 24.

Most notably for current purposes was the precise nature of the authorisation, how it was expressed in UNSC resolutions, and whether the legal basis rested with Article 42 or 51. In addition, the UNSC's delegation of the use of force to Member States (namely, to a unified command under the United States) brought about its own set of questions concerning the legality of such a decision.

i. The Wording and Form of the Authorisation

Resolutions 83 and 84 (1950) serve as the earliest examples of UNSC authorisation of force. The preamble to Resolution 83 (1950) explicitly contains an Article 39 determination, stating that the UNSC had 'determined that the armed attack upon the Republic of Korea by forces from North Korea constitutes a breach of the peace'.[11] Resolution 83 (1950) also recalled Resolution 82 (1950) in which the situation on the Korean peninsula was first determined a threat to the peace.[12] In authorising the use of force, Resolution 83 (1950) '*recommends*' that Member States provide assistance to South Korea to repel the attack.[13] Resolution 84 (1950) then explicitly recommended Member States provide assistance to South Korea as may be necessary to repel the armed attack and explicitly authorised a unified command designated to the United States.[14] Although containing an Article 39 determination and expressly authorising force, Chapter VII did not appear in the resolution. From context it seemed clear that the UNSC was relying on Chapter VII although not invoking it.[15]

ii. The Legal Basis of Resolutions 83 and 84 (1950): Between Article 42 and Article 51

When the UNSC authorises the use of force or acts broadly under Chapter VII, it does not ordinarily invoke a specific article of that chapter.[16] Consequently, not only has this given rise to ambivalence in determining the legal basis of UNSC resolutions, but it has also generated competing arguments favouring military action as being based either on Article 42 or 51 of the UN Charter. This is true not only for the resolutions adopted on the Korean War, but also on those resolutions adopted following the Iraqi invasion of Kuwait. In principle, both articles represent established exceptions to the Article 2(4) prohibition of force. The scope and extent to which force may be used however differs. A resolution

[11] UNSC Res 83 (1950) preamble para 1; UNSC Res 84 (1950) preamble para 1.

[12] UNSC Res 82 (1950), preamble para 4.

[13] UNSC Res 83 (1950) preamble para 6.

[14] UNSC Res 84 (1950) paras 3, 5, 6.

[15] Security Council Report (n 4) 3.

[16] The exception remains the UNSC's occasional invocation of Art 41 in more recent times, and the albeit exceptional invocation of Arts 39 and 40. See for example UNSC Res 54 (1948); UNSC Res 62 (1948); UNSC Res 598 (1987) and UNSC Res 660 (1990). The UNSC has on several occasions also invoked Art 51.

based on Article 42 would arguably authorise the use of force to a greater extent than a resolution based on Article 51.

After all, Article 42 permits the UNSC to authorise the use of force in the broader context of restoring international peace and security. On the contrary, force used in the exercise of individual or collective self-defence under Article 51 must adhere to the principles of necessity and proportionality and remains a response to the limited concept of an armed attack.[17] Moreover, self-defence may only be exercised 'until the Security Council has taken the measures necessary to maintain international peace and security'.[18] Article 51 as a basis for the use of force is therefore more restrictive than Article 42.[19]

The wording used in Resolutions 83 and 84 (1950) suggests a basis under Article 51 of the UN Charter. Both resolutions refer to 'assistance' to South Korea 'as may be necessary to repel the armed attack'. The use of these terms suggests that the UNSC had authorised the use of force not under Article 42, but specifically to repel the armed attack in line with Article 51.[20] Whether the UNSC was in fact authorising force or simply encouraging States to act in collective self-defence remains speculative.[21]

The United States, which led the military operation against North Korea, seemed flexible when implementing the resolutions. Initially, it based its actions on Article 51. This position was supported by statements made by then Secretary of State Dean Acheson, who on one occasion stated that United States military assistance was 'solely for the purpose of restoring the Republic of Korea to its status prior to the invasion from the North'.[22] In fact, a legal justification based on self-defence for an attack against the invasion of South Korea had already been tabled by the United States State Department policy planning staff several days prior to the adoption of Resolution 83 (1950). The State Department identified two legal justifications for the use of force in South Korea:

> The question debated … was whether the US should justify its intervention in the conflict solely on Article 51 of the UN Charter or seek to obtain the approval of the organisation for collective action under Article 39. Article 51 recognises the inherent right of individual or collective self defence in the case of an armed attack against a

[17] *Military and Paramilitary Activities in and against Nicaragua (Nicaragua v United States of America)*, Merits, Judgment, ICJ Reports 1986, p 14, p 94, para 176; Michael Wood, 'Self-Defence and Collective Security: Key Distinctions' in Marc Weller (ed), *The Oxford Handbook of the Use of Force in International Law* (Oxford University Press 2015) 656.

[18] Art 51 UN Charter. For an in-depth analysis of the limits to self-defence and when such a right ceases to exist, see Terry D Gill, 'When Does Self-Defence End?' in Weller (n 17) 737–51; see also Wood, 'Self-Defence and Collective Security' (n 17) 654–55.

[19] Wood, 'Self-Defence and Collective Security' (n 17) 656.

[20] Evan Luard, *A History of the United Nations: Volume 1: The Years of Western Domination 1945–1955* (Macmillan 1982) 245.

[21] Erika de Wet, 'Introduction to Chapter VII: The General Framework' in Bruno Simma et al (eds), *The Charter of the United Nations: A Commentary* (4th edn, vol II, Oxford University Press 2024) 1584.

[22] Luard (n 20) 245–46.

> member, until the Security Council has taken measures necessary to maintain international peace and security. Article 39 provides the Security Council with the overall responsibility for taking the measures required to maintain or restore international peace and security. Specifically the choice for the US was to intervene unilaterally or to obtain a UN umbrella for the operation, which would include the military and material support of other members, and give practical support to the UN approach to the maintenance of peace and security.[23]

The State Department's policy planning staff preferred to base United States action on the right of self-defence, citing concerns that any attempt to seek UNSC authorisation would be vetoed by the Soviet Union.[24] However, the State Department eventually followed the route of UN approval, subsequently proposing a draft resolution which would ultimately be adopted as Resolution 83 (1950).[25] The fact that the United States opted to undertake action through the UN suggests it did not view Article 51 as the legal basis of Resolution 83 (1950).

The implementation of Resolutions 83 and 84 (1950) was realised on 15 September 1950 when amphibious assaults against North Korean forces were initiated at Inchon. The counter-offensive continued until 2 November that year, leading to the eventual withdrawal of North Korean forces behind the 38th parallel.[26] Uncertainty however arose as to the legal position once North Korean forces withdrew. Then United States President Truman's initial response suggested that a new UNSC resolution would be needed to take action against North Korea beyond the 38th parallel.[27] However, the State Department and military authorities thought differently.[28] They suggested that the use of force against North Korea, although having already successfully repelled the attack against South Korea, could be taken by virtue of existing resolutions.[29] In particular, Resolution 83's (1950) wording that Member States were to 'restore international peace and security in the area' was interpreted as sufficient justification for military action against North Korea over and above merely repelling the attack against South Korea.[30] Such interpretation arguably reflects the resolutions' legal basis under Article 42, since the United States considered its actions were based on existing resolutions beyond merely repelling the armed attack.[31]

[23] John D Hickerson Oral History Interview by Richard D McKinzie, 10 November 1972, Harry S Truman Presidential Library and Museum, reproduced in Withana (n 10) 96.

[24] Withana (n 10) 96–97.

[25] ibid. See also the draft resolution in UN Doc S/1508/Rev.1 (1950).

[26] Air Force Historical Research Agency, 'Korean War Campaigns' https://shorturl.at/I7Pcc.

[27] James R Arnold and Roberta Wiener (eds), *Understanding US Military Conflicts Through Primary Sources* (Vol III, ABC-CLIO 2016) 431–33.

[28] Luard (n 20) 247.

[29] Luard (n 20) 248.

[30] Luard (n 20) 247; Withana (n 10) 103–04.

[31] But see however a Memorandum by the Executive Secretary to the National Security Council on US Courses of Action With Respect to Korea which interpreted the political mission of the UN in the respective resolutions as bringing about the 'complete independence and unity of Korea' suggesting that repelling North Korea forces was only part of the UN mission. It did, however acknowledge that mobilising UN troops into North Korean territory (north of the 38th parallel) was not clearly

This interpretation was realised on 25 October 1950 when UN troops under US commander General Douglas MacArthur began mobilising across the North Korean border. The term 'restore international peace and security in the area' was given a wider interpretation to authorise cross-border deployment. The mobilisation of UN troops across the border eventually led to the military involvement of China, forcing UN troops to retreat and eventually allowing North Korean forces to reclaim Seoul.[32] The Chinese involvement in the Korean War, coupled with Soviet vetoes in the UNSC, was the strongest protest to UNSC authorisation of force arguably seen to date. Although the Soviet protest was placed both in its veto power, as well as its miscalculation that its absence would result in the non-adoption of UNSC resolutions, Chinese involvement seemed to have occurred only once UN troops had mobilised into North Korean territory.

Nevertheless, the Korean War and the adoption of Resolutions 83 and 84 (1950) remain a point of debate in so far as their legal basis concern.[33] That UNSC authorisation could at all be based on Article 51 remains unlikely for a number of reasons. First, the wording of Article 51 suggests that it is to be invoked by Member States (and not necessarily by the UNSC).[34] The right of self-defence is after all an inherent right all States possess. Second, States may exercise this right only 'until the Security Council has taken the measures necessary to maintain international peace and security'.[35] This implies that the UNSC may take action to maintain peace and security once a State has already invoked self-defence. This in turn implies that it is not the UNSC that bases its actions on Article 51, but rather a Member State.[36] That the UNSC takes action on a situation does not automatically extinguish the right of self-defence and the two may run concurrently.[37] Logically, any action the UNSC subsequently takes would be based on Article 42.

authorised by existing UNSC resolutions. See Draft Report by the National Security Council on United States Courses of Action With Respect to Korea, Memorandum by the Executive Secretary of the National Security Council, NSC 81, Washington, 1 September 1950 in Executive Secretariat Files NSC 81, Foreign Relations of the United States, 1950, Korea, Volume II at 686 (Draft Report by the NSC on US Action in Korea, 1950); Draft Report by the NSC on US Action in Korea, 1950, 688, stated: 'Military actions north of the 38th parallel which go beyond the accomplishment of this mission … are not clearly authorized by existing Security Council resolutions. Accordingly, United Nations approval for such further military actions is a prerequisite to their initiation.'

[32] Howard Levie, 'How It All Started – And How It All Ended: A Legal Study of the Korean War' (2002) 35(2) *Akron Law Review* 220–22.

[33] White (n 10) 31–32; Christine Gray, *International Law and the Use of Force* (Oxford University Press 2018) 266–67.

[34] Erika de Wet, 'The Gulf War – 1990–91' in Ruys and Corten (n 10) 465; Erika de Wet, *The Chapter VII Powers of the United Nations Security Council* (Hart Publishing 2004) 262.

[35] Art 51 UN Charter; Wood, 'Self-Defence and Collective Security' (n 17) 653–57. See also broadly Terry D Gill, 'When Does Self-Defence End?' in Weller (n 17) 737 and Malvina Halberstam, 'The Right to Self-Defence Once the Security Council Takes Action' (1996) 17(229) *Michigan Journal of International Law* 229.

[36] De Wet, *The Chapter VII Powers* (n 34) 464–65.

[37] Wood, 'Self-Defence and Collective Security' (n 17) 656; De Wet, *The Chapter VII Powers* (n 34) 263.

Third, that the North Korean invasion can qualify both as an armed attack (for purposes of self-defence) and a breach of the peace (for purposes of collective security) is evidenced by the wording of the respective resolutions. While States may come to the aid of a victim State, only the UNSC can take action to 'restore international peace and security'. Assistance furnished in self-defence may ultimately form part of UNSC enforcement measures once the UNSC acts on a situation.[38] Therefore, when the UNSC adopted Resolutions 83 and 84 (1950) it could only have done so by basing its actions on Articles 39 and 42, since it authorised the use of force by Member States to restore international peace and security (even though that authorisation was also to repel the armed attack).[39] The fact that the UNSC recognised South Korea as the victim of an armed attack did not detract from its power to authorise enforcement action under Article 42.[40] Likewise, the mere fact that the UNSC recognises the existence of an armed attack does not automatically mean that it authorises any enforcement action. As will be discussed further below, the mere recognition of a right of self-defence does not in itself necessitate a conclusion that force is authorised.

Finally, it is worth noting that under Resolution 84 (1950), a unified command was designated to the United States. It is notable in so far as this designation was given by the UNSC; such designation being unnecessary when States act in collective self-defence.

iii. The Legality of Delegated Enforcement Action

In the absence of military agreements under Article 43, Resolutions 83 and 84 (1950) were the first instances of what would become known as delegated enforcement action (use of force by Member States on behalf of the UNSC). Since the model of delegated enforcement action is not explicitly mentioned in the UN Charter, its legality has been the subject of significant debate.[41] While the

[38] White (n 10) 31.

[39] That does not mean that the United States could not rely on Article 51 on which to base its own actions, since it may have come to the aid of South Korea to repel the armed attack even before the UNSC adopted its resolutions on the situation. Nigel D White, *The United Nations System: Toward International Justice* (Lynne Rienner Publishers 2002) 153, but see also De Wet, 'Article 42' in Simma (n 21) 1699 as well as the issue of authorising force against a non-UN Member States (North Korea). See however Burns Weston, 'Security Council Resolution 678 and Persian Gulf Decision Making: Precarious Legitimacy' (1991) 85(3) *American Journal of International Law* 519–22.

[40] White (n 10) 31.

[41] See broadly John Quigley, 'The "Privatization" of Security Council Enforcement Action: A Threat to Multilateralism' (1996) 17(2) *Michigan Journal of International Law* 249; Danesh Sarooshi, *The United Nations and the Development of Collective Security: The Delegation by the UN Security Council of its Chapter VII Powers* (Oxford University Press 1999) 143–46; Niels Blokker, 'Is the Authorisation Authorised? Powers and Practice of the UN Security Council to Authorise the Use of Force by "Coalitions of the Able and Willing"' (2000) 11(3) *European Journal of International Law* 542; De Wet, *The Chapter VII Powers* (n 34) 257, and on the Korean War see 275–76.

drafters of the UN Charter did not necessarily foresee delegated enforcement action, it has nonetheless been considered a lawful exercise of its Chapter VII powers and an implied power of the UNSC.[42] After all, the UNSC is able to delegate enforcement action to regional organisations under Article 53, which leaves the question as to why it should not also be lawfully entitled to delegate such action to Member States.[43]

Delegated enforcement action has since become an arguably well-established practice of the UNSC.[44] Scholarly commentary confirms its acceptance and conformity with the UN Charter, but also several limitations. The most notable of these include that the resolution delegating the enforcement action must be validly adopted and in conformity with the UN Charter, and that the action undertaken in pursuance of the resolution must be in conformity with the provisions of that resolution which was validly adopted.[45] It is therefore clear that delegated enforcement action is not without limits.[46] The UN Charter for example provides that the UNSC must retain at least some degree of command and control over operations it authorises.[47] To this end, it will be noted in subsequent chapters that the UNSC has regularly imposed reporting requirements on Member States that seek to implement measures it authorises. This is perhaps the most common way in which the UNSC attempts to retain some degree of control over authorised operations.[48] Since the Korean War and later the Gulf War, delegated enforcement action has become the dominant practice of the UNSC when it authorises force.

Although the adoption of Resolutions 83 and 84 (1950) was heralded as a milestone in UNSC practice, having been the first instance in which the UNSC had authorised the use of force, it was not without criticism. Both China and the Soviet Union maintained arguments against the authorisation.[49] While initially only arguing against United States intervention in North Korea, broader arguments later condemned the entirety of the authorisations granted in Resolutions 83 and 84 (1950).[50] Nonetheless, the adoption of the resolutions on the Korean War opened the way for future UNSC-authorised interventions

[42] Sarooshi (n 41) 146; De Wet, *The Chapter VII Powers* (n 34) 308; Nigel White and Özlem Ülgen, 'The Security Council and the Decentralised Military Option: Constitutionality and Function' (1997) 44 *Netherlands International Law Review* 385–88; Olivier Corten, *The Law Against War: The Prohibition on the Use of Force in Contemporary International Law* (2nd edn, Hart Publishing 2021) 321–34; Blokker, 'Is the Authorisation Authorised?' (n 41) 567–68.

[43] Sarooshi (n 41) 148.

[44] De Wet, 'Article 42' (n 39) 1696–97. See also Corten, *The Law Against War* (n 42) 317–18.

[45] Sarooshi (n 41) 20–22 and 44–46; Corten, *The Law Against War* (n 42) 321–34.

[46] See extensively Sarooshi (n 41) 153–63.

[47] Sarooshi (n 41) 159–63; De Wet, *The Chapter VII Powers* (n 34) 265–66, 308; White and Ülgen (n 42) 387–88.

[48] Sarooshi (n 41) 160–61; 171–72; de Wet, 'Article 42' (n 39) 1698.

[49] Withana (n 10) 99–101.

[50] See Withana (n 10) 100–01. Notably, the adoption of both UNSC Resolutions 83 and 84 (1950) ultimately lead to the adoption of the 'Uniting for Peace' resolution.

through delegated enforcement action, and with a more concise manner when taking measures under Chapter VII.[51]

B. Resolution 221 (1966) | Southern Rhodesia

The continued paralysis of the UNSC during the Cold War years meant that a subsequent authorisation of force only occurred more than a decade later on the situation in Southern Rhodesia. On 11 November 1965, the Rhodesian cabinet adopted a Unilateral Declaration of Independence, announcing its autonomy from the British government. Led by Rhodesian Prime Minister Ian Smith, the regime ensured white minority rule over an overwhelmingly African populace. Having expressed grave concern against the regime and the unilateral declaration of independence by the Rhodesian authorities, the UNSC adopted Resolution 221 (1966) authorising the limited use of force to enforce an oil embargo against Southern Rhodesia.[52]

The adoption of Resolution 221 (1966) raised a number of issues. First, authorisation was specifically granted to the United Kingdom and Northern Ireland (and was not the typical and more generally directed authorisation given to 'Member States of the UN'). Moreover, while the authorisation was explicit, it did not invoke Chapter VII. Second was the limited scope of the authorisation, which was granted specifically for the sole purpose of preventing the arrival of vessels believed to be carrying oil to Southern Rhodesia. As a result, the resolution contained no broad language as such to authorise the use of force to 'restore international peace and security'.

Third, the adoption of the resolution raised many questions in relation to the scope of authorisation for the use of force. Prominent debates in the UNSC questioned why the use of force was not targeted against the Southern Rhodesian regime itself, and not only against oil-ferrying vessels to the region. Finally, the adoption of Resolution 221 (1966) lead to questions about its legal basis. Was authorisation to enforce embargoes a measure under Article 41 or Article 42 of the UN Charter?

i. Explicit Authorisation without a Chapter VII Invocation

Resolution 221 (1966) served as the second instance in which the UNSC authorised the use of force. The resolution's preamble began by expressing concern that large quantities of oil may reach Southern Rhodesia, a regime the UNSC considered illegal.[53] It then considered that supplies of oil to the regime would enable

[51] De Wet, 'Article 42' (n 39) 1698.

[52] UNSC Res 221 (1966).

[53] The UNSC first condemned the racist Southern Rhodesian minority and called on Member States not to recognise or render assistance to the 'illegal regime' in UNSC Res 216 (1965). This was

its continued existence and, therefore, the resulting situation constituted a threat to the peace.[54] The UNSC had already in Resolution 217 (1965) determined that the declaration of independence by Southern Rhodesia and its continuance in time constituted a threat to peace and security.[55] Unlike Resolution 83 (1950) on the Korean War, this determination was not made in the preamble to the resolution, but in the first operative paragraph. The UNSC then explicitly authorised the use of force 'if necessary' by the United Kingdom and Northern Ireland to prevent the arrival of any vessel that was reasonably believed to be delivering oil to Southern Rhodesia.[56] Although authorising the use of force under limited circumstances and with the condition of necessity, Chapter VII was not invoked. However, from context and the subsequent enforcement of the resolution, it was clear that the UNSC had relied on Chapter VII.[57]

ii. Support to, and Contestation of, the Limited Nature of the Authorisation

A point of contention during the adoption of Resolution 221 (1966) concerned the limited nature of the authorisation. The question arose as to whether the authorisation of force should be extended to apply against the illegal Rhodesian regime itself. At the UNSC's 1276th meeting, the United Kingdom submitted a draft resolution on the situation (adopted as Resolution 221 (1966)).[58] The United Kingdom representative said that the resolution would enable it to act in conformity with international law, and to take steps against Southern Rhodesia, including the use of force, to prevent the arrival of ships at Beira, which would otherwise fall into the regime's control.[59] As the United Kingdom representative argued, this was in accordance with Resolution 217 (1965) which had imposed the oil embargo against Rhodesia. Careful attention was paid at ensuring that any authorisation of force was strictly limited only at enforcing an arms embargo and not directed at the regime itself.[60]

The limitation on the use of force only against oil-carrying vessels was criticised by the representatives of Uganda, Mali and Nigeria, who jointly submitted a revised draft resolution.[61] While the United Kingdom resolution proposed only the use of force for the implementation of the embargo, the Ugandan proposal aimed to authorise the use of force to also topple the minority regime

reaffirmed in UNSC Res 217 (1965) in which the declaration of independence was regarded as having no legal validity.

[54] UNSC Res 221 (1966), para 1.

[55] UNSC Res 217 (1965) para 1.

[56] UNSC Res 221 (1966) para 6.

[57] Gray, *International Law and the Use of Force* (n 33) 265–66.

[58] UN Doc S/PV.1276 (1966).

[59] UN Doc S/PV.1276 (1966) 16–24. See also revision to the UK's draft resolution in UN Doc S/7236/Rev.1 (1966) (text eventually adopted as Resolution 221 (1966)).

[60] UN Doc S/PV.1276 (1966) 16.

[61] UN Doc S/7243 (1966).

in Southern Rhodesia.[62] The Ugandan revised draft resolution explicitly added that the United Kingdom would 'employ all measures including the use of armed force to bring down the settler minority regime in Rhodesia'.[63] Uganda's viewpoint on the matter was not widely shared among UNSC representatives. In particular, Argentina explicitly mentioned that measures under Article 42 should be used only in extreme cases. It added that the United Kingdom's resolution could be accepted as paragraph 5 authorising force was clearly defined and limited.[64] The United Kingdom's draft resolution was subsequently adopted as Resolution 221 (1966).[65]

Shortly after the adoption of the resolution, the United Kingdom began what was to be a nine year naval blockade by the Royal Navy which became known as the Beira Patrol.[66] Both the Royal Navy and the British Air Force monitored shipping in the Mozambique Channel to ensure that no oil reached Southern Rhodesia.[67] While significant pressure from UN members had presented itself during the adoption and implementation of Resolution 221 (1996) to authorise force against the Rhodesian regime in its entirety, it was clear at the time that the UNSC was not prepared to authorise any broader use of force.

iii. Conditional Use of Force under Resolution 221 (1966)

Resolution 221 (1966) authorised the United Kingdom to use military force only to enforce the oil embargo under Resolution 217 (1965). The use of force was subject to two conditions, namely, necessity and a reasonable belief that oil was being ferried to Southern Rhodesia. Therefore, in order to use force, the United Kingdom must have reasonably believed that an oil tanker was transporting oil to Southern Rhodesia before it could employ force.

Moreover, the use of force must have been a necessary measure to prevent the arrival of the ships to Southern Rhodesia. This interpretation of Resolution 221 (1966) was in line with opinions expressed by the Attorney-General on the matter at the time.[68] Such a view was also supported prior to the adoption of Resolution 221 (1966) whereby a vessel, Joanna V, was intercepted as it was believed to be carrying oil to the Rhodesian regime.[69] It was at that time that the United Kingdom wished to use force against the vessel, first requesting the Greek government (under which flag the ship was sailing) to order its diversion from Beira. The Greek government expressed its opinion that 'no [g]overnment would

[62] UN Doc S/PV.1276 (1966) 44–57.
[63] UN Doc S/PV.1276 (1966) 56; UN Doc S/7243 (1966).
[64] UN Doc S/PV.1277 (1966) 47.
[65] UN Doc S/PV.1277 (1966).
[66] Richard Mobley, 'The Beira Patrol: Britain's Broken Blockade against Rhodesia' (2002) 55(1) *Naval War College Review* 63.
[67] Mobley (n 66) 63.
[68] Mobley (n 66) 73.
[69] Sarooshi (n 41) 196.

consent to a foreign power intercepting or intimidating merchant ships under its flag'.[70] However, it went on to say that 'if the United Nations authorises the British [g]overnment to intercept the vessel, [Greece] shall respect the decision'.[71] Rigorous UNSC debates surrounding the adoption of Resolution 221 (1966), with its explicit yet limiting language, nevertheless suggested a wide acknowledgment that the authorisation to use force in the resolution was restricted to the United Kingdom for the enforcement of the oil embargo under Resolution 217 (1966). Resolution 221 (1966) therefore remains one of the earliest practices in which, although not invoking Chapter VII, the UNSC had clearly authorised the use of force for a strict and limited mandate using explicit terms for such authorisation.[72]

iv. Resolution 221's (1966) Legal Basis: Article 41 or 42?

One of the more notable debates concerning Resolution 221 (1966) was its exact legal basis under the UN Charter. Making no reference to a specific article under which the UNSC was acting, the question which arose was whether measures were taken under Article 41 or 42. Prior resolutions on the situation in Southern Rhodesia were clearly based on Article 41, with the imposition of economic sanctions under Resolution 217 (1965) being most notable. However, Resolution 221 (1966) authorisation of force opened the question: is the use of force to enforce embargoes based on Article 41 or 42? Some authors suggest that the legal basis for Resolution 221 (1966) is most consistent with Article 42, since the UNSC 'called upon' the UK to use force if necessary, and even 'empower[ed]' it to arrest and detain the tanker Joanna V.[73] This reasoning is supported if one considers arguments contrary to basing the resolution on Article 41. In particular, Article 41's wording expressly excludes military measures; military force and Article 41 would therefore be incompatible.[74]

On the opposing view, some suggest that Article 42 could not have been the legal basis since the UNSC had at the time not had grounds to believe that its Article 41 measures would be inadequate and would therefore not be sure whether it would need to rely on Article 42 measures.[75] Moreover, arguments basing Resolution 221 (1966) on Article 41 point towards instances of 'minimal

[70] Sarooshi (n 41) 196–97.

[71] See Sarooshi (n 41) 196.

[72] When the UNSC subsequently adopted UNSC Res 232 (1966), it explicitly invoked Arts 39 and 41.

[73] Sarooshi (n 41) 198–99; David Schweigman, *The Authority of the Security Council under Chapter VII of the UN Charter: Legal Limits and the Role of the International Court of Justice* (Kluwer Law International 2001) 62.

[74] Sarooshi (n 41) 198–99; Gray (n 125) 265–66.

[75] See the discussion in Martin Fink, *Maritime Interception and the Law of Naval Operations: A Study of Legal Bases and Legal Regimes in Maritime Interception Operations* (Springer 2018) 88.

use of force to enforce sanctions'.[76] This line of argument suggests that Article 42 measures are actually meant as large-scale military actions and blockades, but that Article 41 may empower the UNSC to authorise minimal or limited use of force to enforce sanctions.[77] This argument is supported by those who suggest that Resolution 221 (1966) expressly indicates that force was to be used only by the United Kingdom and only for the enforcement of the oil embargo *if necessary*, therefore constituting minimalistic (and limited) use of force.[78]

The contrary position should however be noted. First, UNSC debates prior to the adoption of the resolution already indicated that Article 41 measures adopted under Resolution 217 (1965) had proven ineffective. Therefore, it would be inaccurate to state that there were no grounds for the UNSC to believe that Article 41 measures would be inadequate. It is also clear today that the UNSC has the discretion to authorise Article 42 measures without the necessity of non-military measures already becoming inadequate.[79] In addition, it would seem that at least one UNSC Member (Argentina) at the time interpreted the wording of paragraph 5 as referring to Article 42.[80]

Second, there is nothing in the drafting history of the UN Charter, or from its very wording, that suggests Article 42 should be interpreted to only authorise large-scale military actions. Authorisation under Article 42, therefore, can take the form of minimalistic uses of force, or large-scale military interventions. This reasoning is support by the principle of *a maiore ad minimus*.[81] Combined with the fact that Article 41 clearly excludes military measures, it is evident that any military action authorised by the UNSC would have to be based on Article 42.[82]

Resolution 221 (1966) therefore paved the way for the UNSC to authorise the use of force to enforce embargoes. Similar resolutions on the enforcement of embargoes were brought up again, particularly in the 1990s during the Gulf War, the situation in the Federal Republic of Yugoslavia (FRY) and the civil unrest in Sierra Leone and Haiti.[83] These situations are discussed in detail below

[76] See the discussion in Penelope Nevill, 'Enforcement in the Absence of Express Authorisation' in Weller (n 17) 287–88.

[77] Nevill (n 76) 288; see also Fink (n 75) 88.

[78] Nevill summarises the debate as follows: The use of minimal force to enforce sanctions could be authorised by the UNSC under art 41 in the same way as a minimal use of force by land-based peacekeeping missions under the 'active self-defence' doctrine might be authorised by reference to art 40. See Nevill (n 76) 288.

[79] Nico Krisch, 'Article 39' in Bruno Simma et al (eds), *The Charter of the United Nation: A Commentary* (3rd edn, Oxford University Press 2012) 1341.

[80] UN Doc S/PV.1277 (1966) 47.

[81] De Wet, *The Chapter VII Powers* (n 34) 182 fn 11.

[82] De Wet, 'Article 42' (n 39) 1700. The authorisation has sometimes been described as a half-way point between Arts 41 and 42 (Article 41½ measures). See Blokker, 'Is the Authorisation Authorised?' (n 41) 543–44; Gray, *International Law and the Use of Force* (n 125) 266; Fink (n 75) 87. But see Sarooshi (n 41) 198–99, basing it on Art 42.

[83] See for example UNSC Res 675 (1990) para 5; UNSC Res 787 (1992) para 12, UNSC Res 917 (1994) and UNSC Res 1132 (1997) on Sierra Leone.

in relation to the legal issues that arose in each situation and their implications for UNSC practice of authorising force to enforce embargoes.

III. EXPLICIT AUTHORISATION AFTER THE COLD WAR ERA

A. Resolutions 665 and 678 (1990) | The Gulf War

On 2 August 1990 Iraqi forces entered Kuwait and began a full-scale invasion and occupation of the oil-rich neighbouring nation.[84] The Iraqi government argued it was reclaiming its territory, and on 8 August 1990 it pronounced an 'eternal merger' of Kuwait as its nineteenth province.[85] The UNSC was swift to act on the situation, adopting Resolution 660 (1990) on the same day of the invasion.[86] It had expressed its alarm at the invasion of Kuwait, determined a breach of the peace and demanded under Articles 39 and 41 that Iraqi forces immediately and unconditionally withdraw.[87] Failed compliance with the resolution resulted in the adoption of, among others, Resolution 665 (1990) on 29 August 1990 and, eventually, Resolution 678 (1990) on 29 November 1990, explicitly authorising the use of force.[88]

The adoption of these resolutions signalled a turning point for the UNSC's authorisation of force. First was the build-up to the adoption of Resolution 678 (1990), with several previous resolutions exhausting Article 41 measures. Resolution 665 (1990), as in the case of Resolution 221 (1966) on Southern Rhodesia, was interpreted to have authorised the limited use of force to enforce an embargo against Iraq. Thereafter, the adoption of Resolution 678 (1990) became the third instance in which the UNSC had authorised force, and the third time it had made use of delegated enforcement action. Most significant was the coining of the term 'all necessary means', which has since become known as the primary operative language by which the UNSC authorises force.

Second were debates raised as to the exact legal basis of Resolution 678 (1990) and whether measures under it were based on Article 42 or Article 51. The adoption of Resolution 678 (1990) also signalled the beginning of a more structured approach when the UNSC authorises force.[89]

[84] Michael Gordon, 'Iraq Army Invades Capital of Kuwait in Fierce Fighting' (2 August 1990) *The New York Times*.

[85] Times Wire Services, 'Iraqis Annex Kuwait in "Eternal Merger": Middle East: Baghdad Describes the Takeover as "Returning the Branch to the Whole"' *Los Angeles Times* (8 August 1990).

[86] UNSC Res 660 (1990).

[87] UNSC Res 660 (1990) preamble paras 2, 3, para 3.

[88] UNSC Res 665 (1990); UNSC Res 678 (1990).

[89] Blokker, 'Is the Authorisation Authorised?' (n 41) 543; see the appendix in Adam Roberts and Dominik Zaum, 'War and the United Nations Security Council since 1945' (2007) 47 (395) *The Adelphi Papers* 81–83.

i. Resolution 665 (1990) and the Build-up to Resolution 678 (1990)

Resolution 660 (1990) was the first resolution to explicitly determine the situation a breach of the peace.[90] Thereafter, Resolutions 661, 662 and 664 (1990) employed Article 41 measures against Iraq. Measures under Resolutions 661 and 664 (1990) were explicitly adopted under Chapter VII of the UN Charter. Having failed to comply with these measures, the UNSC then adopted Resolution 665 (1990). The significance of the resolution concerned the authority it granted to Member States to use force to enforce an embargo against Iraq. This was the second instance in which the UNSC had employed such a measure and, as with Southern Rhodesia, the authorisation granted under Resolution 665 (1990) was strictly limited.

First, only Member States that were 'co-operating with the Government of Kuwait' could rely on the authorisation. Second, Member States whose maritime forces were deployed in the area were to use 'such measures commensurate to the specific circumstances as may be necessary' when exercising the authority. Finally, the authority to use force was strictly limited by the last sentence of the paragraph, namely, to 'halt inward and outward shipping' in order to inspect and verify cargo to ensure the strict implementation of the provisions of Resolution 661 (1990). The use of force under Resolution 665 (1990) was therefore clearly intended only for purposes of enforcing the embargo, an interpretation as authorisation for the minimal use of force.[91] That Resolution 665 (1990) authorised limited use of force was evident from the UNSC debate preceding the adoption of the resolution, despite the fact that it did not invoke Chapter VII.

This conclusion has primarily been attributed to the explicit wording of the resolution which called on Member States to 'use such measures commensurate to the specific circumstances as may be necessary'. In addition, the preamble to the resolution expressly stated that economic sanctions under Resolution 660 (1990) were imposed under Chapter VII, and that resolution was also reaffirmed in Resolution 665 (1990). Moreover, paragraph 4 requested Member States to co-ordinate their actions with the Military Staff Committee and to submit reports to the UNSC concerning the situation. Given that the practice of the UNSC in authorising force to enforce embargoes has become a regular occurrence, it is also reasonable to conclude that Resolution 665 (1990) was based on Article 42, since military measures are not permissible under Article 41.

[90] UNSC Res. 660 (1990) preamble para. 2.

[91] De Wet, 'The Gulf War' (n 34) 457; UN Doc S/PV.2938 (1990); see the United States statement at 26 that '[t]he authority granted in this resolution is sufficiently broad to use armed force – indeed, minimum force – depending upon the circumstances which might require it' and the United Kingdom statement at 48 that '[m]easures include such minimum use of force as may be necessary to achieve the purposes of paragraph 1'; see also Yoshiro Matsui, 'The Gulf War and the United Nations Security Council' in Ronald St John McDonald (ed), *Essays in Honour of Wang Tieya* (Martinus Nijhoff Publishers 1994) 514; Tetsou Ito, 'UN Authorised Use of Force: Recent Changes in UN Practice' (Institute for Forsvarsstudies 1995) 10.

Although the fact that Resolution 665 (1990) did not invoke Chapter VII gave rise to some uncertainty,[92] in context of its earlier practice authorising limited uses of force without invoking Chapter VII, it is inevitable to conclude that the UNSC indeed authorised force.[93]

ii. Resolution 678 (1990) and 'All Necessary Means'

Having determined the situation to be a breach of international peace and security in Resolution 660 (1990),[94] the UNSC more broadly authorised under Resolution 678 (1990) Member States to use force to ensure the withdrawal of Iraqi forces from Kuwait. Force was also authorised to ensure the implementation of decisions of subsequent resolutions to restore international peace and security.[95] Resolution 678 (1990) was the first UNSC resolution authorising the use of force which included both an Article 39 determination and a Chapter VII invocation. This combination of explicit determination and invocation was the beginning of what would become standard UNSC practice. Most notable, however, was the language employed by paragraph 2 of the resolution. The operative paragraph explicitly 'authorised' Member States to use 'all necessary means' to implement Resolution 660 (1990) and all subsequent resolutions; authorising the use of force to 'restore international peace and security in the area'.[96]

UNSC debates prior to and after the adoption of the resolution widely acknowledged the term to have authorised force. Yemen referred to the resolution as 'in effect authorising states to use force to ensure compliance', Cuba affirmed that 'the text before us … authoris[e]s some [s]tates to use military

[92] Lacking reference to Chapter VII, the Soviet Union and China suggested a level of uncertainty as to whether force was authorised. The lack of such reference has led to arguments in favour of implied authorisation. See also Ian Johnstone, 'When the Security Council is Divided: Imprecise Authorisations, Implied Mandates and the "Unreasonable Veto"' in Weller (n 17) 238; see also Marc Weller, *Iraq and the Use of Force in International Law* (Oxford University Press 2010) 27 and Christopher John Sabec, 'The Security Council Comes of Age: An Analysis of the International Legal Response to The Iraqi Invasion of Kuwait' (1991) 63 *Georgia Journal of International and Comparative Law* 72.

[93] China was of the view that the resolution in fact did not authorise the use of force, not even for embargo enforcement. It cited the removal of the reference of 'minimum use of force' from an earlier version of the resolution as an explanation. See UN Doc. S/PV.2938 (1999) 53. See also See Sarah Rumage, 'The Return of Article 42: Enemy of the Good for Collective Security' (1993) 5(1) *Pace International Law Review* 280–81.

[94] UNSC Res 660 (1990) preamble para 2.

[95] These include UNSC Res 661 (1990), UNSC Res 662 (1990), UNSC Res 664 (1990), UNSC Res 665 (1990), UNSC Res 666 (1990) and UNSC Res 667 (1990).

[96] UNSC Res 678 (1990) para 2, read together with UNSC Res 660 (1990) and UNSC Res 674 (1990). Para 2 of UNSC Res 678 (1990) reads: '[The UNSC] [a]uthorises Member States co-operating with the Government of Kuwait, unless Iraq on or before 15 January 1991 fully implements, as set forth in paragraph 1 above, the above-mentioned resolutions, to use all necessary means to uphold and implement resolution 660 (1990) and all subsequent resolutions and to restore international peace and security in the area.'

force', and China added that the wording 'use all necessary means' in essence permitted the use of military action.[97] A similar sentiment was echoed by the representatives of Canada, the Soviet Union, the United Kingdom and the United States.[98] Addressing the UNSC after its adoption, Malaysia interpreted its authorisation of force to extend only within the context of Resolutions 660 (1990), 662 (1990) and 664(1990).[99]

The introduction of the term 'all necessary means' was initially supplemented by the words 'including the use of force'. The latter part was however left out during negotiations. Framed by then US Secretary of State James Baker III,[100] the preferred phrasing to indicate the permissibility of the use of force by using the term 'all necessary means' has since regularly been used in UNSC resolutions and is undoubtedly understood as authorising force.[101]

iii. Legal Basis of Resolution 678 (1990)

The adoption of Resolution 678 (1990) was not spared from issues of legality. In particular, and as with the resolutions on the Korean War, a central question raised was whether the resolution was based on Article 42 or 51. Arguments in favour of Article 51 as a legal basis proposed that Resolution 678 (1990) did not by itself constitute an 'autonomous' legal basis for force, but rather re-affirmed the right of self-defence as both an inherent right and a right under Article 51 of the UN Charter.[102] Notwithstanding the argument to the contrary detailed under Resolutions 83 and 84 (1950) that it is States which invoke Article 51, this position may be noted as follows. First, Kuwait had been the victim of an armed attack and, therefore, would be entitled to exercise its right of self-defence. Several

[97] UN Doc S/PV.2963 (1990) 32, 58, 62.

[98] UN Doc S/PV.2963 (1990) 71–72, 82, 91, 103. See the Soviet Union's statement that '[at] those who have breached the peace should know that "all necessary means" will indeed inexorably be used against them' and the United States' statement that '[t]oday's resolution is very clear. The words authorise the use of force.'

[99] UN Doc. S/PV.2963 (1990) 76–77.

[100] James A Baker III, 'The Politics of Diplomacy: Revolution, War and Peace, 1989–1992 (GP Putman's Sons, 1995) in James A Baker III, 'Baker Presses Security Council Members' Global Policy Forum www.globalpolicy.org/component/content/article/169-history/36387.html. Baker stated: 'I wanted the resolution to include a clean, unambiguous statement that authorized the use of force but didn't mandate it. My suggested language was "all necessary means", including the use of force. Skilful diplomacy, however, is grounded in the art of the possible. So we had a backup position. At my request, Bob Kimmitt had researched the legalities and concluded that if the Soviets and other allies objected to such specificity, the simple phrase, "all necessary means" conferred sufficient authority to wage war.'

[101] Niels Blokker, 'Outsourcing the Use of Force: Towards More Security Council Control of Authorised Operations?' in Weller (n 17) 211; Arend and Beck (n 10) 54.

[102] De Wet, 'The Gulf War' (n 34) 464; Det Wet, 'Article 42' (n 39) 1701. See also De Wet, *Introduction to Chapter VII* (n 21) 281; Frederic Kirgis, 'The Security Council's First Fifty Years' (1995) 89 *American Journal of International Law* 521–22; Oscar Schachter, 'United Nations Law in the Gulf Conflict' (1991) 85(3) *American Journal of International Law* 459–60; cf Colin Warbrick, 'The Invasion of Kuwait by Iraq – Part II' (1991) 40 *International and Comparative Law Quarterly* 487.

Communiqués issued to the UNSC following the Iraqi invasion confirmed that Member States at that time were acting in either collective defence at the request of, among others, Kuwait and Saudi Arabia.[103] Although the UNSC had not referred to an 'armed attack' as it did in Resolution 83 (1950), referring rather to the invasion of Kuwait, it had already affirmed Kuwait's right to individual or collective defence under Resolution 661 (1990).[104] The fact that Resolution 678 (1990) specifically recalled and reaffirmed Resolution 661 (1990), read together with the operative paragraph under Resolution 678 (1990), has been put forward as not only basing enforcement action on self-defence, but also modifying it in so far as paragraph 2 authorising the use of force mandated a compulsory waiting period before Member States could take action against Iraq.[105]

However, basing Resolution 678 (1990) purely on Article 51 measures has faced criticism in literature. One particularly convincing argument put forward is that a legal basis under Article 51 confuses distinctions between self-defence and collective security.[106] In so doing, such confusion may have considerable consequences for the limits to which force may be used. As is recalled, Article 42 permits the use of force to a greater extent than that permitted by self-defence.[107] For this reason, important distinctions between self-defence and collective security must be noted. First, while self-defence does not require UNSC authorisation, actions based on Article 42 can only be authorised by the UNSC. Hence, the UNSC did not need to authorise Article 51 self-defence under Resolution 678 (1990). Second, whereas Article 42 measures are preconditioned on the determination of a threat to the peace under Article 39,[108] self-defence is preconditioned on the existence of an armed attack (although an armed attack may also be considered a threat to the peace).[109] Hence, Article 42 measures may be taken even if the possibility of self-defence does not exist. Third, under Article 42, it is the UNSC that determines which Member States may undertake

[103] See letters sent to the UNSC following the Iraqi invasion but preceding the adoption of UNSC Res 678 (1990), the United States position in UN Doc S/21492 (1990); the United Kingdom position in UN Doc S/21501 (1990); and Saudi Arabian position in UN Doc S/21554 (1990). See also the position of Kuwait in UN Doc S/21498 (1990). The position of the United States in UN Doc S/21537 (1990) also raises some questions, suggesting that the United States was willing to use force, if necessary, to enforce trade sanctions under UNSC Res 661 (1990). This suggests that the United States interpreted a right to use force under that resolution.

[104] UNSC Res 661 (1990) preamble para 5.

[105] UNSC Res 678 (1990) para 2; De Wet, 'The Gulf War' (n 34) 465.

[106] See broadly, Derek W Bowett, 'Collective Security and Collective Self-Defence: The Errors and Risks of Identification' in Manuel R Montaldo (ed), *El derecho internacional en un mundo en transformación: Liber amicorum: en homenaje al profesor Eduardo Jiménez Aréchaga* (vol 1, Fundación de Cultura Universitaria 1994) 425–40 quoted in Wood, 'Self-Defence and Collective Security' (n 17) 658–59. See also De Wet, 'Article 42' (n 39) 1702.

[107] Wood, 'Self-Defence and Collective Security' (n 17) 652.

[108] Wood, 'Self-Defence and Collective Security' (n 17) 652.

[109] The UNSC may however determine an armed attack as a breach of the peace, as was the case in UNSC Res 83 (1950). See also Jan Klabbers, 'Intervention, Armed Intervention, Armed Attack, Threat to Peace, Act of Aggression, and Threat or Use of Force: What's the Difference' in Weller (n 17) 496.

delegated enforcement action, whereas under self-defence, it is the victim State that decides which States may assist it. Fourth, self-defence is limited by the principles of necessity and proportionality, whereas Article 42 measures are limited when peace and security have been restored (a determination left to the UNSC's discretion).[110]

This in mind, there are several reasons why Resolution 678 (1990) could only be based on Article 42.[111] First, the wording of Article 51 clearly reserves the right of self-defence to Member States but only until such time as the UNSC has taken measures necessary to maintain peace and security. It follows from this that the very adoption of Resolutions 665 and 678 (1990) indicates that the UNSC had already become involved, thereby (potentially) terminating or supplementing the right of self-defence under Article 51. This line of argument holds that Article 42 and Article 51 measures are mutually exclusive and that it is only States that may invoke Article 51, while the UNSC authorises action under Article 42.[112] Further support to Article 42 as the basis of Resolution 678 (1990) is credited to the wording of the resolution itself. The second paragraph is clear that the UNSC 'authorises' Member States to take action and, under paragraph 3, 'all states' were requested to provide support in pursuance of paragraph 2.[113] If one considers the wording of Article 48(1) of the UN Charter, namely, that the UNSC may determine who carries out actions (whether all Member States, or just some of them) in maintaining international peace and security, it is clear that such 'instruction' would be given under Article 42.[114]

Nonetheless, the implementation of Resolution 678 (1990) served as a second instance in which a broader interpretation of the provisions authorising force were evident from the subsequent practice of States.

B. Resolution 794 (1992) | Somalia

In 1991, as a result of increasing instability in Somalia, Somali President Mohammed Siad Barre was overthrown and forced to flee the country. Shortly afterwards, the collapse of the central Somali government and intensive fighting

[110] Wood, 'Self-Defence and Collective Security' (n 17) 652.

[111] But note the report of the Secretary-General in which he suggests that the UNSC has yet not made use of Article 42 measures in UN Doc S/24111 (1992) 42, 43. In paragraph 42, the Secretary-General states: 'The Security Council has not so far made use of the most coercive of these measures – the action by military force foreseen in article 42.'

[112] De Wet, 'The Gulf War' (n 34) 465.

[113] UNSC Res 678 (1990) paras 2, 3. See also the Repertoire of the Practice of the Security Council (1989–1992) 913–14 which considers UNSC Res 678 (1990) in the discussions relating to Art 42 of the UN Charter.

[114] Ar 48(1) UN Charter; De Wet, 'The Gulf War' (n 34) 465. see Simon Chesterman, *Just War or Just Peace? Humanitarian Intervention and International Law* (Oxford University Press 2003) 168 for an explanation as to why Art 48 cannot be used directly to justify delegated enforcement action.

between political factions saw the country fall into a period of civil war.[115] The UNSC first took action in Somalia by establishing a peacekeeping mission, the United Nations Operation in Somalia (UNOSOM I).[116] Conceived as a classic peacekeeping mission, it could therefore use force only in self-defence – possibly its greatest hinderance in achieving its mandate.[117] When the situation in Somalia worsened, the UNSC adopted Resolution 794 (1992) in which it authorised Member States to use all necessary means to establish a secure environment for humanitarian relief operations.[118] The United States-led United Task Force (UNITAF) began its deployment under the name *Operation Restore Hope*. UNITAF served only as an interim operation until its transition into a more robust UNOSOM II operation with the adoption of Resolution 814 (1993).[119] For current purposes, two aspects of the resolutions need specific examination. First was the fact that the adoption of Resolution 794 (1992) was the first time the UNSC had authorised the use of force by Member States in an internal situation for the provision of humanitarian assistance.[120] Second was the somewhat convoluted division of labour between UNITAF and UNOSOM, which led to divergent approaches in mandate implementation.[121]

i. Explicit Authorisation to Member States

The UNSC first determined the situation in Somalia a threat to international peace and security in Resolution 733 (1992), a determination in line with the report of the Secretary-General made at the time.[122] Thereafter, Resolutions 746 (1992), 751 (1992), 767 (1992) and 775 (1992) determined the continuation of the situation in Somalia a threat to international peace and security.[123] With the adoption of Resolution 794 (1992), the UNSC determined that the 'magnitude of human tragedy caused by the conflict in Somalia', exacerbated by obstacles to the delivery of humanitarian assistance, constituted a threat to international peace and security.[124] Invoking Chapter VII, the UNSC 'authorise[d]' Member States (co-operating with the Secretary-General) to use 'all necessary means' to establish a secure environment for humanitarian operations.[125] Resolution 794

[115] See Terry Gill and Kinga Tibori-Szabó, 'The Intervention in Somalia – 1992–95' in Ruys and Corten (n 10) 482.

[116] UNSC Res 751 (1992) para 2.

[117] Christiane E Philipp, 'Somalia – A Very Special Case' (2005) 9 *Max Planck Yearbook of United Nations Law* 530.

[118] UNSC Res 794 (1992) para 10.

[119] UNSC Res 814 (1993) paras 5, 6, 14.

[120] Philipp (n 117) 534.

[121] For an analysis of UNOSOM and UNOSOM II, see ch 5.

[122] UNSC Res 733 (1992) preamble para 4.

[123] UNSC Res 746 (1992) preamble par 6; UNSC Res 751 (1992) preamble para 6; UNSC Res 767 (1992) preamble para 7; UNSC Res 775 (1992) preamble para 6.

[124] UNSC Res 794 (1992) preamble para 3.

[125] UNSC Res 794 (1992) para 10.

(1990) was therefore the fourth instance of authorisation of force, the second instance of explicit authorisation and the first resolution to subsequently use the phrasing 'all necessary means'.

ii. UN-authorised Humanitarian Intervention

Resolution 794 (1992) was the first instance in which the UNSC had authorised the use of force for humanitarian purposes based on a purely internal conflict.[126] Moreover, it was the first time the UNSC had determined that an internal situation resulting in human rights violations had constituted a threat to peace and, authorised the use of force based on this determination.[127] The UNSC subsequently took similar action in a range of other situations, including those in the FRY and Haiti. However, the issue pertaining to Resolution 794 (1992) concerned the determination of a threat to peace based on the internal or domestic affairs of a State. When the UNSC authorised the use of force in the Korean War, and again during the Gulf War, it did so based on 'trans-border wars' which had constituted a threat to peace. The question posed on Somalia was whether the UNSC could determine the internal situation there as a threat to peace; thereby allowing it to authorise the use of force as an authorised humanitarian intervention.[128] Consequently, the resulting debate concerned whether a 'threat to international peace and security' could be interpreted broadly to include domestic issues. Arguments in favour of a narrow interpretation suggest that human rights violations could not constitute a threat to international peace. These violations (even on a large scale) that took place within the borders of a State and, therefore, contained no internationally present element, could not warrant UNSC action as they did not fall under the meaning of Article 39.[129] Unlike Resolution 866 (1991) in which the UNSC first determined human rights violations a threat to peace and security, namely, the repression of Iraqi civilians resulting in refugee flows across international borders, Resolution 794 (1992) indicated no international nexus to the situation.[130]

With that said, however, arguments favouring a narrower interpretation of threats to peace find support neither in the wording of the UN Charter nor

[126] See also Philipp (n 117) 534; see also Richard B Lillich, 'The Role of the UN Security Council in Protecting Human Rights in Crisis Situations: UN Humanitarian Intervention in the Post-Cold War World' (1995) 3 *Tulane Journal of International and Comparative Law* 7–8, who discusses also the significance of UNSC Res 688 (1991).

[127] Lillich (n 126) 7–8. The UNSC had already in UNSC Res 688 (1991) made a similar determination concerning the repression of Iraqi civilians. However, it did not authorise forcible measures under that resolution. See also UNSC Res 418 (1977) on South Africa.

[128] Art 2(7) of the UN Charter expressly excludes UNSC action under Chapter VII.

[129] See Lori Fisler Damrosch, 'Commentary on Collective Military Intervention to Enforce Human Rights' in Lori Fisler Damrosch and David J Scheffer (eds), *Law and Force in the New International Order* (Boulder Westview Press 1991) 217; Mary O'Connell, 'Continuing Limits on UN Intervention in Civil War' (1992) 67 *Indiana Law Journal* 910, 912–13.

[130] See UNSC Res 688 (1991) preamble para 3.

in extensive UNSC practice. For one, the drafting history of the UN Charter suggests that the term 'threat to peace' was deliberately left undefined to give the UNSC a broad discretion when making an Article 39 determination.[131] Moreover, the concept of a threat to the peace has since developed to include a broad range of not only external or cross-border situations, but also internal situations arising from armed conflicts.[132] If one considers later developments, such as the Responsibility to Protect doctrine, it is evident that the UNSC has a wide margin to decide on a threat to peace. Consequently, its authority to authorise force in maintaining or restoring international peace and security is undeniable.[133]

iii. Parallel Authorisation and the Division of Labour between UNOSOM and UNITAF

As mentioned earlier, the establishment of UNOSOM I was intended as a classic peacekeeping operation under Resolution 751 (1992).[134] Its mandate was subsequently expanded under Resolution 767 (1992) and its force was increased under Resolution 775 (1992).[135] Despite this, it was unable to handle the situation, resulting in the deployment of UNITAF. While UNOSOM I was under the command of the UN Secretary-General, UNITAF was under the unified command of the United States. Resolution 794 (1992) notably requested the Secretary-General and Member States participating under UNITAF to 'establish appropriate mechanisms for coordination between the United Nations and their military forces'.[136] Effectively, this meant that two parallel operations were present in Somalia at the time – one with a peacekeeping mandate and the other peace enforcement under Chapter VII to complement the peacekeeping operation.

[131] Erika de Wet and Michael Wood, 'Threat to the Peace' *Max Planck Encyclopedia of Public International Law* (online edn, last updated January 2022). See also Nigel White, 'The Relationship Between the UN Security Council and General Assembly in Matters of International Peace and Security' in Weller (n 17) 298–99; Mónica Lourdes de la Serna Galván, 'Interpretation of Article 39 of the UN Charter (Threat to the Peace) by the Security Council: Is the Security Council a Legislator for the Entire International Community?' (2011) XI *Anuario Mexicano de Derecho Internacional* 153–54.

[132] Erika de Wet, 'Article 39' in Simma et al (n 21) 1633–34. See for example UNSC Res 1295 (2000) on the situation in Angola, UNSC Res 1291 (2000) on the situation in the Democratic Republic of the Congo, UNSC Res 1333 (2000) on the situation in Afghanistan and UNSC Res 1474 (2003) on the situation in Somalia.

[133] Dire Tladi, 'Security Council, the Use of Force and Regime Change: Libya and Côte d'Ivoire' (2012) 37(1) *South African Yearbook of International Law* 24–25. The fact that the resolution authorised humanitarian intervention was also raised during the respective UNSC debates. See UN Doc S/PV.3145 (1992), for example 30 (France), 31 (Australia), 36 (United States), 46 (Morocco) and 51 (Hungary).

[134] UNSC Res 751 (1992) paras 2, 7.

[135] UNSC Res 751 (1992) paras 2, 7; UNSC Res 775 (1992) para 3.

[136] UNSC Res 794 (1992) para 13.

This division of labour proved practically problematic, especially considering the respective mandates given to UNOSOM and UNITAF and the corresponding command over these operations. The issue was first raised during UNSC debates preceding the adoption of Resolution 794 (1992). Although the general response to the situation was welcomed, the shared sentiment was that the authorisation and implementation should be at the behest of the UN. The Zimbabwean representative welcomed the draft resolution, emphasising that the UN Secretary-General was at the controlling centre of the operation.[137] This was not the opinion of the Chinese representative who noted that, while the Secretary-General had been given 'some authorisation', it expressed its reservation at the draft resolution as it had 'taken the form of authorising certain countries to take military actions, which may adversely affect the collective role of the UN'.[138] Nonetheless, it voted in favour of the resolution. Belgium expressed its preference to have a purely UN operation in line with the fifth proposal by the Secretary-General in his report on Somalia, but conceded that the fourth option of authorising Member States to take action was also acceptable.[139] The Russian delegation said that the situation in Somalia clearly required the use of force 'under the auspices of the Security Council' to deliver humanitarian assistance and, therefore, it would also vote in favour of the draft resolution.[140]

Concerns raised in the Council debate were soon realised. Issues of practicality were especially highlighted when two missions that were not under a unified UN command operated simultaneously, involving somewhat diverging mandates. Disagreements pertaining to the interpretation of the respective mandates were present from the start. UNOSOM was mandated to, among others, monitor a ceasefire agreement in Mogadishu, to provide protection to UN personnel and to escort deliveries of humanitarian supplies. Under Resolution 775 (1992), its mandate was expanded to include the protection of humanitarian convoys throughout Somalia. UNITAF's mandate, on the other hand, was to establish a secure environment for humanitarian assistance and it predominantly operated in Mogadishu (although later on also in the southern parts of the country).[141] Under its mandate, unlike that of UNOSOM, disarmament was not considered part of its objectives.[142] In contrast, the UN Secretariat considered disarmament as essential before the UNITAF transition to UNOSOM II under UN command.[143] In addition, the UN also continuously requested that UNITAF expand its operations in Northern Somalia. The directive given to UNITAF,

[137] UN Doc S/PV.3145 (1992) 7.

[138] UN Doc S/PV.3145 (1992) 17.

[139] UN Doc S/PV.3145 (1992) 24.

[140] UN Doc S/PV.3145 (1992) 26–27.

[141] See UNSC Res 775 (1992) para 3. See also US Army Centre of Military History, 'The United States Army in Somalia 1992–1994' (CMH Pub 40-81-1).

[142] Gill and Tibori-Szabó, 'The Intervention in Somalia' (n 115) 492; see also Major Robert Allen, 'Lessons From Somalia: The Dilemma of Peace Enforcement' (1997) Global Security CSC Paper.

[143] Allen (n 142) 29.

however, was that such an expansion could constitute 'mission creep' and, as a result, effect was not given to the requests by the UN.[144] By March 1993, UNITAF considered the situation in Somalia secure, sufficiently enough to transition to UNOSOM II and to allow it to begin efforts of its broader mandate of rehabilitation. The UN Secretary-General, however, disagreed with the timing of the transition and expressed concern that UNITAF's mandate had not been entirely fulfilled.[145] Nonetheless, by 31 March 1994 UNITAF had completely withdrawn from Somalia.

On 26 March 1993 the UNSC adopted Resolution 814 (1993) establishing the expanded UNOSOM II operation. Citing the Secretary-General's concerns, the UNSC explicitly provided UNOSOM II with a mandate under Chapter VII.[146] In addition, the UNSC also stressed the importance of disarmament which had notably been raised during UNITAF's mandate, demanding that all Somali parties comply with modalities of disarmament.[147] With the adoption of Resolution 837 (1993), the UNSC explicitly authorised the expanded UNOSOM II peacekeeping operation to use 'all necessary measures' beyond self-defence to establish effective authority of UNOSOM II throughout Somalia and to arrest and detain persons acting against it.[148] This was seen as an improvement of the mandate originally assigned to UNOSOM. UNOSOM II was terminated under Resolution 954 (1994), which extended its mandate for a final period until 31 March 1994.

In essence, the presence of two parallel UNSC-authorised operations was not ideal, and the fact that the UN did not have overall command of both operations proved practically and logistically challenging.[149] Nevertheless, it would not be the first time in which such challenges arose, having authorised several similar parallel operations in other situations. As for its authorisation of humanitarian assistance, the adoption of Resolution 794 (1992) signalled the beginning of a new era where human rights violations constituted a central consideration by the UNSC.[150] At the time, the UNSC's competence to make such a determination and subsequently to take action for humanitarian purposes was sceptically assessed. However, given its extensive practice, particularly during the 1990s, it is clear today that the UNSC has the power to act under Chapter VII for humanitarian purposes.

[144] Allen (n 142) 29.
[145] Allen (n 142) 29.
[146] UNSC Res 814 (1993) paras 5, 6.
[147] UNSC Res 814 (1993) paras 7, 8.
[148] UNSC Res 837 (1993) para 5.
[149] See also Philipp (n 117) 535; Neyire Akpinarli, *The Fragility of the 'Failed State' Paradigm: A Different International Law Perception of the Absence of Effective Government* (Martinus Nijhoff Publishers 2010) 40–47.
[150] Even so, it is important to note that while the UNSC has become more concerned with human rights violations, its actions (and inaction), particularly during the 1990s exposed its failures to prevent atrocities committed during the Rwandan Genocide (1994) and the Bosnian Genocide (1995).

C. Resolutions Pertaining to the Situation(s) in Haiti

i. Resolutions 875 (1993), 917 and 940 (1994)

On 29 September 1991 a military coup led by Lieutenant General Rauol Cedras overthrew Haitian President Jean-Bertrand Aristide. Widely regarded as Haiti's first democratic elections, Aristide had won the election only nine months prior. In the months that followed, Human Rights Watch estimated political killings and civil unrest to have led to the deaths of more than a thousand people.[151] Beginning on 19 October 1993, in a bid to remove the military junta that had rebelled against the Haitian government and to restore democracy in the country, the UNSC adopted a series of resolutions authorising and eventually authorised force against the Haitian regime.

The adoption of these resolutions served as another example in which the UNSC had explicitly authorised the use of force. More specifically, the unique action by the UNSC saw a dual approach in attempting to remove the military junta: First was the authorisation for the use of force to enforce an embargo (similar to Resolution 221 (1966) on Southern Rhodesia and Resolution 665 (1990) on Iraq), and second was the authorisation for the use of force against the regime itself. With the adoption of Resolution 940 (1994), the UNSC for the first time authorised the use of force to restore a democratically elected government.[152]

a. Explicit Authorisation for Embargo Enforcement: Resolutions 875 (1993) and 917 (1994)

Resolution 875 (1993) reaffirmed the threat to international peace and security the UNSC had first made in Resolution 841 (1993).[153] Subsequently, this determination was reaffirmed in Resolution 861 (1993) and recalled in Resolutions 862 (1993), 867 (1993) and 873 (1993).[154] Resolution 875 (1993) called upon Member States acting nationally or through regional organisations to 'use such measures commensurate' with specific circumstances 'as may be necessary … to ensure strict implementation' of a petroleum, arms and related embargo in line with Resolutions 841 (1993) and 873 (1993).[155] The language used in the resolution deviated from the express mention of the use of force or the term 'by all necessary means'. Instead, the term 'such measures commensurate with the specific

[151] Human Rights Watch, 'Human Rights Watch World Report 1993 – Haiti (1 January 1993)' https://shorturl.at/eMPFr.

[152] UNSC Res 940 (1994).

[153] UNSC Res 841 (1993) preamble para 14.

[154] UNSC Res 861 (1993) preamble paras 1, 6; UNSC Res. 862 (1993) preamble para 6; UNSC Res 867 (1993) preamble para 7; UNSC Res 873 (1993) preamble para 4.

[155] UNSC Res 875 (1993) para 1; UNSC Res 873 (1993) para 1, 2, 3; UNSC Res 841 (1993) para 3.

circumstances as may be necessary' appeared in the resolution's first operative paragraph.

This was precisely the language used in Resolution 665 (1990) which had authorised the use of force to enforce an embargo against Iraq.[156] UNSC debates show the resolution was interpreted as an authorisation of force: the United States said that it would use its 'diplomatic and military power to see that economic sanctions work' and the United Kingdom viewed the resolution based on Chapters VII and VIII.[157] China acknowledged the resolution's authorisation of force adding that the resolution authorised 'special actions taken under the unique and exceptional circumstances in Haiti' and should not establish a precedent.[158] The President of the UNSC at the time, in his capacity as the Brazilian representative, said that not only were the 'unique measures' taken in exceptional circumstances, but that they were taken 'in response to a formal and explicit request by the legitimate [g]overnment of Haiti for the strengthening of the provisions of Resolution 873 (1993)'.[159]

Seven months later, following continued instability in Haiti and non-compliance with embargo measures, the UNSC adopted its second authorising resolution, Resolution 917 (1994).[160] Reaffirming all previous Resolutions including authorising Resolution 875 (1993), the UNSC imposed a broad range of increased, comprehensive embargo measures.[161] Acting under Chapter VII, it again called upon Member States 'to use such measures commensurate with the specific circumstances as may be necessary under the authority of the Security Council to ensure strict implementation of the provisions of the present resolution and earlier relevant resolutions'.[162] Among these were the partial interruption of flights to and from Haiti; preventing the of entry of certain persons into their states' territories; freezing the funds and resources of certain individuals; and preventing the supply of all commodities and products originating in Haiti.[163] Resolution 917 (1994) also demanded the return of the democratically-elected government in Haiti in accordance with the Governors Island Agreement.[164]

b. Resolution 940 (1994) Explicit Authorisation for the Restoration of Democracy

Continued non-compliance by the military junta with UNSC demands then lead to the adoption of Resolution 940 (1994). It was the first instance in which the use

[156] UNSC Res 665 (1990) para 1.
[157] UN Doc S/PV.3293 (1993) 7, 12.
[158] UN Doc S/PV.3293 (1993) 18.
[159] UN Doc S/PV.3293 (1993) 23.
[160] UNSC Res 917 (1994).
[161] UNSC Res 917 (1994) paras 3–9.
[162] UNSC Res 917 (1994) para 10.
[163] UNSC Res 917 (1994) para 2; paras 3(a)–(c); paras 4–7.
[164] UNSC Res 917 (1994) para 18(e).

of force was specifically authorised to restore democratic rule.[165] Resolution 940 (1994) determined the situation a threat to peace and security in the region.[166] It subsequently authorised Member States to form a multinational force under a unified command and use 'all necessary means' to achieve its mandate.[167] The authorisation to use force was approved for three main tasks: first, to remove the illegal military leadership from Haiti; second, to allow for the return of the legitimately-elected President; and, third, to restore the legitimate authorities of the government of Haiti.[168] The resolution has on occasion been argued as being a prime example of the development of the right to assist to restore democracy.[169] However, it is important to note that the UNSC was clear that the situation in Haiti was of a 'unique character' and required an 'exceptional response'. This evidently was to limit the interpretation of Resolution 940 (1994) from setting a precedent for the use of force to restore democratic rule.[170] Nonetheless, the intervention in Haiti was not an isolated instance in which force was employed by the UNSC for the restoration of democracy, the UNSC having on no less than three subsequent occasions acted similarly.[171] In addition to authorising enforcement action, the resolution explicitly stated that its mission would be terminated upon a determination by the UNSC of the establishment of a secure and stable environment in Haiti.[172] Resolution 940 (1994), therefore, was one of the first UNSC resolutions to contain a 'functional deadline' after the which the use of force would be terminated.[173]

As with other authorising resolutions, Resolutions 875 (1993) 917 (1994) and 940 (1994) authorised force explicitly. They explicitly determined and reaffirmed a threat to peace and security, invoked both Chapters VII and VIII and used explicit language in their operative paragraphs.

ii. Resolution 1529 (2004)

Nearly a decade after the UNSC had authorised the intervention force to restore democratic rule in Haiti, in February 2004 a conflict lasting several weeks broke

[165] Gray, *International Law and the Use of Force* (n 33) 343.

[166] UNSC Res 940 (1994) preamble para 10.

[167] UNSC Res 940 (1994) para 4.

[168] UNSC Res 940 (1994) para 4.

[169] See for example Lois Fielding, 'Taking the Next Step in the Development of New Human Rights: The Emerging Right of Humanitarian Assistance to Restore Democracy' (1995) 5 *Duke Journal of Comparative and International Law* 343–55 and Christopher Ward, 'Drawing a Line in the Sand: The United Nations Security Council' (1998) *Australian International Law Journal* 112.

[170] Gray, *International Law and the Use of Force* (n 33) 66. See Repertoire of the Practice of the Security Council (1993–1995) 1128, discussion surrounding concerns of Latin American States since a previous draft of the resolution contained language similar to that of UNSC Res 678 (1990). These Latin American States, for one, argued against the situation in Haiti as being a threat to international peace and security.

[171] See for example the UNSC's actions in Côte d'Ivoire in 2011.

[172] UNSC Res 940 (1994) para 8.

[173] Blokker, 'Is the Authorisation Authorised?' (n 41) 563.

out across the country, engulfing it in civil unrest and violence. The outbreak of violence was the result of long-lasting political tensions building up from a sweeping election win by President Jean-Bertrand Aristide in 2000. The election win was widely argued to have been flawed. By February 2004 rebels had gained control of much of the country and, under mounting domestic and international pressure, led to the eventual resignation of President Aristide.[174] On 29 February 2004, expressing its concern at the continuing violence, the UNSC adopted Resolution 1529 (2004), again authorising the use of force in Haiti.[175] The resolution followed a similar path as in the previous three resolutions that had authorised the use of force in Haiti in 1993, namely, that such authorisation had been explicitly provided. Resolution 1529 (2004), however, differed in two respects. First, the Article 39 determination expressly indicated that the threat to international peace and security also constituted a threat to the stability of the Caribbean sub-region as a result of potential refugee outflows. Second was the slight deviation from the usual wording of 'all necessary means', the resolution instead having referred to 'all necessary measures'.

a. Explicit Authorisation

Resolution 1529 (2004), determining the situation in Haiti a threat to international peace and security and acting under the Chapter VII, authorised the immediate deployment of a multinational interim force for a period of three months to facilitate humanitarian assistance.[176] It explicitly authorised all Member States participating in the multinational force to 'take all necessary measures' to fulfil its mandate.[177] The objectives of the interim force were predominantly humanitarian orientated, including facilitating the provision of humanitarian assistance.[178]

Notably however, was how a threat to peace and security within the resolution was articulated. Previous UNSC resolutions on Haiti determined the internal situation a threat to peace and security in the region; applying ample caution not to set any precedent on domestic intervention nor purely internal situations constituting a threat to the peace.[179] With the adoption of Resolution 1529 (2004), however, the UNSC did not condition its words. Not only did it consider the internal situation in Haiti to constitute a threat to international peace and security, but it also explicitly included an international nexus to the situation. The resolution firmly expressed that the situation in Haiti also threatened the stability of the Caribbean sub-region and, principally because of the potential

[174] See broadly Anne Street, *Haiti 2004: A Nation in Crisis* (Catholic Institute for International Relations 2004).
[175] UNSC Res 1529 (2004).
[176] UNSC Res 1529 (2004) para 2.
[177] UNSC Res 1529 (2004) para 6.
[178] UNSC Res 1529 (2004) paras 2(a)–(e).
[179] The UNSC referred to the situation in Haiti in 1993 as 'unique' and 'exceptional'.

outflow of people from the country.[180] It was clear that the authorisation of force in Haiti in 2004 considered the cross-border impact of the domestic situation, which at the time stood in direct contrast to the previous resolutions adopted on the situation in 1993.

A second aspect under Resolution 1529 (2004) was the precise wording of the operative paragraph authorising the use of force by the multinational force. It was the first time the UNSC had opted for the term 'all necessary measures' rather than its previous phrasing of 'all necessary means'. While appearing to be a matter of semantics, Kirgis suggests some significance in the difference.[181]

Whereas the term 'all necessary means' has been interpreted as simply authorising the use of force, Kirgis suggests that the term 'all necessary measures' could in addition to including authorisation of force, also include additional actions to achieve the resolution's goals (including humanitarian goals).[182] Kirgis therefore proposes that the word 'measures', may be interpreted more broadly and consequently suggests action beyond the mere use of force. This may be a justifiable interpretation since the UNSC in more recent practice has engaged in providing more extensive mandates when authorising force. This in turn suggests that authorising resolutions concern the achievement of certain objectives (often humanitarian objectives) that may require action beyond the mere use of force.

This is evident from resolutions adopted in the 1990s on the situation in the FRY, in particular, which consistently authorised the use of all necessary 'measures' rather than 'means'.[183] Kirgis points to, for example, the language used in Resolution 1528 (2004) on the situation in Côte d'Ivoire adopted just two days before. Paragraph 16 explicitly authorised a strictly security-related mandate to French forces to use 'all necessary means' (and not 'measures') to support the United Nations Operation in Côte d'Ivoire, therefore suggesting only the use of force to ensure security.[184] With that said, however, as Blokker points out, the broader UNSC practice does not suggest much of a distinction between the terms.[185] The most recent use of the word 'means'

[180] UNSC Res 1529 (2004) preamble para 9.

[181] In this context, the term 'all necessary measures' was first used by the UNSC in UNSC Res 169 (1961), when it requested the Secretary-General, under a peacekeeping operation in the Congo, to 'prevent the entry or return' of foreign military and paramilitary elements into the Congo. See UNSC Res 169 (1961) para 5. See also the interpretation of these two terms by Kirgis in Frederic Kirgis, 'Security Council Resolution on Multinational Interim Force in Haiti' (2004) 8(4) *American Journal of International Law Insights*.

[182] Kirgis (n 181). See also Blokker, 'Outsourcing the Use of Force' (n 101) 213.

[183] See for example UNSC Res 770 (1992); UNSC Res 781 (1992); UNSC Res 816 (1993) and UNSC Res 908 (1994).

[184] Kirgis (n 181). UNSC Res 1528 (2004) para 16, but see also contrast to the term 'all necessary means' in para 8.

[185] Blokker, 'Outsourcing the Use of Force' (n 101) 213. Blokker suggests that there is no indication from UNSC practice that the difference in terms would have a bearing on the scope or mandate of a

rather than 'measures' was only seen under Resolutions 1816 and 1838 (2008) on instances of piracy in Somalia. In all other authorising resolutions since Resolution 1529 (2004), the UNSC has opted to consistently employ the phrase 'all necessary measures' when authorising the use of force, at least when authorising Member States or regional organisations, whether for humanitarian purposes or not.[186] In any case, it is also clear that the incorporation of either of the terms may be interpreted affirmatively for the authorisation of the use of force.[187]

The implementation of Resolution 1529 (2004) came with the deployment of the United States-led *Operation Secure Tomorrow* (French *Operation Carbet*; Canadian *Operation Halo*), with forces from the United States, Chile, Canada and France contributing to the multinational force. The force consisted of some 3,500 troops under the overall command of the United States. On the one hand, the operation was widely seen to have assisted in improving the situation in Haiti, allowing for the establishment of the subsequent follow-up United Nations Stabilisation Mission in Haiti (MINUSTAH).[188] On the other hand, the operation was criticised on several fronts. The United States contribution to the multinational force was far too insignificant, especially considering that it had intervened in Haiti in 1994 with a much larger force.[189] Contributing factors, in particular, its commitments in Afghanistan and Iraq at the time, were attributed to the lack of resources for the operation.[190] Roughly midway through its deployment, the multinational force was still unable to completely accomplish its mandate, specifically its objective of securing a stable environment across Haiti.[191]

The interim multinational force had fully withdrawn by July 2004 and, in line with the Secretary-General's recommendation, MINUSTAH was established.[192] The interim multinational force was entirely succeeded by MINUSTAH through the adoption of Resolution 1542 (2004).[193]

resolution and that the use of the terms was a 'coincidental outcome of the negotiations preceding the adoption of the relevant resolutions'.

[186] See Blokker, 'Outsourcing the Use of Force' (n 101) 213. The most recent example includes UNSC Resolution 2699 (2023).

[187] Blokker, 'Outsourcing the Use of Force' (n 101) 225. See also Penelope Nevill, 'Military Sanctions Enforcement in the Absence of Express Authorisation?' in Weller (n 17) 289 that the authorisation to 'use all necessary means' does not encompass forcible enforcement of sanctions at sea.

[188] MINUSTAH was first envisaged under UNSC Res 1529 (2004) para 3 and established under UNSC Res 1542 (2004).

[189] See UNSC Res 940 (1994) above and the discussion pertaining to the United States *Operation Uphold Democracy*.

[190] Nathaniel T Crain, 'Haiti: Two Decades of Intervention and Very Little to Show' (School of Advanced Military Studies 2012) 35.

[191] UN Doc S/2004/300 (2004) paras 25–26.

[192] UN Doc S/2004/300 (2004) para 69.

[193] UNSC Res 1542 (2004). See ch 5 at p 147–148 on MINUSTAH's authorisation of force.

iii. Resolution 2699 (2023)

Despite intensive intervention by the UNSC, instability persisted in Haiti. In 2020, a gang war erupted in the country's capital, leading to large-scale clashes between Haitian authorities and gangs. By 2023, some estimates claimed that gangs controlled over 90 per cent of Port-au-Prince. On 2 October 2024, the UNSC adopted Resolution 2699 (2024) in response to the situation and after the Haitian government requested international assistance.[194] In a letter to the UNSC requesting the assistance, Haiti explicitly indicated the importance of securing 'Security Council Authorisation under Chapter VII'.[195]

By the time the UNSC adopted its Resolution 2699 (2024), its modus operandi for authorising force to Member States had been well-established.[196] Resolution 2699 (2024) represents one of the most recent explicit authorisations of force.

That Resolution 2699 (2024) authorises force is explicit within the resolution's provisions. The resolution determined the situation in Haiti 'continues to constitute a threat to international peace and security and to stability in the region'.[197] Invoking Chapter VII, Resolution 2699 (2024) authorised Member States to establish a multinational security support mission in Haiti. The UNSC then 'authorise[d]' Member States participating in the mission to 'take all necessary measures' to fulfil its mandate.[198] As was mentioned above, it is interesting to note the use of the term 'all necessary measures' given that the mission was to address a variety of security related objectives ultimately securing conditions conducive to the holding of free and fair elections. Given that the mission was also to assist the Haitian National Police, the mission likely had to take actions beyond the mere use of force.

In addition, the deployment of the mission was limited to an initial period of 12 months. The UNSC also reaffirmed that the rules of engagement and any directives on the use of force were to be developed by the mission in consultation with Haiti and participating States in full respect of Haiti's sovereignty and in conformity with international humanitarian law.[199]

In line with Resolution 2699 (2023), the mission was deployed to Haiti in June 2024 under Kenya, which initially proposed to lead the deployment. At the time of writing, the deployment was explicitly extended under Resolution 2751 (2024), explicitly determining the situation continued to constitute a threat to international peace and security and invoking Chapter VII.[200]

[194] UNSC Res 2699 (2023).
[195] UN Doc S/RES/2023/726 (2023) 2.
[196] Marko Svicevic, 'Resolution 2699's (2023) Authorisation of the Use of Force: A Cautious Return to the Security Council's Chapter VII Authorisation Model?' (12 October 2023) *EJIL:Talk!*
[197] UNSC Res 2699 (2023) preamble para 24.
[198] UNSC Res 2699 (2023) para 5.
[199] UNSC Res 2699 (2023) para 9.
[200] UNSC Res 2751 (2024) para 1.

D. Resolution 929 (1994) | Rwanda

On 4 August 1993 the signing of the Arusha Agreement intended to end a four-year civil war in Rwanda. The conflict, which occurred between 1990 and 1994, was the result of long-standing differences between the Hutu-led Rwandan government and the Tutsi-led rebel Rwandan Patriotic Front. The UNSC first took action in Rwanda on 5 October 1993 when it established the United Nations Assistance Mission for Rwanda (UNAMIR), meant to assist with the implementation of the Arusha Agreement.[201] UNAMIR's weak mandate, which lacked any reference to Chapter VII, was only authorised to use force in line with classic peacekeeping principles.[202] An ineffective mandate together with a lack of resources meant that it could not effectively handle the situation.[203] Combined with violations of the Arusha Agreement and the onslaught of a genocide on a scale not seen since World War II, on 22 June 1994 the UNSC adopted Resolution 929 (1994).[204]

Following widespread killings and displacement of Rwandan civilians, Resolution 929 (1994) established a temporary multinational force to protect persons at risk.[205] In addition, it reiterated support for UNAMIR's mandate under Resolution 925 (1994) by authorising Member States to take action in this respect. The situation in Rwanda was therefore similar to that in Somalia whereby an already-existing UN peacekeeping mission was complemented by Chapter VII authorisation to Member States to assist the mission.

i. Explicit Authorisation under Resolution 929 (1994)

Resolution 929 (1994) followed a similar approach in authorising force by Member States as with previous authorising resolutions. It explicitly determined that the magnitude of the humanitarian crisis in Rwanda constituted a threat to peace and security in the region. The resolution also explicitly invoked Chapter VII when in its operative paragraph three it *authorised* Member States to use 'all necessary means' to conduct the operation.[206] Moreover, paragraph two of the resolution welcomed the offer by Member States to cooperate with the Secretary-General in order to establish a temporary operation under national command and control to achieve the objectives of the UN. These objectives were listed under operative paragraph two of the resolution, indicating the operation was to 'in an impartial way' contribute to the security and protection

[201] UNSC Res 872 (1993) paras 2, 3. See also arts 1, 5, Peace Agreement between the Government of the Republic of Rwanda and the Rwandese Patriotic Front' (4 August 1993).
[202] Several resolutions were adopted on UNAMIR, however, none were under Chapter VII.
[203] See also Haidi Willmot and Ralph Mamiya, 'Mandated to Protect: Security Council Practice on the Protection of Civilians' in Weller (n 17) 384.
[204] UNSC Res 929 (1994).
[205] UNSC Res 929 (1994) para 2.
[206] UNSC Res 929 (1994) para 3.

of displaced persons, refugees and civilians at risk.[207] Paragraph three invoked Chapter VII authorising force, specifically to 'conduct the operation referred to in paragraph 2 above using all necessary means to achieve the humanitarian objectives set out in paragraph 4(a) and (b) of Resolution 925 (1994)'.[208]

ii. Authorisation by Reference to a Previous Non-authorising Resolution

In effect, with the adoption of Resolution 929 (1994), the UNSC authorised the use of force to not only ensure the implementation of the provisions under paragraph 2 of Resolution 929 (1994), but also to ensure the implementation of specific provisions of Resolution 925 (1994). Resolution 925 (1994) specifically extended UNAMIR's mandate and expanded it under paragraphs 4(a) and (b). Resolution 925 (1994), however, did not authorise force for purposes of its own implementation. Paragraphs 4(a) and (b) of Resolution 925 (1994) reaffirmed the mandate of UNAMIR which, similar to paragraph 2 of Resolution 929 (1994), involved the protection of displaced persons, refugees and civilians.[209] Additionally, it included as part of its mandate the provision of security and support for the distribution of relief supplies and humanitarian relief operations.[210]

Essentially, UNAMIR was not mandated under Chapter VII of Resolution 925 (1994) (nor under Resolution 872 (1993)), which in itself proved detrimental to UNAMIR's performance in Rwanda. Rather, the invocation of Chapter VII in Resolution 929 (1994), combined with the reference to UNAMIR's mandate in Resolution 925 (1994), seemed to have remedied this in that force was authorised to implement the provision of a previous resolution which did not initially allow for force to be used.[211] Authorisation to use force was of course granted to Member States and not to UNAMIR. With the exception of Resolution 770 (1990) on the situation in Bosnia, it was one of the first instances in which the UNSC had authorised force to explicitly implement listed provisions of a non-authorising resolution.

This did not transform Resolution 925 (1994) into a Chapter VII resolution, but merely ensured that Chapter VII measures under the subsequent Resolution 929 (1994) could be employed to effect provisions under it. As such, the UNSC debate preceding the adoption of Resolution 929 (1994) proposed caution when proceeding with such authorisation. For example, Brazil, raising the issue of Chapter VII invocation, stated that 'the Council should do its utmost to avoid invoking the extraordinary powers conferred upon it by Chapter VII of

[207] UNSC Res 929 (1994) para 2.

[208] UNSC Res 929 (1994) para 3, read together with para 2 and UNSC Res 925 (1994).

[209] UNSC Res 925 (1994) para 4(a).

[210] UNSC Res 925 (1994) para 4(b).

[211] Ibrahim A Gambari, 'Rwanda: An African Perspective' in David M Malone (ed), *The UN Security Council: From the Cold War to the 21st Century* (Lynne Rienner Publishers 2004) 518–19, authorisation was given to France.

the United Nations Charter', highlighting the fact that UNAMIR's mandate was not given under Chapter VII.[212] In a post-adoption statement, underlining the scope of the operation's mandate and recognising scepticism with its authorisation to use force, the United States pointed out that the mandate had been narrowed to addressing only humanitarian needs under paragraphs 4(a) and (b) of Resolution 925 (1994).[213]

iii. Implementation of Resolution 929 (1994)

On 2 July 1994 France announced that it would send troops to assist the UN-mandated temporary force under *Operation Turquoise*.[214] The multinational operation under Resolution 929 (1994) was approved for a period of two months subject to a shorter time should the Secretary-General find that UNAMIR was able to carry out its mandate without the operation.[215] Subsequently, the withdrawal of French forces was to commence on 31 July 1994 but only occurred on 21 August that year.[216] *Operation Turquoise* was conducted in four phases, the first two of which included its deployment in several regions in Rwanda and the establishment of safe humanitarian zones in the south-west of the country.[217] The third phase involved reducing troop numbers and gradually transferring control over safe humanitarian zones to UNAMIR.[218] The final phase of *Operation Turquoise* involved logistical support to French-speaking African contingents for necessary replenishments and supply operations. According to the French government, the operation put an end to the massacre in Rwanda, ensured the protection of the population and allowed for the transition of the safe humanitarian zones to UNAMIR 'under satisfactory circumstances'.[219] It concluded that the operation, which aimed 'to re-establish, through the use of force, a situation in which humanitarian activities could be carried out', was considered successful. A decisive factor to which it attributed this success was the strict observance of neutrality.[220]

While the French operation was described as a success, at least under its mandate concerning humanitarian assistance, the UN's (in)action in Rwanda was later deemed its greatest failure. This was partially attributable to UNAMIR's weak mandate at the time, which failed to prevent the ensuing genocide. In particular, the UN-sponsored Report of the Independent Inquiry

[212] UN Doc S/PV.3392 (1994) 2. Brazil abstained from the vote.
[213] UN Doc S/PV.3392(1994) 6.
[214] UN Doc S/1994/924 (1994) 3.
[215] UNSC Res 929 (1994) para 4. See also UN Doc S/1994/832 (1994).
[216] UN Doc S/1994/1133 (1994) 6.
[217] UN Doc S/1994/1100 (1994) 4.
[218] UN Doc S/1994/1133 (1994) 6.
[219] UN Doc S/1994/1133 (1994) 5.
[220] UN Doc S/1994/1133 (1994) 6.

into the Actions of the United Nations During the 1994 Genocide in Rwanda exposed several failures by the UN and French forces.[221] Moreover, as was expressed by the Brazilian delegate during the adoption of Resolution 929 (1994), the report also found it problematic that there were two operations in Rwanda with UNSC authorisation but with 'such divergent powers'.[222] Nonetheless, the criticism stemming from the UN action in Rwanda exposed organisational inefficiencies, including political unwillingness where peace operations were concerned.

Political and logistical considerations aside, the authorisation given to the operation under Resolution 929 (1994) was a clear example of explicit authorisation, having determined a threat to peace and security, invoking Chapter VII and using specific authorising language.

E. Resolution 1080 (1996) | Great Lakes Region

Following the Rwandan genocide of 1994, an estimated two million Rwandan refugees had fled to neighbouring countries of the Great Lakes Region. By spring of 1996, over one million refugees were displaced into (then) Zaire, mainly Hutu Rwandese and Burundian Hutus who had fled the civil war.[223] The large-scale refugee crisis was exacerbated by the fact that many of the persons (including government officials) who had been involved in the Rwandan genocide were present among refugees in the region. As a result, refugee camps became militarised and an eventual Rwandan Patriotic Front-rebel invasion occurred against Zaire. Considering increasing tensions and conflict in the region, on 14 November 1996 Canada proposed the establishment of a temporary multinational force to facilitate humanitarian assistance. To this end, Canada requested 'as a legal framework for this intervention, a resolution under Chapter VII' to meet humanitarian objectives and be terminated by 31 March 1997.[224]

The UNSC's response to the Canadian proposal came one day later with the adoption of Resolution 1080 (1996) in which it authorised a temporary multinational force to assist with humanitarian efforts.[225] Resolution 1080 (1996) served as yet another instance in which the UNSC had explicitly authorised the use force in line with humanitarian considerations. It was also notable that Member States (Canada in particular) would only be willing to engage in operations under a Chapter VII mandate. Although of limited significance, since the

[221] UN Doc S/1999/1257 (1999) 30.
[222] UN Doc S/1999/1257 (1999) 49; UN Doc S/PV.3392 (1994) 5.
[223] Howard Adelman 'The Use and Abuse of Refugees in Zaire: April 1996 to March 1997' Stanford University. https://shorturl.at/Loza2.
[224] UN Doc S/1996/941 (1996) 2.
[225] UNSC Res 1080 (1996).

implementation of the resolution's provision became unnecessary due to changing circumstances, its explicit authorisation needs brief mention.

i. Explicit Authorisation

Resolution 1080 (1996), much like previous Chapter VII resolutions, explicitly determined the situation in Eastern Zaire to constitute a threat to international peace and security. Similarly, this determination was also made in Resolution 1070 (1996). It welcomed the establishment of the temporary multinational force and authorised Member States co-operating with the Secretary-General to conduct the operation using 'all necessary means' to achieve its humanitarian objectives.[226] In line with the Canadian envisagement, the Resolution also explicitly invoked Chapter VII. It was however during the UNSC debates in which the changing situation on the ground had been raised, with reports of thousands of refugees returning to Rwanda. Rwanda urged changing circumstances should be taken into account by the multinational force and that its mandate should accordingly be reconsidered.[227]

While the Canadian proposal was praised in the UNSC debate preceding the adoption of Resolution 1080 (1996), the changing situation had significant impacts. This development prompted some troop-contributing States to reassess the need for the multinational force.[228] The United States alone scaled down on its intended contribution from 4,000 to fewer than 1 000 troops, none of which were to be deployed in Zaire.[229] While over 20 nations contributed to the operation (financially) and a multinational headquarters was set up in the country, eventually only Canadian troops were deployed to Zaire under *Operation Assurance*.[230] Although the operation was scheduled to terminate at the end of March 1997 and was authorised to use force to achieve its objectives, by December 1996 the Canadian force had completely withdrawn.[231]

In hindsight, the mandate under Resolution 1080 (1996) seemed almost unnecessary, given the rate at which circumstances on the ground had changed. Nonetheless, the UNSC's adoption of Resolution 1080 (1996) clearly authorised force for humanitarian purposes. This was evident in both the wording of the resolution and the UNSC debates preceding its adoption.

[226] UNSC Res 1080 (1996) preamble para 11, para 3; see also UNSC Res 1078 (1996) preamble para 18.

[227] UN Doc S/PV.3731 (1997) 5.

[228] John Hay, 'Conditions of Influence: A Canadian Case Study in the Diplomacy of Intervention' (1999) Centre for Security and Defence Studies Occasional Paper 19–20; see also remarks by the UN Secretary-General in UN Doc S/1996/993 (1996) para 2.

[229] Hay (228) 22.

[230] Hay (233) 25. See also Michael Hennessy, 'Operation "Assurance": Planning a Multinational Force for Rwanda/Zaire' (Spring 2001) *Canadian Military Journal* 17.

[231] Hay (n 233) 28; Simon Massey, 'Operation Assurance: The Greatest Intervention that Never Happened' [1998] *The Journal of Humanitarian Assistance* 10; 'Canadian-Led Zaire Force to Pull Out' *Reuters* (14 December 1996).

F. Resolutions 1101 and 1114 (1997) | Albania

During 1996–97, nation-wide civil unrest engulfed Albania. The unrest was the result of the collapse of an intricate system of pyramid schemes in the country which saw Albania lose an estimated $1, 2 billion, amounting to almost half the country's gross domestic product.[232] What resulted was months of civil unrest described as a near civil war and the deaths of some 2 000 people. Italy was the first to suggest a UNSC-sanctioned operation in Albania. In a letter to the UN Secretary-General, the Italian Permanent Representative said that Albania had requested an international response and confirmed that it would take the initiative in line with consultation between the Organisation for Security and Cooperation in Europe (OSCE) and Albania, to create a multinational protection force which would 'act under Chapter VII of the Charter'.[233] In a subsequent letter to the UNSC, Albania indicated the multinational force should have the 'necessary support and authorisation of the UNSC'.[234]

Both the letters of the Italian and Albanian permanent representatives were clear that the envisaged multinational force would have a humanitarian function – assisting in delivery of humanitarian aid and creating a safe environment across the country. On the same day, an Italian-sponsored draft resolution was adopted as Resolution 1101 (1997).[235] The most notable aspect of the resolution was that it lacked the standard reference authorising the use of 'all necessary means'. Nonetheless, it was clear that the invocation of Chapter VII in this context, read together with the provisions of the resolution, authorised force.

i. Explicit Authorisation under 'Conditional Chapter VII Invocation'

Resolution 1101 (1997), similarly to Resolution 940 (1994) on the situation in Haiti, determined the situation in Albania to be a threat to peace and security in the region, and not to international peace and security generally.[236] It welcomed the establishment of a temporary and limited multinational protection force to facilitate humanitarian assistance and authorised participating Member States to act in a neutral and impartial way to achieve its objectives.[237] These included facilitating the delivery of humanitarian assistance and helping create a secure environment for the provision of assistance by international organisations.[238]

The resolution invoked Chapter VII specifically where it authorised Member States participating in the multinational protection force

[232] Christopher Jarvis, 'The Rise and Fall of Albania's Pyramid Schemes' (March 2000) 37(1) *Finance and Development International Monetary Fund* 1.
[233] UN Doc S/1997/258 (1997) 1.
[234] UN Doc S/1997/259 (1997).
[235] UNSC Res 1101 (1997).
[236] UNSC Res 1101 (1997) preamble para 9.
[237] UNSC Res 1101 (1997) para 4.
[238] UNSC Res 1101 (1997) para 2.

'to ensure the security and freedom of movement of the personnel [of the force]'.[239] Kritsiotis has pointed out that Resolution 1101's (1997) 'qualified invocation' of Chapter VII presented a 'narrow field of application' of the UNSC's enforcement actions.[240] The consequence thereof is that the UNSC's Chapter VII powers were not attributable to the multinational forces' mandate, but only to the security and movement of its personnel.[241] Such a conclusion is supported both by the limited Chapter VII invocation as well as the fact that the UNSC chose not to authorise more broadly the use of 'all necessary means [or] measures].'

In so far as the authorisation may be considered explicit, it is also worth noting that the UNSC expressly limited the operation to a period of three months and participating Member States were to report every two weeks to the UNSC (through the Secretary-General).[242]

The fact that Resolution 1101 (1997) lacked reference to the terms 'by all necessary means' did not detract from its authorisation of force. The invocation of Chapter VII combined with the UNSC having 'authorise[d]' the operation to be conducted in a 'neutral and impartial way' and for the protection of and freedom of movement of the force was interpreted affirmatively as an authorisation of force.[243] This was particularly evident with China's reservation against the invocation of Chapter VII in relation to a State's domestic affairs.[244] This was however not at dispute in the present case since the protection force had been requested by the Albanian government. The multinational protection force under Resolution 1101 (1997) was deployed as the Italian-led *Operation Alba*, with 11 additional nations participating. Italy assumed command and operational control of the operation, which conducted several hundred humanitarian aid escorts, securing 27 aid distribution points, and over 1,500 OSCE mission escorts.[245]

In its sixth report to the UNSC on *Operation Alba*, the Italian representative sought to extend the multinational force's mandate, at the request of the Albanian authorities for a period not exceeding 45 days upon the termination of the originally mandated three-month period.[246] Subsequently, the UNSC adopted its second authorising resolution on the situation in Albania on 19 June 1997. Resolution 1114 (1997), reiterating that the situation in Albania

[239] UNSC Res 1101 (1997) para 4.

[240] Dino Kritsiotis, 'Security Council Resolution 1101 (1997) and the Multinational Protection Force of Operation Alba in Albania' (1999) 12 *Leiden Journal of International Law* 531.

[241] Kritsiotis (n 240) 533, but see also 540–41 on the obscure link between the authorisation and the Chapter VII invocation.

[242] UNSC Res 1101 (1997) paras 6, 9; As Blokker, 'Is the Authorisation Authorised?' (n 41) 544 notes, these reports for the first time had to fulfil certain conditions.

[243] Gray, *International Law and the Use of Force* (n 33) 346.

[244] UN Doc S/PV.3758 (1997) 3.

[245] Colonel Riccardo Marchio, '"Operation Alba": A European Approach to Peace Support Operations in the Balkans' (2000) USAWC Strategy Research Report 7.

[246] UN Doc S/1997/460 (1997) paras 4, 12.

remained a threat to peace and security in the region, explicitly extended the mandate of the operation by a period of 45 days.[247]

Although both Resolutions 1101 and 1114 (1997) determined the situation in Albania to be a threat to peace and security in the region and invoked Chapter VII, explicit authorisation for the use of force did not follow the usual wording of the UNSC's 'by all necessary means [or] measures' phrasing. Nevertheless, the resolutions were interpreted to have authorised force for very specific reasons, essentially because of the limited Chapter VII invocation to (only) ensure the security and freedom of movement of personnel. In practice, however, it seemed that the multinational force did not rely on any force in conducting its operations and, at most, was involved in cracking down on armed groups, counter-insurgency and patrolling.[248] Most operations involved mission escorts, securing routes and government buildings and preventing looting and arson.

G. Resolutions 1264 and 1272 (1999) | INTERFET and UNTAET

On 11 June 1999 the UNSC established the United Nations Mission in East Timor (UNAMET). UNAMET's predominant goal was to organise and conduct an UN-sponsored referendum for East Timor. On 30 August 1999 the referendum was held and showed majority support for independence from Indonesia. On 4 September, following the announcement of the referendum results, violent clashes erupted in the region. In response to escalating violence, the UNSC adopted Resolution 1264 (1999) authorising the establishment of a multinational International Force for East Timor (INTERFET).[249]

i. Explicit Authorisation

Resolution 1264 (1999) determined the situation in East Timor a threat to peace and security and authorised the deployment of the Australian-led INTERFET under Chapter VII. INTERFET was mandated to restore peace and security in East Timor, protect UNAMET in carrying out its tasks and facilitate humanitarian assistance operations.[250] It explicitly authorised States participating in the multinational force to 'take all necessary measures to fulfil this mandate'.[251]

[247] UNSC Res 1114 (1997) para 6. See also UN Doc S/PV.3791 (1997), the UNSC debate favouring the extension.

[248] James Pettifer and Miranda Vickers, *The Albanian Question: Reshaping the Balkans* (IB Tauris & Co Ltd 2007) 73–74 who question whether such actions could in themselves be considered a use of force.

[249] UNSC Res 1264 (1999) para 3. See also Gray, *International Law and the Use of Force* (n 33) 314, 349.

[250] UNSC Res 1264 (1999) para 3.

[251] UNSC Res 1264 (1999) para 3.

Further, it requested the Secretary-General to make recommendations as soon as possible on the deployment of a United Nations transitional administration in East Timor. In line with these recommendations, the UNSC established the United Nations Transitional Administration in East Timor (UNTAET) under Resolution 1272 (1999).[252]

UNTAET was established under Chapter VII and given a broad mandate to, among others, provide security and maintain law and order throughout the territory of East Timor, establish an effective administration and ensure coordination of humanitarian assistance. UNTAET was set up with a military component of 8,950 troops and up to 200 military observers and was authorised to take 'all necessary measures' to fulfil its mandate.[253]

Resolution 1272 (1999) also requested that both INTERFET and UNTAET cooperate closely with each other with a view to UNTAET replacing INTERFET's enforcement powers 'as soon as possible'. This authorisation given to UNTAET was underlined in Resolution 1319 (2000), although not explicitly. Resolution 1319 (2000) stated that UNMAET should 'respond robustly to the militia threat in East Timor, consistent with Resolution 1272 (1999)'.[254] Although recalling Resolution 1272 (1999), it contained neither an Article 39 determination nor a Chapter VII invocation. Similar phrasing was referenced in Resolution 1338 (2001) extending UNTAET's mandate but without explicitly invoking Chapter VII, determining the situation there to be a threat to peace and security, and lacked any authorising language.

While explicitly extending UNTAET's mandate, UNTAET's authorisation of force was not renewed in subsequent resolutions.[255] In February 2000 INTERFET's military command was transferred to UNTAET. It was eventually replaced by the United Nations Mission of Support in East Timor (UNMISET) and thereafter by the United Nations Integrated Mission in Timor Leste (UNMIT). Neither UNMISET nor UNMIT were subsequently authorised to use force beyond self-defence and remained in line with classic peacekeeping missions.[256] UNMIT was eventually terminated in 2012. All resolutions adopted on the situation in East Timor establishing authorisation were therefore done

[252] UNSC Res 1272 (1999) para 1. For purposes of feasibility, the authorisation accorded to UNTAET is analysed here as it was authorised on the same situation and in the same time span as the authorisation accorded to INTERFET. For a further analysis on specifically authorisation for the use of force to UN peacekeeping missions, see ch 5.

[253] UNSC Res 1272 (1999) paras 3(c), 4.

[254] UNSC Res 1319 (2000) para 6.

[255] See UNSC Res 1319 (2000) para 6; UNSC Res 1338 (2001) para 7; UNSC Res 1392 (2002) para 2. The two former resolutions both state that 'UNTAET should respond robustly to the militia threat in East Timor, consistent with its Resolution 1272 (1999) of 22 October 1999' but without invoking Chapter VII.

[256] See also Gray (n 125) 314 who notes that UNMISET was not established under Chapter VII but was given some Chapter VII powers under UNSC Res 1410 (2002) para 6 to 'take the necessary actions, for the duration of its mandate, to fulfil its mandate'. UNMISET was extended under UNSC Res 1480 (2003), UNSC Res 1543 and UNSC Res 1573 (2004).

under Chapter VII and determined that the situation there constituted a threat to peace and security. UNSC authorisation of UN peacekeeping missions which, among others, examines the establishment and renewal of authorisation of force, is addressed in chapter five.

H. Resolutions 1511 and 1546 (2003) | Multinational Force in Iraq

In March 2003, the United States, supported by the United Kingdom and Australia, commenced *Operation Iraqi Freedom*. The operation, which is discussed in relation to implicit UNSC authorisation in chapter six, was meant to 'disarm Iraq of weapons of mass destruction [and] to end Saddam Hussein's support for terrorism'.[257] The operation in part led to the eventual overthrow and incarceration of Hussein in December 2003. At present, it suffices to say that the legal basis of the operation remains controversial.[258] In the months during and after the invasion, the UNSC adopted a series of notable resolutions on the situation in Iraq.

The first of these was Resolution 1483 (2003), citing the need for the Iraqi people to determine their own political future and gain control over their natural resources.[259] It encouraged efforts at creating a new representative government of Iraq and expressed its resolve at assisting the Iraqi people with humanitarian support and the reconstruction and restoration of national and local institutions of governance. Thereafter, Resolution 1500 (2003) welcomed the establishment of the Governing Council of Iraq and formally established the United Nations Mission for Iraq for an initial period of 12 months and in line with a mandate given under Resolution 1483 (2003).[260] Reaffirming all previous resolutions on the situation and in an effort to ensure stability in Iraq and affirming a series of terrorist bombings as being an attack directed against the Iraqi people, the UNSC adopted Resolution 1511 (2003), its first Chapter VII resolution explicitly authorising force in Iraq.[261]

i. Explicit Authorisation to the Multinational Force

Resolution 1511 (2003) was adopted five months after the United States had ended its major combat operation in Iraq. It determined that the situation in Iraq, 'although improved', continued to constitute a threat to international peace

[257] Office of the Press Secretary, The White House, 'Operation Iraqi Freedom: President Discusses Beginning of Operation Iraqi Freedom' (22 March 2003) https://shorturl.at/wsr0M.

[258] See ch 6 at p 168–176.

[259] UNSC Res 1483 (2003) preamble para 1.

[260] UNSC Res 1500 (2003) paras 1, 2.

[261] UNSC Res 1511 (2003). While not the first Chapter VII resolution adopted on Iraq, it was certainly the first Chapter VII resolution explicitly authorising force after the Second Gulf War.

and security.[262] Acting under Chapter VII, the UNSC, reaffirming its appeal to Member States to assist the people of Iraq and to contribute to its safety and stability under Resolution 1483 (2003), *authorised* a multinational force with a unified command to 'take all necessary measures to contribute to the maintenance of security and stability in Iraq'.[263] The resolution also *urged* Member States to contribute assistance 'including military forces' to the multinational force.[264] The multinational force would have its mission reviewed no later than one year from the adoption of the resolution. The mandate of the multinational force would only expire upon the completion of the political process described in the resolution, namely, when an internationally recognised democratically-elected government assumed responsibility for Iraq.[265] While the authorisation to the multinational force was explicit, it is worth noting that the mandate was criticised at the time as being open-ended without a functional limit – a fact also evident during the UNSC debate.[266]

That said, by June 2004 an Iraqi Interim Government was formed and eventually replaced the CPA. The UNSC then adopted Resolution 1546 (2004), determining the situation continued to constitute a threat to international peace and security and invoking Chapter VII.[267] *Endorsing* the formation of the interim government, and *noting* its request for the presence of the multinational force, the UNSC *reaffirmed* the authorisation for the multinational force under unified command established under Resolution 1511 (2003).[268] It further *decided* that the multinational force 'shall have the authority to take all necessary measures to contribute to the maintenance of security and stability in Iraq'.[269] The authorisation provided to the multinational force was in effect a response to a request by the Prime Minister of the Iraqi Interim Government which had requested 'a new resolution on the Multinational Force (MNF) mandate to contribute to maintaining security in Iraq'.[270] The mandate of the multinational force was to be reviewed at the request of the Iraqi government or 12 months from the date of adoption of Resolution 1546 (2004).[271] Additionally, its mandate was to terminate either at the completion of Iraq's political transition to a democratic government or earlier if requested by the Iraqi government – highlighted in particular during the UNSC debate.[272] The UNSC also explicitly *requested* the United States report to it on behalf of the multinational force

[262] UNSC Res 1511 (2003) preamble para 7.
[263] UNSC Res 1511 (2003) para 13.
[264] UNSC Res 1511 (2003) para 14.
[265] UNSC Res 1511 (2003) para 15, read together with paras 4–7, 10 and 13.
[266] De Wet, *The Chapter VII Powers* (n 34) 290; UN Doc S/PV.4844 (2003) at 3, 4.
[267] UNSC Res 1546 (2004) preamble para 20.
[268] UNSC Res 1546 (2003) para 9, having regard to the request for the multinational force by the Iraqi government.
[269] UNSC Res 1546 (2004) paras 1, 10.
[270] UNSC Res 1546 (2004), Annex.
[271] UNSC Res 1546 (2004) para 12.
[272] UNSC Res 1546 (2004) para 12; S/PV.4987 (2004) 7 (France), 9 (Russia), 12 (Spain).

within three months on efforts and progress of the force, and on a quarterly basis thereafter.[273]

The mandate of multinational force was subsequently extended in Resolution 1637 (2005), Resolution 1723 (2006) and for a final time in Resolution 1790 (2007). In each subsequent resolution, the UNSC explicitly *decided* on the mandate extension and explicitly *reaffirmed* the 'authorisation for the multinational force as set forth in resolution 1546 (2004)'.[274]

Throughout all resolutions adopted on the situation in Iraq pertaining to authorisation of the multinational force, the UNSC consistently determined a threat to international peace and security, invoked Chapter VII and used explicit language to authorise force (*reaffirming* the authorisation for the force established under Resolution 1511 (2003) and later Resolution 1546 (2004)). Resolutions extending the mandate of the multinational force also explicitly *noted* that the presence of the force was at the request of the Iraqi government and that its mandate would be terminated if the government so requested. In addition, mandate extensions were complimented by explicit requests for reporting on a quarterly basis.[275]

Resolution 1511 (2003) and subsequent authorising resolutions were therefore a prime example of explicit UNSC authorisation of force. However, the complexity of the United States' presence and its preceding invasion of Iraq meant that for the most part, attention was primarily directed toward the initial unilateral action by the United States and its allies, rather than the subsequent UN-authorised operation.

IV. 'COMBINED' AUTHORISATION OF FORCE TO MULTIPLE ENTITIES

From the above assessment, it is clear that the UNSC may authorise force to one or more entities. At times, UNSC authorisation is employed by States under a multinational force. Alternatively, and as will be examined in the subsequent chapter, UNSC authorisation may be employed by States 'acting through' regional organisations. At times however, the distinction between authorisation to States and authorisation to regional organisations is not always clear.

On occasion, the UNSC has authorised two or more distinct and separate entities to use force and, in practice, these entities have made extensive use of this authorisation. The principal distinction with combined authorisation, as opposed to, for example, other resolutions that also authorised multiple entities to use force, is that combined authorisation tends to explicitly authorise different

[273] UNSC Res 1546 (2004) para 31. See also UN Doc S/PV.4987 (2004) 9, 12.

[274] UNSC Res 1637 (2005) para 1; UNSC Res 1723 (2006) para 1; UNSC Res 1970 (2007) para 1.

[275] UNSC Res 1546 (2003) para 31; UNSC Res 1637 (2005) para 6; UNSC Res 1723 (2006) para 6; UNSC Res 1970 (2007) para 5.

entities with different degrees of authorisation, and this authorisation is usually demonstrated in practice. This contrasts with, for example, resolutions that authorise force solely to Member States or even Member States 'acting through regional organisations' where such authorisation is usually only made use of by the organisation leading the operation.[276] Such was the case with, for example, most resolutions adopted on the FRY which authorised member states, yet were implemented by NATO-led operations. As will be seen below, the clearest set of practice pertaining to hybrid authorisation involves the UNSC's resolutions on the situations of piracy off the Somalian coast.[277]

A. Resolutions on Piracy off the Somalian Coast (2008–present)

Between 2008 and 2017, an estimated 458 cases of piracy were recorded across the waters off the Somalian coast.[278] Coordinated international efforts significantly reduced the number of these cases. In response to the piracy situation, several States began military operations to deter acts of maritime piracy and protect shipping vessels in the region.

In 2008, the UNSC adopted its first series of authorising resolutions pertaining to the situation of piracy, a practice of explicit authorisation it would repeat for over a decade onward. In addition to the fact that the UNSC authorised force explicitly in more than a dozen resolutions, it also raised several legal implications. Most notable was that the authorisation under the respective resolutions was accorded in adherence with the United Nations Convention on the Law of the Seas (UNCLOS). It therefore meant that States making use of the authorisation, in addition to adhering to the respective resolutions, also had to act in accordance with UNCLOS.

[276] See the detailed categories to which the UNSC has authorised the use of force in Simon Chesterman, *Just War or Just Peace? Humanitarian Intervention and International Law* (Oxford University Press 2001) 171, 174–77. Chesterman identifies five 'classes' of delegated enforcement action: authorisation under Art 42 by the UNSC using troops contributed pursuant to Art 43 agreements; authorisation to the Secretary-General; authorisation to any state; authorisation to a certain nominated state(s); and authorisation to regional organisations.

[277] A similar situation of combined authorisation is found with the operations by ECOWAS, UNOCI and French Forces in the Ivory Coast. These authorising resolutions are however considered in the subsequent chapter.

[278] Statista, 'Number of Actual and Attempted Piracy Attacks in Somalia From 2008 to 2017' https://shorturl.at/gTVvL. Subsequently, debates about the use of force against piracy were abundant. See for example Tullio Treves, 'Piracy, Law of the Sea, and Use of Force: Development off the Coast of Somalia' (2009) 20 *European Journal of International Law* 400; Douglas Guilfoyle, 'Piracy off Somalia: UN Security Council Resolution 1816 and IMO Regional Counter-Piracy Efforts' (2008) 57 *International and Comparative Law Quarterly* 690; Laurie R Blank, 'The Use of Force Against Pirates' in Michael P Scharf, Michael A Newton and Milena Sterio, *Prosecuting Maritime Piracy: Domestic Solutions to International Crimes* (Cambridge University Press 2015) 103; Douglas Guilfoyle, 'The Use of Force Against Pirates' in Weller (n 17) 1057.

i. Resolution 1816 (2008)

On 2 June 2008 the UNSC adopted Resolution 1816 (2008) determining that the

> incidents of piracy and armed robbery against vessels in the territorial waters of Somalia and the high seas off the coast of Somalia exacerbate the situation in Somalia which continues to constitute a threat to international peace and security in the region.

It is first and foremost important to note that the UNSC determined the situation in Somalia and not actual acts of piracy to constitute a threat to peace and security.[279] Acting under Chapter VII, the UNSC *decided* that for a period of six months, States cooperating with the Transitional Federal Government (TFG) in Somalia could take certain actions in the fight against piracy and armed robbery off its coast.

First, the UNSC authorised States to enter into the territorial waters of Somalia for purposes of repressing acts of piracy and armed robbery in a manner consistent with such action permitted on the high seas and with respect to relevant international law.[280] Second, the UNSC authorised States to use, within the territorial waters of Somalia, in a manner consistent with action permitted on the high seas with respect to piracy under relevant international law, *all necessary means* to repress acts of piracy and armed robbery.[281] In addition to the time limit attached to the authorisation, the UNSC explicitly requested States cooperating with the TFG to inform it of actions making use of the authorisation.[282]

Essentially, the authorisation given to Member States under Resolution 1816 (2008) pertained to the use of force against acts of piracy and armed robbery and was subject to such acts being in conformity with relevant international law.[283] Read together with the applicable international legal framework against piracy, namely UNCLOS, the resolution therefore affirmed and expanded the use of force against acts of piracy (including the seizure of a pirate ship, the detention of persons guilty of piracy and hot pursuit) within the territorial waters of Somalia.[284] The resolution also specifically limited its authorisation to

[279] UNSC Res (2008) preamble para 12; UN Doc S/PV.5902 (2008) 4 (South Africa). See also Guilfoyle (n 278) 694–95. The UNSC had first expressed its concern against situations of piracy in UNSC Res 1676 (2006). This exact phrasing was again used in UNSC Res 1801 (2008). See also UNSC Res 1772 (2007) para 18 and UNSC Res 1801 (2008) para 12.

[280] UNSC Res 1816 (2008) para 7(a).

[281] UNSC Res 1816 (2008) para 7(b). Somalia at the time consented to this authorisation. See Guilfoyle, 'Piracy off Somalia' (n 278) 695.

[282] UNSC Res 1816 (2008) para 12.

[283] The relevant international law being the United Nations, United Nations Convention on the Law of the Sea (adopted 10 December 1982, entered into force 16 November 1994) 1833 UNTS 3 (UNCLOS). As Guilfoyle points out, the relevant international law may be summarised as maritime action that is necessary, proportionate and includes the preceding acts of warning shots. See Guilfoyle (n 278) 696.

[284] UNSC Res 1816 (2008) preamble para 4; Arts 101–03, 105, 107, 111 UNCLOS.

the situation in Somalia, and expressly confirming it shall not be considered as establishing customary international law.[285]

ii. Resolution 1838 (2008) and Subsequent Authorising Resolutions

Four months later, the UNSC adopted Resolution 1838 (2008), its second authorising resolution on the situation.[286] It followed an identical manner of formulation when it again authorised force: explicitly determining a threat to international peace and security, explicitly invoking Chapter VII, and explicitly *calling upon* Member States to use the necessary means to repress acts of piracy.[287] In addition, it *called upon* States and regional organisations to coordinate their actions. Thereafter, Resolution 1846 (2008) explicitly extended the authorisation given to Member States for a further period of 12 months from the date of its adoption.[288] Increasing acts of piracy and the continuation of the situation off the coast of Somalia then resulted in several more authorising resolutions. The authorisation to use such measures was subject to advance notification to the Secretary-General and the TFG.

Subsequently, Resolution 1851 (2008) called upon Member States and regional organisations that have the necessary capacity to actively take part in the fight against piracy and expand the use of force against piracy to land-based operations on Somalian territory.[289] Resolution 1851 (2008) arguably expanded the scope of authorised force given it was no longer limited to acts purely at sea and governed by UNCLOS.[290] This was to be done by 'deploying naval vessels and military aircraft and through seizure and disposition of boats, vessels, arms and other related equipment used in the commission of piracy and armed robbery at sea off the coast of Somalia'.[291] The authorisation provided for in Resolutions 1846 (2008) and 1851 (2008) was again explicitly renewed under over a dozen subsequent resolutions.[292]

[285] UNSC Res 1816 (2008) para 9. Guilfoyle notes that this provision aims to extinguish concerns among states that UNCLOS not be modified in any manner. Guilfoyle, 'Piracy off Somalia' (n 278) 696. See also the position of South Africa in UN Doc S/PV.5902 (2008) 4 and UN Doc SC/9344 (2008).

[286] UNSC Res 1838 (2008). See also Eugene Kontorovich, 'International Legal Responses to Piracy off the Coast of Somalia' (2009) 13(2) *American Journal of International Law Insights.*

[287] UNSC Res 1838 (2008) paras 3, 4.

[288] UNSC Res 1846 (2008) paras 10, 11.

[289] UNSC Res 1851 (2008) para 6; Blank (n 278) 111; Kontorovich (n 286).

[290] Robin Geiβ and Anna Petrig, *Piracy and Armed Robbery at Sea: The Legal Framework for Counter-Piracy Operations in Somalia and the Gulf of Aden* (Oxford University Press 2011) 83 note that UNSC Res 1851 (2008) and the use of all necessary measures phrase meant that enforcement action was significantly broadened since it was not read restrictively with UNCLOS.

[291] UNSC Res 1846 (2008) para 2; Geiβ and Petrig (n 278) 83–84.

[292] UNSC Res 1897 (2009) para 7; UNSC Res 1950 (2010) para 7; UNSC Res 2020 (2011) 9; UNSC Res 2077 (2012) para 12; UNSC Res 2125 (2013) para 12; UNSC Res 2184 (2014) para 13; UNSC Res 2246 (2015) para 14; UNSC Res 2316 (2016) para 14; UNSC Res 2383 (2017) para 14; UNSC Res 2442 (2018) para 14; UNSC Res 2500 (2019) para 14; UNSC Res 2554 (2020) para 14; UNSC Res 2608 (2021) para 14.

The resolutions adopted on acts of piracy have been significant in establishing several aspects of UNSC practice. It has been well pointed out that the UNSC has adopted more resolutions pertaining to piracy as a threat to international peace and security than it has on terrorism.[293] The UNSC practice in this regard may be highlighted as follows. First, all UNSC resolutions adopted on the situation explicitly contained an Article 39 determination and invoked Chapter VII. Second, the terms 'by all necessary measures [or] means' does not appear in every resolution.[294] Rather, in those resolutions that did not contain this phrasing, the UNSC authorised the use of force by directly stating that Member States (and, under later resolutions, regional organisations) were to combat piracy 'by deploying naval vessels and military aircraft' to combat this threat – an explicit indication that force could be used. In addition to calling for the use of military assets, the UNSC unequivocally expressed that the legal framework applicable to combating piracy was reflected under UNCLOS.[295] This suggests that the UNSC considered UNCLOS as the primary instrument governing the use of force against piracy.[296]

The implementation of the various UNSC resolutions on the fight against piracy has enjoyed overwhelming support from both Member States and international organisations. In December 2008 the EU launched *Operation Atlanta* (European Union Naval Force EU NAVOFOR) under EU Council Joint Action 851.[297] *Operation Atlanta*'s legal basis was founded upon the relevant UNSC resolutions when acting within Somali territorial waters, and functions under Article 100 of UNCLOS when acting on the high seas.[298] In May 2012 the EU force launched its first inland operation against a pirate base.[299] *Operation Atlanta* was most recently extended by the EU in December 2022 for a period of two years.[300]

On 12 January 2009 the United States-led Combined Maritime Forces established Combined Task Force 151 (CTF 151), operating with a mission-based mandate 'currently endorsed under UNSCR 2608'.[301] It operates in conjunction with the EU's *Operation Atlanta* and NATO's *Operation Ocean Shield* (a component under NATO's *Operation Enduring Freedom – Horn of Africa*). NATO concluded *Operation Shield* in December 2016, although it expressed

[293] Guilfoyle, 'The Use of Force Against Pirates' (n 278) 1058.

[294] The term is contained in UNSC Res 1816 (2008) para 7(b).

[295] Arts 105, 107, 110(1)(a) UNCLOS; Blank (n 278) 105–06, but see also 107 specifically regarding the use of force minimum requirements of proportionality and necessity.

[296] See the position of UNSC Members in UN Doc S/PV.5902 (2008) 2, 4. The exception to this is of course those resolutions that contained the 'all necessary means' phrasing and expanded the authorisation to land-based operations; as noted above by Geiβ and Petrig (n 278) 84.

[297] European Union Council Joint Action 2008/851/CFSP of 10 November 2008 (EU Council Joint Action 851).

[298] Art 1(1), 2, EU Council Joint Action 851.

[299] Frank Gardner, 'Somali Piracy: EU Forces in First Mainland Raid' (15 May 2012) *BBC News*.

[300] European Union Council Decision (CFSP) 2022/2441 of 12 December 2022.

[301] Combined Maritime Forces (CMF), 'CTF 151: Counter-Piracy' https://shorturl.at/9g5hz.

its readiness to restart operations should the need arise.[302] In addition to the three international naval operations conducted against piracy off the coast of Somalia, numerous other States have contributed forces under the relevant resolutions. These include forces from China, India, Japan, South Korea, Russia and Turkey. Reports from the Secretary-General confirm that the authorisation provided for in respective resolutions was widely made use of, with numerous States deploying naval assets off the coast of Somalia.[303]

The resolutions adopted on the situation with piracy off the Somalian coast represent extensive UNSC authorising force. Resolutions explicitly determined an Article 39 determination in connection with the situation, consistently invoking Chapter VII, and carefully employing explicit authorising language.

V. CONCLUSION

The analysis above has examined some two dozen resolutions, predominantly focusing on authorisation to Member States. In comparison to the total number of UNSC resolutions authorising force to date, it forms part of just under a third of all practice, the rest of which is analysed in the following three chapters. From the above, several conclusions may be drawn pertaining to both an empirical analysis and a substantive examination of UNSC practice.

First, early UNSC practice shows that it had authorised force without explicitly invoking Chapter VII.[304] Resolutions 83 and 84 (1950) on North Korea, Resolution 221 (1966) on Southern Rhodesia and Resolution 665 (1990) on Iraq did not expressly invoke Chapter VII. These resolutions nonetheless were interpreted to have authorised force. Further, the manner in which the UNSC invokes Chapter VII has taken two forms. The first is where Chapter VII is invoked at the end of the preamble in which a resolution states that the UNSC is 'acting under Chapter VII'. This manner of invocation thereby encompasses a resolution's operative paragraphs in their entirety. Examples include Resolution 678 (1990) on Iraq; Resolution 1080 (1996) on the Great Lakes Region; and Resolutions 875 (1993) and 1529 (2004) on Haiti. The second form of invocation is where the UNSC invokes Chapter VII under a specific operative paragraph(s), thereby implying that it only applies to that paragraph(s) of the resolution.[305] This form of invocation seems more prevalent, with examples such as Resolution 794 (1992) on Somalia; Resolutions 917 (1994) and 940 (1994) on Haiti; Resolution 929 (1994) on Rwanda; and Resolutions 1101 and 1114 (1997) on Albania.

[302] NATO, 'NATO Concludes Successful Counter-Piracy Mission' (15 December 2016) https://shorturl.at/eRfmj.

[303] UN Doc S/2011/662 (2011) paras 39–47; UN Doc S/2012/783 (2012) paras 33–37; UN Doc S/2013/623 (2013) paras 37–41; UN Doc S/2014/740 (2014) paras 31–34; UN Doc S/2015/776 (2015) paras 43–47; UN Doc S/2019/867 (2019) paras 41–47; UN Doc S/2021/920 (2021) paras 39–45.

[304] Security Council Report (n 4) 3, 16.

[305] Blokker, 'Outsourcing the Use of Force' (n 171) 210.

A first preliminary conclusion is therefore that while the UNSC did not initially invoke Chapter VII, it has since developed a custom of doing so, thereby unequivocally expressing the legal effect of such authorisation.[306] With that said, and as has been discussed above, it is equally important to note that the mere invocation of Chapter VII does not necessarily authorise the use of force.[307]

The second aspect evident from UNSC practice above is the manner in which it has expressed an Article 39 determination. Its early practice has either referred to a 'breach of the peace' or a 'threat to the peace'. More recent practice has formulated the Article 39 determination as a 'threat to international peace and security' or a 'threat to peace and security in the region'. On occasion, the UNSC has also expanded this formulation to include certain qualifications to the threat. For example, it has determined that a threat to peace also threatens the 'stability' of a region or subregion due to potential refugee outflows.[308] Yet, the fact that the UNSC has made an Article 39 determination in authorising resolutions is probably one of the most consistent practices to date. Even its earlier resolutions which did not invoke Chapter VII included this determination. Only one resolution thus far did not explicitly make such a determination, namely, Resolution 665 (1990) on Iraq. It nonetheless *recalled* Resolution 660 (1990) in which an Article 39 determination was made (no doubt an indication that the situation generally had already reached this threshold). In this light it is worth noting that in that same situation, Resolution 678 (1990) contained no explicit Article 39 determination but rather the UNSC's phrasing that it was 'mindful of its duties and responsibilities under the [UN Charter] for the maintenance of international peace and security'. It too recalled Resolution 660 (1990) which had already determined the situation a threat to international peace and security.

A second preliminary conclusion therefore regards an Article 39 determination, namely, that when authorising the use of force, the UNSC determines a situation to be a threat to peace and security in an authorising resolution. Alternatively, the UNSC may recall or reaffirm such a determination made in a previous resolution that is on the same situation (provided that that resolution is sufficiently connected in time and the determination directly relates to the initial situation). In addition, UNSC practice overwhelmingly indicates that an Article 39 determination is a threshold requirement before it employs coercive military measures.

A third aspect to be noted is the consistency the UNSC has shown when its authorising resolutions invoke previous or existing resolutions that either already determined a situation a threat to peace and security or invoked Chapter VII. The only resolutions to not have done so were those on North Korea (1950), Haiti (2004) and Albania (1997). This implies that authorising resolutions are usually preceded by previous resolutions that have taken some

[306] Security Council Report, *In Hindsight: Chapter VII* (October 2013).

[307] Blokker, 'Outsourcing the Use of Force' (n 171) 210.

[308] UNSC Res 1529 (2004) preamble para 9.

other form of action or UNSC decision, potentially non-coercive measures.[309] This in turn implies that the UNSC very rarely, if ever, authorises coercive military measures under a first resolution it adopts on a situation. In the case of the Korean War, the UNSC in fact determined a breach of the peace in Resolution 82 (1950) before it subsequently authorised force. In the case of the two other exceptions, one must consider that the 1997 resolutions on Albania were actually adopted as a result of a request by the Albanian government, and the resolutions on Haiti in fact recalled a presidential statement (although the statement was not made under Chapter VII) and 'previous resolutions' although the UNSC did not specify which resolutions.

The third preliminary conclusion under this chapter is that UNSC authorisation for the use of force to Member States usually occurs only *after* a range of other actions (non-military) the UNSC has taken which have not been able to sufficiently restore international peace and security. In addition, it is rare for an authorising resolution to be the first resolution adopted on a situation also the first to make and Article 39 determination.

In so far as the language the UNSC employs when authorising force, UNSC practice shows it has only ever opted for a very specific set of formulations: It *recommends*,[310] *calls upon*,[311] *authorises*[312] or *decides*[313] that Member States use force. On occasion, the UNSC has also *reaffirmed* authorisation of force to Member States.[314] These 'instructive verbs' are usually used in combination with explicit authorisation for Member States to use 'all necessary means' or 'all necessary measures'. On one occasion, the UNSC even expressly referred to the 'use of force, if necessary' when authorising a member state to use force.[315] The combination of such language as an authorisation of force remains without doubt today.

From its historical practice, it is evident that the UNSC has developed methods in international law that the drafters of the UN Charter could most probably not have foreseen. Earlier discussions focused on the legality of

[309] For UNSC Res 221 (1966) on Southern Rhodesia, and see UNSC Res 217 (1965). For UNSC Res 665 and UNSC Res 678 (1990), see UNSC Res 660 (1990). For UNSC Res 794 (1992) on Somalia, generally UNSC Res 733 (1992), UNSC Res 746 (1992), UNSC Res 751 (1992) and UNSC Res 767 (1992).

[310] UNSC Res 83 (1950), UNSC Res 84 (1950).

[311] UNSC Res 221 (1966), UNSC Res 665 (1990), UNSC Res 875 (1993), UNSC Res 917 (1994), UNSC Res 1838 (2008).

[312] UNSC Res 678 (1990), UNSC Res 794 (1992), UNSC Res 940 (1994), UNSC Res 929 (1994), UNSC Res 1080 (1996), UNSC Res 1101 (1997), UNSC Res 1114 (1997), UNSC Res 1264 (1999), UNSC Res 1511 (2003), UNSC Res 1529 (2004), UNSC Res 2699 (2023) para 4.

[313] UNSC Res 1546 (2004), UNSC Res 1816 (2008), UNSC Res 1846 (2008), UNSC Res 1851 (2008), UNSC Res 1897 (2009), UNSC Res 1950 (2010), UNSC Res 2020 (2011), UNSC Res 2077 (2012), UNSC Res 2125 (2013), UNSC Res 2184 (2014), UNSC Res 2246 (2015), UNSC Res 2316 (2016), UNSC Res 2382 (2017), UNSC Res 2442 (2018), UNSC Res 2500 (2019) para 14, UNSC Res 2554 (2020) para 14; UNSC Res 2608 (2021) para 14.

[314] UNSC Res 1637 (2005), UNSC Res 1723 (2006), UNSC Res 1790 (2007).

[315] UNSC Res 221 (1966) para 5.

delegated enforcement action. Despite the absence of the Article 43 agreements, the delegation of its enforcement powers today seems to be widely accepted inherent power of the UNSC.

Equally significant are issues of legality pertaining to the precise legal basis of authorising resolutions. As has been detailed, the most plausible basis for UNSC authorisation of force rests with Article 42 of the UN Charter. Arguments basing UNSC authorisation of force on Article 51 arguably conflate differences between collective security under the UN Charter and that of individual and collective self-defence. In addition, UNSC practice indicates it has consistently authorised the use of force either explicitly for the 'maintenance of international peace and security' or for purposes that plainly fall outside the scope of Article 51.

In concluding, it should be stressed that there is sufficient UNSC practice suggesting it has developed a systematic approach when it authorises force. This approach is composed of four elements. First, an authorising resolution usually *recalls* or *reaffirms* a previous resolution which has either already determined a situation to constitute a threat to peace or has invoked Chapter VII. Second, the authorising resolution itself usually also explicitly determines the situation a breach of the peace or a threat to the peace. Third, Chapter VII (and, on occasion, Chapter VIII) has been invoked either in application to the resolution in its entirety or under a specific operative paragraph of the resolution. Finally, an authorising Resolution contains in its operative paragraphs that the UNSC *recommends*, *calls upon* or, more frequently, *authorises* or *decides* that Member States are to use 'force' or 'all necessary means' or 'all necessary measures'. In addition, resolutions that authorise force in the first instance, without the UNSC having at the least employed alternative (non-military) measures, are few and far between.

Finally, the UNSC has included in this systematic approach two forms of control. It either limits its authorisation of force in time or on the basis of a function limitation determining when a mandate accompanied by authorisation to use force expires or is terminated. Correspondingly, the UNSC has also made it a habit of explicitly request reporting from entities it has authorised to use force. Such reporting obligations ensure to some extent that the UNSC remains, albeit to a limited extent, in control over operations and mandates it authorises.

3

Explicit Authorisation to Regional Organisations and Regional Peacekeeping Initiatives

I. INTRODUCTION

THE PREVIOUS CHAPTER has outlined and examined explicit United Nations Security Council (UNSC) authorisation to Member States. This chapter now turns its focus on authorisation to regional arrangements and agencies (regional organisations) – at least those regarded as such under Chapter VIII of the Charter of the United Nations (UN Charter).[1] Resolutions explicitly authorising force to three regional organisations in particular are examined: the African Union (AU), the European Union (EU) and the Economic Community of West African States (ECOWAS).

As mentioned, on several occasions the UNSC has authorised the use of force to more than one entity. Presently, the most notable example examined is the situation which arose in Chad and the Central African Republic (CAR), which is addressed separately below. Authorisation of force in the Ivory Coast (2004–2011), including authorisation to the relevant UN peacekeeping missions and Member States, is addressed in the context of authorisation to the Economic Community of West African States.

While authorisation to UN peacekeeping missions is more broadly dealt with in chapter five, for feasibility, several UN missions are also examined here based on topical and chronological characteristics, since they were established

[1] Arts 52, 53, United Nations, Charter of the United Nations (adopted 26 June 1945, entered into force 24 October 1945) UNCIO XV, 335 (UN Charter). On the definition of regional organisations, see Erika de Wet, 'Regional Organisations and Arrangements: Authorisation, Ratification, or Independent Action?' in Marc Weller (ed), *The Oxford Handbook of the Use of Force in International Law* (Oxford University Press 2015) 315–17. On the classification of organisations, see Nishkala Suntharalingam, 'The UN Security Council, Regional Arrangements, and Peacekeeping Operations' in Hillary Charlesworth and Jean-Marc Coicaud (eds), *Fault Lines of International Legitimacy* (Cambridge University Press 2012) 206–09. See also the topic of regional organisations and their use of force, extensively covered in Ademola Abass, *Regional Organisations and the Development of Collective Security: Beyond Chapter VIII of the UN Charter* (Hart Publishing 2004).

and authorised in the same time span and on the same situations as those resolutions that authorised force to the respective regional organisations.

The chapter aims to demonstrate that as with authorisation to Member States, the authorisation of force to regional organisations follows a routine practice of prior explicit authorisation. That is, authorising resolutions determine or recall an existing determination of a threat to international peace and security under Article 39, invoke Chapter VII or VIII of the UN Charter and use specific authorising language.

II. AUTHORISATION TO THE AFRICAN UNION

A. Resolution 1744 (2007) | AMISOM

In 2004, following the Somali presidential elections, Colonel Abulah Yusuf requested AU peacekeeping forces to assist his government with security and stability in Somalia. Initially, the Intergovernmental Authority on Development (IGAD) was meant to deploy a Peace Support Mission in Somalia (IGASOM).[2] Although such a deployment never materialised, in 2006, the adoption of Resolution 1725 (2006) authorised IGAD and AU Member States to take action in Somalia.[3] In 2007 the AU Peace and Security Council (AU PSC) formally replaced IGASOM with the African Union Mission in Somalia (AMISOM). AMISOM's mandate was subsequently authorised under Resolution 1744 (2007).[4] AMISOM was the first UN-authorised, AU-led regional peacekeeping mission with a mandate to use force under Chapter VII. Serving as another example of explicit UNSC authorisation of the use of force to a regional peacekeeping mission, it later received explicit authorisation and mandate expansion under two dozen subsequent authorising resolutions.

Determining that the situation in Somalia and acts of violence and extremism constituted a threat to international peace and security, the UNSC, acting under Chapter VII, authorised Member States of the AU to establish AMISOM in Somalia for an initial period of six months.[5] AMISOM was authorised to 'take all necessary measures as appropriate' to carry out its mandate.[6] After six months of AMISOM operations in Somalia, the situation had not improved. A failure by the force to deploy effectively, combined with continuous attacks

[2] IGASOM was mandated under UNSC Res 1725 (2006) under Chapter VII, but it was not authorised to use force.

[3] UNSC Res 1725 (2006). See Niels Blokker, 'Outsourcing the Use of Force: Towards More Security Council Control of Authorised Operations?' in Weller (n 1) 211–12 who considers UNSC Res 1725 (2006) as authorising force, although such authorisation is 'unclear' and is 'exceptional'.

[4] UNSC Res 1744 (2007) para 4; AU Doc PSC/PR/Comm (LXIX) para 8.

[5] UNSC Res 1744 (2007) preamble para 10, para 4.

[6] UNSC Res 1744 (2007), paras 4(a)–(e).

against its troops meant that it could not carry out much of its mandate.[7] On 20 August 2007 the UNSC adopted Resolution 1772 (2007) again authorising it to use 'all necessary measures as appropriate' under Chapter VII.[8] Thereafter, AMISOM's mandate was extended in seven subsequent resolutions.[9] In 2012, under Resolution 2036 (2012), the UNSC then authorised an expansion of AMISOM to cover four sectors across Somalia and authorised an increase in troops.[10] This mandate was subsequently affirmed in Resolution 2072 (2012)[11] and, under Resolution 2073 (2012), AMISOM was also authorised to assist UN personnel carrying out functions in Somalia.[12]

Increasing threats of terrorist activities, in particular of Al-Shabaab, prompted the UNSC to include under Resolution 2093 (2013) an additional task of extending state authority over areas recovered from Al-Shabaab.[13] The expansion to AMISOM's mandate to include anti-terrorism activities was renewed under seven further resolutions.[14]

Under Resolution 2297 (2016), the UNSC further expanded AMISOM's anti-terrorist operations by authorising it to conduct offensive operations against Al-Shabaab.[15] AMISOM's authorisation was renewed one final time in Resolution 2431 (2018).[16]

The UNSC's authorisation to AMISOM was therefore a clear demonstration of prior explicit authorisation, having consistently determined a threat to international peace and security, invoked Chapter VII, and made use of the 'all necessary measures' phrasing.

B. Resolution 2628 (2022) | ATMIS

In 2022, the AU decided to reconfigure AMISOM into the AU Transition Mission in Somalia (ATMIS). By Resolution 2628 (2022), the UNSC endorsed this reconfiguration. Determining the situation in Somalia continued to constitute a threat to regional and international peace and security, and acting under Chapter VII, the UNSC in paragraph 22 authorised, for an initial period of 12 months, AU

[7] Christine Gray, *International Law and the Use of Force* (Oxford University Press 2018) 398.

[8] UNSC Res 1772 (2007).

[9] UNSC Res 1801 (2008) para 1; UNSC Res 1831 (2008) para 1; UNSC Res 1863 (2009) paras 1–2; UNSC Res 1872 (2009) para 16; UNSC Res 1910 (2010) paras 1–2; UNSC Res 1964 (2010) paras 1–2; UNSC Res 2010 (2011) paras 1–2; UNSC Res 2036 (2012) preamble para 18, para 1.

[10] UNSC Res 2036 (2012) para 2.

[11] UNSC Res 2072 (2012) preamble para 5.

[12] UNSC Res 2073 (2012) para 1.

[13] UNSC Res 2093 (2013) para 1, read together with paras 10, 14, 15.

[14] UNSC Res 2124 (2013), UNSC Res 2182 (2014), UNSC Res 2232 (2015), UNSC Res 2232 (2015) para 3; UNSC Res 2289 (2016) para 1; UNSC Res 2355 (2017) para 1; UNSC Res 2372 (2017) paras 5–7; UNSC Res 2415 (2018) para 1.

[15] UNSC Res 2297 (2016) paras 4–7.

[16] UNSC Res 2431 (2018) paras 5–8.

Member States to 'take all necessary measures' to carry out ATMIS's mandate.[17] Notably, by Resolution 2670 (2022), the UNSC accepting a request by the AU to extend the drawdown of ATMIS, extended its authorisation by reference to Resolution 2628 (2022). Invoking Chapter VII, Resolution 2670 (2022) reaffirming its decisions in Resolution 2628 (2022) including the decision to authorise ATMIS, *recalled* in paragraph 1 the relevant 'paragraphs 22, 23, 24 and 26' of Resolution 2628 (2022) authorising the use of 'all necessary means'.[18] While extending the authorisation given to ATMIS, the UNSC itself acknowledged that it 'exceptionally extends its authorisation until 30 June 2023.' This 'exceptional' extension of authorisation to ATMIS was explicitly repeated in Resolution 2687 (2023) when the UNSC recalled its authorisation in 'paragraph 22 of Resolution 2628 (2022), extended in paragraph 1 to Resolution 2670 (2023)' until 31 December 2023.[19] By Resolution 2710 (2023), such authorisation was extended by a further year. Both Resolutions 2628 and 2710 (2023) were explicit in so far as determining the situation in Somalia a threat to international peace and security and invoking Chapter VII.

UNSC practice of authorisation of force to AMISOM remains significant in that it has repeated its explicit authorisation over two dozen resolutions, first authorising and extending AMISOM and later AMIS. Moreover, every resolution adopted in relation to AMISOM determined the situation in Somalia to be a threat to international peace and security, invoked Chapter VII and authorised force using explicit language. Notably, the UNSC authorised AMISOM under Chapter VII, and not Chapter VIII, despite the AU falling within the meaning of a regional organisation for purposes of Article 53(1).

C. Resolution 1769 (2007) | UNAMID

In 2007, the UNSC adopted Resolution 1769 (2007) in response to ongoing violence in Darfur, authorising and mandating the establishment of the AU-UN Hybrid Operation in Darfur (UNAMID) for an initial period of 12 months.[20] UNAMID became the legal successor to both the AU and UN missions in Sudan.

Determining the situation in Darfur continued to constitute a threat to international peace and security and acting under Chapter VII, the UNSC authorised UNAMID to 'take the necessary action, in the areas of deployment of its forces and as it deems fit within its capabilities' to undertake its mandate, which included the protection of civilians and facilitating the delivery of humanitarian

[17] UNSC Res 2628 (2022) para 10.

[18] UNSC Res 2670 (2023) para 1.

[19] UNSC Res 2687 (2023) para 17.

[20] UNSC Res 1769 (2007) para 1; see also Suyash Paliwal, 'The Primacy of Regional Organisations in International Peacekeeping: The African Example' (2010) 51 (1) *Virginia Journal of International Law* 200.

assistance.[21] Notably, Chapter VII was invoked only in paragraph 15 which authorised UNAMID's to take the necessary action.

UNAMID's mandate was extended in several subsequent resolutions, although interestingly no Chapter VII invocation occurred even when the UNSC *underlined* the need for it to make full use of its mandate and capabilities.[22] From Resolution 2003 (2011), the UNSC extended UNAMID's mandate while also explicitly *encouraging* implementation of its 'Chapter VII mandate' and *emphasising* its 'Chapter VII mandate, as defined in resolution 1769'.[23] This practice was repeated in Resolution 2063 (2012), Resolution 2133 (2013), and in Resolution 2173 (2014) in which the UNSC additionally *recalled* that UNAMID 'is authorised to take all necessary action in fulfilment of [its] mandate'.[24] UNAMID's mandate and its authorisation were subsequently extended explicitly under seven resolution until December 2020.[25]

III. AUTHORISATION TO THE EUROPEAN UNION

A. Resolution 1484 (2003) | EUFOR in the DRC (*Operation Artemis*)

Set off following the second Congo War, the Ituri conflict erupted between the Balendru and BaHima peoples of the Ituri region in the Democratic Republic of the Congo (DRC). To assist in the region, the UNSC established the United Nations Mission in the Democratic Republic of the Congo (MONUC) in 1999 to, among others, observe and implement ceasefire agreements.[26] Although the conflict first began in 1972, violence significantly intensified between 1999 and 2003. Over 50,000 deaths and 500,000 displaced persons prompted the adoption of Resolution 1484 (2003), authorising the deployment of an Interim Emergency Multinational Force (IEMF).[27]

Resolution 1484 (2003) in essence gave effect to a request by the Secretary-General (along with the President of Rwanda, the President of the DRC and Ituri parties) to authorise the IEMF. Its Article 39 determination deviated slightly from usual UNSC practice in that it had determined the situation in the Ituri region and in Bunia in particular 'constitute[d] a threat to the peace process in the [DRC] and to the peace and security in the Great Lakes Region'.[28]

[21] UNSC Res 1769 (2008) par 15(a).

[22] UNSC Res 1828 (2008) para 1; UNSC Res 1881 (2009) paras 1, 2; UNSC Res 1935 (2010) paras 1, 2.

[23] UNSC Res 2003 (2011) preamble para 12, para 5.

[24] UNSC Res 2173 (2014) para 9.

[25] UNSC Res 2228 (2015); UNSC Res 2363 (2017); UNSC Res 2425 (2018); UNSC Res 2429 (2018); UNSC Res 2479 (2019); UNSC Res 2495 (2019); UNSC Res 2525 (2020).

[26] UNSC Res 1279 (1999) paras 4–5.

[27] UNSC Res 1484 (2003) read together with UN Doc S/PRST/2003/6 (2003); see also UN Doc S/PV.4764 (2003) 2.

[28] UNSC Res 1484 (2003) preamble para 8.

The resolution also expressly invoked Chapter VII when it approved the deployment of the IEMF and authorised participating Member States to 'take all necessary measures to fulfil its mandate'.[29] The IEMF was to be deployed on a strictly temporary basis to allow for the reinforcement of MONUC operations in Bunia.[30] With that said, however, it is interesting to note that no invocation of Chapter VIII occurred even though the measures under the resolution were implemented by the EU. Despite its authorisation to a regional organisation, the resolution contained no Chapter VIII invocation even though the EU operation clearly derived legal authority from Resolution 1484 (2003).[31]

i. Operation Artemis

The implementation of Resolution 1484 (2003) came with the first ever EU-led peacekeeping mission – *Operation Artemis*, which was launched on 12 June 2003 (although the first troops under the IEMF were already deployed on 6 June 2003).[32] Its mandate under Resolution 1484 (2003) was to contribute to the stabilisation of security conditions and the improvement of the humanitarian situation in Bunia, to protect the airport in Bunia, internationally displaced persons and, if required, to contribute to the safety of the civilian population, UN personnel and the humanitarian presence there.[33] On 6 June 2003 IEMF forces secured the airport without much resistance. By July the situation had improved significantly: Bunia was declared a weapon-free town and rebel militia had withdrawn.[34] Its authorisation to use force was made use of on several occasions – 'the IEMF used the threat or the use of force in a convincing manner, managing quickly to establish its presence and stabilise the area of its deployment'.[35]

The EU-led operation in the DRC was therefore regarded as a success, providing time for logistical arrangements and the UNSC to authorise the expansion of MONUC. On 14 August 2003 the Secretary-General recommended the UNSC

[29] UNSC Res 1484 (2003) preamble para 8, paras 1, 4.

[30] UNSC Res 1484 (2003) para 1; Walter Dorn, 'Combat Air Power in the Congo, 2003' in Walter Dorn (ed), *Air Power in UN Operations: Wings for Peace* (Routledge 2014) 242–43.

[31] Christine Gray, 'Peacekeeping and Enforcement Action in Africa: The Role of Europe and Obligations of Multilateralism' (2005) 31 *Review of International Studies* 215–16; Suntharalingam (n 1) 221.

[32] Council Decision 2003/432/CFSP of 12 June 2003.

[33] UNSC Res 1484 (2003) para 1. See also Abou Abass, 'The Security Council and the Use of Peace United Nations Peace Operations to Protect Civilians. The Case of MONUC/MONUSCO in the Democratic Republic of Congo' (2017) https://shorturl.at/lwjxH 53; Suntharalingam (n 1) 221.

[34] Michael Koenig, 'Operation Artemis': The Efficiency of EU Peacekeeping in the Congo' *e-Relations* (5 October 2012); Walter Dorn, 'Combat Air Power in the Congo, 2003' in Walter Dorn (ed), *Air Power in UN Operations: Wings for Peace* (Routledge 2014) 245.

[35] United Nations Department of Peacekeeping Operations (UNDPK, 2004) in Koenig (n 34). See also Emeric Rogier, 'MONUC and the Challenges of Peace Implementation in the Democratic Republic of Congo' Institute for Security Studies. Report on ISS International Expert Workshop, Pretoria, 17–19 September 2003 9; Dorn (n 34) 245.

authorise the IEMF to assist to the best of its capabilities in the transition of the IEMF to MONUC.[36] These recommendations were adopted in Resolution 1501 (2003) in which the UNSC, acting under Chapter VII, authorised the IEMF to provide assistance to MONUC at its request.[37] It also listed a final date of the IEMF's disengagement of 15 September 2003, after which its mandate would be terminated.[38] Before the IEMF handed over responsibility to MONUC, the UNSC adopted several resolutions providing MONUC a robust mandate, strengthening the number of troops at its disposal, and explicitly authorising it to use force to achieve its mandate. The authorisation given to MONUC and to the transformed United Nations Organisation Stabilisation Mission in the Democratic Republic of Congo (MONSUCO), is discussed in chapter five.[39]

The authorisation for the use of force under Resolution 1484 (2003) and the subsequent EU *Operation Artemis* were clear examples of the UNSC's Chapter VII powers to authorise the use of force to a regional peacekeeping initiative, and again explicitly so. It is also important to note that while the EU was not willing to assist in the UN force (MONUC), it preferred to operate more independently under separate Chapter VII authorisation.[40]

B. Resolution 1575 (2004) | EUFOR (*Operation Althea*)

On 29 June 2004 at its Istanbul Summit, NATO announced that it would be concluding its Stabilisation Force in Bosnia and Herzegovina (SFOR). In a Communiqué issued by the Heads of State and Government, NATO indicated it would continue to maintain a presence in Bosnia and Herzegovina to assist in defence reform and the pursuit of persons indicted for war crimes.[41] Several days later, the EU announced its intention to carry out an EU-led operation with a military component, taking over from SFOR. The UNSC through Resolution 1551 (2004) welcomed the EU's intention to launch the operation.

On 29 September 2004 the EU proposed a concept for the mission dubbed *Operation Althea* which outlined the political and military objectives,

[36] UN Doc S/2003/821 (2003).

[37] UNSC Res 1501 (2003) para 2.

[38] UNSC Res 1501 (2003) para 2. On 1 September 2003 responsibility for regional security was handed over to MONUC.

[39] See ch 5 at p 136–139.

[40] See Kees Homan, 'Operation Artemis in the Democratic Republic of Congo' in *European Commission: Faster and More Unified? The Debate About Europe's Crisis Response Capacity* (European Commission 2007) 154 specifically that none of the forces of the IEMF were willing to be rehatted into MONUC. See also Claudia Major, 'EU-UN Cooperation in Military Crisis Management: The Experience of EUFOR RD Congo in 2006' (September 2008) *European Union Institute for Security Studies* 13.

[41] NATO, 'Istanbul Summit Communiqué, Issued by the Heads of State and Government participating in the meeting of the North Atlantic Council' (28 June 2004) NATO Press Release (2004) 96 paras 3, 7–9.

limitations and exit strategy of the EU-led force. It also included a set of assumptions pending the deployment of the mission. Notably, its third assumption conditioned the deployment: '[a] *new* UNSCR will be adopted *prior* to the deployment of EUFOR detailing its mandate and role, based on *Chapter VII of the UN Charter* and will grant EUFOR full authority under the GFAP [Peace Agreement]'.[42]

The EU's desire for UNSC authorisation came with the adoption of Resolution 1575 (2004). Acting under Chapter VII, the UNSC welcomed the establishment of EUFOR, along with the establishment of a NATO headquarters in the country.[43] Both EURFOR and the NATO presence were to be the legal successors to SFOR with the mandate of implementing the Peace Agreement. The UNSC recognised that the Peace Agreement and the provisions of its previous resolutions, and any reference to IFOR or SFOR or NATO shall be read as applying to EUFOR and the NATO presence.[44] Much in the same manner in which the UNSC authorised the use of force by IFOR and SFOR, so too did it accord authorisation to EUFOR and NATO. The UNSC authorised the use of force by the two organisations to ensure the implementation of the Peace Agreement, in defence of the organisations, and to assist them in carrying out their missions.[45] EUFOR was to have the main peace stabilisation role under the military aspects of the Peace Agreement.

On 2 December 2004 the EU launched *Operation Althea*.[46] The operation was described as largely a change of name and commanders, with 80 per cent of SFOR troops having been reassigned to the operation.[47] An initial deployment of 7,000 troops occurred, with some 19 EU and non-EU countries contributing to EURFOR.[48] *Operation Althea* was controlled under the direction of the Political and Security Committee of the EU (EU PSC) and, in line with Resolution 1575 (2004), was to report on its activities on three-month intervals. With the situation in Bosnia and Herzegovina having improved, resulting in the gradual reduction of troop numbers under EUFOR over the years, the UNSC

[42] Emphasis added. EU, 'Concept for the European Union (EU) Military Operation in Bosnia and Herzegovina (BiH) – Operation Althea, Council of European Union' (Brussels, 29 September 2004), EU Doc 12576/04 para 1(g)(3).

[43] UNSC Res 1575 (2004) paras 7, 9–11.

[44] UNSC Res 1575 (2004) para 12. On the EUFOR transition from SFOR, see Julie Kim, 'Bosnia and the European Union Military Force (EUFOR): Post-NATO Transition' in M Clausson (ed), *NATO: Status, Relations, and Decision-Making* (Novinka Books 2007) 96.

[45] UNSC Res 1575 (2004) paras 14–16; note that Winther describes the authorisation given to EUFOR as broad, adding that the resolution was another example in which the EU had to practice a division between peacekeeping and peace enforcement. Dace Winther, *Regional Maintenance of Peace and Security under International Law: The Distorted Mirrors* (Routledge 2013) 175.

[46] Council Decision 2004/803/CFSP of 25 November 2004 on the Launching of the European Union Military Operation in Bosnia and Herzegovina' (17 November 2004) *Official Journal of the European Union* L 353/21 art 1.

[47] Nick Hawton, 'EU Troops Prepare for Bosnia Swap' *BBC* (23 October 2004).

[48] Operation Althea functioned under the Berlin Plus Agreement, a comprehensive arrangement between the EU and NATO for EU use of NATO capabilities in crisis management operations.

extended the authorisation to use force on several more occasions. The UNSC has explicitly extended the EUFOR (and NATO) mandates and authorisation to use force 19 times.[49]

Since its deployment, *Operation Althea* has generally been regarded as having successfully implemented its mandate, having significantly reduced conflict and violence in the country. More so, many EUFOR tasks have since been handed over to local authorities.[50] To date, the extension of *Operation Althea* makes it the longest EU running military operation since its establishment.[51]

Throughout all resolutions adopted on the situation in Bosnia and Herzegovina (including those which are assessed in the subsequent chapter on the NATO presence in the former Federal Republic of Yugoslavia) UNSC practice has been incredibly consistent. All authorising resolutions on the situation either determined a threat to peace and security or recalled a resolution that had previously made such a determination. Moreover, all authorising resolutions have invoked Chapter VII and used specific operative paragraphs, usually stating that the UNSC 'decides' or 'authorises' the EU or NATO (or both) to take 'all necessary measures'. Additionally, UNSC practice on the situation in Bosnia and Herzegovina undoubtedly affirms its preference for prior explicit authorisation of the use of force, a practice it has committed to for nearly two and a half decades across two dozen resolutions.

C. Resolution 1671 (2006) | EUFOR RD Congo in DRC

In July 2002, the signing of the Pretoria Accord formally ended the decade-long second Congo war when Rwanda agreed to withdraw troops from the DRC. In 2003 the transitional government of the DRC was established as an interim government tasked to set up a national constitution and to facilitate a general election. Following the adoption of a draft Constitution on 18 February 2006 and in preparation for general elections across the DRC, the EU expressed its willingness to assist in the democratic process in the DRC, in particular, with the objective of supporting the existing MONUC mission (later MONUSCO).[52] The EU's willingness to deploy the assistance force was welcomed by the DRC,

[49] UNSC Res 1639 (2005) paras 14–16; UNSC Res 1722 (2006) paras 14–16, UNSC Res 1785 (2007) UNSC paras 14–16; UNSC Res 1845 (2008) paras 14–16; SC Res 1895 (2009) paras 14–16; SC Res 1948 (2010) paras 14–16; SC Res 2019 (2011) paras 14–16; SC Res 2074 (2012) paras 14–16; SC Res 2123 (2013) paras 14–16; SC Res 2183 (2014) paras 14–16; SC Res 2247 (2015) paras 5–7; SC Res 2315 (2016) paras 5–7; UNSC Res 2384 (2017) paras 5–7; UNSC Res 2443 (2018) paras 5–7; UNSC Res 2496 (2019) paras 5–7; UNSC Res 2549 (2020) paras 5–7; UNSC Res 2604 (2021) paras 3–5; UNSC Res 2658 (2022) paras 3–5; UNSC Res 2706 (2023) paras 3–5.

[50] EU, 'Common Security and Defence Policy EUFOR Operation Althea' (May 2018) www.euforbih.org/eufor/images/pdfs/EUTM_Mission_Factsheet.pdf.

[51] Winther (n 45) 175.

[52] See UNSC Res 1279 (1999); UN Doc S/2006/219 Annex II, 4.

which requested the UNSC to endorse the initiative.[53] In turn the EU requested UNSC approval of the deployment and the use of force:

> The adoption of a [UNSC] resolution under Chapter VII is essential to enable the involvement of the European Union ... A key point of the resolution will be autonomy for the European Union in deciding on the use of force.[54]

The EU operation was to operate for a four-month period and the UN would be informed on a regular basis on the progress of the operation.[55] Twelve days later the UNSC gave effect to the initiative under Resolution 1671 (2006), approving the EU force (EUFOR RD Congo).[56] For current purposes, Resolution 1671 (2006) was the third instance in which the UNSC had explicitly authorised the use of force to the EU, having also expressly indicated, without invoking Chapter VIII, that it was authorised to use force under Chapter VII.

The resolution determined that the situation in the DRC continued to constitute a threat to international peace and security in the region; recalling six previous resolutions which had also made such a determination.[57] Acting under Chapter VII, the UNSC authorised EUFOR RD Congo to 'take all necessary measures, within its means and capabilities' to carry out tasks listed under the resolution.[58] Moreover, the UNSC stressed that the deployment was authorised 'immediately to take all appropriate steps' to prepare for its full operational capability.[59] The authorisation for the operation to use force was also given under a listed five-point mandate. In addition to assisting MONUC, EUFOR RD Congo was also to contribute to the protection of civilians under imminent threat of physical violence in the areas of its deployment.[60]

One point of concern that arose with Resolution 1671 (2006) was its precise implications pertaining to when the EUFOR RD Congo mandate would be terminated. Although the operation was terminated on 30 November 2006 in line with the envisaged four-month mandated period, additional phrasing under the resolution needs brief mention. Resolution 1671 (2006) explicitly authorised the deployment for a period 'ending four months after the date of the first round of the presidential and parliamentary elections'.[61] However, unlike standard UNSC practice of adopting a subsequent resolution specifically extending the authorisation, the resolution seemed in itself to allow for a subsequent

[53] UN Doc S/2006/203 (2006) 2.
[54] UN Doc S/2006/219 (2006) Annex II, 4–5.
[55] UN Doc S/2006/219 (2006) Annex II, 4–5.
[56] UNSC Res 1671 (2006) para 1.
[57] UNSC Res 1671 (2006). See also UNSC Res 1493 (2003); UNSC Res 1565 (2004); UNSC Res 1592 (2005); UNSC Res 1596 (2005); UNSC Res 1621 (2005); and UNSC Res 1635 (2005).
[58] UNSC Res 1671 (2006) para 8. See also Council Decision 2006/412/CFSP of 12 June 2006 and Council Joint Action 2006/319/CFSP of 27 April 2006.
[59] UNSC Res 1671 (2006) para 6.
[60] UNSC Res 1671 (2006) paras 8(a)–(e). For an analysis on the authorisation given to MONUC, see ch 5 at 136–137.
[61] UNSC Res 1671 (2006) para 2.

extension of the force's deployment beyond the four-month period. According to the fourth operative paragraph, the authorisation for the deployment in line with paragraph 2 was not to exceed the term of MONUC's mandate.[62] Moreover, beyond 30 September 2006, the authorisation for the deployment was subject to the extension of MONUC's mandate.[63] Therefore, the authorisation for the deployment could be extended as long as its extension did not exceed MONUC's mandated period. This implied that should MONUC's mandate be extended, then so too would the mandate of the EUFOR RD Congo deployment. The potential for such an extension seemed contradictory to the initial outline of a four-month mandated period.

The convoluted formulation of such an extension was specifically raised during the UNSC debate during the adoption of the resolution. The French delegate explicitly referred to the interpretation of operative paragraph 4, stating that 'it will not be necessary to adopt another resolution to renew the European force's mandate when the Council decides, by 30 September, to extend [MONUC's] mandate'.[64] Read together with preambular paragraph 11 of Resolution 1671 (2006) in which the UNSC expressed its intention to extend MONUC's mandate beyond 30 September 2006, it seems that the EU force's deployment had already implicitly the potential for extension under the same resolution that authorised its deployment.

Another question concerning potential mandate extension was weather any extension of MONUC's mandate also extended EUFOR RD Congo's authorisation to use force. One possible interpretation is that the wording of Resolution 1671 (2006) suggests that any extension of the EU force beyond 30 September 2006 (in line with the extension of MONUC's mandate) was merely an extension of the deployment, and not an extension of its authorisation to use force. Specifically, the phrasing that the EU force deployment would be extended subject to MONUC's extension was contained in paragraph 4 of the resolution. Paragraph 4 specifically referred to an extension of authorisation under paragraph 2. Paragraph 2 merely authorised the EU force deployment, while its authorisation to use all necessary measures (within its means and capabilities) was authorised under paragraph 8.

In any case, practical implications never resulted since the force had withdrawn by the end of November resulting in the termination of the operation in line with the initial four-month mandated period.

On 30 July 2006, the first of the EUFOR RD Congo troops began arriving in the DRC. The largest contributors to the force came from France, Germany, Spain, Poland and Belgium, with the EUFOR RD Congo total troop disposal at the time of operations standing at 4,000.[65] Operations were predominantly based in

[62] UNSC Res 1671 (2006) para 4.
[63] UNSC Res 1671 (2006).
[64] UN Doc S/PV.5421 (2006) 2.
[65] Major (n 40) 18.

Kinshasa, with occasional out-of-area activities on request allowing it to operate over other parts of the DRC. National provisions by some contributing Member States, particularly those of Germany and Spain, restricted operations by their troops beyond EUFOR RD Congo's area of deployment.[66] On 30 July 2006 a general election in the DRC was held for the first time in over four decades in which, although not without some contestation, Joseph Kabila was elected president. The operation was officially terminated on 30 November 2006, therefore adhering to Resolution 1671 (2006)'s four-month period reference, although the force was effectively deployed in the DRC for six months inclusive of pre-deployment preparation and the withdrawal period.

The operation's use of force during its deployment seemed limited, having only resorted to it on three predominant occasions. The most significant of these incidents occurred on 21 August 2006 when the residence of the Vice-President was attacked.[67] Subsequently, violence also broke out following the announcement of the first round of the presidential elections. EUFOR RD Congo, at the request of MONUC, was able to prevent the spread of violence and significantly contribute to stabilising the volatile situation during the election period.[68] In so doing, the EU operation in the DRC was hailed a success and its capacity to intervene militarily was considered a highlight in accomplishing its mandate under Resolution 1671 (2006).[69] The convoluted language pertaining mandate extension aside, Resolution 1671 (2006) was another example in which the UNSC explicitly authorised force by a regional organisation. Although not invoking Chapter VIII (but rather Chapter VII), it had clearly and expressly referred to the EU in its resolutions.

D. Resolution 2240 (2015) | Migrant Smuggling in the Mediterranean and *Operation Sophia*

On 19 April 2015 the migration crisis in the Mediterranean experienced one of the worst human losses of life when a vessel alleged to be smuggling migrants capsized, leading to the deaths of over 800 people.[70] On 18 May 2018 the EU Council established EUNAVFOR MED, a naval operation aimed at 'disrupting the business model of human smuggling and trafficking networks in the Southern

[66] Major (n 40) 18.

[67] Major (n 40) 21.

[68] Major (n 40) 19; Council of the European Union, Report Operation EUFOR RD Congo – Report to the United Nations' 5139/07 DG E VIII para 11.

[69] Major (n 40) 21.

[70] Francesca Mussi, 'Countering Migrant Smuggling in the Mediterranean Sea under the Mandate of the UN Security Council: What Protection for the Fundamental Rights of Migrants?' (2018) 22 (4) *The International Journal of Human Rights* 490. See also Alessandra Bonomolo and Stephanie Kirchgaessner, 'UN Says 800 Migrants Dead in Boat Disaster as Italy Launches Rescue of Two More Vessels' (20 April 2015) *The Guardian*.

Central Mediterranean'.[71] The operation was launched on 22 June 2015.[72] EUNAVFOR MED, subsequently renamed *Operation Sophia*, consists of three phases, the first of which, monitoring migrant smuggling activities, has been completed. Phase two involves two stages, namely, monitoring and seizing, searching, or diverting vessels either in (a) international waters, or (b) Libyan territorial waters. In accordance with the EU Council's decision, the legal basis of phase two stage one would either constitute the 1982 United Nations Convention on the Law of the Seas (UNCLOS), and for phase two stage two, would be conducted either with the consent of the Libyan government or alternatively under applicable UNSC resolutions.[73]

i. Explicit Authorisation

On 9 October 2015 the UNSC adopted Resolution 2240 (2015), its first resolution addressing the migrant smuggling crisis and authorising EUNAVFOR MED activities.[74] Its affirmative authorisation in favour of the use of force rested with several unique characteristics. First, Resolution 2240 (2015) did not explicitly determine a threat to international peace and security. Citing Libyan concerns against linking other issues in Libya to migrant smuggling as well as the invocation of Chapter VII, the determination of a threat to peace and security from a previous draft resolution was removed.[75]

Instead, Resolution 2240 (2015) in its preamble indicated that the UNSC was 'mindful of its primary responsibility for the maintenance of international peace and security under the [UN Charter]'.[76] It will be recalled that the UNSC in several previous situations authorised force without explicitly determining a threat to peace and security and instead opted for that or similar phrasing. The 'mindful of primary responsibility' phrasing was notably used in Resolution 678 (1990) on the Iraqi invasion of Kuwait, and again when the UNSC renewed authorisation to UNOCI and French forces to use force in Côte d'Ivoire in 2016.[77]

The UNSC was therefore careful not to explicitly declare the situation in Libya a threat to peace and security or, at least, not to link the situation there

[71] Mussi (n 70) 489–90. See also European Union, Council Decision (CFSP) 2015/778 of 18 May 2015.

[72] Mussi (n 70) 491. European Union, Council Decision (CFSP) 2015/972 of 22 June 2015.

[73] Mussi (n 70) 490–91; Giorgia Bevilacqua, 'Exploring the Ambiguity of Operation Sophia Between Military and Search and Rescue Activities' in Gemma Andreone (ed), *The Future of the Law of the Sea: Bridging Gaps Between National, Individual and Common Interests* (SpringerOpen 2017) 170–74.

[74] UNSC Res 2240 (2015).

[75] What's In Blue, 'Vote on a Resolution on Human Trafficking and Migrant Smuggling in the Mediterranean' (8 October 2015) What's In Blue: Insight on the Work of the UN Security Council https://shorturl.at/lX6L4.

[76] UNSC Res 2240 (2015) preamble para 12.

[77] UNSC Res 678 (1990), preamble para 3; Res 2248 (2016) preamble para 21.

with the migrant crisis.[78] The UNSC employed similar caution when acting on the situations of piracy off the Somalian coast. In those resolutions, the UNSC did not per se determine piracy a threat to peace and security but rather indicated that its occurrence exacerbated the situation in Somalia which constituted a threat to international peace and security in the region.[79]

The UNSC was equally cautious when invoking Chapter VII. The invocation was conditional to the need to put an end to the proliferation and endangerment of lives by the smuggling of migrants and the trafficking of person. Therefore, the phrasing 'for these specific purposes, acting under Chapter VII of the Charter of the United Nations' was used to indicate that its actions were taken only in this regard. The strict conditioning of its Chapter VII invocation was seemingly attributed to Libyan concerns, and that its territory and territorial waters were to be respected by Member States.[80] Resolution 2240 (2015) in its operative paragraphs then authorised Member States, acting nationally or through regional organisations, to inspect and seize vessels that were believed to be used for migrant smuggling.[81]

Most significant, however, were the provisions of operative paragraph 10 in which the UNSC *decided* to authorise Member States acting nationally or through regional organisations to use 'all measures commensurate with the specific circumstances' in confronting migrant smugglers or human traffickers.[82] The UNSC affirmed that authorisation provided for in the respective paragraphs applied only to the migrant smuggling situation on the high seas off the coast of Libya.[83]

Despite no reference to 'all necessary means [or] measures' phrasing, the resolution was interpreted authorising force. It is worth recalling that the UNSC had previously authorised force under the 'all measures commensurate with the specific circumstances' phrasing. UNSC practice suggests that while this phrasing is meant to authorise force, it is used only when the use of force is limited in purpose.[84] For example, in Resolution 665 (1990), the UNSC authorised limited force to enforce an embargo against Iraq. Similar language authorising limited force was used in Resolution 794 (1992) on Somalia; Resolutions 875 (1993) and 917 (1994) on Haiti; and Resolution 787 (1992) on Bosnia and Herzegovina.[85]

[78] Mussi (n 70) 492. The instability in Libya at the time was nonetheless determined to constitute a threat to peace and security in several other resolutions. See eg, UNSC Res 2208 (2015) preamble para 7; UNSC Res 2213 (2015) preamble para 13 and recalled in UNSC Res 2238 (2015) preamble para 20 and UNSC Res 2259 (2015) preamble para 24.

[79] See for example UNSC Res 1816 (2008).

[80] What's In Blue (n 75).

[81] UNSC Res 2240 (2015) paras 6–8.

[82] UNSC Res 2240 (2015) para 10.

[83] UNSC Res 2240 (2015) para 11.

[84] Bevilacqua (n 73) 176.

[85] UNSC Res 794 (1992) para 16; UNSC Res 875 (1993) para 1; UNSC Res 917 (1994) para 10; UNSC Res 787 (1992) para 12.

As has been pointed out, such authorisation is not a 'blanket mandate' to use force as with resolutions referencing 'all necessary means [or] measures'.[86]

That the UNSC authorised force under Resolution 2240 (2015) was evident in the UNSC debate. Chad acknowledged the resolution authorised the existing EU operation in the Mediterranean,[87] France indicated recourse to force was precisely defined,[88] and Chile expressed the view that the use of force was limited in scope.[89] Venezuela was the only UNSC member which abstained from the vote, stating that military force would not contribute meaningfully to addressing the issue of migrant smuggling.[90]

ii. Limitations on the Use of Force

While authorising force, Resolution 2240 (2015) applied ample restraint. First, the UNSC opted for the terms 'all measures commensurate' and not 'all necessary means [or] measures', indicating explicitly the limited nature of the authorisation. Second, the authorisation provided for in operative paragraph 10 was applicable to the provisions of operative paragraphs 7 and 8. Paragraph 7 specifically referred to Member States *inspecting* vessels that were reasonably suspected of being used to smuggle migrants or traffic persons. Member States had to also make good faith efforts in obtaining consent from vessels' flag States before making use of the authorisation. Therefore, Member States would have to reasonably suspect that a vessel was involved in smuggling or trafficking and had to attempt to at least obtain consent to inspect these vessels before they could make use of measures under the resolution. Additionally, the authorisation provided for was for a period of one year from the date of adoption of the resolution.

Under paragraph 8, Member States were authorised to *seize* vessels inspected under paragraph 7. This authorisation was provided only for those vessels that were confirmed to have been used for migrant smuggling or the trafficking of persons. In addition, Member States were also authorised to *dispose* of these vessels.

The measures provided for under paragraphs 7, 8 and 10 was subject to additional restrictions. These measures were to be taken only against those vessels on the high seas off the coast of Libya and in full compliance with international human rights laws.[91] The use of force to combat migrant smuggling and human trafficking was therefore limited and did not extend to Libya's territorial waters. Member States acting under measures provided for to inspect or seize vessels

[86] Bevilacqua (n 73) 176.
[87] UN Doc S/PV.7531 (2015) 2.
[88] UN Doc S/PV.7531 (2015) 6.
[89] UN Doc S/PV.7531 (2015) 7.
[90] UN Doc S/PV.7531 (2015) 9.
[91] UNSC Res 2240 (2015) para 10; Mussi (n 70) 495.

also had to keep flag States informed of measures taken against their vessels.[92] Additionally, Member States making use of the measures under paragraphs 7 to 10 were to keep the UNSC informed within three months of the adoption of the resolution and every three months thereafter.[93]

iii. Implementation of Resolution 2240 (2015) and Operation Sophia

On 7 October 2015 the EUNAVFOR MED officially launched its second phase, which includes the boarding, search, seizure and diversion of vessels suspected of being used for smuggling or trafficking. According to reports by the Secretary-General, EU Member States had relied on these measures on several occasions.[94] On 9 and 18 July 2016, the EU military operation had for the first time inspected and seized vessels.[95] By 9 August 2016 the EU had reported that 241 vessels had been disposed of in accordance with the provisions of Resolution 2240 (2015).[96]

Since its adoption of Resolution 2240 (2015), the UNSC has renewed its authorisation in eight subsequent resolutions.[97] All subsequent authorising resolutions have invoked Chapter VII, explicitly renewed measures under paragraphs 7 to 10 of Resolution 2240 (2015), and imposed reporting obligations on Member States acting pursuant to the respective resolutions.

IV. AUTHORISATION TO THE ECONOMIC COMMUNITY OF WEST AFRICAN STATES

A. Resolutions Authorising Force in the Ivory Coast

In 2002, ethnic violence in Côte d'Ivoire erupted into a national civil war. Prior to the outbreak of the war, instability in the surrounding region coupled with a prosperous Ivorian economy resulted in a massive change in its population. A foreign African population in Côte d'Ivoire was estimated at 26 per cent of the total population. Over half of these were Burkinabes.[98] In the months preceding a general election in 2000, the Ivorian government adopted legislation that required both parents of a presidential candidate to be of Ivorian descent.

[92] UNSC Res 2240 (2015) para 9.

[93] UNSC Res 2240 (2015) para 17.

[94] UN Doc S/2017/761 (2016) paras 11, 12. See also UN Doc S/2018/807 (2018) paras 9–14.

[95] UN Doc S/2016/766 (2016) para 13.

[96] UN Doc S/2016/766 (2016) para 14.

[97] UNSC Res 2312 (2016) para 7; UNSC Res 2380 (2017) para 7; UNSC Res 2437 (2018) para 2; UNSC Res 2491 (2019) para 2; UNSC Res 2456 (2020) para 2; UNSC Res 2598 (2021) para 2; UNSC Res 2652 (2022) para 2; UNSC Res 2698 (2023) para 3.

[98] James Copnall, 'Ivory Coast's Cultural Divide' (17 July 2004) *BBC*; Lara Pawson, 'French Fears in Ivory Coast' (19 January 2004) *BBC*; Barrie Amadu, 'Guinea: Unstoppable Exodus' (18 May 2004) *BBC*.

Presidential candidate Alassane Outtarra, who represented the predominantly Muslim North population, was thus excluded.[99] Troops from the north of the country began attacks against major cities, particularly against the Christian government held south. By the end of 2002, ceasefire agreements had failed to deter the fighting. It was only on 26 January 2003 that the parties to the conflict met in Paris and signed the Linas-Marcoussis Agreements, agreeing to, among others, a ceasefire, a government of national reconciliation and UN involvement.[100] In particular, the UNSC was requested to affirm the deployment of an ECOWAS force to the Ivory Coast.[101]

In response, the UNSC adopted a series of resolutions on the situation in Côte d'Ivoire and over a period spanning a decade, authorised force to several entities. These included ECOWAS and, most notably, French forces that had been authorised to assist ECOWAS in its mandate implementation. As will be seen below, the UNSC accorded such authorisation explicitly and in no uncertain terms. With the exception of its later Resolution 1975 (2011) adopted on the post-election situation, all other resolutions served as clear instances in which it had authorised the use of force under clear and robust mandates.

i. Resolutions 1464, 1498 (2003), 1527 and 1528 (2004)

The UNSC's response to the Linas-Marcoussis Agreement and the ECOWAS request for UNSC involvement came with the adoption of Resolution 1464 (2003).[102] Welcoming the progress that had been made in stabilising the security situation, the UNSC noted the existence of challenges to stability and determined the situation to be a threat to international peace and security. Acting under Chapter VII, it authorised Member States participating in the ECOWAS force 'in accordance with Chapter VIII' together with French forces to 'take the necessary steps' to, among others, guarantee the security and movement of their personnel and protect civilians immediately threatened with physical violence within their zones of operation.[103] It would seem that the UNSC in this case invoked both Chapter VII and VII; likely given that the authorisation was to be made use of by both French Forces (Member States) and ECOWAS as a regional organisation operating in one of its Member States.

[99] 'Timeline: Ivory Coast/West African Nation's Key Events From 1960 Independence Until Present Day Events' (30 November 2011) *Aljazeera*; see also Citizenship Rights in Africa, 'Côte d'Ivoire' http://citizenshiprightsafrica.org/region/cote-divoire/ and UN High Commissioner for Refugees (UNHCR), 'Statelessness and Nationality in Côte d'Ivoire – A Study for UNHCR' December 2016, www.refworld.org/docid/58594d114.html.

[100] UN Doc S/2003/99 (2003) Annex I.

[101] UN Doc S/2003/99 (2003) Annex II, para 14.

[102] UNSC Res 1464 (2003); see Gray, *International Law and the Use of Force* (n 7) 352 and UN Doc SC/7657 (2003).

[103] UNSC Res 1464 (2003) para 9. See also Ralph Zacklin, 'The Use of Force in Peacekeeping Operations' in Niels Blokker and Nico Schrijver (eds), *The Security Council and the Use of Force: Theory and Reality – A Need for Change?* (Marinus Nijhoff Publishers 2005) 99.

The UNSC limited the authorisation to a six-month period and both ECOWAS and France were obliged to report periodically to the UNSC.[104]

Three months later, aiming to assist the continuing situation in Côte d'Ivoire, the UNSC established MINUCI under Resolution 1479 (2003). While its mandate included a military component, it was not authorised to use force beyond self-defence.[105] The UNSC also welcomed ECOWAS and French forces' intentions to assist MINUCI in its mandate.[106] By August of that year, the UNSC adopted Resolution 1498 (2003) in which it *decided* to renew the authorisation given to ECOWAS Member States and French forces for a further period of six months.[107] Although not explicitly referencing the authorisation under Resolution 1464 (2003) in context it was clear that the authorisation renewed was that given under Resolution 1464 (2003).[108] Resolution 1498 (2003) therefore remains exceptional in that it neither explicitly determined the situation a threat to international peace and security nor did it invoke Chapter VII. In addition, the reporting requirements laid down in Resolution 1464 (2003) were not mentioned under Resolution 1498 (2003).

When the UNSC subsequently extended the authorisation to ECOWAS and French forces under Resolutions 1527 and 1528 (2004), it did so in clearer terms. Resolution 1527 (2004) recalled Resolution 1464 (2003), determined the situation continued to constitute a threat to international peace and security in the region, and invoked Chapter VII when it renewed this authorisation.[109] Under Resolution 1528 (2004) the UNSC established the United Nations Operation in Côte d'Ivoire (UNOCI), from which authority from MINUCI and ECOWAS was to be transferred to. It authorised UNOCI to use 'all necessary measures' to implement its mandate.[110] The UNSC also renewed the authorisation given to ECOWAS and French forces initially under Resolution 1527 (2004).[111] It explicitly authorised French forces to use 'all necessary means' to support UNOCI in its mandate.[112] Among these, French forces were to intervene at the request of UNOCI, intervene against belligerent actions, and protect civilians in its areas of deployment. The authorisation given to both UNOCI and French forces supporting it was explicitly renewed again in 16 subsequent resolutions.[113]

[104] UNSC Res 1464 (2003) paras 9, 10.

[105] Its mandate was extended under UNSC Res 1514 (2003).

[106] UNSC Res 1479 (2003) paras 3, 12.

[107] UNSC Res 1498 (2003) para 1.

[108] Blokker, 'Outsourcing the Use of Force' (n 3) 209 similar views the resolution as having authorised force.

[109] UNSC Res 1527 (2004).

[110] UNSC Res 1528 (2004) para 8. See specifically Zacklin (n 103) 99 who indicates that UNOCI's mandate under UNSC Res. 1528 (2004) 'contains elements where the use of force beyond self-defence is clearly authorised'; see also Antonio Tzanakopoulos, 'The UN/French Use of Force in Abidjan: Uncertainties Regarding the Scope of UN Authorisations' *EJIL: Talk!* (9 April 2011).

[111] UNSC Res 1528 (2004) para 15.

[112] UNSC Res 1528 (2004) para 16.

[113] UNSC Res 1572 (2004) para 2; UNSC Res 1584 (2005) para 2; UNSC Res 1594 (2005) para 1; UNSC Res 1600 (2005) para 5; UNSC Res 1603 (2005) para 11; UNSC Res 1609 (2005) para 1; UNSC

ii. Resolution 1975 (2011)

While both UNOCI and French forces received regular renewals to use force in Côte d'Ivoire over the next seven years, in 2011 the UNSC was forced to act on yet another situation brewing in the country. Less than two weeks after authorising the use of force in Libya, on 30 March 2011 the UNSC adopted Resolution 1975 (2011) on the situation in Côte d'Ivoire.[114] The resolution was adopted following the election defeat of then President Laurent Gbagbo and his refusal to relinquish power to successor Alassane Ouattara.

The resolution is significant for two reasons. On the one hand, it was another example of explicit UNSC authorisation of force. On the other hand, measures taken under the resolution ultimately forced President Gbagbo to relinquish power. Consequently, Resolution 1973 (2011) has been cited as in part authorising force to enforce regime change; an aspect of authorisation that remains controversial.[115]

a. Authorisation to UNOCI and French Forces

Determining that the situation in Côte d'Ivoire continued to constitute a threat to international peace and security, and acting under Chapter VII of the UN Charter, the UNSC recalled its authorisation given to UNOCI and French forces in previous resolutions. It authorised UNOCI 'to use all necessary means to carry out its mandate to protect civilians under imminent threat of physical violence, within its capabilities and its areas of deployment, including to prevent the use of heavy weapons against the civilian population'.[116] The authorisation given to UNOCI was renewed in seven subsequent resolutions until it was eventually terminated in 2017.[117] All resolutions subsequently renewing the initial authorisation were made under Chapter VII, contained an Article 39 determination, and explicitly referred to the use of all necessary means.

Res 1652 (2006) para 1; UNSC Res 1726 (2006) para 1; UNSC Res 1739 (2007) paras 5, 8(a)–(f); UNSC Res 1763 (2007) para 1; UNSC Res 1765 (2007) para 1; UNSC Res 1795 (2008) para 4; UNSC Res 1826 (2008) para 1; UNSC Res 1865 (2009) para 15; UNSC Res 1880 (2009) paras 19, 30; UNSC Res 1911 (2010) paras 14, 20. UNOCI was given a new mandate and subsequent authorisation to use force under UNSC Res 1933 (2010) para 17, French forces were given authorisation under para 24, and this authorisation was extended under UNSC Res 1962 (2010) paras 3, 14, 17, and UNSC Res 1975 (2011) para 6.

[114] UNSC Res 1975 (2011).

[115] On the UNSC and regime change in Côte d'Ivoire (and Libya), see Dire Tladi, 'Security Council, the Use of Force and Regime Change: Libya and Côte d'Ivoire' (2012) 37 *South African Yearbook of International Law* 22. On the broader topic of the UNSC and regime change, see Steven Wheatley, 'The Security Council, Democratic Legitimacy and Regime Change in Iraq' (2006) 17(3) *European Journal of International Law* 531; Mehrdad Payandeh, 'The United Nations, Military Intervention, and Regime Change in Libya' (2012) 52(2) *Virginia Journal of International Law* 355.

[116] UNSC Res 1975 (2011) para 6.

[117] UNSC Res 1981 (2011) para 1; UNSC Res 2000 (2011) para 1; UNSC Res 2062 (2012) paras 1, 5; UNSC Re 2112 (2013) paras 1, 7; UNSC Res 2162 (2014) paras 18, 20, 28; UNSC Res 2226 (2015) paras 18, 20, 28; UNSC Res 2284 (2016) paras 14, 16, 25.

b. Authorised Regime Change?

While no doubt explicitly authorising force, one question which arose with Resolution 1975 (2011) is whether it had authorised force for purposes of regime change. As has been noted elsewhere, suggestions that the UNSC may have intended regime change under a resolution is arguably contrary to the principles of *jus ad bellum* and the prohibition of supporting rebels against the government of a state.[118] Nevertheless, some scholars have argued that UNOCI, bound by the principles of neutrality, interpreted its mandate broadly. In so doing, it sided with pro-Ouattara forces in protecting them and actively fighting against pro-Gbagbo forces.[119] In addition, that UNSC measures were adopted solely against pro-Gbagbo loyalists was a clear indication that it wished to put pressure to ensure Gbagbo's eventual removal from office.[120] The fact that the UNSC formally recognised Ouattara as the election winner has also been equated as a tacit approval for the ousting of Gbagbo.

In contrast to this line of argument, Resolution 1975 (2011) does not expressly indicate any objective aimed at the eventual removal of Gbagbo from office. The resolution notably welcomed a political solution to the situation, urged Gbagbo forces to fully cooperate with UNOCI and even called upon Gbagbo to lift a siege of the Golf Hotel.[121] While it expressly urged Gbagbo to step aside and urged all Ivorian institutions to yield to Ouattara's presidential authority, no indication suggested that force was authorised by UNOCI (or any other entity) to remove Gbagbo from office.[122]

Nonetheless, as in the case of Libya, it became clear through subsequent reports that UN forces under UNOCI, with the assistance of French forces, were instrumental in Gbagbo's capture. Although a carefully phrased narrative was later put forward by both the UN and France that its forces were not directly involved in Gbagbo's capture, this result was evidently attributable to their involvement in fighting pro-Gbagbo forces.[123] In essence however, while

[118] See ch 5 on the analysis of Resolution 1973 (2011). See also Olivier Corten and Vaios Koutroulis, 'The Illegality of Military Support to Rebels in the Libyan War: Aspects of *Jus Contra Bellum* and *Jus in Bello*' (2013) 18 *Journal of Conflict* and *Security Law* 63, 91–93.

[119] Sean Butler, 'Separating Protection from Politics: The UN Security Council, the 2011 Ivorian Political Crisis and the Legality of Regime Change' (2015) 20(2) *Journal of Conflict and Security Law* 259.

[120] Butler (n 119) 259–60.

[121] UNSC Res 1975 (2011) paras 2, 7, 11.

[122] UNOCI's mandate had already been made clear in several previous resolutions. UNSC Res 1975 (2011) merely reaffirmed its right to use all necessary means for the protection of civilians, adding also that it was to protect civilians from the use of heavy weaponry.

[123] Tladi (n 115) 42. See also interview given by Alain Juppe, French Minister of Foreign and European Affairs, to 'France Info' www.ambafrance-uk.org/Alain-Juppe-interviewed-France,188688. See also Butler (n 119) 260 in which he quotes a keynote address by former UN Secretary-General Ban Ki-Moon interpreting it as saying that Gbagbo's removal from office at most was a side effect of UNOCI's actions.

Resolution 1975 (2011) explicitly authorised force by UNOCI, it did not grant such authorisation to the extent required to remove Gbagbo from office.[124]

Controversy surrounding Resolution 1975 (2011) and regime change aside, the broader UNSC practice in Côte d'Ivoire remains clear. Authorisation for the use of force to UN peacekeeping missions (UNOCI), regional organisations (ECOWAS) and Member States (France), was granted explicitly in every authorising resolution. Interestingly however, when authorising force in Resolution 1464 (2003), the UNSC opted to invoke both Chapter VII and VIII, possibly because it had authorised both individual Member States (France) and a regional organisation under Article 53(1) (ECOWAS).

B. Resolution 1497 (2003) | ECOMIL in Liberia

In April 1999 the emergence of the Liberians United for Reconciliation and Democracy (LURD) sparked the beginning of the second Liberian civil war. By 2003, the emergence of a second rebel group, the Movement for Democracy in Liberia (MODEL), eventually led to the seizure of Monrovia and the resignation of President Charles Taylor. The UNSC responded to these developments with Resolution 1497 (2003), establishing an UN-authorised, ECOWAS-led Multinational Force and authorising it to use force under a robust Chapter VII mandate.[125] Although explicitly authorising force, Resolution 1497 (2003) based its authorisation not on Chapter VIII but on Chapter VII.

The decision to authorise a multinational force in Liberia was first proposed by Secretary-General Kofi Annan in which an explicit request that the force 'be authorised under Chapter VII' was made.[126] Subsequently, the UNSC adopted Resolution 1497 (2003), explicitly determining the situation in Liberia constituted a threat to international peace and security and to the stability of the West African sub-region.[127] Acting under Chapter VII, the UNSC authorised Member States to establish a multinational force in Liberia to support the implementation of a ceasefire agreement signed on 17 June 2003.

The multinational force was given a robust mandate, which included the establishment of conditions for the initial stages of disarmament, demobilisation and reintegration activities; the establishment and maintenance of security in the period after the departure of President Taylor and the installation of a

[124] Several UNSC members disapproved of regime change as a potential consequence under the resolution. See Bulter (n 119) 260 who notes statements made by India, China and Russia to this effect. On that topic, see also Claus Kreβ, 'Pro-Democratic Intervention in Current International Law: The Case of The Gambia in January 2017' (2017) 4(2) *Journal on the Use of Force and International Law* 239; Julie Gagnon, 'ECOWAS's Right to Intervene in Côte d'Ivoire to Install Alassane Ouattara as President-Elect' (2013) 3(1) *Notre Dame Journal of International and Comparative Law* 52.

[125] UNSC Res 1497 (2003).

[126] UN Doc S/2003/678 (2003) Annex.

[127] UNSC Res 1497 (2003) preamble para 8.

successor authority; securing the environment for the delivery of humanitarian assistance; and preparation for the introduction of a longer-term UN stabilisation force to succeed the multination force.[128] Member States participating in the multinational force were authorised to 'take all necessary measures to fulfil its mandate'.[129]

ECOWAS was first to respond affirmatively to the Secretary-General's proposal, indicating that it was ready to deploy 1,500 troops to Liberia by mid-August 2003.[130] Supported by the United States, ECOWAS officially deployed the ECOWAS Vanguard Interposition Force in Liberia (ECOMIL), consisting of troops from Nigeria, Ghana, The Gambia, Guinea-Bissau, Mali, Senegal, Togo and Benin.[131]

By 11 September, the Secretary-General had reported that the situation had significantly improved and that logistical planning for the deployment of a follow-up UN peacekeeping mission to succeed the multinational force was underway.[132] He also highlighted the successful and swift deployment of ECOMIL with United States support, having been instrumental in stabilising the situation in Liberia.[133] In line with the recommendations of the Secretary-General, on 19 September 2003 the UNSC adopted Resolution 1509 (2003), establishing and mandating the United Nations Mission in Liberia (UNMIL).[134] On 1 October 2003 ECOMIL transferred all authority to UNMIL.

a. Action under Chapter VII or VIII?

The operations in Liberia were predominantly carried out by ECOMIL with support of the United States. ECOMIL's involvement in Liberia was essentially an instance of regional enforcement action. Resolution 1497 (2003) specifically authorised 'Member States' to establish the multinational force. Moreover, it neither invoked Chapter VIII nor made reference to the usual wording in its operative paragraphs in which the UNSC authorised Member States 'acting nationally or through regional agencies or arrangements'.[135] ECOWAS was only mentioned once in the resolution's preamble in which the UNSC 'commend[ed]' it for its role in facilitating ceasefire agreements in Liberia. Additionally, it 'recognis[ed]' the 'critically important role [ECOWAS] played and necessarily

[128] UNSC Res 1497 (2003) para 1.

[129] UNSC Res 1497 (2003) para 5; Gray, *International Law and the Use of Force* (n 7) 356; James Sloan, *The Militarisation of Peacekeeping in the Twenty-First Century* (Hart Publishing 2011) 221.

[130] UN Doc S/2003/769 (2003).

[131] ECOWAS, 'Final Communiqué: Extraordinary Summit of ECOWAS Heads of State and Government on the Situation in Liberia' (Accra, 31 July 2003) Art 13.

[132] UN Doc S/2003/875 (2003) paras 20, 51–101. While the United States did not directly become involved, some 2 000 US troops were positioned off the Liberian coast. See Sloan (n 129) 221; Gray, *International Law and the Use of Force* (n 7) 356.

[133] UN Doc S/2003/875 (2003) paras 102–04.

[134] UNSC Res 1509 (2003) paras 1, 3(a)–(s). See also ch 5 on UNMIL.

[135] This was in contrast to, for example, UNSC Res 794 (1992) and UNSC Res 875 (1993).

will continue to play in the Liberia peace process, consistent with Chapter VIII of the Charter of the United Nations'.

ECOWAS's swift response indicating its readiness to the Secretary-General to assist in Liberia was one reason behind the adoption of Resolution 1497 (2003).[136] As a result, the resolution actually authorised enforcement action by ECOMIL under Chapter VII, and not under Chapter VIII. Although the precise implications thereof remain unclear, it is evident that authorisation under either of these chapters may involve the use of force.[137] Moreover, the subsequent adoption of Resolution 1509 (2003) commending the ECOMIL deployment 'pursuant to Resolution 1497 (2003)' suggests that ECOMIL was indeed authorised to act in Liberia under that resolution.[138]

C. Resolutions Adopted on the Situation in Mali | 2012–present

i. Resolution 2085 (2012) | AFISMA

In January 2012 armed conflict broke out between the Malian government and Tuareg rebels from the National Movement for the Liberation of Azawad (MNLA). The MNLA, fighting for an independent Azawad, had taken control of most of the region by April of that year.[139] While fighting in the north continued, dissatisfaction with the government's response and a perceived ill-equipping of military forces resulted in a *coup* against President Amadou Toumani Toure on 22 March 2012, one week before scheduled presidential elections.[140]

International condemnation and pressure against the *coup*, in particular by the AU and ECOWAS, led the military junta to agree to a transition toward elections.[141] ECOWAS political efforts, especially those of ECOWAS mediator for Mali, President Compaore of Burkina Faso, resulted in the signing of a framework agreement and transitional government pending presidential elections.[142] In response to these events, the UNSC adopted Resolution 2085 (2012), authorising the deployment of an AU-led International Support Mission to Mali (AFISMA).[143] The authorisation given to AFISMA was, in the regional context, a clear example of prior explicit authorisation of regional enforcement action.

[136] See UN Doc S/2003/769 (2003). See also UN Doc S/2003/678 (2003).

[137] The UNSC debate confirms this. See UN Doc S/PV.4803 (2003) 3 (Mexico), 5 (United States), 6 (China).

[138] UNSC Res 1509 (2003).

[139] Marina Caparini, 'The Mali Crisis and Responses by Regional Actors' (2015) *Norwegian Institute of International Affairs* Working Paper 849 4.

[140] Caparini (n 139) 5.

[141] Caparini (n 139) 7.

[142] Caparini (n 139) 7.

[143] UNSC Res 2085 (2012).

Resolution 2085 (2012) determined the situation in Mali constituted a threat to international peace and security.[144] Acting under Chapter VII, the UNSC authorised the deployment of AFISMA for an initial period of one year.[145] Furthermore, it authorised AFISMA to 'take all necessary measures, in compliance with applicable international humanitarian law and human rights law' to carry out its tasks.[146]

AFISMA's mandate included capacity building of the Malian Defence and Security Forces, support in recovering territory under rebel control, and supporting Malian authorities to create a secure environment for the civilian-led delivery of humanitarian assistance and the voluntary return of internally-displaced persons and refugees.[147] The UNSC also requested the AU, in close coordination with ECOWAS, the Secretary-General and other international organisations, to report back to it every 60 days on the deployment and activities of AFISMA.[148] On 19 January 2013 ECOWAS authorised AFISMA's immediate deployment. While the deployment of AFISMA was initially set for September 2013, unexpected rebel advances prompted ECOWAS to deploy the mission earlier.

The AFISMA deployment was however plagued by shortfalls. From the start of operations, AFISMA lacked the necessary logistical and financial support to deploy, resulting in Mali's request for assistance to France.[149] The French intervention, *Operation Serval*, was therefore the first external military response, having begun in January 2013, even prior to that of ECOWAS which had been planning a military response since the coup in Mali first took place.[150]

ii. Resolution 2100 (2013) and Subsequent Authorising Resolutions | MINUSMA and French Forces

Before AFISMA could deploy, the situation on the ground began changing drastically when rebel forces made unprecedented advances that were unexpected by most. This development prompted the UNSC to release a press statement on 10 January 2013 in which it recalled among others, Resolutions 2085 (2012); iterated an *urgent need* to counter terrorist activities in Mali; reiterated its call to Member States to assist Mali by, in particular, providing assistance to the defence and security forces; and expressed its determination to fully implement the provisions of Resolution 2085 (2012). The UNSC also called for the

[144] UNSC Res 2085 (2012) preamble para 15; see also UNSC Res 2056 (2012); UNSC Res 2071 (2012).

[145] UNSC Res 2085 (2012) para 9.

[146] UNSC Res 2085 (2012) para 9.

[147] UNSC Res 2085 (2012) paras 9(a)–(f).

[148] UNSC Res 2085 (2012) para 10.

[149] UN Doc S/2013/17 (2013).

[150] See also Johan Tejpar and Adriana Lins de Albuquerque, 'Challenges to Peace and Security in West Africa: The Role of ECOWAS' (August 2015) *Studies in African Security* Swedish Defence Research Agency 2.

rapid deployment of AFISMA.[151] In addition, the press statement considered that the 'serious deterioration of the situation threatens even more the stability and integrity of Mali' and constitutes 'a direct threat to international peace and security'.

The UNSC therefore considered that the rapidly changing circumstances in Mali warranted action by Member States pending AFISMA's deployment. The press statement is also significant in that it has on at least one occasion been interpreted in favour of a legal basis for the subsequent French *Operation Serval*.[152]

Indeed, the UNSC recognised the urgent nature of the situation unfolding in Mali, and the need to assist it to prevent a deterioration in the situation. It has even been suggested that the press statement was an 'urgent interpretation' of Resolution 2085 (2013) authorising intervention in Mali.[153] While this book's analysis is primarily concerned with UNSC resolutions, the following should be noted.

First, an ECOWAS statement on 12 January 2013 suggested it viewed the UNSC press statement as a legal basis for intervention in Mali.[154] Be that as it may, one day after the UNSC statement and one day before the subsequent ECOWAS statement, Mali had in fact sent an official request to France for military assistance.[155] Given that a state may legally request military assistance, it seems that the French operation would first and foremost be based on intervention by invitation and that, by extension, an alternative legal basis would be unnecessary.[156]

a. UNSC Authorisation of Force in a Press Statement?

Despite the sound legal basis of the French operation, a central question was whether the UNSC could in fact authorise force in a press statement. Such a conclusion is unlikely for a number of reasons. First, the UNSC ordinarily authorises force in resolutions, arguably its primary instrument for effecting binding decisions. While press statements may serve as evidence of the interpretation of UNSC resolutions, it would be difficult to regard them as instruments which could embody any binding rights or obligations.[157] Despite the urgency

[151] See UN Doc SC/10878-AFR/2502 (2013).

[152] Theodore Christakis and Karine Bannelier, 'French Military Intervention in Mali: It's Legal But … Why? Part II: Consent and UNSC Authorisation' *EJIL: Talk!* (25 January 2013).

[153] Christakis and Bannelier (n 152).

[154] ECOWAS, 'Statement of the President of the ECOWAS Commission on the Situation in Mali' (12 January 2013) No 006/2013 (12 January 2013).

[155] 'Mali Asks for Help From France as Islamist Rebels Push Forward' *The Telegraph* (11 January 2013). See also UN Doc S/1013/17 (2013).

[156] See also Amy Laird, 'Mali: A Legally Justifiable Intervention by France?' (2012) 10 *New Zealand Yearbook of International Law* 127.

[157] The United States and the United Kingdom, however, have on at least one occasion indicated that UNSC press statements are binding as they add on to existing Chapter VII measures. See Marko Milanovic, 'Can UNSC Presidential Statements be Legally Binding?' *EJIL: Talk!* (15 April 2009). On

concerning the situation in Mail at the time, the UNSC does not convey a decision to authorise force (whether they can at all be considered decisions) in a press statement.

If one considers that the press statement does have such an effect, and conscious of the fact that it determined the situation to be a threat to peace and security, it nonetheless did not invoke Chapter VII. It suffices at present to say that an interpretation of a UNSC press statement as having authorised force would entirely erode the legal certainty it has in recent decades espoused within its resolutions. Additionally, neither France nor any other State has proposed the press statement as a legal basis for *Operation Serval*.[158]

What can however be noted is that France was not authorised to use force under Resolution 2085 (2012). Despite subsequently indicating it was acting 'in line with Security Council resolutions', France has never explicitly based its actions on Resolution 2085 (2012).[159] In addition, it never raised arguments of implicit authorisation, or even on retroactive authorisation upon the adoption of subsequent resolutions which in fact later authorised French forces to use force to assist the follow-up UN mission in Mali, MINUSMA.

To this end, it was clear that the French operation assisting MINUSA was based on subsequent UNSC resolutions (only to the extent provided for in those resolutions), and that all other activities outside this scope would be based on the request for assistance by the Malian government.[160] The fact that the UNSC recognised the French presence in Mali prior to authorising them in subsequent resolutions was a recognition of the *fait accompli* at the time around which MINUSMA would have to work with.[161]

That said, subsequent to AFISMA's deployment, the UNSC adopted Resolution 2100 (2013), welcoming the swift response by French forces in combating extremist activities and commending the support of these forces to restore Mali's territorial integrity along with AFISMA and the Malian defence and security forces.[162] Resolution 2100 (2013), again determining the

this topic, see also Stefan Talmon, 'The Statements by the President of the Security Council' (2003) 2 *Chinese Journal of International Law* 448 who indicates that statements by the President of the Security Council to the press do not constitute decisions of the UNSC, at least not under Article 27 of the UN Charter; Michael Wood, 'Security Council Working Methods and Procedure: Recent Developments' (1996) 45(1) *International and Comparative Law Quarterly* 154.

[158] Karine Bannelier and Theodore Christakis, 'The Intervention by France and Others in Mali' in Tom Ruys and Olivier Corten (eds), *The Use of Force in International Law: A Case-Based Approach* (Oxford University Press 2018) 824–25.

[159] Bannelier and Christakis (n 158) 824. See also the legal basis claimed by France at the time in UN Doc S/2013/17 (2013).

[160] Bannelier and Christakis (n 158) 826.

[161] Bannelier and Christakis (n 158) 825. Although they indicate that since the UNSC was aware of the impending French deployment, it may have implicitly approved of the intervention or at the least accepted the soundness of its legality based on intervention by invitation.

[162] UNSC Res 2100 (2013). It however did not retroactively authorise the French operation. In any case, France did not claim that it was authorised under it or preceding resolutions. Bannelier and Christakis (n 158) 825.

situation in Mali to constitute a threat to peace and security and acting under Chapter VII, established MINUSMA, handing over all authority from AFISMA to it.[163] MINUSMA was authorised to use 'all necessary means' to fulfil its mandate which, in particular, included a protection of civilians component.[164]

In addition to the authorisation given to MINUSMA, the UNSC authorised French troops, within their capabilities and areas of deployment, to use 'all necessary means'. Such means were to be used from the commencement of MINUSMA's activities in support of its elements when it was under imminent and serious threat. In turn, France was requested to report to the UNSC on the implementation of the resolution. The authorisation given to MINUSMA and French forces, as well as the corresponding reporting obligation to the French forces, was extended under Chapter VII in eight subsequent resolutions.[165] French forces subsequently withdrew from Mali in 2022 and MINUSMA was terminated in 2023.[166]

In short, all authorisation given, first to AFISMA and subsequently to MINUSMA and French forces, was given in explicit terms. Every resolution establishing or extending authorisation on the situation in Mali determined a threat to international peace and security, invoked Chapter VII and authorised the use of 'all necessary means'.

V. COMBINED AUTHORISATION OF FORCE: RESOLUTIONS ADOPTED ON CHAD AND THE CENTRAL AFRICAN REPUBLIC

Towards the end of 2003, conflict in Sudan's Darfur region spilled over into Chad. The resulting situation saw a mass refugee influx from Sudan into Chad as well as the north-eastern regions of the Central African Republic (CAR). Among the refugees were also rebel forces present at refugee camps. These forces at the time were in part armed by the Sudanese government that attempted to overthrow Chadian President Idriss Deby. At the same time, rebel forces in Sudan were also being armed by the Chadian government. By December 2005, a civil war had engulfed Chad and violence had spread across the country. In response to the escalating regional conflict, the UNSC authorised the establishment of

[163] African Union, 'African-Led International Support Mission in Mali (AFISMA) Press Release *AFISMA Transfers its Authority to MINUSMA*' (1 July 2013); UNSC Res 2100 (2013) para 7.

[164] UNSC Res 2100 (2013) paras 16–17.

[165] UNSC Res 2164 (2014) paras 12, 26; UNSC Res 2227 (2015) paras 13, 27; UNSC Res 2295 (2016) paras 17, 35; UNSC Res 2364 (2017) paras 18, 37; UNSC Res 2423 (2018) paras 32, 53; UNSC Res 2480 (2019) paras 19, 42; UNSC Res 2531 (2020) paras 18, 41; UNSC Res 2584 (2021) paras 20, 43. UNSC Res 2640 (2022) para 17 only extended MINUSMA's authorisation of force given that French forces had withdrawn by this time.

[166] UNSC Res 2690 (2023) para 1.

the United Nations-African Union Mission in Darfur (UNAMID). Two months later, the UNSC responded to the escalating situation in Chad and the CAR by establishing the United Nations Mission in the Central African Republic and Chad (MINURCAT). In addition to establishing MINURCAT, Resolution 1778 (2007) also authorised an EU operation (EUFOR Tchad/RCA) as a multidimensional response to the ongoing situation.

A. Resolution 1778 (2007) | EU Force in Chad and the CAR

Resolution 1778 (2007) was the fourth instance in which the UNSC explicitly authorised the EU to take action and was the third instance in which the EU conducted an UNSC-authorised military operation in Africa.[167] Under Resolution 1778 (2007), the UNSC determined that the situation in the region of the border between Sudan and the CAR constituted a threat to international peace and security. Moreover, it welcomed Chad and the CAR's approval for the deployment of an international presence by the EU and UN. It also established MINURCAT in the region for a period of one year as an element to the multidimensional EU/UN presence. Acting under Chapter VII, it authorised a one-year deployment of an EU operation authorised to take 'all necessary measures within its capabilities and its area of operation'.[168] The area of operation was expressly indicated as Eastern Chad and North-Eastern CAR.

While the operation was able to achieve some degree of success in its tasks, continued instability prompted the UNSC to consider an extension of its mandate in 2008.[169] Subsequently, it adopted Resolution 1861 (2009) extending the EU operation and commencing its transition to a follow-up UN mission.[170] It, however, did not extend the authorisation of force to the operation since the Chapter VII invocation was attributable only to MINURCAT's mandate. Under paragraph 9 it 'recalled' its authorisation to the EU force to 'take all appropriate measures' to achieve an orderly disengagement, essentially also terminating its mandate under the resolution as of 15 March 2009 and replacing it with MINURCAT.[171] In the same resolution, the UNSC also explicitly authorised the use of force by MINURCAT under a Chapter VII mandate.[172] The resolution also set a final date of transfer of authority from the EU operation to MINRUCAT.[173] While MINURCAT was authorised

[167] UNSC Res 1778 (2007) para 6(a).

[168] UNSC Res 1778 (2007) para 6(a); Gray, *International Law and the Use of Force* (n 7) 346–47.

[169] UNSC Res 1834 (2008) para 4 merely expressed the UNSC's intention to extend the mandate.

[170] UNSC Res 1861 (2009) paras 1, 8.

[171] UNSC Res 1861 (2009) para 9; Gray, *International Law and the Use of Force* (n 7) 347.

[172] UNSC Res 1861 (2009) paras 7(a), (b). For an analysis of the authorisation provided to MINURCAT, see ch 5 at p 142.

[173] UNSC Res 1861 (2009) para 3.

under a robust Chapter VII mandate, in December 2010 Chad withdrew consent to the mission on the basis that it had the capacity to protect civilians on its territory. MINURCAT was subsequently extended for a final period until 31 December 2010.[174] Although the resolutions adopted on both the EU operation and MINURCAT explicitly authorised the use of force, the effectiveness of their implementation was short-lived. The situation in the CAR remained unstable and by 2014, the UNSC had again resorted to its Chapter VII powers to act on the situation.

B. Resolution 2127 (2013) | MISCA and French Forces in the CAR

The continuing deterioration of the situation in the CAR in what the UNSC characterised as a 'total breakdown in law and order' prompted renewed authorisation to restore peace and security in the region. Determining the situation in the CAR constituted a threat to international peace and security, the UNSC in Resolution 2127 (2013) authorised the deployment of the African-led International Support Mission in the CAR (MISCA).[175] The authorisation under Resolution 2127 (2013) was in fact the UNSC's response to a request by the AU Peace and Security Council in which it urged the adoption of a resolution endorsing and authorising MISCA.[176] Acting under Chapter VII, the UNSC authorised MISCA to 'take all necessary measures' for a period of 12 months to, among others, protect civilians; restore security and public order; stabilise the country and restore state authority.[177]

In that same vein, the UNSC also authorised French forces present in the CAR 'within the limits of their capacities and areas of deployment, and for a temporary period, to take all necessary measures to support MISCA' in its mandate.[178] Both the MISCA and French force deployments were to be reviewed six months after the adoption of the resolution. In addition, the AU, UN Secretary-General and all relevant bilateral partners were to report to the UNSC every 60 days on the deployment and activities of MISCA.[179] France was also requested to report on its mandate implementation in coordination with the AU.[180] For its part, France's implementation of Resolution 2127 (2013) came with *Operation Sangaris*, when it deployed a 2,000 strong force in the CAR to assist with security conditions and support the MISCA force.

[174] UNSC Res 1923 (2010) para 1. See also UN Doc S/2010/470; Gray, *International Law and the Use of Force* (n 7) 347.
[175] UNSC Res 2127 (2013) preamble para 31, para 28.
[176] UNSC Res 2127 (2013) preamble para 27.
[177] UNSC Res 2127 (2013) paras 28(i)–(iv).
[178] UNSC Res 2127 (2013) para 50.
[179] UNSC Res 2127 (2013) para 16.
[180] UNSC Res 2127 (2013) para 50.

C. Resolutions 2134, 2181 and 2149 (2014) | EU Operation in the CAR

Less than two months after it had authorised the use of force by MISCA and French forces, the UNSC then authorised a second EU operation to assist both MISCA and French forces. Resolution 2134 (2014) was the result of an EU initiative in which it expressed its willingness to contribute to the security and stability of the situation in the CAR.[181]

Giving effect to this, Resolution 2134 (2014), determining that the situation in the CAR continued to constitute a threat to peace and security, authorised under Chapter VII the EU operation which was to 'take all necessary measures within the limits of its capabilities and areas of deployment'.[182] In addition, the EU was requested to report to the UNSC on the implementation of its mandate every 60 days.[183]

The EU deployment's assistance to MISCA and French forces was evident with it rapidly contributing to security in Bangui, the country's capital, along with securing its international airport seven kilometres outside of Bangui. By September that year, the situation in the CAR had improved significantly and the UNSC replaced MISCA with the United Nations Multidimensional Integrated Stabilisation Mission in the CAR (MINUSCA).[184]

Citing violent reprisals across the CAR remained a threat to peace and security, MINUSCA was authorised under Chapter VII to take 'all necessary means' to implement its mandate, which included the protection of civilians and the delivery of humanitarian assistance.[185] The authorisation for the use of force to the EU deployment was explicitly extended under Resolution 2181 (2014). Determining that the situation in the CAR continued to constitute a threat to international peace and security and invoking Chapter VII, the UNSC *decided* to 'extend the authorisation of the European Union operation contained in paragraph 44 of Resolution 2134 (2014) until 15 March 2015'.[186]

i. Authorisation to MINUSCA and French Forces

In addition to the authorisation granted to MINSUCA, the UNSC again under Resolution 2149 (2014) authorised French forces to use force. French forces in the CAR were authorised to 'use all necessary means' to provide support to MINUSCA. The authorisation accorded to French forces was again strictly based on time limits, effective only from the 'commencement of the activities of MINUSCA until the end of MINUSCA's mandate'.[187] France was again requested

[181] UN Doc S/2014/45 (2014).
[182] UNSC Res 2134 (2014) paras 43, 44.
[183] UNSC Res 2134 (2014) para 45 read together with UNSC Res 2127 (2013) para 32.
[184] UNSC Res 2149 (2014) para 21.
[185] UNSC Res 2149 (2014) paras 29, 30(a)–(g).
[186] UNSC Res 2181 (2014) para 1.
[187] UNSC Res 2149 (2014) para 47; Gray, *International Law and the Use of Force* (n 7) 348.

to report on the implementation of this mandate. Authorisation of the French forces mandate and the corresponding reporting obligations were explicitly renewed in two subsequent resolutions.[188] Interestingly, from Resolution 2387 (2017) onward, French forces were authorised to use *only* 'all means' (and not *all necessary means*) to provide operational support to MINUSCA, at the request of the Secretary-General, and *only* when MINUSCA was under serious threat.[189] It would seem from Resolution 2387 (2017) onward, authorisation to use force by French forces was therefore strictly limited.

The UNSC's resolutions on the CAR and Chad were again a definitive concretisation of explicit authorisation (to EU, AFISMA, MINUSCA and French forces). Over the course of a decade, the UNSC consistently and explicitly authorised such force. All resolutions establishing authorisation were adopted under Chapter VII, and the UNSC had on numerous occasions declared that the situation in the CAR and Chad constituted a threat to international peace and security. In addition to opting for explicit phrasing ('all necessary means [and] measures'), it also imposed specific timelines on the renewal of authorisation as well as corresponding reporting requirements on all entities so authorised.

VI. CONCLUSION

The chapter has focused its attention on UNSC authorisation to regional organisations, namely, authorisation to the AU, the EU and ECOWAS. In addition, it also examined selected UN peacekeeping missions as well as regional peacekeeping initiatives undertaken by these organisations. In so doing, the chapter consider over 50 resolutions which either established, extended or expanded authorising for the use of force. The analysis shows that as with authorisation to Member States, the UNSC consistently *decides*, *authorises* or *calls upon* Member States acting through regional organisations to use 'all necessary measures' (on occasion expressed as 'all measures necessary'). One resolution also employed the use of 'such measures commensurate' phrasing when authorising limited use of force.

Its determination of a threat to peace and security has similarly been consistent. Every resolution authorising or extending authorisation for the use of force has consistently and explicitly made such a determination. Only one resolution presented a deviation from this consistent practice, Resolution 2240 (2015), which did not explicitly determine a threat to peace and security. However, it nonetheless employed the 'mindful of its primary responsibilities for the maintenance of international peace and security' phrasing, which was repeated in three resolutions extending the authorisation. A similar observance in consistency was

[188] UNSC Res 2217 (2015) para 50; UNSC Res 2301 (2016) para 56.

[189] UNSC Res 2387 (2017) para 65; UNSC Res 2448 (2018) para 69; UNSC Res 2499 (2019) para 52; UNSC Res 2552 (2020) para 52; UNSC Res 2605 (2021) para 56.

seen in relation to the UNSC recalling previous Article 39 determinations and invoking Chapter VII. The only exception remains Resolution 1484 (2003), when the UNSC authorised the IEMF in Bunia. With that said, the UNSC, although recalling previous resolutions and statements by its president, did not specify which resolutions were being recalled. To this exception one may again also add Resolution 2240 (2015), although that resolution was adopted in response to the tragic loss of 800 lives on the Mediterranean and was also not preceded by any other resolutions on the situation.

The chapter's analysis has also shown that the UNSC has to date probably relied on regional organisations to implement its decisions more so than on individual states. Even though it has resorted to authorising 'Member States' per se, the implementation of those resolutions in which regional organisations have played a predominant role has surely emphasised the phrased authorisation of Member States 'acting nationally or through regional arrangements or agencies'. More so, the practice also indicates that when authorising regional organisations, the UNSC has consistently relied on Chapter VII measures, rather than invoking Chapter VIII. A similar practice is outlined in the following chapter, which examines UNSC authorisation to NATO under Chapter VII. As with that analysis, it suffices to say that when a regional organisation acts militarily against a Member State or within its geographical area, the UNSC may legally rely on Chapter VIII or, more specifically, Article 53(1).[190]

Given the extensive and consistent invocation of Chapter VII, arguments that UNSC authorisation is based on Articles 42 therefore, seem to be maintained, in part by virtue of the UNSC's practice overwhelmingly supporting such a conclusion. It is therefore a strong conclusion under this chapter that when the UNSC authorises the use of force by regional organisations against non-Member States or authorises an out-of-area deployment, it relies on Articles 42 and 48(1). Where the UNSC authorises the use of force by a regional organisation in its own area or against one of its member states, it may, of course, not only rely on Chapter VII, but also on Chapter VIII measures.[191]

It is also interesting to observe the purpose for which the UNSC has authorised the use of force to regional organisations. As in the case of authorisation to Member States examined in the previous chapter, the authorisation of force has been given to, among others, counter terrorism, support peacekeeping operations, for humanitarian purposes such as the protection of civilians and the provision of humanitarian assistance, and at the request of a state or regional organisation.

[190] See also extensively Abass (n 33) 66–69, 71–78; see broadly Danesh Sarooshi, *The United Nations and the Development of Collective Security: The Delegation by the UN Security Council of its Chapter VII Powers* (Oxford University Press 1999) 247–53; see also the remarks in Mary O'Connell, 'The UN, NATO, and International Law after Kosovo' (2000) 22(1) *Human Rights Quarterly* 65–69.

[191] See broadly however the observations in Nigel White, 'From Korea to Kuwait: The Legal Basis of United Nations' Military Action' (1998) 20(3) *The International History Review* 597.

However, in comparison to resolutions which are argued as examples in which the UNSC has purportedly authorised the use of force in response to an armed attack (to which self-defence would also be available), it has yet to 'authorise' the equivalent for an international organisation. Put differently, the UNSC has yet not authorised the use of force by regional organisations in response to an armed attack (even though authorisation for self-defence is legally not required).[192]

The manner in which the UNSC has extended authorisation of force is also worth noting. On occasion, certain mandates have been extended but without extending the original authorisation for the use of force. In effect, these instances mean that the initial authorisation was limited in time, and that subsequent resolutions merely extended an operation's mandate but not its authorisation to use force. This was evident in Resolution 1861 (2009) which extended the EU operation in the CAR. Although Chapter VII was invoked in the resolution, it was only attributable to the mandate of MINURCAT. This was also the case when the UNSC authorised the use of force by the multinational force in Haiti in 2004 under Resolution 1529 (2004). Resolution 1542 (2009), adopted thereafter, explicitly extended the force's mandate but without extending its authorisation to use force. Similarly, the invocation of Chapter VII was attributable to the mandate of MINUSTAH and not to the multinational force.[193]

With that said, the above analysis has undoubtedly shown that when the UNSC authorises the use of force, it does so systematically. With the exceptional few deviations, UNSC practice shows that the authorisation of force is given after a threat to peace and security has been determined, such force is authorised under Chapter VII (although sometimes recalling the provisions of Chapter VIII), and that it has made a custom of referring to military measures in its operative paragraphs, almost always employing the 'all necessary measures' phrasing.

[192] If one considers the 2001 military action in Afghanistan as falling under 'regional enforcement action', although initially based on self-defence claimed by the United States and United Kingdom, it in fact was authorisation under Chapter VII for the subsequent NATO-led ISAF deployment.

[193] See ch 5 at p 148.

4

Explicit Authorisation to the North Atlantic Treaty Organisation

I. INTRODUCTION

THE PREVIOUS CHAPTER has analysed and made some preliminary conclusions on United Nations Security Council (UNSC) practice authorising force to regional organisations. Consequently, this chapter examines authorisation to collective defence alliances, namely, the North Atlantic Treaty Organisation (NATO). While under Article 53(1) of the United Nations Charter (UN Charter), the UNSC may authorise the use of force by regional organisations, whether collective defence alliances such as NATO are authorised under this article remains uncertain.[1] The precise distinction between regional organisations (for purposes of Article 53(1)) and collective defence alliances is particularly relevant when considering under which chapter the UNSC authorises their use of force and against whom such organisation acts. The analysis therefore also focuses on the manner of authorisation and whether any distinctions exist between authorisation to regional organisations and authorisation to NATO.[2]

As with the analysis in previous chapters, it is also worth noting that UNSC resolutions have on occasion authorised force to more than one entity. Presently, the most notable examples concern those resolutions adopted on the former Yugoslavia and Afghanistan in which force was authorised to Member States (acting through NATO), as well as UN peacekeeping missions and individual operations. While UN peacekeeping missions are more broadly dealt with in chapter five, for feasibility, relevant UN peacekeeping missions are grouped and assessed here since they were established and authorised in the same time span and on the same situation.

As was detailed in previous chapters, the UNSC routinely employs a uniform regime of explicit authorisation. Authorising resolutions determine a threat

[1] Art 53(1), United Nations, Charter of the United Nations (adopted 26 June 1945, entered into force 24 October 1945) UNCIO XV, 335 (UN Charter).

[2] It does not engage in debates as to whether NATO is considered an Article 53 organisation. On the nature of NATO and discussions on whether it falls within Chapter VIII, see broadly Marten Zwanenburg, 'NATO, its Member States, and the Security Council' in Niels Blokker and Nico Schrijver (eds), *The Security Council and the Use of Force: Theory and Reality – A Need for Change?* (Martinus Nijhoff Publishers 2005) 189–211, 251–65.

to international peace and security under Article 39, invoke Chapter VII (or Chapter VIII) of the UN Charter, and contain one or several operative paragraphs explicitly authorising force. Moreover, explicit authorising resolutions are adopted prior to the use of force.

II. RESOLUTIONS ADOPTED ON THE FORMER YUGOSLAVIA, INCLUDING BOSNIA AND HERZEGOVINA AND KOSOVO

During the early 1990s, political unrest and conflict erupted in Yugoslavia; beginning with its dissolution in 1991 when Croatia and Slovenia unilaterally declared independence.[3] Over the course of the decade, Yugoslavia would eventually disintegrate into five successor states.[4] Serbian leadership, holding centralised control, strongly resisted the dissolution.[5] The Yugoslav People's Army (YNA) intervened militarily to prevent secessionist activities, which later led to years of war between the republics. The outbreak of hostilities and increasing tensions led the UNSC to quickly declare the situation a threat to international peace and security.[6] Over the subsequent years, the UNSC adopted numerous resolutions implementing embargoes against weapons and military equipment. In February 1992 the UNSC established the United Nations Protection Force (UNPROFOR), a peacekeeping operation as an 'interim arrangement' to create conditions of peace and security to negotiate a settlement to the Yugoslav crisis.[7]

After numerous arms and trade embargoes were imposed against Yugoslavia and failure to comply with demands for the cession of hostilities, the UNSC passed several resolutions authorising force by Member States (acting through regional organisations). The UNSC also authorised UNPROFOR under a Chapter VII mandate allowing it to act more robustly.[8] Authorisation of force

[3] Catherine Baker, *The Yugoslav Wars of the 1990s* (Palgrave 2015) 49–50.

[4] In 2006, Montenegro seceded from Serbia and in 2008 Kosovo unilaterally declared independence from Serbia.

[5] Marc Weller, 'The International Response to the Dissolution of the Socialist Federal Republic of Yugoslavia' (1992) 86(3) *The American Journal of International Law* 569–70; Susan Woodward, *Balkan Tragedy: Chaos And Dissolution After the Cold War* (The Brookings Institute 1995) 99–100.

[6] UNSC Res 713 (1991) preamble para 4. On its Art 39 determination, see Jan Klabbers, 'Intervention, Armed Intervention, Armed Attack, Threat to peace, Act of Aggression, and Threat or Use of Force: What's the Difference?' in Marc Weller (ed), *The Oxford Handbook of the Use of Force in International Law* (Oxford University Press 2015) 496.

[7] UNSC Res 743 (1992) paras 2, 5; Pierre Klein, 'The Intervention in Bosnia and Herzegovina – 1992–95' in Tom Ruys and Olivier Corten (eds), *The Use of Force in International Law: A Case-based Approach* (Oxford University Press 2018) 496.

[8] Jon E Fink, 'From Peacemaking to Peace Enforcement: The Blurring of the Mandates for the Use of Force in Maintaining International Peace and Security' (1995) 19 *Maryland Journal of International Law and Trade* 30–31, 37; James Sloan, *The Militarisation of Peacekeeping in the Twenty-First Century* (Hart Publishing 2011) 143–44. As Sloan argues, UNPROFOR became militarised with the adoption of UNSC Res 807 (1993) when it was given a Chapter VII mandate. See

under these resolutions was not a new phenomenon; having in that same decade authorised force in Iraq (1990), Somalia (1992) and Haiti (1993).[9] It was however the first time the UNSC would authorise the use of force by NATO and UNPROFOR under the circumstances of solely providing humanitarian assistance, particularly under Resolution 770 (1992), and later for the protection of safe areas under Resolution 836 (1993).

Moreover, resolutions adopted on the situation in Yugoslavia consistently and explicitly determined or referenced a threat to international peace and security. Additionally, UNSC debates unambiguously confirmed that States viewed the invocation of Chapter VII as a prerequisite for the authorisation of force.[10]

A. Resolution 770 (1992)

i. Explicit Authorisation to Member States Acting Through NATO

On 3 March 1992 Bosnia and Herzegovina proclaimed independence, leading to an immediate response from the Bosnian Serbian Army along with the YNA. The resulting conflict led to a prolonged siege of the state's capital, Sarajevo. The UNSC adopted several resolutions on the situation concerning the violence and humanitarian suffering. Resolution 770 (1992) was the first of such resolutions invoking Chapter VII. The resolution determined the humanitarian crisis in Bosnia constituted a threat to international peace and security. This determination was first made in Resolution 713 (1991) and consistently either determined or *reaffirmed* in 13 subsequent resolutions.[11] The Article 39 determination made in Resolution 770 (1992), however, seemed to go one step further: It stated that an important element in the UNSC's efforts at restoring peace and security in the area was the provision of humanitarian assistance.[12]

also Christine Gray, *International Law and the Use of Force* (Oxford University Press 2018) 290–91; Trevor Findlay, *The Use of Force in UN Peace Operations* (Oxford University Press 2002) 219.

[9] See ch 4.

[10] Klein, 'The Intervention in Bosnia' (n 7) 500.

[11] UNSC Res 713; UNSC Res 721 (1991); UNSC Res 724 (1991); UNSC Res 727; UNSC Res 740 (1992); UNSC Res 743 (1992); UNSC Res 749 (1992); UNSC Res 752 (1992); UNSC Res 758 (1992); UNSC Res 760 (1992); UNSC Res 761 (1992); UNSC Res 762 (1992); UNSC Res 764 (1992); UNSC Res 769 (1992).

[12] UNSC Res 770 (1992) preamble para 5. See also Lois Fielding, 'Taking a Closer Look at Threats to Peace: The Power of the Security Council to Address Humanitarian Crises' (1996) 73 *University of Detroit Mercy Law Review* 564; Jost Delbruck, 'A More Effective International Law or A New "World Law"? Some Aspects of the Development of International Law in a Changing International System' (1993) 68(3) *Indiana Law Journal* 709–10. As pointed out by Schachter, Delbruck finds that the UNSC used its Chapter VII powers under Resolution 733 to deliver humanitarian assistance to Bosnia and Herzegovina. See also Marc Weller, 'Peace-Keeping and Peace-Enforcement in the Republic of Bosnia and Herzegovina' (*Max-Planck-Institut für ausländisches öffentliches Recht und Völkerrecht* 1996) 97.

Acting under Chapter VII, the UNSC called on Member States to take nationally or through regional organisations 'all measures necessary' to facilitate humanitarian assistance in Sarajevo and wherever needed in other parts of the country.[13] The decision to invoke Chapter VII and to include the use of force to provide humanitarian assistance was generally welcomed by UNSC Member States.[14] While the resolution directed that Member States 'acting nationally or through regional agencies or arrangements' were to use force, its authorisation was attributable to NATO.[15]

ii. Concerns Over UNSC Oversight

A predominant concern raised during UNSC debates was that of control over and accountability for the use of force in Bosnia and Herzegovina. India pointed out that the use of force should be resorted to only in exceptional circumstances, stressing the importance of UN command whenever the UNSC authorised force.[16] Similarly, Zimbabwe stressed that any coercive action should be taken under the full control and accountability of the UNSC.[17]

Despite these objections, it has been pointed out that Resolution 770 (1992) established several reporting and control mechanisms.[18] These mechanisms included that Member States were to report to the Secretary-General on measures taken in implementing the resolution and that such measures were to be taken in 'coordination with the United Nations'.[19] Additionally, the Secretary-General was mandated to report to the UNSC on a periodic basis on the implementation of the resolution.[20]

While these concerns persist when the UNSC authorises force, it has developed some mechanisms to ensure, at the least, some UNSC oversight. These include not only mandatory reporting obligations but, as is seen with more recent resolutions, mandated operations usually contain strict time limits, after which a new UNSC resolution would need to extend such mandates. Nonetheless, the wording of Resolution 770 (1991) together with the sentiment shared during the UNSC debate made clear the fact that the resolution undoubtedly authorised the use of force.

[13] UNSC Res 770 (1992) para 2.
[14] UN Doc S/PV.3106 (1992) 6, 8–9, 34.
[15] Dace Winther, *Regional Maintenance of Peace and Security under International Law: The Distorted Mirrors* (Routledge 2014) 196.
[16] UN Doc S/PV.3106 (1992) 11–12.
[17] UN Doc S/PV.3106 (1992) 16–17.
[18] Klein, 'The Intervention in Bosnia' (n 7) 501.
[19] UNSC Res 770 (1992) para 4.
[20] UNSC Res 770 (1992) para 7.

B. Resolutions 776 and 781 (1992)

One month later, the UNSC adopted Resolutions 776 and 781 (1992).[21] These resolutions brought up specific questions pertaining to UNPROFOR's authorisation to use force. Unlike its practice with other peacekeeping missions during the 1990s of explicitly authorising in a single resolution that a mission was authorised to use force beyond self-defence, the UNSC opted to incorporate the use of force by referencing a previous authorising resolution, namely, Resolution 770 (1992).

Resolution 776 (1992) was also the first instance in which UNPROFOR's mandate began to shift towards a peace enforcement operation. It is worth mentioning that UNPROFOR was initially established under Resolution 743 (1992) as a classic peacekeeping operation and was therefore authorised to use force only in self-defence.[22] With the adoption of Resolution 776 (1992), UNPROFOR was authorised to use force to secure the delivery of humanitarian aid.[23] The way in which UNPROFOR received this authorisation was of significant concern. Resolution 776 (1992) authorising UNPROFOR's enlargement contained neither an Article 39 determination, nor did it invoke Chapter VII. Instead, the second paragraph of the resolution *authorised* the implementation of paragraph two of Resolution 770 (1992) to enlarge UNPROFOR's mandate and strength.[24]

In effect, the resolution authorised UNPROFOR to use force by reference to Resolution 770 (1992).[25] That Resolution 776 (1992) had indeed authorised UNPROFOR to use force was widely acknowledged in the UNSC debate.[26] However, the manner of authorisation was criticised. Zimbabwe considered UNPROFOR's enlargement in such a manner unfortunate[27] and India found it had distorted the purpose and objective of UNPROFOR enlargement.[28] The greatest protest against UNPROFOR's authorisation came from China.[29] Citing the link created between UNPROFOR's mandate and Resolution 770 (1992), the delegate concluded that the resolution authorised UNPROFOR to use force beyond the usual limits of self-defence.[30] Despite its reservations against the

21 UNSC Res 776 (1992); UNSC Res 781 (1992).

22 UNSC Res 743 (1992) para 2; Sloan (n 8) 143–45.

23 Gray, *International Law and the Use of Force* (n 8) 290; Sloan (n 8) 143.

24 UNSC Res 776 (1992) para 2.

25 Gray, *International Law and the Use of Force* (n 8) 290; Scott Sheeran, 'The Use of Force in United Nations Peacekeeping Operations' in Weller (n 6) 353; Sloan (n 8) 143–45.

26 UN Doc S/PV.3114 (1992) 4, 7, 9–10, 12.

27 UN Doc S/PV.3114 (1992) 4. Chiyuki Aoi, *Legitimacy and the Use of Armed Force: Stability Missions in the Post-Cold War Era* (Routledge 2010) 54.

28 UN Doc S/PV.3114 (1992) 8; Aoi (n 27) 54–55.

29 UN Doc S/PV.3114 (1992) 11–12.

30 UN Doc S/PV. 3114 (1992) 11–12. See, however, Michael Bothe, 'Peacekeeping' in Bruno Simma et al (eds), *The Charter of the United Nations: A Commentary, Volume II* (3rd edn, Oxford

resolution, China did not veto its adoption. The resolution was subsequently adopted with 12 votes in favour and three abstentions. Although authorised to use force, in practice UNPROFOR made little use of the authorisation, and even less so when specifically protecting humanitarian assistance missions.[31]

Shortly thereafter, the UNSC adopted Resolution 781 (1992), again with a reference to Resolution 770 (1992) – this time however only in its preamble.[32] Acting 'pursuant to Resolution 770 (1992) aimed at ensuring the delivery of humanitarian assistance', it established a ban on military flights over Bosnian airspace and called upon States acting nationally or through regional arrangements to take 'all measures necessary' to provide assistance to UNPROFOR in its task of monitoring the ban.[33] Resolution 781 (1992) therefore did not itself authorise force and contained neither an explicit Article 39 determination nor Chapter VII invocation.[34] The UNSC debate preceding its adoption nevertheless again raised concerns surrounding its incorporation of Resolution 770 (1992) and its authorisation of force.[35] The resolution was nonetheless adopted with 14 votes in favour.

C. Resolutions 787 (1992), 820 and 816 (1993)

On 16 November 1992, the UNSC adopted Resolution 787 (1992). Acting under Chapters VII and VIII, it called upon Member States to act nationally or through regional arrangements to use 'such measures commensurate with the specific circumstances as may be necessary' to halt inward and outward maritime shipping for inspection and verification of cargo and to ensure strict implementation of the provisions of Resolutions 713 (1991) and 757 (1992).[36] Through this resolution, the UNSC authorised force to ensure compliance with

University Press 2012) 1178–79 who states that '[a]s a matter of principle, UNPROFOR was not given a mandate to use force beyond the traditional authorization to use force in self-defence and against attempts to prevent the force to execute its mandate'.

[31] Klein, 'The Intervention in Bosnia' (n 7) 497.

[32] UNSC Res 781 (1992) preamble para 9.

[33] UNSC Res 781 (1992) paras 2, 5.

[34] There is some debate as to whether the resolution authorised force. See Ralph Zacklin, *The United Nations Secretariat and the Use of Force in a Unipolar World v Principle* (Cambridge University Press 2010) 55; Kenneth Manusama, *The United Nations Security Council in the Post-Cold War Era* (Marthinus Nijhoff Publishers 2006) 223; Jules Nobel and Michael Ratner, 'Bypassing the Security Council: Ambiguous Authorisations to Use Force, Cease-Fires and the Iraqi Inspection Regime' (1999) 93(1) *The American Journal of International Law* 141 fn 68; Tarcisio Gazzini, 'NATO Coercive Military Activities in the Yugoslav Crisis (1992–1999) (2001)12 (3) *European Journal of International Law* 395–96 who argues that despite the reference to Resolution 770 (1992), Resolution 781 (1992) did not authorise the use of force. Gazzini also cites the fact that US attempts at adopting the resolution under Chapter VII had failed thereby indicates that the resolution did not authorise the use of force.

[35] UN Doc S/PV.3122 (1992) 7; 9–11; Manusama (n 34) 223.

[36] UNSC Res 787 (1992) para 12.

the maritime embargo in its previous resolutions.[37] The resolution contained an Article 39 determination and, as in the case of Resolution 770 (1992), indicated several reporting and oversight mechanisms.[38] The UNSC subsequently adopted Resolution 820 (1993). Acting under Chapter VII, it *reaffirmed* 'the authority of States acting under paragraph 12 of Resolution 787 (1992)' to 'use such measures commensurate with the specific circumstances as may be necessary' to enforce its resolutions also in the territorial waters of Yugoslavia.[39]

The implementation of Resolution 787 (1992) was realised by Member States through NATO, swiftly establishing *Operation Maritime Guard*. During its operation, more than 1,000 ships were inspected under the blockade.[40] The operation was succeeded by *Operation Sharp Guard*, under a unified NATO command, which resulted in the boarding of more than 6 000 ships, 1 000 being diverted for further inspection and more than a dozen that were found to be in violation of the embargo.[41] With the adoption of Resolution 787 (1992) and 820 (1993), NATO's role in Bosnia and Herzegovina changed from monitoring to enforcement.[42]

On 31 March 1993, in reaction to continued violence and allegations of ethnic cleansing in Bosnia and Herzegovina, the UNSC gradually broadened the authorisation of force, this time under Resolution 816 (1993). It authorised Member States to take 'all necessary measures' to enforce a ban on military flights in Bosnian airspace in accordance with Resolution 781 (1992).[43] Acting under Chapter VII, the UNSC authorised Member States to take such action only seven days after the adoption of the resolution and 'under the authority of the Security Council and subject to close coordination with the Secretary-General and UNPROFOR'.[44] In response, NATO again took a leading role in ensuring the implementation of the resolution. It had in fact been involved in monitoring the military ban in accordance with Resolution 781 (1992) under its *Operation Sky Monitor*. With the adoption of Resolution 816 (1993), like its maritime activities, its role transitioned from monitoring to enforcement. On 12 April 1993 NATO commenced its *Operation Deny Flight* and in accordance with the resolution, was authorised to use force to ensure strict implementation.[45]

[37] China however opposed the authorisation of force. See UN Doc S/PV.3135 (1992) 16.

[38] UNSC Res 787 (1992) para 14.

[39] UNSC Res 820 (1993) para 29.

[40] NATO's monitoring of UNSC imposed embargoes began with Operation Maritime Monitor and was also NATO's first 'out of area' operation. Its successor, Operation Maritime Guard, commenced on 22 November 1992. Operation Maritime Guard, Global Security.org www.globalsecurity.org/military/ops/maritime_guard.htm.

[41] NATO/WEU Operation Sharp Guard, IFOR Final Factsheet (2 October 1996) NATO www.nato.int/ifor/general/shrp-grd.htm.

[42] Klein, 'The Intervention in Bosnia' (n 7) 497.

[43] UNSC Res 816 (1993) para 4; UNSC Res 781 (1992) para 1. See also UN Doc S/PV.3191 (1993).

[44] UNSC Res 816 (1993) para 4. The authorisation provided for under Resolution 816 (1993) was applicable only to Member States and not to UNPROFOR.

[45] Klein, 'The Intervention in Bosnia' (n 7) 497–98.

In particular, it was authorised to use force in cases of further violations, against all fixed-wing and rotary-wing aircraft in the airspace over Bosnia and Herzegovina, except for flights authorised for UNPROFOR.[46] The authorisation was most notably used when four Bosnian Serbian aircraft were shot down on 28 February 1994 which were reported to have bombed munitions plants over the country.[47] The NATO engagement against the aircraft represented its first ever offensive action since its establishment in 1949.[48]

D. Resolutions 836 (1993) and 908 (1994) | UNPROFOR

Although Resolution 776 (1992) first authorised UNPROFOR to use force (at least beyond self-defence), the UNSC subsequently adopted additional resolutions authorising the broader use of force by the mission. Resolution 836 (1993) explicitly authorised UNPROFOR to 'take the necessary measures, including the use of force' in carrying out its mandate under Resolutions 770 (1992) and 776 (1992).[49] The resolution also extended UNPROFOR's mandate and consequently its authorisation to use force. UNPROFOR was authorised to use force in addition to its mandate under Resolutions 770 and 776 (1992), acting in self-defence, to also deter attacks against safe areas in line with Resolution 824 (1993), to monitor cease-fire agreements, and to promote the withdrawal of military and paramilitary units other than those of the Bosnian government.[50] It further authorised UNPROFOR to use force in reply to bombardments against safe areas by any party or any armed incursion in the event of the deliberate obstruction of freedom of movement of UNPROFOR or protected humanitarian convoys.[51]

In addition to authorising UNPROFOR, Resolution 836 (1993) authorised Member States acting in co-operation with UNPROFOR and the Secretary General to take 'all necessary measures, through the use of air power' to assist UNPROFOR in its mandate.[52] Again, the implementation of Resolution 836 (1993) was primarily conducted by NATO through airstrikes against Bosnian Serbian forces.[53] On 31 March 1994 the UNSC then adopted Resolution 908

[46] As UNSC Res 836 (1993) paras 1, 4; Woodward (n 5) 307.

[47] Michael Gordon, 'Conflict in the Balkans; NATO Craft Down Four Serb Warplanes Attacking Bosnia' *The New York Times* (1 March 1994).

[48] Klein, 'The Intervention in Bosnia' (n 7) 498.

[49] UNSC Res 836 (1993) para 9; Sloan (n 8) 143–45; Woodward (n 5) 314.

[50] UNSC Res 836 (1993) para 9; Sloan (n 8) 143–45.

[51] UNSC Res 836 (1993) paras 5, 9.

[52] UNSC Res 836 (1993) para 10; Gazzini (n 34) 398.

[53] The interpretation of UNSC Res 836 (1993) in favour of the use of force first appeared in a letter by the Secretary-General in which he stated that two incidents that had occurred in Sarajevo at the time merited urgent preparation for air strikes to deter further attacks, in line with paras 9 and 10 of UNSC Resolution 836 (1993). See UN Doc S/1994/131 (1994). Subsequently, NATO conducted several air strikes in accordance with the request by the Secretary-General.

(1994) authorising the use of force over the Republic of Croatia in defence of UNPROFOR personnel.[54] The authorisation was again subject to 'close coordination with the Secretary-General and UNPROFOR'. The authorisation given in Resolution 836 (1993) was then extended with the adoption of Resolution 958 (1994).[55] The UNSC in Resolution 958 (1994), acting under Chapter VII, *decided* that the authorisation provided in paragraph 10 of Resolution 836 (1993) was to apply also to measures taken in Croatia.[56] Member States, acting nationally or through regional organisations, were therefore authorised to take all necessary measures through the use of air power to support UNPROFOR in its mandate.

The resolutions authorising force by Member States through NATO and by UNPROFOR in relation to UNSC practice on the situation in Bosnia and Herzegovina are indicative of several aspects. The first of these is the NATO involvement in the situation. Although NATO's constituent document allows for the use of force based on self-defence, its involvement has been argued as an 'admission by NATO that an authorisation from the Security Council [is] required for the Alliance to resort to coercive measures involving the use of force outside of the situation of self-defence'.[57] Moreover, NATO's actions in Bosnia and Herzegovina constituted its first ever out-of-area engagement and its actions were not based on collective self-defence under its constituent instrument.

Essentially, NATO engagements in Yugoslavia were based on UNSC authorisation. It is also pertinent to note that the UNSC did not invoke Chapter VIII or Article 53, instead basing its authorisation on Chapter VII of the UN Charter. In effect, the UNSC was probably also making use of measures under Chapter VIII when it authorised NATO to act when it specifically referred to 'member states acting nationally or through regional agencies or arrangements' although invoking Chapter VII.[58]

The resolutions adopted on the situation in Bosnia and Herzegovina constituted a considerable degree of practice of explicit authorisation, with the determination of a threat to peace and security and the invocation of Chapter VII

[54] UNSC Res 908 (1994) para 8.

[55] UNSC Res 958 (1994).

[56] UNSC Res 958 (1994).

[57] Klein, 'The Intervention in Bosnia' (n 7) 501. See also Ige Dekker, 'Air Strikes on Bosnian Positions: Is NATO Also Legally the Proper Instrument of the UN?' (1996) 9 *Leiden Journal of International Law* 413; Niels Blokker, 'NATO as the UN Security Council's Instrument: Question Marks from the Perspective of International Law' (1996) 9 *Leiden Journal of International Law* 418.

[58] The UNSC's preference (and subsequent practice) of invoking Chapter VII rather than Chapter VIII has resulted in significant discussion behind the precise reasoning. See specifically Laurence Boisson de Chazournes, *Les relations entre organisations régionals et organisations universelles: Recueil des cours de l'Académie de droit international de La Haye* (Matinus Nijhoff Publishers 2013) 296–300; Ademola Abass, *Regional Organisations and the Development of Collective Security: Beyond Chapter VIII of the UN Charter* (Hart Publishing 2004) 8–9; Christian Walter, 'Article 53' in Simma et al (n 30) 1484, 1499. Walter describes the reliance on Chapter VII measures (specifically Article 48), rather than Chapter VIII, as a 'migration of regionalism to Chapter VII'.

being considered prerequisites for the use of force. The most significant bearing was the authorisation of force accorded in subsequent resolutions by reference to Resolution 770 (1992), without characteristically making an Article 39 determination or invoking Chapter VII. With that said, however, such manner of authorisation was met with significant criticism from UNSC members and remains an exceptional occurrence under UNSC practice. Moreover, it is worth noting that despite the reference to Resolution 770 (1992) in subsequent resolutions, Resolution 770 (1992) itself was adopted under Chapter VII and expressly determined the situation in Bosnia and Herzegovina a threat to international peace and security.

E. Resolution 981 (1995) | UNCRO

Until early 1995, UNPROFOR had carried out peacekeeping tasks in Bosnia and Herzegovina, Croatia and Macedonia. In January of that year, however, Croatian President Franjo Tudjman terminated consent to UNPROFOR and demanded its withdrawal from Croatian territory, citing its presence as counterproductive to peace processes.[59] What resulted from negotiations between, among others, the United States and Croatia, was a decision to replace UNPROFOR in Croatia with a new mission using the existing structure and personnel there.[60] In response, the UNSC adopted Resolution 981 (1995), formally establishing the United Nations Confidence Restoration Operation in Croatia (UNCRO).

Interestingly, Resolution 981 (1995) did not in itself explicitly determine the situation in Croatia a threat to international peace and security, although it did recall 'all previous relevant resolutions on the conflicts in the territory of the former Yugoslavia'.[61] Acting under Chapter VII to 'ensure the freedom and movement of [UN] personnel … in the territory of the former Yugoslavia', it established UNCRO for an initial period of eight months.[62] The UNSC authorised Member States, acting nationally or through regional organisations under its authority and in close coordination with the Secretary-General, to take 'all necessary measures' to extend close air support in the territory of Croatia in defence of UNCRO and in the performance of its mandate.[63] The Secretary-General was obliged to report periodically on any use of close air support.[64] As with UNPROFOR, force was, however, not authorised to the peacekeeping mission, but rather to Member States in defence of UNCRO, its mandate and freedom of movement.

[59] UN Doc S/1995/28 (1995) 4.
[60] UN Doc S/1995/28 (1995) 167; see also UN Doc S/1995/206 (1995).
[61] UNSC Res 981 (1995) preamble para 1.
[62] UNSC Res 981 (1995) para 2.
[63] UNSC Res 981 (1995) para 6.
[64] UN Doc S/1995/650 (1995) paras 12–15 which suggests that while there were restrictions on freedom of movement, no close air support was made use of.

The fact that force was authorised under Resolution 981 (1995) was an evident interpretation of the resolution. On 5 August 1995 three UN personnel were killed as a direct consequence of fighting between Croatian and Serbian forces. In response and to deter hostilities, a request was made to NATO for an air presence over the sector in which the incident occurred, although it seemed that there was no actual use of force.[65] UNCRO eventually handed over to the United Nations Transitional Authority in Eastern Slavonia, Baranja and Western Sirmium (UNTAES) the following year, in line with the Basic Agreement signed between the government of Croatia and local Serb authorities.[66] Despite what would later be considered a failure on UNCRO's part to contribute to a lasting peaceful settlement to the conflict, the adoption of Resolution 981 (1995) authorising force in defence of UNCRO served as another example of explicit UNSC authorisation.

F. Resolution 1031 (1995) | IFOR

On 21 November 1995 Yugoslavia, the Republic of Croatia and Bosnia and Herzegovina signed the General Framework Agreement for Peace in Bosnia and Herzegovina (Dayton Peace Agreement), ending the three and a half year-long conflict in the Balkans.[67] Part of the Dayton Peace Agreement included that the UNSC adopt a resolution that would establish a 'multinational military implementation force' (IFOR), which 'may' be composed of ground, air and maritime units from NATO and non-NATO members.[68] The parties also agreed that IFOR would begin the implementation of the provisions of the agreement upon the transfer of authority from the UNPROFOR commander to the IFOR commander and that, until such time, UNPROFOR would continue executing its mandate.[69] The authority for IFOR to operate under NATO's command and political control was also explicitly agreed upon.[70] Moreover, the parties also agreed with the objective to authorise IFOR to 'take such action as required, including the use of necessary force, to ensure compliance with [the agreement at hand] and to ensure its own protection'.[71]

One day after the signing of the Dayton Peace Agreement, the UNSC adopted Resolution 1031 (1995), complementing the consensual basis of the agreement with formal UNSC authorisation of IFOR's mandate. Determining the situation in the region continued to constitute a threat to peace and security

[65] UN Doc S/1995/730 (1995) para 8.
[66] UNSC Res 1037 (1996).
[67] The General Framework Agreement for Peace in Bosnia and Herzegovina (21 November 1995, Dayton, Ohio) (Dayton Peace Agreement).
[68] Art I(1)(a), Dayton Peace Agreement.
[69] Art I(1)(a), Dayton Peace Agreement.
[70] Art I(1)(b), Dayton Peace Agreement.
[71] Art 1(2)(b), Dayton Peace Agreement.

and acting under Chapter VII, the UNSC authorised the establishment of IFOR under unified command and control.[72] Member States participating in IFOR were authorised to 'take all necessary measures' to effect the implementation of the peace agreement. The UNSC also stressed in the same paragraph that the parties to the peace agreement would be equally subjected to IFOR's enforcement action as may be necessary and that the UNSC had taken note that 'the parties have consented to IFOR's taking of such measures'.[73] The UNSC also authorised Member States to take all necessary measures, at IFOR's request, to protect or assist it in carrying out its mandate.[74] In addition, the UNSC 'recognised' IFOR's right to take all necessary measures to defend itself from attack or threat of attack.[75]

Under Resolution 1031 (1995), upon the transfer of authority from UNPROFOR to IFOR, the authority to take certain measures (including the use of force) conferred upon states under Resolutions 770 (1992), 781 (1992), 816 (1993), 836 (1993), 844 (1993) and 958 (1994) was to be terminated.[76] The provisions of Resolution 824 (1993) and subsequent resolutions pertaining to safe areas would similarly be terminated upon such a date.[77]

Member States participating in IFOR were to report to the UNSC on a monthly basis.[78] The UNSC also authorised Member States to use all necessary measures to assist in the withdrawal of UNPROFOR.[79]

On 1 December 1995, the NATO Council authorised the Supreme Allied Commander Europe to deploy forces into Croatia and Bosnia and Herzegovina, signalling the beginning of NATO's *Operation Joint Endeavour*. At that time, the acting NATO Secretary-General announced that 14 non-NATO members had been invited to participate in the operation. Some 60,000 soldiers were involved in the one-year mandated operation, with three predominant land components spread across Bosnia and Herzegovina, as well as Croatia.[80] Forces from NATO members included those from Belgium, Canada, Denmark, France, Germany, Italy, Luxembourg, The Netherlands, Norway, Portugal, Spain, Turkey, the United States and the United Kingdom. Non-NATO members most notably included Romania, Ukraine and Russia.

The adoption of Resolution 1031 (1995) was therefore a unique example of Chapter VII authorisation to Member States participating in IFOR, essentially a regional peacekeeping operation authorised to use force beyond self-defence.

[72] UNSC Res 1031 (1995) para 14.
[73] UNSC Res 1031 (1995) para 15.
[74] UNSC Res 1031 (1995) para 17.
[75] UNSC Res 1031 (1995) para 17.
[76] UNSC Res 1031 (1995) para 19.
[77] UNSC Res 1031 (1995) para 19.
[78] UNSC Res 1031 (1995) para 25.
[79] UNSC Res 1031 (1995) para 36.
[80] NATO, 'Peace Support Operations in Bosnia and Herzegovina' (23 November 2017) www.nato.int/cps/ie/natohq/topics_52122.htm.

G. Resolutions 1037 (1996) and 1120 (1997) | UNTAES

At the same time that the UNSC authorised the deployment and mandate of IFOR to assist in the post-conflict situation in Bosnia and Herzegovina, it also turned its attention to the situation in Croatia. Two particular resolutions it adopted concerned explicit authorisation of the use of force, and both resolutions were directed at Member States acting through regional organisations in support of its peacekeeping efforts in the region. On 15 January 1996 it adopted Resolution 1037 (1996) establishing UNTAES.[81] The establishment of UNTAES followed the signing of the Erdut Agreement on 12 March 1995 on the peaceful resolution of the Croatian War of Independence.[82] Under Resolution 1037 (1996) UNTAES was established for an initial period of 12 months as a peacekeeping operation with military and civilian components. The resolution, determining that the situation in Croatia constituted a threat to international peace and security and invoking Chapter VII, outlined four elements to UNTAES's mandate and included a military component with an initial deployment of 5,500 troops.[83] UNTAES was also instructed to cooperate closely with IFOR.

Member States, acting nationally or through regional organisations, were authorised to take all necessary measures, including close air support in defence of UNTAES and to assist with its withdrawal. The authorisation to use force was subject to 'the request of UNTAES and on the basis of procedures communicated to the [UN]'.[84] Thus, the authorisation to use force was accorded to Member States in defence of UNTAES, and not to the mission itself. With that said, however, UNTAES represented a classic peacekeeping mission in that its deployment occurred with the consent of the Croatian government and its authorisation to use force was strictly based on self-defence. UNTAES was subsequently extended through Resolutions 1079 (1996) and 1120 (1997).[85]

Both resolutions determined that the situation in Croatia continued to constitute a threat to international peace and security, and invoked Chapter VII.[86] Specifically, the invocation of Chapter VII was referenced for the purposes of 'ensur[ing] the security and freedom of movement of the personnel of the [UN] peacekeeping operations in the Republic of Croatia'. Resolution 1079 (1996) although having made an Article 39 determination and invoking Chapter VII, contained no operative paragraph authorising force. On the other hand, the UNSC in Resolution 1120 (1997) explicitly *reiterated* its decision in Resolution 1037 (1996) that Member States acting nationally or through

[81] UNSC Res 1037 (1996) para 1.

[82] UN Doc S/1995/951 (1995) Annex (Basic Agreement on the region of Eastern Slavonia, Baranja and Western Sirmium) (Erdut Agreement). The Erdut Agreement was first acknowledged by the UNSC in Res 1023 (1995) para 1.

[83] UNSC Res 1037 (1996) paras 10(a)–(d).

[84] UNSC Res 1037 (1996) para 14.

[85] UNSC Res 1079 (1996) para 7(a); UNSC Res 1120 (1997) para 8.

[86] UNSC Res 1079 (1996) preamble paras 8, 9; Res 1120 (1997) preamble paras 12, 13.

regional organisations may use force at the request of UNTAES for its defence and assistance in withdrawal.[87]

The implications, therefore, were similar to Resolution 1037 (1996) itself in that authorisation to use force was in fact only granted to Member States (acting through regional arrangements) and not to UNTAES. The UNSC subsequently terminated UNTAES through the establishment of a civilian police support group for a once-off period of nine months with the adoption of Resolution 1145 (1997).[88]

H. Resolutions 1088 (1996) and Subsequent Authorising Resolutions | SFOR

On 12 December 1996, the UNSC adopted Resolution 1088 (1996) establishing a multinational stabilisation force (SFOR), the legal successor to IFOR. As with IFOR, the UNSC again took the opportunity to authorise SFOR with a robust mandate under Chapter VII and also authorised it to use force. Resolution 1088 (1996) determined that the situation in the region continued to constitute a threat to international peace and security and, acting under Chapter VII, authorised Member States participating through or in cooperation with SFOR to take all necessary measures to ensure compliance with the Dayton Peace Agreement.[89] The UNSC again underlined that in accordance with the peace agreement, the parties consented to SFOR taking measures against them, including the use of force.[90] Along with SFOR, the UNSC also authorised Member States to take all necessary measures 'at the request of SFOR' in its defence or in carrying out its mission.[91] It also recognised the right of the operation to use force to defend itself from attack or threat of attack.[92] Additionally, Member States were authorised to take all necessary measures to ensure compliance with the rules and procedures governing command and control over Bosnia and Herzegovina.[93] Member States participating in SFOR were mandated to report to the UNSC on a monthly basis.[94]

As with IFOR, it was NATO that began the implementation of Resolution 1088 (1996) with its deployment of *Operation Joint Guard* on 21 December 1996. By December 1997 NATO had informed the UN Secretary-General that approximately 35,600 troops were deployed across Croatia and Bosnia and Herzegovina as part of the mission. All NATO Members contributed forces,

[87] UNSC Res 1120 (1997) para 12.
[88] UNSC Res 1145 (1997) paras 1, 13.
[89] UNSC Res 1088 (1996) para 19.
[90] UNSC Res 1088 (1996) para 19.
[91] UNSC Res 1088 (1996) para 20.
[92] UNSC Res 1088 (1996) para 20.
[93] UNSC Res 1088 (1996) para 21.
[94] UNSC Res 1088 (1996) para 26.

along with 20 non-NATO Members.[95] Further reports from the NATO Secretary-General indicated that the authorisation to use force was not broadly used, and only on several occasions did SFOR resort to it.[96]

The authorisation granted to SFOR was explicitly reaffirmed in 10 subsequent resolutions where the UNSC repeatedly *authorised* Member States to 'take all necessary measures'.[97] All subsequent authorising resolutions recalled previous authorising resolutions which contained an Article 39 determination, invoked Chapter VII, and explicitly authorised the use of force by Member States participating in SFOR to ensure compliance with the Peace Agreement, at the request of SFOR in self-defence or to ensure implementation of its mandate.

I. UNSC Practice on the Situation in Yugoslavia: Summary

In general, UNSC practice on the situation in the former Yugoslavia highlighted several notable aspects. First, except for the authorisation by incorporation technique used in Resolutions 776 (1992), all authorising resolutions explicitly contained an Article 39 determination and invoked Chapter VII. Second, resolutions authorising force again confirmed that both the terms 'all necessary measures' and 'such measures commensurate to the specific circumstances' were affirmatively interpreted to have authorised force. The phrasing of Resolution 836 (1993) that necessary measures included 'the use of force' was the second instance in the UNSC's history in which it had authorised force by explicitly using the term in a resolution, having on only one other occasion opted for that choice of wording.[98]

Additionally, the fact that UNPROFOR's mandate was extended under Chapter VII suggests a transition from its classic peacekeeping role to a broadened peace enforcement role. Moreover, the UNSC also notably authorised the use of force by Member States, implemented by NATO and by its peacekeeping operation, as well as UNPROFOR. Measures authorised included the use of force to enforce an embargo (such as that of Resolution 665 (1990) on Iraq), and for the broader purposes of ensuring humanitarian assistance by UNPROFOR, IFOR and SFOR.

[95] UNSC UN Doc S/1997/975 (1997) para 1.

[96] UN Doc S/1997/975 (1997) para 21. See also UN Doc S/1997/369 (1997); UN Doc S/1997/602 (1997) and UN Doc S/1997/794 (1997). Most incidents involved actions taken against Bosnian Serb military activities.

[97] UNSC Res 1174 (1998) paras 10–13; UNSC Res 1247 (1999) paras 11–13; UNSC Res 1305 (2000) paras 10–13; UNSC Res 1357 (2001) paras 10–13; UNSC Res 1418 (2002); UNSC Res 1420 (2002); UNSC Res 1421 (2002); UNSC Res 1423 (2002) paras 10–13; UNSC Res 1491 (2003) paras 10–13; UNSC Res 1551 (2004) paras 13–15.

[98] UNSC Res 836 (1993) para 9; see also UNSC Res 221 (1966) para 4.

It is also worth noting that the UNSC extensively invoked Chapter VII in its authorising resolutions (and not Chapter VIII).[99] Its practice in this regard has been argued as implicitly employing the collective security framework under Chapter VII of the UN Charter.[100] With that said, a question that specifically arises regarding the above authorisations is whether the UNSC could legally authorise NATO under Chapter VIII, more specifically under Article 53(1). This is because the UNSC's powers under Article 53(1) relate to the authorisation of regional enforcement action arguably within that organisation's 'territory' and against a Member State of that organisation.[101] NATO's enforcement actions in the Yugoslavia were considered an out-of-area engagement and, more so, against non-Member States.

Even if for current purposes NATO was to be regarded as a regional organisation under Article 53(1), the UNSC would not necessarily rely on that article in cases where it authorises regional organisations to act 'out of area'.[102] For the UNSC to legally authorise NATO out-of-area deployments, it would have to rely on Articles 42 and 48(1), which would allow for regional enforcement action outside of NATO's territory and against non-NATO Member States.[103]

This argument is supported if one examines the resolutions on the Yugoslavia and the consistency in invoking Chapter VII rather than VIII. Furthermore, if one considers that NATO represents more of a collective defence alliance rather than an Article 53 regional organisation, it is evident that its use of force would be based either on Article 42 UNSC authorisation or Article 51 individual and collective self-defence.[104] Since its actions in the former Yugoslavia did not fall under the scope of collective defence, and bearing in mind that the UNSC invoked Chapter VII consistently when authorising it to engage in enforcement action, it is reasonable to conclude that the UNSC relied on Chapter VII (Articles 42 and 48(1) in this instance).[105]

[99] The exception to this is UNSC Res 743 (1992) preamble para 7, in which Art 25 and Chapter VIII were *recalled* when it established UNPROFOR. UNSC Res 787 (1992) specifically invoked both Chapters VII and VIII when it authorised Member States to use force to enforce an embargo against the FRY. UNSC Res 816 (1993) also *recalled* Chapter VII in its preamble, although not invoking it. See, broadly, Brandt Chu, 'The Forgotten Chapter: The Legality of Peacekeeping, Peace Enforcement, and Military Intervention under Chapter VIII of the UN Charter' (2017) 20 *Gonzaga University Journal of International Law*.

[100] Alexander Orakhelashvili, *Collective Security* (Oxford University Press 2011) 306–07.

[101] Erika de Wet, *The Chapter VII Powers of the United Nations Security Council* (Hart Publishing 2004) 294; see also Walter, 'Article 53' (n 58) 1845.

[102] De Wet, *The Chapter VII Powers* (n 101) 293. See also Walter, 'Article 53' (n 30) 1498–99.

[103] De Wet, *The Chapter VII Powers* (n 101) 294.

[104] De Wet, *The Chapter VII Powers* (n 101) 292; Albrecht Randelzhofer and George Nolte, 'Article 51' in Simma et al (n 30) 1420–21; Bruno Simma, 'NATO, the UN and the Use of Force: Legal Aspects' (1999) 10 *European Journal of International Law* 3.

[105] See also Rosalyn Higgins, *Themes and Theories: Selected Essays, Speeches, and Writings in International Law* (Oxford University Press 2009) 255–60; cf Tarcisio Gazzini, 'NATO's Role in The Collective Security System' (2003) *Journal of Conflict and Security Law* 8(2) 250–51, 255–56.

It is worth noting that broader UNSC practice of invoking Chapter VIII supports such a conclusion. The UNSC has in fact very rarely invoked Chapter VIII in its resolutions. Only a handful of resolutions have expressed the UNSC's 'acting under Chapter VIII' formulation when invoking that chapter, which includes Resolution 917 (1994) on Haiti and Resolution 1132 (1997) on Sierra Leone. In both cases, the UNSC had first and foremost invoked Chapter VII, and in further operative paragraphs expressed that it was 'acting *also* under Chapter VIII'.[106] Instead, the UNSC more commonly prefers to 'recall' Chapter VIII in its resolutions without formally invoking it, as was the case with some of the resolutions examined in the previous chapter.

In contrast, the UNSC tends to always formally invoke Chapter VII when it authorises enforcement action, and has never merely 'recalled' the chapter when authorising such action, potentially indicating that it is definitively and authoritatively taking measures under that chapter. To this end, in contrast to the occasional invocation of Chapter VII rather than Chapter VIII suggests the former is the principal basis on which the use of force is based. As mentioned above, the fact that Chapter VIII was not formally invoked on the situation in the former Yugoslavia additionally suggests that the NATO action there was in fact authorised under Chapter VII and was not an instance of regional enforcement action under Article 53(1).

J. Resolution 1244 (1999) | Kosovo

i. Explicit Authorisation to KFOR

Less than five years following from the conflicts which arose across the former Yugoslavia, gross human rights atrocities and accusations of a genocide against Kosovar Albanians by Serbian military and paramilitary forces began to emerge.[107] At the same time as events began to unfold in Kosovo, NATO was engaged in an air campaign against the Milosevic regime in Belgrade which began on 24 March 1999 and would last until 10 June of that year. The NATO campaign ended when Yugoslav armed forces withdrew from Kosovo, culminating in the Kumanovo Agreement which specified the terms of deployment of an International Security Force (KFOR) to Kosovo.[108] The Kumanovo Agreement expressly stated that KFOR was authorised to use all necessary actions to establish and maintain a secure environment for Kosovo's citizens. Moreover, it

[106] Emphasis added. UNSC Res 917 (1994) para 10 and UNSC Res 1132 (1997) para 8 where the UNSC in both cases was 'acting *also* under Chapter VIII'.

[107] 'US says "Genocide is Unfolding in Kosovo"' *CNN* (29 March 1999); 'NATO: Kosovo on Brink of "major Humanitarian Disaster"' *CNN* (28 March 1999).

[108] Arts I, II, Military Technical Agreement between the International Security Force (KFOR) and the Governments of the Federal Republic of Yugoslavia and the Republic of Serbia (9 June 1999, Kosovo) (Kumanovo Agreement).

conditioned its deployment pending the adoption of a resolution by the UNSC.[109] On 10 June 1999 the UNSC adopted Resolution 1244 (1999) giving effect to the agreement under Chapter VII.[110] At this point it is prudent to note that Resolution 1244 (1999) has been cited as the legal basis for the NATO's *Operation Allied Force* against Yugoslavia two months earlier. Presently, it suffices to say that the authorisation to the NATO air campaign under Resolution 1244 (1999) has been disputed. The argument that it constituted implicit and even *ex post facto* authorisation along with Resolutions 1160 and 1199 (1998) is addressed in subsequent chapters.[111] The analysis of Resolution 1244 (1999) having authorised the use of force by the international security presence is addressed here.

Having considered the violence against the Kosovo population, the UNSC determined the situation in the region to constitute a threat to international peace and security.[112] It authorised Member States and 'relevant international organisations' to establish an international security presence in Kosovo as set out in Annex II of Resolution 1244 (1999).[113] Acting under Chapter VII, Member States and international organisations were authorised to use 'all necessary means' to fulfil the mandate of the international security presence which included deterring hostilities, maintaining and enforcing a ceasefire and establishing a secure environment in which refugees and displaced persons could return home in safety.[114]

In terms of the political agreement reached with the Yugoslavia on Kosovo as authorised under Resolution 1244 (1999), the international security presence would be composed of substantial NATO participation and would be deployed under its unified command and control.[115] Two days after the adoption of Resolution 1244 (1994), the NATO-led KFOR entered Kosovo. By 20 June 1999 all Yugoslav and Serbian military and paramilitary forces had withdrawn from Kosovo, signalling a success in one of KFOR's first objectives.[116] KFOR had on several occasions resorted to the use of force, although reports by the Secretary-General indicate that force was resorted to predominantly in self-defence.[117] By November of that year, there were approximately 48,000 KFOR troops across Kosovo, which included forces from NATO, the United States, the United Arab Emirates, Ukraine and Russia.[118] While close cooperation between

[109] Arts I(1)–(2), Kumanovo Agreement.

[110] UNSC Res 1244 (1999). See also UN Doc S/1999/516 (1999) and UN Doc S/1999/649 (1999) (Annex I and Annex II of UNSC Res 1244 (1999), respectively).

[111] See chs 6 and 7.

[112] UNSC Res 1244 (1999) preamble para 12. Such a determination was also made in UNSC Res 1199 (1998) preambul para 14 and UNSC Res 1203 (1998) preamble para 15.

[113] UNSC Res 1244 (1999) para 7.

[114] UNSC Res 1244 (1999) paras 9(a)–(h).

[115] UNSC Res 1244 (1999) Annex II, para 4.

[116] NATO, 'NATO's Role in Kosovo/The Evolution of NATO's Role in Kosovo' (9 March 2017) www.nato.int/cps/en/natolive/topics_48818.htm.

[117] See for example UN Doc S/1999/692 (1999) paras 1(e), 2(a); UN Doc S/2012/169 (2012) para 7.

[118] UN Doc S/1999/1266 (1999) paras 1–2.

the FRY, Serbian military forces, the KLA and KFOR assisted in significantly stabilising the situation, the Secretary-General on numerous occasions reported that no significant changes in the situation had occurred, citing continuing attacks against minorities and escalating tensions.[119]

At its height, KFOR comprised of some 50,000 troops from 39 countries, including troops from four of the five permanent UNSC members.[120] Today, less than 5,000 troops remain present in Kosovo.

ii. Perpetual Deployment?

Although there have been no subsequent authorising resolutions since the adoption of Resolution 1244 (1999), KFOR, although in a limited capacity, currently remains present in Kosovo. The significance thereof is that Resolution 1244 (1999) lacks reference to a termination period. Paragraph 19 of the resolution specifically states that 'the international civil and security presence are established for an initial period of 12 months, *to continue thereafter unless the Security Council decides otherwise*' (emphasis added). This means that a new UNSC resolution would be needed to terminate the mission.[121] By implication, any resolution that seeks to terminate KFOR could in theory be vetoed by a permanent member, thereby rendering the KFOR mandate indefinite under Resolution 1244 (1999).[122]

iii. Explicit Authorisation of Force?

There has been some debate as to whether Resolution 1244 (1999) in fact authorised force. One argument suggests that the operative paragraph containing the term 'all necessary means' was not a decision of the UNSC but, rather, a compromised formula borrowed from the preceding political agreements as expressed in the annex of the resolution.[123] This argument is supported by sentiments shared by both Russia and China during the adoption of the resolution. The Russian delegate stressed that the resolution's reference to

[119] See UN Doc S/1999/868 (1999) para 4; UN Doc S/1999/982 (1999) para 12; UN Doc S/1999/1062 (1999) para 14; UN Doc S/1999/1185 (1999) para 14; UN Doc S/1999/1266 (1999) para 17.

[120] China was the only UNSC permanent member that did not deploy troops to Kosovo.

[121] UNSC Res 1244 (1999) para 19; De Wet, *The Chapter VII Powers* (n 101) 308; see also Niels Blokker, 'Is the Authorisation Authorised? Powers and Practice of the UN Security Council to Authorise the Use of Force by "Coalitions of the Able and Willing"' (2000) 11(3) *European Journal of International Law* 563 who points out the need for deadlines to authorisations; Herman Schaper, 'The Security Council and NATO' in Sebastian von Einsiedel et al (eds), *The UN Security Council in the 21st Century* (Lynne Rienner Publishers 2015) 402.

[122] De Wet, *The Chapter VII Powers* (n 101) 308; Blokker, 'Is the Authorisation Authorised' (n 121) 563, fn 95.

[123] Gray, *International Law and the Use of Force* (n 8) 356–57. Gray states: 'The Resolution spelled out in detail the responsibilities of KFOR; it did not expressly authorise force and it did not say that member states could use or take all necessary means to carry out its mandate.' Gray indicates that the use of the terms 'all necessary means' was attributed to its mere establishment.

Chapter VII 'relates exclusively to ensuring the safety and security of international personnel and compliance with the provisions of the [resolution]'.[124] The delegate added that there should be no hint that force could be used beyond the limits of the objectives set out in the resolution.[125] The Chinese delegate abstaining from the vote, stressed that the resolution failed to impose necessary restrictions on the invocation of Chapter VII – particularly with regard to time limits.[126]

To the contrary, several arguments favouring authorisation of force under Resolution 1244 (1999) point predominantly to the language used in the resolution. Like the first time the UNSC used the term 'all necessary means' in Resolution 678 (1990) on the Iraqi invasion of Kuwait, at that time there existed no UNSC resolution that incorporated those terms under such a resolution that in fact did not authorise force. Moreover, Resolution 1244 (1999) contained an Article 39 determination, recalled two previous resolutions that had made such a determination, and invoked Chapter VII.[127] Moreover, the Kumanovo Agreement preceding the adoption of Resolution 1244 (1999) expressly indicated that KFOR could take 'all necessary action' to establish a secure environment for citizens of Kosovo.[128]

Combined with the fact that, in practice, KFOR on several occasions had made use of force in implementing its mandate suggests that force had indeed been authorised, and at least anticipated. Such a conclusion is also strongly supported by statements of several other UNSC delegates at the UNSC debate during the adoption of the resolution, who regarded the resolution as having clearly authorised the use of force.[129]

III. RESOLUTIONS ADOPTED ON THE SITUATION IN AFGHANISTAN

A. Resolutions Adopted on ISAF

Following the 2001 United States *Operation Enduring Freedom* in Afghanistan, on 5 December the Agreement on Provisional Arrangements in Afghanistan Pending the Re-Establishment of Permanent Government Institutions (Bonn Agreement)

[124] UN Doc S/PV.4011 (1999) para. 7; Gray, *International Law and the Use of Force* (n 8) 357.

[125] UN Doc S/PV.4100 (1999) para 7.

[126] UN Doc S/PV.4011 (1999) para 9; Gray, *International Law and the Use of Force* (n 8) 357. Blokker, however, lists UNSC Res 1244 (1999) as an instance of UNSC authorisation for the use of force. See Blokker, 'Is the Authorisation Authorised?' (n 121) 543, 563 fn 95.

[127] UNSC Res 1244 (1999) preamble para 12; UNSC Res 1199 (1998) preamble para 14; UNSC Res 1203 (1998) preamble paras 7, 15.

[128] Arts I(2), B(1), Kumanovo Agreement.

[129] UN Doc S/PV.4011 (1999), see specifically at 10 (Slovenia). Gray, *International Law and the Use of Force* (n 8) 357 refers to the compromised formula used in the resolution which was 'seen by the West as wide enough to cover enforcement action'.

was adopted in an attempt to assist the establishment of a nationally agreed-upon government.[130] The Bonn Agreement paved the way for UNSC authorisation of the International Security Assistance Force (ISAF). Between 2001 and 2003 the UNSC adopted four explicit authorising resolutions, and over the subsequent years numerous more extending its authorisation. However, the matter was complicated when the United States became involved in Afghanistan under *Operation Enduring Freedom*, as this effectively meant that two operations, one under UNSC authorisation and another under United States command, were simultaneously present in Afghanistan. The United States presence, however, as will be seen below, remained distinct from the UNSC authorised ISAF operation.

In December 2001, under the Bonn Agreement, an interim authority in Afghanistan was created, pending the establishment of a permanent government through democratic elections.[131] Under Annex I of the Bonn Agreement, the participants thereto agreed to a request for an international security force that would assist in the maintenance of security in Kabul and surrounding areas. The request was directed to the UNSC 'to consider authorising the early deployment to Afghanistan of a United Nations mandated force'.[132] The agreement also made provision for the expansion of the force to other urban areas across the country. Initially, no mention of Chapter VII was not made despite the listed mandate suggesting force should be authorised. Although initially indicating the deployment 'on the basis of Chapter VI',[133] Afghanistan subsequently requested that the security force 'could be deployed under Chapters VI *or VII* of the Charter'.[134] On 19 December, the United Kingdom expressed its willingness to lead the formally named ISAF in Afghanistan.[135] It added that it would lead ISAF for an initial period of three months, that it had the support of the United States, that it sought a UNSC resolution authorising the operation and that it would exercise command over the force.[136]

i. Resolutions 1386 (2001), 1413 and 1444 (2002)

On 20 December 2001, taking note of the request for security assistance and the United Kingdom proposal to lead ISAF, the UNSC adopted Resolution 1386 (2001).[137] Determining that the situation continued to constitute a threat to international peace and security, the UNSC invoked Chapter VII to ensure

[130] UN Doc S/2001/1154 (2001) ('Bonn Agreement').
[131] Art 1(4), Bonn Agreement (n 130).
[132] Annex I, para 3, Bonn Agreement (n 130).
[133] UN Doc S/2001/1223 (2001).
[134] Emphasis added. UN Doc S/2001/1223 (2001) Annex, para 2.
[135] UN Doc S/2001/1217 (2001).
[136] UN Doc S/2001/1217 (2001) Annex, paras 2, 4, 6.
[137] UNSC Res 1386 (2001).

the implementation of ISAF's mandate in line with the Bonn Agreement.[138] It authorised the creation of ISAF as envisaged under the agreement and authorised Member States to 'take all necessary measures' to fulfil its mandate.[139]

The implementation of Resolution 1386 (2001) came through NATO's involvement, with over 130,000 troops from 51 NATO and non-NATO states deployed to Afghanistan at the height of operations.[140] On 23 May 2002 the UNSC adopted Resolution 1413 (2002), extending ISAF's mandate for a period of six months.[141] Determining the situation continued to constitute a threat to international peace and security and invoking Chapter VII, the UNSC again authorised Member States participating in ISAF to use 'all necessary measures' to fulfil ISAF's mandate.[142] Authorisation was extended for a further period of one year with the adoption of Resolution 1444 (2002), in the same manner that it was first extended under Resolution 1413 (2002).[143] The NATO-led force operated only around Kabul, until 13 October 2003, when the UNSC adopted Resolution 1510 (2003) which expanded its area of operations.[144] In addition to the explicit authorisation, an explicit reporting request was also made. In Resolution 1386 (2001) and Resolution 1444 (2002), ISAF leadership was requested to provide 'periodic reports' on implementation, and in Resolution 1413 (2002) a request for 'monthly reports' was made.[145]

ii. Resolution 1510 (2003) and Subsequent Mandate Extensions

Resolution 1510 (2003) was the first resolution to both extend and expand ISAF's mandate beyond the area of Kabul. The adoption of the resolution came in response to a NATO decision to expand ISAF to enable operations across Afghanistan. The NATO decision was first communicated to the Secretary-General on 2 October 2003.[146] Although not necessarily formally requesting the UNSC expand ISAF's mandate, the NATO Secretary-General stated that '[a]n expanded ISAF mandate will require a specific [UNSC] resolution'.[147] The NATO Secretary-General, however, added that '[s]uch an expansion would be

[138] UNSC Res 1386 (2001) preamble para 11.

[139] UNSC Res 1386 (2001) para 3; Gray, *International Law and the Use of Force* (n 8) 358; Michael Byers, 'The Intervention in Afghanistan – 2001' in Ruys and Corten (n 7) 626.

[140] NATO, 'ISAF's Mission in Afghanistan (2001-2014)' (archived) (1 September 2015) www.nato.int/cps/en/natohq/topics_69366.htm.

[141] UNSC Res 1413 (2002) para 1.

[142] UNSC Res 1413 (2002) para 2.

[143] UNSC Res 1444 (2002) paras 1, 2.

[144] UNSC Res 1510 (2003); UN Doc SC/7894 (2003); UN Doc S/PV.4840 (2003).

[145] UNSC Res 1368 (2001) para 9; UNSC Res 1413 (2002) para 4; UNSC Res 1444 (2002) para 4.

[146] UN Doc S/2003/970 (2003).

[147] UN Doc S/2003/970 (2003) Annex I, para 2 states: 'Enclosure Longer-Term Strategy for the North Atlantic Treaty Organization in its International Security Assistance Force role in Afghanistan'.

subject to the adoption of a [UNSC] resolution providing appropriate authority and the identification and provision of appropriate assets'.[148]

By 11 August 2003, NATO had assumed full command, control and coordination of ISAF and, under Resolution 1510 (2003), was authorised, resources permitting, to support the Afghan Transitional Authority in the maintenance of security outside Kabul.[149] Member States participating in ISAF were again authorised to use all necessary measures and ISAF's mandate was extended for a further 12 months.[150] The expanded ISAF mandate was explicitly extended for 12-month periods again in 10 subsequent resolutions.[151]

iii. ISAF, Operation Enduring Freedom, and Resolution 1373 (2001)

The deployment and expansion of ISAF notably occurred during the United States presence in Afghanistan under its *Operation Enduring Freedom*. The operation was aimed at combating terrorism in the country and was in part its response to the September 11 terrorist attacks. The United States operation seemed to have multiple legal bases, including that of intervention by invitation and self-defence.[152] The adoption of Resolution 1373 (2001) on 28 September 2001, merely a week before the launch of *Operation Enduring Freedom*, has on occasion been cited as an additional legal basis.[153] Alternatively, it has been argued that rather than authorising the use of force, Resolution 1373 (2001), read together with Resolution 1368 (2001), merely reaffirmed the right of States to act in self-defence under Article 51 of the UN Charter.[154] These resolutions are assessed in detail in subsequent chapters. For current purposes, it is worth mentioning that *Operation Enduring Freedom* and the ISAF deployment functioned as two distinct operations.

[148] UN Doc S/2003/970 (2003) Annex II.

[149] UNSC Res 1510 (2003) para 1; Byers, 'The Intervention in Afghanistan' (n 139) 626; Gray, *International Law and the Use of Force* (n 8) 358.

[150] UNSC Res 1510 (2003) paras 3, 4.

[151] UNSC Res 1563 (2004); UNSC Res 1623 (2005); UNSC Res 1707 (2006); UNSC Res 1776 (2007); UNSC Res 1833 (2008); UNSC Res 1890 (2009); UNSC Res 1943 (2010); UNSC Res 2011 (2011); UNSC Res 2069 (2012); UNSC Res 2120 (2013).

[152] See broadly, Michael Byers, 'Terrorism, the Use of Force and International Law After 11 September' (2002) 51 *International and Comparative Law Quarterly* 401.

[153] But see Byers, 'The Intervention in Afghanistan' (n 139) 636; Patrick Terry, 'The War in Afghanistan – Was the Use of Force Legal and/or Wise?' (2011) 9(3) *New Zealand Yearbook of International Law* 70–71.

[154] Sikander Shah, 'War on Terrorism: Self-Defence, Operation Enduring Freedom, and the Legality of US Drone Strikes on Pakistan' (2010) 9(1) *Washington University Global Studies Law Review* 96–97, 101–03; Terry (n 153) 73–74; Nicholas Rostow, 'Before and After: The Changed UN Response to Terrorism Since September 11th' (2002) 35(3) *Cornell International Law Journal* 481. See broadly Yoram Dinstein, 'Terrorism and Afghanistan' in Michael Schmitt (ed), *The War in Afghanistan: A Legal Analysis* (Naval War College 2009) and Lindsay Moir, *Reappraising the Resort to Force: International Law,* Jus ad Bellum *and the War on Terror*' (Hart Publishing 2010) 41. See also Mary O'Connell, 'Lawful Self-Defence to Terrorism' (2002) 63 *University of Pittsburgh Law Review* 908.

Operation Enduring Freedom brought about the eventual overthrow of the Taliban government at the time and, in part, resulted in the need for the Bonn Agreement and the subsequent ISAF deployment. Effectively, this meant that the two operations (one led by the United States functioning outside of UNSC authority, the other, UNSC-mandated), operated across Afghanistan during the same period. While the ISAF deployment was meant to assist in stabilisation efforts, the United States operation was mandated under the 'war on terror' acting outside of the scope of the UNSC.[155]

From 2011 onward, responsibility for security was gradually transferred to Afghan security forces and ISAF was formally terminated in 2014. Even with the initial presence of both ISAF and the *Operation Enduring Freedom* (and the subsequent *Operation Resolute Support* and *Operation Freedom's Sentinel*)[156] the Taliban ultimately regained power in 2021.

Nonetheless, the operation there under the UNSC Chapter VII-authorised mandate was yet another example in which the UNSC explicitly authorised the use of force (and stood in contrast to the *Operation Enduring Freedom* which was not authorised under UNSC resolutions). All resolutions adopted on Afghanistan and the ISAF deployment, whether extending or expanding its mandate, were made under Chapter VII, contained an Article 39 determination, and authorised the use of 'all necessary measures'.

IV. RESOLUTION 1973 (2011) | NATO ENFORCEMENT ACTION IN LIBYA

The Libyan civil war of 2011 was an armed conflict between Libyan armed forces loyal to Colonel Muammar Gaddafi and rebel groups seeking to overthrow his government. Confrontations between the rebel-led interim National Transition Council and Libyan security forces, combined with mass civil unrest, soon turned the conflict into a full-scale civil war. On several occasions, Libyan forces had used live ammunition in an attempt to quell protests and the violent crackdown prompted the UN High Commissioner for Human Rights to call for an investigation into crimes against humanity.[157] On 26 February 2011 the UNSC adopted its first resolution on the situation in Libya in which it expressed concern at the use of force used against civilians and acting under Chapter VII, demanded an immediate end to the violence.[158]

[155] Erika de Wet, 'The Invocation of the Right to Self-Defence in Response to Armed Attacks Conducted by Armed Groups: Implications for Attribution' (2019) 32(1) *Leiden Journal of International Law* 94; O'Connell (n 190) 908; Sikander Ahmed Shah, 'War on Terrorism: Self Defense, Operation Enduring Freedom, and the Legality of US Drone Attacks in Pakistan' (2010) 9(1) *Washington University Global Studies Law Review* 88–92.

[156] Byers, 'The Intervention in Afghanistan' (n 139) 627.

[157] Stephanie Nebehay, 'Update 3-Libya Attacks May Be Crimes Against Humanity – UN' *Reuters* (22 February 2011).

[158] UNSC Res 1970 (2011) paras 1, 2.

It also referred the situation to the Prosecutor of the International Criminal Court (ICC), imposed an arms embargo on Libya and imposed a travel ban and asset freezes on certain government officials close to Gaddafi, on Gaddafi himself and his family members.

The deteriorating humanitarian situation in Libya and the country's escalating civil war led the UNSC to adopt Resolution 1973 (2011), authorising the use of force by Member States and regional organisations, specifically for the protection of civilians, the imposition of a no-fly zone and for the enforcement of an arms embargo.[159] While the resolution no doubt authorised force, as will be seen below, concerns predominantly concerned the mandate given under the resolution. In particular, the protection of civilians' mandate was interpreted to give protection to rebel forces in the country, thereby assisting them in the eventual overthrowal of the Libyan authorities.

Consequently, questions of legality included whether the protection of civilians mandate was correctly interpreted in line with international humanitarian law to assist rebel forces; whether the resolution's provisions in fact did authorise assistance to rebel forces; whether the UNSC could legally authorise these provisions given the prohibition against assisting forces in overthrowing a government; and, as a result, whether the resolution could have been interpreted to have authorised a regime change in Libya.[160]

A. Explicit Authorisation and the Protection of Civilians

Deploring the Libyan authorities' failure to comply with demands under Resolution 1970 (2011), Resolution 1973 (2011) determined that the situation continued to constitute a threat to international peace and security.[161] Acting under Chapter VII, the UNSC authorised the use of force by Member States and regional organisations under three predominant categories, namely, the protection of civilians, the establishment of a no-fly zone and the enforcement of an arms embargo. The two latter categories were also rooted in the first, in that both the no-fly zone and arms embargo enforcement were aimed at protecting civilians. At present it suffices to say that the resolution's authorisation of the use of force remains undisputed and was widely acknowledged during UNSC

[159] UNSC Res 1973 (2011); Gray, *International Law and the Use of Force* (n 18) 377–78; see also Paul Williams, 'Security Council Resolution 1973 on Libya: A Moment of Legal and Moral Clarity' (2011) 44(1) *Case Western Reserve Journal of International Law* 233, 235–37.

[160] On the UNSC and regime change, see extensively Mehrdad Payandeh, 'The United Nations, Military Intervention, and Regime Change in Libya' (2012) 52 *Virginia Journal of International Law* 383–84, 386, 387–88; Christian Henderson, 'International Measures for the Protection of Civilians in Libya and Côte d'Ivoire' (2011) 60(3) *The International and Comparative Law Quarterly* 772–73; see broadly also Dire Tladi, 'Security Council, the Use of Force and Regime Change: Libya and Côte d'Ivoire' (2012) 37(1) *South African Yearbook of International Law* 22.

[161] UNSC Res 1973 (2011) preamble paras 1, 8, 21.

debates.[162] The interpretation of the mandate and scope of authorisation, however, requires considerable attention.[163]

Regarding the protection of civilians component, Member States acting nationally or through regional organisations were authorised to take all necessary measures to protect civilians and civilian populated areas under attack.[164] This authorisation extended to the area of Benghazi. The authorisation was subject to notification to, and in cooperation with, the Secretary-General. The provision was also explicit that such authorisation excluded a 'foreign occupation force of any form on any part of Libyan territory.' Recognising the importance of the League of Arab States in the situation, the UNSC '*bearing in mind*' Chapter VIII of the UN Charter, requested Member States of the League of Arab States to cooperate with other Member States in the implementation of the protection of civilians.[165] The second objective under which authorisation for the use of force was granted was for the enforcement of a no-fly zone over Libya, again in order to protect civilians.[166] Member States, acting nationally or through regional organisations, were authorised to take all necessary measures to enforce compliance with the ban on flights.[167] The authorisation was again subject to notification to the UN Secretary-General as well as notification to the Secretary-General of the League of Arab States.

The third objective under the resolution authorising the use of force concerned the enforcement of an arms embargo.[168] The UNSC called on Member States to 'use all measures commensurate to the specific circumstances' to carry out inspection of vessels and aircraft to ensure compliance with the embargo. Measures taken by Member States in pursuit of the first objective, the protection of civilians, was to be immediately reported to the UNSC.[169] Measures in pursuit of the second and third objectives, the enforcement on flight bans and

[162] UN Doc S/PV.6498 (2011) 4 (Lebanon), 5 (Germany), 6 (India and Brazil), 7 (Colombia), 8 (Russia), 10 (China). Ashley Deeks, 'The NATO Intervention in Libya – 2011' in Ruys and Corten (n 7) 751; Gray, *International Law and the Use of Force* (n 8) 377.

[163] The interpretation of such mandates has been extensively addressed in scholarship. See Dire Tladi, 'Interpretation of Protection of Civilians Mandates in United Nations Security Council Resolutions' in Dan Kuwali and Frans Viljoen (eds), *By All Means Necessary: Protecting Civilians and Preventing Mass Atrocities in Africa* (Pretoria University Law Press 2017) 82–83; Dapo Akande, 'What Does UN Security Council Resolution 1973 Permit?' *EJIL: Talk!* (23 March 2011); Williams (n 159) 233.

[164] UNSC Res 1973 (2011) para. 4. Scott Sheeran and Catherine Kent, 'Protection of Civilians, Responsibility to Protect, and Humanitarian Intervention: Conceptual and Normative Interactions' in Haidi Willmot et al (eds), *Protection of Civilians* (Oxford University Press 2016) 59–60; Williams (n 159) 238–39.

[165] UNSC Res 1973 (2011) para 5.

[166] UNSC Res 1973 (2011) para 6.

[167] UNSC Res 1973 (2011) para 8; Deeks, 'The NATO Intervention in Libya' (n 162) 751.

[168] UNSC Res 1973 (2011) para 13.

[169] UNSC Res 1973 (2011) para 4; Deeks, 'The NATO Intervention in Libya' (n 162) 751.

the arms embargo, were to be reported to the UN Secretary-General and the Secretary-General of the League of Arab States.[170]

B. Implementation of Resolution 1973 (2011)

The first week of operations saw several individual States use force against Libya under Resolution 1973 (2011). The French *Operation Harmattan* was among the first to make use of the authorisation when, on 19 March 2011, French combat jets attacked four Libyan army tanks.[171] During its 13-day operation, French targets predominantly revolved around those in breach of the no-fly zone, although on occasion also targeting ground forces. The United Kingdom, under *Operation Ellamy*, began a naval blockade on 19 March 2011. On 20 March the United Kingdom's Defence Ministry reported that it had targeted Libyan ground forces (along with forces which had breached the no-fly zone), in order to enforce the protection of civilians mandate.[172] The United Kingdom's operation continued to target both air and land targets for the duration of its operation, which it considered posed a threat to civilians or civilian occupied areas. Similarly, the Canadian *Operation Mobile* reported attacks on Libyan ammunition depots,[173] and the United States-led *Operation Odyssey Dawn* was reported to have destroyed Gaddafi's compound on 21 March 2011.[174]

On 31 March 2011 NATO took full command and control of operations under *Operation Unified Protector*. Forces under unified command, in addition to the international operations mentioned above, included troops from Belgium, Bulgaria, Greece, Italy, The Netherlands, Spain and Turkey. Throughout its operations, NATO maintained that all efforts it engaged in were to protect civilians and civilian populated areas, and that it was guided by the principle of using 'minimum force'.[175]

[170] UNSC Res 1973 (2011) paras 10, 14.

[171] Colin Freeman and Sean Rayment, 'Libya: British Forces Fire Missiles at Gaddafi' *The Telegraph* (19 March 2011). On the French operation, see Camille Grand, 'The French Experience: Sarkozy's War' in Karl Mueller et al (eds), *Precision and Purpose: Airpower in the Libyan Civil War* (RAND Corporation 2015) 183; see also Jolyon Howorth, '"Operation Harmattan" in Libya: A Paradigm Shift in French, European and Transatlantic Security Arrangements?' (2014) 12(4) *Journal of Transatlantic Studies* 405.

[172] United Kingdom Ministry of Defence, 'Libya Update' (20 March 2011).

[173] 'Canadian Jets Bomb Libyan Targets' (23 March 2011) *CBC News*.

[174] CNN Wire Staff, 'US Official: Gadhafi's Momentum Stopped' (21 March 2011) *CNN*.

[175] Operation Unified Protector Protection of Civilians and Civilian Populated Areas Fact Sheet; Operation Unified Protector NATO No-Fly Zone over Libya Fact Sheet; Operation Unified Protector NATO Arms Embargo against Libya Fact Sheet. Karl Sorenson and Nima Damidez, 'Fragments of an Army: Three Aspects of the Libya Collapse' in Kjell Engelbrekt et al (eds), *The NATO Intervention in Libya: Lessons Learned from the Campaign* (Routledge 2014) 141. See further Eric Myjer and Nigel White, 'Peace Operations Conducted by Regional Organisations and Arrangements' in Terry Gill and Dieter Fleck (eds) *The Handbook of the International Law of Military Operations* (Oxford University Press 2015) 191.

Finally, it is worth noting that the implementation of Resolution 1973 (2011) in part eventually led to the overthrow of Gaddafi. Consequently, although outside of the current scope of discussions, one question which has arisen is whether Resolution 1973 (2011) may have authorised regime change. That question has been widely addressed in scholarship and need to be discussed here, suffice it to say however that conclusions both favouring or disfavouring such an outcome are directly related to the interpretation of Resolution 1973 (2011) and its provisions. More specifically, the fact that force had been authorised alongside the protection of civilians mandate accorded within the resolution has faced significant debate.[176] They are however a prime example of the significance and far-reaching effects of UNSC resolutions authorising the use of force.

V. CONCLUSION

The chapter has examined some 50 UNSC resolutions authorising force. Of these, more than a dozen resolutions have established authorisation, with over three dozen resolutions have renewed the authorisation originally provided for under previous UNSC resolutions. While principally focusing on the authorisation given to NATO, it has also considered authorisation to UN peacekeeping missions, most notably, UNCRO, UNPROFOR and UNTAES, as well as regional peacekeeping missions, namely, IFOR, ISAF, KFOR and SFOR. The analysis above, which constitutes considerable UNSC practice, has shown the following.

Of the resolutions considered above, the term 'all necessary measures' on occasion expressed as 'all measures necessary' appears in the majority of both authorising resolutions as well as resolutions extending authorisation. One resolution employed the term 'all necessary means,' equivalent in consequence to 'all necessary measures' where the use of force is concerned. One other resolution employed the term 'use such measures commensurate' and three resolutions authorised the use of force by directly referring to a previous authorising resolution. Only in one instance has the UNSC authorised the use of force by referring to a previous authorising resolution without specifically invoking Chapter VII.[177]

[176] See for example Geir Ulfstein and Føsund Christiansen, 'The Legality of the NATO Bombing in Libya' (2013) 62(1) *International and Comparative Law Quarterly* 162–63; Jennifer Welsh, 'Civilian Protection in Libya: Putting Coercion and Controversy Back into RtoP' (2011) 25(3) *Ethics and International Affairs* 258; Dapo Akande, 'France Admits to Arming Libyan Rebels – Was this Lawful?' (1 July 2011) *EJIL: Talk!*; cf Deeks, 'The NATO Intervention in Libya' (n 162) 757; Ben Smith and Arabella Thorp, 'Interpretation of Security Council Resolution 1973 on Libya' (6 April 2011) House of Commons Library SN/IA/5916; Chris de Cock, 'Operation Unified Protector and the Protection of Civilians in Libya' in Michael Schmitt and Louise Arimatsu (eds), *Yearbook of International Humanitarian Law, Volume 14* (Asser Press 2011) 217; Corten and Koutroulis in Olivier Corten and Vaios Koutroulis, 'The Illegality of Military Support to Rebels in the Libyan War: Aspects of *Jus Contra Bellum* and *Jus in Bello*' (2013) *Journal of Conflict and Security Law* 59.

[177] UNSC Res 776 (1992).

Moreover, in giving effect to its decisions, the UNSC opted to use the words *authorises*,[178] *decides*[179] or *calls upon*,[180] when authorising force in its operative paragraphs. Only on one occasion did it choose to *reiterate* that Member States take 'all necessary measures', although the resolution was extending this authorisation and not establishing it in the context of assisting UNTAES.[181]

Where the determination of a situation to constitute a threat to peace and security concerns, UNSC practice indicates that almost every resolution authorising or extending authorisation to use force has consistently and explicitly made such a determination. Only four resolutions constitute exceptions to this and all four related to the situation in the FRY. Resolutions 776 (1992), 781 (1992), 908 (1994) and 981 (1994) merely reaffirmed an Article 39 determination made in previous resolutions. Equally as notable is the fact that only the first two of these resolutions also lacked a Chapter VII invocation, opting to authorise the use of force by referring to a previous resolution that had invoked Chapter VII, namely, Resolution 770 (1992). The third resolution, Resolution 908 (1994), authorised the use of force in support of UNPROFOR. Again, however, it recalled a previous resolution in which such a determination was made. In essence, however, these resolutions lacking an explicit Article 39 determination did not in themselves establish authorisation, but rather extended authorisations based on previous resolutions.

Similarly, that the UNSC recalls previous resolutions in an authorising resolution has again been confirmed in the above analysis. Every resolution authorising or extending the use of force recalled either a previous resolution that had made an Article 39 determination, invoked Chapter VII, or both. Only one exception exists: Resolution 1386 (2001) authorising ISAF in Afghanistan. With that said, the authorisation for ISAF was granted at the request of the Afghan government (and was thus not preceded by any UNSC resolution that had first considered the situation there a threat to peace and security).

Noteworthy in the current context of authorisation to NATO as a collective defence alliance is the UNSC's reliance on Chapter VII measures, rather than invoking Chapter VIII.[182] A reasonable justification for this has been

[178] UNSC Res 776 (1992); UNSC Res 816 (1993); UNSC Res 836 (1993); UNSC Res 1031 (1995); UNSC Res 1088 (1996); UNSC Res 1174 (1998); UNSC Res 1247 (1999); UNSC Res 1305 (2000); UNSC Res 1357 (2001); UNSC Res 1423 (2002); UNSC Res 1491 (2003); UNSC Res 1551 (2004); UNSC Res 1244 (1999); UNSC Res 1386 (2001); UNSC Res 1413 (2002); UNSC Res 1444 (2002); UNSC Res 1510 (2003); UNSC Res 1563 (2004); UNSC Res 1623 (2005); UNSC Res 1707 (2006); UNSC Res 1776 (2007); UNSC Res 1833 (2008); UNSC Res 1890 (2009); UNSC Res 1943 (2010); UNSC Res 2011 (2011); UNSC Res 2069 (2012); UNSC Res 2120 (2013); UNSC Res 1973 (2011).

[179] UNSC Res 836 (1993); UNSC Res 908 (1994); UNSC Res 958 (1994); UNSC Res 981 (1995); UNSC Res 1037 (1996); UNSC Res 1418 (2002); UNSC Res 1420 (2002); UNSC Res 1421 (2002).

[180] UNSC Res 770 (1990); UNSC Res 787 (1992).

[181] UNSC Res 1120 (1997).

[182] Gill and Tibori-Szabó note the UNSC's reliance on Chapter VII over VIII, acknowledging reliance on either chapter is of a secondary importance. See Terry Gill and Kinga Tibori-Szabó, *The Use of Force and the International Legal System* (Cambridge University Press 2024) 82–83. See also

analysed above, but it suffices to say that when a regional organisation (or collective defence alliance such as NATO) acts militarily against a Member State or within its geographical area, the UNSC could legally rely on Chapter VIII or Article 53(1).[183] Where such organisation or collective defence alliance takes military measures 'out of area' or against a non-Member State, UNSC practice particularly in Yugoslavia undoubtedly confirms it authorises action under Chapter VII. Implicitly, such UNSC action is in turn based on Articles 42 and 48(1).[184] The only exception evidenced in UNSC practice is the invocation of Chapter VIII in Resolutions787 (1992) which authorised the use of force for embargo enforcement. However, in that case, it is important to note that paragraph 12 authorising force for embargo enforcement was limited as such, to only enforce Article 41 measures (albeit with the use of force).

Instead, UNSC practice overwhelmingly points to the fact that when the UNSC authorises force by a collective defence alliance against non-Member States or authorises an out-of-area deployment, it would rely on Chapter VII. Where the UNSC authorises the use of force by a collective defence alliance in its own area or against one of its member states, it may, of course, not only rely on Articles 42 and 48(1), but also on Chapter VIII measures.[185]

The above analysis has also drawn attention to resolutions that do not impose some form of time limit to entities they authorise, rendering such authorisation potentially perpetual Because authorisation of force is granted under Chapter VII, a subsequent resolution is needed to terminate that authorisation. This presents a dangerous situation in which the UNSC may authorises force indefinitely and then subsequently be unable to adopt a resolution (given the veto power) to terminate such authorisation.[186] The most notable example in this regard remains Resolution 1244 (1999).

With that said, however, the above analysis has undoubtedly shown, as has the previous chapter, that when the UNSC authorises the use of force, it

Schaper (n 121) 409 who considers the question of NATO being a Chapter VIII organisation as moot given its out-of-area engagements under UNSC authorisation.

[183] See also extensively Abass (n 58) 66–69, 71–78; Danesh Sarooshi, *The United Nations and the Development of Collective Security: The Delegation by the UN Security Council of its Chapter VII Powers* (Oxford University Press 1999) 248–53; Mary O'Connell, 'The UN, NATO, and International Law after Kosovo' (2000) 22(1) *Human Rights Quarterly* 66–67, 69.

[184] See also De Wet, 'Article 42' in Bruno Simma et al (eds), *The Charter of the United Nations: A Commentary* (4th edn, vol II, Oxford University Press 2024) 696–97.

[185] See also the previous chapter's analysis of UNSC Res 1464 (2003) invocation of Chapters VII and VIII when it authorised ECOWAS along with French forces in the Ivory Coast. See also Orakhelashvili (n 129) 301, 310–11; Nigel White, 'From Korea to Kuwait: The Legal Basis of United Nations' Military Action' (1998) 20(3) *The International History Review* 598–600.

[186] Karine Bannelier and Théodore Christakis, 'Between Flexibility and Accountability: How Can the Security Council Strengthen Oversight of Use-of-Force Mandates?' in Jeremy Farrall and Hilary Charlesworth (eds), *Strengthening the Rule of Law Through the UN Security Council* (Routledge 2016) 211–12.

does so systematically. With the exceptional few deviations, the UNSC tends to authorise the use of force only once a situation is determined to be a threat to peace and security. In addition, it authorises such action under Chapter VII, rarely invoking Chapter VIII. Finally, the UNSC has made a custom of referring to military measures in its operative paragraphs, either by stating that 'force' may be used or, more regularly, by employing the 'all necessary measures' phrasing.

5

Explicit Authorisation to UN Peacekeeping Missions

I. INTRODUCTION

THE THREE PREVIOUS chapters have analysed some 150 resolutions in which the United Nations Security Council (UNSC) has authorised force to Member States, regional organisations and collective defence alliances (NATO). These chapters have to a limited extent already examined several UN peacekeeping missions which were either authorised to use force or where force was authorised to Member States in support of these missions. This chapter now turns its attention to the authorisation of force to UN peacekeeping missions more broadly.

The chapter considers both explicit authorisation as well as 'mandated authorisation'. The latter concerns those resolutions authorising force to UN peacekeeping missions through their respective mandates.[1] The reference to 'mandated authorisation' therefore refers to authorisation of force derived not necessarily from explicit phrasing such 'all necessary measures' but instead, based on a UN mission's mandate. It is of course through the interpretation of these robust mandates that the use of force is clearly attributable (and authorised) beyond self-defence. As will be seen, this authorisation is almost always granted in relation to the protection of a mission's mandate and more specifically, for the protection of civilians.

[1] The use of force by peacekeeping missions is widely addressed in literature. See for example Hanna Bourgeois and Patryk I Labuda, 'When May UN Peacekeepers Use Lethal Force to Protect Civilians? Reconciling Threats to Civilians, Imminence and the Right to Life' (2023) 28(1) *Journal of Conflict and Security Law* 1; Trevor Findlay, *The Use of Force in UN Peace Operations* (SIPRI 2002); Scott Sheeran, 'The Use of Force in United Nations Peacekeeping Operations' in Marc Weller (ed), *The Oxford Handbook of the Use of Force in International Law* (Oxford University Press 2015) 347–74; Katherine E Cox, 'Beyond Self-Defense: United Nations Peacekeeping Operations and the Use of Force' (1999) 27(2) *Denver Journal of International Law and Policy* 239; Lise Morjé Howard and Anjali Kaushlesh Dayal, 'The Use of Force in UN Peacekeeping' (2018) 72(1) *International Organizations* 71–103; John Karlsrud, 'The UN at War: Examining the Consequences of Peace-Enforcement Mandates for the UN Peacekeeping Operations in the CAR, the DRC and Mali' (2015) 36(1) *Third World Quarterly* 40–54. See also Christine Gray, *International Law and the Use of Force* (Oxford University Press 2018) 262–340 and James Sloan, *The Militarisation of Peacekeeping in the 21st Century* (Hart Publishing 2011).

II. EXPLICIT AUTHORISATION TO UN PEACEKEEPING MISSIONS

While it is not the purpose of this chapter to delve into the very nature of what constitutes peacekeeping and how it has evolved over the years, its relation to the use of force requires brief mention. Peacekeeping is founded upon three principles, namely, consent, impartiality and the non-use of force except for self-defence and defence of the mandate. Beyond these principles, peacekeeping forces are not permitted to use force, unless of course they are authorised to do so by the UNSC. The Report on the High-Level Independent Panel on Peace Operations in particular confirmed the exceptions to the use of force by peacekeeping missions.[2] Specifically, it affirmed that defence of the mandate was interpreted to always include the responsibility to protect civilians.[3] In addition, it indicated that different threats should be met with the appropriate use of military force, from deterrence and coercion to direct confrontation.[4] It is in this context that the following section will detail instances in which the UNSC has explicitly authorised the use of force, and particularly for the protection of a peacekeeping mission's mandate. As in the case of other authorising resolutions, primary focus is vested in the way the UNSC has accorded this authorisation.

As will be seen, an increasing number of peacekeeping operations are given mandates under Chapter VII. This was particularly brought about after the UN's peacekeeping operations in the former Yugoslavia and Somalia, during which time it became clear that peacekeeping forces needed more robust mandates. In addition, peacekeeping missions began to receive mandates that authorised the use of force beyond self-defence.

In assessing UNSC authorisation of force, the three previous chapters have already examined authorisation to UNOSOM I and II in Somalia; UNPROFOR in Bosnia and Herzegovina; UNCRO and UNTAES in Croatia; and UNTAET in East Timor.[5] In addition, regional peacekeeping missions already assessed include IFOR and SFOR in Bosnia and Herzegovina; KFOR in Kosovo; MISCA in the Central African Republic; AFISMA in Mali; and AMISOM in Somalia.[6]

Beyond these peacekeeping missions, the UNSC has on several occasions acted on a situation solely through peacekeeping initiatives, without having relied on delegated enforcement action to Member States or regional organisations. On other occasions, authorisation of force to Member States and regional organisations has complemented its peacekeeping efforts in a situation. In any case, both scenarios constitute the examination in which the use of force has been authorised to peacekeeping missions. As with the previous chapters, the

[2] UN Doc A/70/95 – S/2015/446 (2015) para 116.

[3] UN Doc A/70/95 – S/2015/446 (2015) para 128. Sheeran (n 1) 366; Mats Berdal, 'The Security Council and Peacekeeping' in Vaughan Lowe et al (eds), *The United Nations Security Council and War: The Evolution of Thought and Practice since 1945* (Oxford University Press 2008) 188–90.

[4] UN Doc A/70/95, paras 124, 128.

[5] See chs 2 at p 38–40, 3 at p 71–72 and 4 at p 108–111.

[6] See chs 3 at p 69–71, 72–79 and 4 at p 111–112, 114–115, 117–118.

analysis below aims to identify and draw a methodology on the manner in which authorisation is provided to these peacekeeping missions, particularly considering whether the UNSC follows a similar route as it does when it authorises Member States and regional organisations, namely, that authorising resolutions contain an Article 39 determination, invoke Chapter VII and use specific language in the resolutions' operative paragraphs.[7]

A. Early UN Security Council Practice: The Case of ONUC

When analysing UNSC practice, its earlier resolutions present particular complexities in ascertaining if and to what extent it had authorised force to a peacekeeping mission. As has been seen in previous chapters, the same may be said when it authorised Member States to use force, particularly in that resolutions adopted in its earlier days did not necessarily invoke Chapter VII.[8] As a result, whether the UNSC was acting under that chapter only became clear from the wording and context of its resolutions. A specific example worth considering here is that of the United Nations Operation in the Congo (ONUC) following its independence from Belgium.[9]

In 1961 the UNSC adopted two specific resolutions concerning peacekeeping and the use of force. Facing the impending possibility of a civil war in the Congo and following the execution of three Congolese leaders, the UNSC adopted Resolutions 161 and 169 (1961).[10] Resolution 161 (1961) concerned the prevalence of conditions that seriously imperilled peace, order and unity in the Congo, consequently determining the situation to constitute a threat to international peace and security.[11] It recalled three previous resolutions on the situation, among which included Resolution 146 (1960) declaring that the entry of the United Nations force into the Katanga province of the Congo was necessary for the implementation of the resolution.[12] To this end, it established ONUC as a peacekeeping mission with the consent (at the request) of the Congolese government at the time.

The UNSC explicitly *urged* the United Nations to 'take immediately all appropriate measures to prevent the occurrence of a civil war in the Congo', including ceasefire arrangements, the halting of military operations, prevention of clashes and the use of force, if necessary, in the last resort.[13] The UNSC

[7] As has already been seen in previous resolutions on peacekeeping missions. See also Sloan (n 1) 143–45.

[8] See the discussions in ch 2 at p 18.

[9] The United Nations Emergency Force (UNEF I) is not analysed here since it was established and mandated (exceptionally so) by the United Nations General Assembly and not the UNSC.

[10] UNSC Res 161 (1961); UNSC Res 169 (1961).

[11] UNSC Res 161 (1961) Part A, preamble para 1, Part B, preamble paras 1, 5; Sloan (n 1) 134.

[12] UNSC Res 146 (1960) para 3.

[13] UNSC Res 161 (1960) Part A, para 1.

subsequently adopted Resolution 169 (1961) some nine months later. Although itself not determining a threat to international peace and security, it had referenced a previous resolution that had made such a determination.[14] Moreover, using similar language, the UNSC *authorised* the Secretary-General 'to take vigorous action, including the use of the requisite measure of force, if necessary, for the immediate apprehension, detention pending legal action and/or deportation of all foreign military and paramilitary personnel and political advisers not under [UN] command, and mercenaries'.[15] Resolution 169 (1961) also *requested* the Secretary-General 'take all necessary measures' to prevent the entry or return into the Congo of mercenaries and all foreign military and paramilitary personnel and political advisers not under UN command.[16]

ONUC, which was initially set up as a classic peacekeeping mission, was therefore later transformed into, at the least, a quasi-enforcement mission. This was evident under Resolutions 161 (1960) and 169 (1961) which, for the first time in UN peacekeeping history, explicitly authorised force beyond self-defence to a peacekeeping mission.[17] Attributable to this interpretation was the wording employed in the resolutions, and it was evident that the UNSC was acting under Chapter VII, although not invoking it.[18] The extent to which the UNSC transformed a classic peacekeeping mission into a peace enforcement mission remains a topic of debate today. What can be said, though, and as will be seen below, is that the UNSC has become more clear and methodological when authorising force to peacekeeping missions.

B. Explicit Authorisation to Peacekeeping Missions under Chapter VII

Previous chapters have already examined a number of peacekeeping missions authorised to use force on similar situations. These include authorisation to UNOSOM II, UNTAET, UNAMID, UNOCI, MINUSMA, UNPROFOR and UNCRO. Attention may now be directed at considering other UN peacekeeping missions explicitly authorised under Chapter VII.

[14] UNSC Res 169 (1961), preamble para 1.

[15] UNSC Res 169 (1961) para 4.

[16] UNSC Res 169 (1961) para 5 read together with para 4.

[17] Sloan (n 1) 131–32; Mohamed Osman, *The United Nations and Peace Enforcement: Wars, Terrorism and Democracy* (Ashgate 2002) 155. Note also the comment by Månsson who states that 'ONUC (1960–64) remains one of the *de facto* peace enforcement missions among the "traditional" peacekeeping operations during the Cold War' and that '[w]hile classified as a peacekeeping mission, there is little doubt that Resolution 161 implicitly provided ONUC with a peace enforcement mandate in accordance with article 42 of the UN Charter'. See Katarina Månsson, 'Use of Force and Civilian Protection: Peace Operations in the Congo' (2005) 12(4) *International Peacekeeping* 504. Månsson also adds that it was the first time that the UNSC authorised a military operation under UN command to use force in order to implement a resolution.

[18] See the discussion in Sloan (n 1) 134, and also in relation to the *Certain Expenses ICJ* case; Osman (n 16) 155–56. See, broadly, Thomas Franck, 'United Nations Law in Africa: The Congo Operation as a Case Study' (1962) 27 *Law and Contemporary Problems* 632.

i. Resolution 1291 (2000) | MONUC

The United Nations Organisation Mission in the Democratic Republic of the Congo (DRC) (MONUC) was established under Resolution 1279 (1999) to monitor ceasefire agreements in the Democratic Republic of the Congo (DRC). Although not initially authorised to use force beyond self-defence, continuing instability in the DRC saw a gradual expansion of MONUC's mandate. Under Resolution 1291 (2000), MONUC was first authorised to 'take the necessary action, in its areas of deployment of its infantry battalions and as it deems it within its capabilities' to use force not only in self-defence, but also to protect civilians under imminent threat of physical violence.[19] The resolution authorising MONUC contained both a Chapter VII invocation and an Article 39 determination.

While MONUC's mandate was extended on several occasions, under Resolution 1417 (2002) the UNSC again specifically extended MONUC's authorisation to 'take the necessary action' to, beyond self-defence, protect civilians under imminent threat of physical violence.[20] Thereafter, by Resolution 1493 (2003) the UNSC strengthened its authority to use force. Determining that the situation continued to constitute a threat to peace and security and acting under Chapter VII, MONUC was authorised to 'take the necessary measures' to carry out, in addition to its existing mandate, the protection of humanitarian workers, and to contribute to the security situation in which humanitarian assistance was to be provided.[21] Moreover, MONUC was also authorised to use 'all necessary means' to fulfil its mandate in the Ituri district and in North and South Kivu.[22] From 26 August 2003, the Interim Multinational Emergency Force in Bunia was to assist MONUC in its mandate.[23]

The authorisation to MONUC given under Resolution 1493 (2003) was then explicitly extended under Resolution 1533 (2004) and Resolution 1555 (2004)[24] and, citing increased instability in the country, MONUC was again authorised under Chapter VII and increased in force size under Resolution 1565 (2004).[25] This authorisation was extended and emphasised in Resolution 1592 (2005), Resolution 1628 (2005), Resolution 1711 (2006), Resolution 1742 (2007),

[19] UNSC Res 1291 (2000) para 8; Jason Stearns, 'Can Force be Useful in the Absence of a Political Strategy? Lessons From the UN Missions to the DR Congo' (2015) Global Peace Operations Review.

[20] UNSC Res 1417 (2002) para 7.

[21] UNSC Res 1493 (2003) para 25.

[22] UNSC Res 1493 (2003) para 26. See also Jim Terrie, 'The Use of Force in UN Peacekeeping: The Experience of MONUC' (2009) 18(1) *African Security Review* 25; Findlay (n 1) 359.

[23] See ch 3 at p 72–73.

[24] UNSC Res 1555 (2004) para 1; Res 1533 (2004) para 3; Findlay (n 1) 296 fn 115. Interestingly, under UNSC Res 1533 (2004) para 3, the UNSC *requested* MONUC use 'all means' and not 'all necessary means' as in previous resolutions. Since the resolution referred to its mandate under UNSC Res 1493 (2003), determined a threat to peace and security and invoked Chapter VII, it is reasonable to conclude that the resolution also authorised force.

[25] UNSC Res 1565 (2004) paras 1, 3, 4, 6.

Resolution 1751 (2007) and Resolution 1756 (2006).[26] With the exception of Resolutions 1649 (2005) and 1693 (2006), each resolution renewing MONUC's authorisation did so by explicitly stating it was authorised to 'use all necessary means' to implement its mandate. This authorisation was merely *emphasised* in Resolution 1649 (2005) and *recalled* in Resolutions 1693 (2006) and 1794 (2007). With that said, however, all subsequent resolutions were adopted under Chapter VII and contained an Article 39 determination. Explicit authorisation in such a manner was given under two additional resolutions, Resolution 1856 (2008) and Resolution 1906 (2009) before it was rehatted as the United Nations Organisation Stabilisation Mission in the Democratic Republic of the Congo (MONUSCO).[27]

ii. Resolution 1545 (2004) | ONUB

In 2004 the UNSC authorised the establishment of the United Nations Operation in Burundi (ONUB). ONUB was established for an initial period of six months and was to consist of a maximum of 5,650 military personnel, including 200 observers and 125 staff officers. ONUB was authorised to 'use all necessary means' to carry out its mandate within its capacity and areas wherein its military components were deployed.[28] It was given a broad mandate under Resolution 1545 (2004) to, among others, ensure respect of ceasefire agreements, carry out disarmament and demobilisation, monitor the illegal flow of arms and protect civilians under imminent threat of physical violence.[29] ONUB's mandate was subsequently extended explicitly under Resolutions 1577 (2004), 1602 (2005), 1641 (2005), 1650 (2005) and Resolution 1692 (2006) until it was succeeded by the United Nations Integrated Office in Burundi.[30]

In the case of Resolution 1545 (2004) and in every resolution extending its mandate, the UNSC explicitly determined that the situation in Burundi constituted a threat to international peace and security in the region. More so, Chapter VII was invoked each time. The main distinction between the manner of authorisation to ONUB and subsequent resolutions extending that authorisation is that only in Resolution 1545 (2004) did the UNSC refer to the use of 'all necessary means'. Subsequent resolutions merely renewed authorisation under Resolution 1545 (2004) without again explicitly using this phrasing. Nonetheless,

[26] UNSC Res 1592 (2005) paras 1, 7; UNSC Res 1628 (2005) para 1. The authorisation was again *emphasised* in UNSC Res 1649 (2005) para 11 and *recalled* in UNSC Res 1693 (2006) para 5. It was also *renewed* in UNSC Res 1711 (2006) para 1; UNSC Res 1742 (2007) para 1; UNSC Res 1751 (2007) para 1; UNSC Res 1756 (2007) para 4 and UNSC Res 1794 (2007) para 8.

[27] UNSC Res 1856 (2008) para 5; Res 1906 (2009) para 6.

[28] UNSC Res 1545 (2004) para 5.

[29] UNSC Res 1545 (2004) para 5.

[30] UNSC Res 1577 (2004) para 1; UNSC Res 1602 (2005) para 1; UNSC Res 1641 (2005) para 1; UNSC Res 1650 (2005) para 2; UNSC Res 1692 (2006) para 1.

it was clear in context that the UNSC was renewing its authorisation to ONUB under Resolution 1545 (2004) for it to use force to carry out its mandate.[31]

iii. Resolutions 1925 (2010) and 2098 (2013) | MONUSCO

Despite the presence of two international forces in the DRC and MONUC having engaged in peacekeeping for nine years, the situation remained volatile. In 2010 the UNSC rebranded MONUC into MONUSCO.[32] Under Resolution 1925 (2010) the UNSC gave one final extension of MONUC's mandate until 30 June 2010, thereafter, employing MONUSCO with a robust Chapter VII mandate. MONUSCO's mandate in order of priority was, first, to protect civilians and, second, to contribute towards stability and peace consolidation. MONUSCO was authorised to take 'all necessary means' to implement its protection of civilians mandate.[33] This authorisation was renewed in Resolutions 1991 (2011) and 2053 (2012).[34] It was, however, not authorised to use force to accomplish its objectives of stability and peace consolidation.

However, while it was initially tasked as a peacekeeping force, by 2013 the situation in the DRC had changed significantly. Active conflict in the country had prompted the UNSC to consider a shift in its mandate. The UN Secretary-General specifically called on the UNSC to establish a peace enforcement brigade to carry out offensive operations in the DRC.[35] This proposal was also supported by the DRC government at the time. In response the UNSC unanimously adopted Resolution 2098 (2013). Considering the proposal by the Secretary-General, the UNSC expanded MONUSCO's mandate to include an 'intervention brigade' tasked with neutralising armed groups. In the same vein, the UNSC stressed that this intervention brigade was on an exceptional basis and was not to create any precedent or to prejudice agreed principles of peacekeeping.[36]

With this new mandate, MONUSCO was authorised to take 'all necessary measures' to protect civilians, *neutralise armed groups through its intervention brigade*, monitor implementation of arms embargoes and provide support to national and international judicial processes.[37] The shift in MONSUCO's role from a peacekeeping mission to peace enforcement, even under exceptional circumstances, was not universally welcomed. Even so, with the reinforced peace enforcement mandate, MONUSCO, together with DRC's armed forces, were able to quickly succeed in taking down several armed groups, most notably the

[31] Sloan (n 1) 260.

[32] See also Menent Savaz-Cazala, 'Offensive Use of Force in Peace Operations: The Force Intervention Brigade' (2016) 2(2) *European Journal of Interdisciplinary Studies* 116.

[33] UNSC Res 1925 (2010) para 11.

[34] UNSC Res 1991 (2011) para 1; Res 2053 (2012) para 2.

[35] Gray, *International Law and the Use of Force* (n 2) 331–32.

[36] UNSC Res 2098 (2013) para 9; Gray, *International Law and the Use of Force* (n 2) 332; Savas-Cazala (n 32) 117.

[37] UNSC Res 2098 (2013) paras 12(a)–(d).

M23 which had protested against MONSUCO's new mandate and announced attacks against it. While the impact of Resolution 2098 (2013) on peacekeeping principles remained divided, what was clear at the time was that the UNSC had undoubtedly authorised the peacekeeping mission to use offensive force in the DRC.[38] This was clearly and explicitly contained in the operative paragraphs of the resolution, together with the invocation of Chapter VII and the preamble's determination of a threat to peace and security. The explicit nature in which the UNSC authorised MONUSCO to use offensive force against armed groups was again repeated when it extended its mandate under eleven subsequent resolutions until its eventual planned withdrawal from 2024 onward.[39]

iv. Resolution 2149 (2014) | MINUSCA

Following the resolutions adopted on the situation in the Central African Republic (CAR), in which the UNSC authorised the AU-led MISCA and later an EU force in the country, the UNSC established the United Nations Multidimensional Integrated Stabilisation Mission in the Central African Republic (MINUSCA).[40] To assist the CAR authorities in stabilising the country, MINUSCA was to deploy from the re-hatted MISCA by 15 September 2015 with both a civilian and military component. MINUSCA was authorised under Resolution 2149 (2014) to 'use all necessary means' within its capabilities and areas of deployment to carry out its extensive mandate. MINSUCA was assigned with six predominant tasks, which among others included, to protect civilians, support and implement a transition process in favour of extending state authority, and to facilitate immediate, full, safe and unhindered delivery of humanitarian assistance.[41] Particularly where its mandate of the protection of civilians was concerned, MINUSCA was to protect civilians from the threat of physical violence, including through active patrolling.

Resolution 2149 (2014) establishing and authorising MINUSCA explicitly determined a threat to international peace and security and invoked Chapter VII when it authorised MINUSCA to use 'all necessary means' to carry out its mandate. This authorisation was extended in four subsequent resolutions, using the same explicit language.[42] When the UNSC thereafter extended MINUSCA's mandate under Resolution 2446 (2018), it did so without referring

[38] Savas-Cazala (n 32) 117 notes that that the brigade has 'the first-ever offensive mandate in UN history to use all necessary means to neutralize and disarm armed groups in Congo'.

[39] UNSC Res 2147 (2014) para 1; UNSC Res 2211 (2015) para 1; UNSC Res 2277 (2016) paras 24, 34; UNSC Res 2348 (2017) paras 26, 33; UNSC Res 2409 (2018) paras 29, 35; UNSC Res 2463 (2019) paras 21, 28; UNSC Res 2502 (2019) paras 22, 27; UNSC Res 2556 (2020) paras 22, 27; UNSC Res 2612 (2021) paras 22, 27; UNSC Res 2666 (2022) paras 19, 22; UNSC Res 2717 (2023) paras 29, 32.

[40] UNSC Res 2149 (2014) para 18.

[41] UNSC Res 2149 (2014) paras 29, 30(a)–(g).

[42] UNSC Res 2217 (2015) para 30; UNSC Res 2281 (2016) paras 1, 2; UNSC Res 2301 (2017) para 32; UNSC Res 2387 (2017) para 41.

explicitly to its authorisation to use 'all necessary means'.[43] Rather, the UNSC *decided* to extend its mandate 'as set out in Resolution 2387 (2017)'.[44] Given that Resolution 2387 (2017) explicitly mandated MINUSCA to 'use all necessary means', its mandate extension under Resolution 2446 (2018) also extended its authorisation to use force. Additionally, Resolution 2446 (2018) invoked Chapter VII and included in its preamble the determination that the situation in the CAR continued to constitute a threat to peace and security. Granted, the resolution only extended MINSUCA for one month, after which the UNSC again explicitly extended MINUSCA citing its use of 'all necessary means' under Resolution 2448 (2018).[45] With that said, every resolution authorising and extending MINUSCA's mandate also explicitly authorised its use of force.

From the above analysis it is clear that the UNSC has on several occasions explicitly authorised the use of force to UN peacekeeping missions, and this authorisation has gone beyond self-defence to include the protection of the mission's mandate. It has accorded this authorisation using two kinds of explicit phrasing, namely, either stating in the operative paragraphs that it authorises 'all necessary measures' or authorises the mission to 'take the necessary action'. In both cases the authorisation was clearly preceded by an Article 39 determination and the invocation of Chapter VII. Nonetheless, as will be seen below, despite the divergence in the use of language in its operative paragraphs, both forms have been interpreted as affirmatively authorising the use of force.

III. EXPLICIT AUTHORISATION: 'ALL NECESSARY MEASURES' AND 'TAKE THE NECESSARY ACTIONS/MEASURES'

Beyond the resolutions examined above, which authorised UN peacekeeping missions to use force beyond self-defence, the UNSC has also on several occasions authorised peacekeeping missions to 'take the necessary action' to implement their mandates. This term has been affirmatively interpreted to authorise the use of force for purposes of mandate implementation. As is recalled above, this was particularly the language used when the UNSC authorised MONUC in its mandate. On occasion, peacekeeping missions initially authorised to 'take the necessary action, in the areas of deployment of its forces and as it deems within its capabilities' are later authorised to take 'all necessary means [or] measures' when implementing their mandates. As will be seen, these measures are always related to a peacekeeping mission's mandate, and usually relate to the protection civilians element.[46]

[43] UNSC Res 2446 (2018) para 1.
[44] UNSC Res 2446 (2018) para 1.
[45] UNSC Res 2448 (2018) para 38.
[46] See also Haidi Willmot and Ralph Mamiya, 'Mandated to Protect: Security Council Practice on the Protection of Civilians' in Weller (n 18) 385–88.

This practice is evidenced in Resolution 1270 (1999) which established and authorised the United Nations Mission in Sierra Leone (UNAMSIL). Acting under Chapter VII, the UNSC *decided* that UNAMSIL may 'take the necessary action to ensure the security and freedom of movement of its personnel and, within its capabilities and areas of deployment, to afford protection to civilians under imminent threat of physical violence'.[47] Chapter VII was invoked only in paragraph 14 in relation to this mandate. Using the same language, the UNSC then revised UNAMSIL's mandate under Resolution 1289 (2000) to again include authorisation of force for civilian protection.[48] It *authorised* UNAMSIL to 'to take the necessary action to fulfil the additional tasks' and *affirmed* that UNAMSIL may 'take the necessary action to ensure the security and freedom of movement of its personnel and, within its capabilities and areas of deployment, to afford protection to civilians under imminent threat of physical violence'.[49] Chapter VII was again invoked only in paragraph 10 in relation to UNAMSIL's revised mandate. While several subsequent resolutions extending its mandate did not invoke Chapter VII, the UNSC *reiterated* its authorisation in Resolution 1389 (2002) that UNAMSIL was authorised to 'take the necessary action' in line with Resolution 1270 (1999) and Resolution 1289 (2000) and determined the situation in Sierra Leone continued to constitute a threat to international peace and security in the region.[50]

The UNSC also used similar phrasing when it authorised the United Nations Mission of Support in East Timor (UNMISET) under Resolution 1410 (2002) to 'to take the necessary actions, for the duration of its mandate, to fulfil its mandate'.[51] Chapter VII was invoked only in paragraph 6 in relation to the 'take the necessary actions' phrasing. However, in the case of UNMISET, its mandate predominantly concerned law enforcement and the maintenance of security; no protection of civilians element formed part of its mandate.[52] Subsequent resolutions which downscaled UNMISET and extended its mandate however made no mention of Chapter VII or the 'take the necessary actions' phrasing.[53]

The UNSC repeated a similar practice when it established the United Nations Mission in Sudan (UNMIS) in Resolution 1590 (2005). Acting under Chapter VII, the UNSC *decided* to authorise UNMIS to 'take the necessary action, in the areas of deployment of its forces and as it deems within its capabilities' to, among others, protect civilians under imminent threat of physical

[47] UNSC Res 1270 (1999) para 14.
[48] UNSC Res 1289 (2000) para 10.
[49] UNSC Res 1289 (2000) para 10.
[50] UNSC Res 1389 (2002) para 2.
[51] UNSC Res 1410 (2002) para 6.
[52] UNSC Res 1410 (2002) para 2(a)–(c).
[53] See for example UNSC Res 1473 (2003); UNSC Res 1480 (2003); UNSC Res 1543 (2004); UNSC Res 1573 (2004).

violence.[54] Chapter VII was invoked only in relation to its authorisation of force in paragraph 16 of the resolution. UNMIS was later authorised under Resolution 1706 (2006) to 'use all necessary means, in the areas of deployment of its forces and as it deems within its capabilities' to implement its mandate, again among others, where the protection of civilians was concerned.[55] Chapter VII was similarly invoked only in relation to its authorisation of force in paragraph 12 of the resolution. In 2007, when the UNSC established the African Union-United Nations Hybrid Operation in Darfur (UNAMID) in Sudan under Resolution 1769 (2007), it again opted to use the terms 'take the necessary action, in the areas of deployment of its forces and as it deems within its capabilities' when authorising UNAMID to use force. The authorisation given to UNAMID was similar to UNMIS in that it was also for purposes of protecting civilians.[56] Chapter VII was again invoked only in paragraph 15 in relation to this mandate.

A similar practice was seen with Resolution 1990 (2011) when the UNSC established the United Nations Interim Security Force for Abyei (UNISFA) in Sudan.[57] Acting under Chapter VII, the UNSC authorised UNISFA to 'within its capabilities and its area of deployment to take the necessary actions' to, among others, protect civilians in the Abyei Area under imminent threat of physical violence, from incursions by unauthorised elements, and ensure security in the area.[58] Notably, Chapter VII was invoked specifically in paragraph 3 outlining the protection of civilians mandate. The authorisation was on numerous occasions extended and expanded.

In contrast, the UNSC has on other occasions preferred to authorise UN peacekeeping missions by explicitly referring to 'all necessary means [or] measures' phrasing. For example, under Resolution 1778 (2007) the UNSC established the United Nations Mission in the Central African Republic and Chad (MINURCAT). It was given a protection of civilians mandate and was also mandated to contribute to human rights and the rule of law in Chad and the CAR.[59] Subsequently the UNSC under Resolution 1861 (2009), acting under Chapter VII, authorised MINURCAT to 'take all necessary measures within

[54] UNSC Res 1590 (2005) para 16(i); Wendy Fenton and Sean Loughna, 'The Search for Common Ground: Civil-Military Coordination and the Protection of Civilians in South Sudan' (2013) Humanitarian Policy Group Working Paper 8 who acknowledge further that there was also explicit authorisation to use 'deadly force' reinforced under the Rules of Engagement. On this point, see Victoria Holt and Glyn Taylor, 'Protecting Civilians in the Context of UN Peacekeeping Operations: Success, Setbacks and Remaining Challenges' Independent Study Jointly Commissioned by the Department of Peacekeeping Operations and the Office for the Coordination of Humanitarian Affairs (United Nations 2009) 323.

[55] UNSC Res 1706 (2006) para 12(a). See also UN Doc S/PV.5520 (2006) 2–4 on the United Kingdom position.

[56] UNSC Res 1769 (2007) paras 15(a)(i)–(ii).

[57] UNSC Res 1990 (2011) para 1.

[58] UNSC Res 1990 (2011) para 3(a)–(f).

[59] UNSC Res 1778 (2007) para 2.

its capabilities and area of operation' to fulfil its mandate relating to, among others, the protection of civilians and facilitating the delivery of humanitarian aid.[60] In the same resolution, it was also authorised to 'take all necessary measures' to contribute to the creation of a more secure environment and to extract civilians and humanitarian workers in danger.[61] MINURCAT's mandate was subsequently extended by Resolutions 1913 (2010), 1922 (2010), and finally by 1923 (2010) outside of Chapter VII.[62] It was therefore not authorised to use 'all necessary measures' beyond Resolution 1861 (2009).[63]

The UNSC followed the same route when it established the United Nations Mission in the Republic of South Sudan (UNMISS). Under Resolution 1996 (2011), UNMISS was authorised under a robust Chapter VII mandate to use 'all necessary means, within the limits of its capacity and in the areas where its units are deployed, to carry out its protection mandate'.[64] Part of its protection mandate included the protection of civilians under imminent threat of physical violence.[65] Seventeen subsequent resolutions have since extended or expanded the UNMISS mandate; all of them invoking Chapter VII and all explicitly *authorising* UNMISS 'to use all necessary means' particularly to carry out its protection mandate.[66] In addition, Under UNSC Resolution 2304 (2016), the UNSC established a Regional Protection Force to form part of UNMISS which was also *authorised* to 'use all necessary means, including undertaking robust action where necessary and actively patrolling' to among others, facilitate conditions for safe and free movement, engage any actor that is credibly found to be preparing attacks or engages in attacks against the UN or civilians.[67]

Finally, the UNSC repeated its practice of explicit authorisation when it established the United Nations Multidimensional Integrated Stabilisation Mission in Mali (MINUSMA).[68] Under Resolution 2100 (2013) MINUSMA was authorised to 'take all necessary measures' (along with French troops) to carry out its mandate, and particularly for the protection of civilians.[69] That

[60] UNSC Res 1861 (2009) para 7(a).

[61] UNSC Res 1861 (2009) para 7(b).

[62] UNSC Res 1913 (2010) para 1; UNSC Res 1922 (2010) para 1; UNSC Res 1923 (2010) para 1.

[63] Chad had requested a reduction of its military component and the extension of MINURCAT was done on a roller-over basis. See UN Doc S/2010/115 (2010) and UN Doc S/2010/129 (2010).

[64] UNSC Res 1996 (2011) para 4.

[65] UNSC Res 1996 (2011) para 3(b)(v).

[66] UNSC Res 2057 (2012) para 5; UNSC Res 2109 (2013) para 8; UNSC Res 2155 (2014) para 4; UNSC Res 2187 (2014) para 4; UNSC Res 2223 (2015) para 4; UNSC Res 2241 (2015) para 4; UNSC Res 2252 (2015) para 8; UNSC Res 2302 (2016) para 1; UNSC Res 2304 (2016) para 4; UNSC Res 2326 (2016) para 2; UNSC Res 2392 (2017) para 1; UNSC Res 2406 (2018) para 7; UNSC Res 2459 (2019) para 7; UNSC Res 2567 (2021) para 3; UNSC Res 2625 (2022) para 3; UNSC Res 2677 (2023) para 3; UNSC Res 2729 (2024) para 3.

[67] UNSC Res 2304 (2016) para 10.

[68] UNSC Res 2100 (2013) para 7.

[69] UNSC Res 2100 (2013) paras 16, 17.

authorisation was explicitly extended under Chapter VII in nine subsequent resolutions until MINUSMA was eventually terminated in Resolution 2690 (2023).[70]

If one compares the peacekeeping missions outlined above to other missions not established or authorised under Chapter VII, or those without explicit authorisation to use force to implement their mandate, it is clear that the UNSC authorises these missions based on several specific elements and almost always includes a protection of civilians mandate.[71] In so doing, the UNSC has consistently established and authorised these missions under Chapter VII, explicitly determining the situation to be a threat to peace and security, and has employed either the phrasing 'all necessary means [or] measures' or 'take the necessary action'.[72] Where these missions are not initially established under Chapter VII, they are on occasion later given mandates under this chapter.

IV. 'MANDATED AUTHORISATION' OF FORCE

An assessment of the extensive UNSC practice of authorising force to peacekeeping missions suggests that when such authorisation is given, it takes one of two forms (on occasion, elements from both coexist). The first form of authorisation has been addressed above. In such a form, the UNSC authorises force using the 'all necessary means [or] measures' or 'take the necessary action/measures' phrasing within a resolution's operative paragraphs. In addition, these resolutions determine the respective situation to constitute a threat to international peace and security and invoke Chapter VII.

A second form of authorisation, termed 'mandated authorisation' differs to the extent that while the authorising resolutions determine a situation constitutes a threat to international peace and security and invoke Chapter VII, they do not contain operative clauses explicitly authorising force. Consequently, no

[70] UNSC Res 2164 (2014) paras 11, 12; UNSC Res 2227 (2015) paras 12, 13; UNSC Res 2295 (2016) paras 14, 17; UNSC Res 2364 (2017) paras 15, 18; UNSC Res 2423 (2018) paras 24, 32; UNSC Res 2480 (2019) paras 17, 19; UNSC Res 2351 (2020) paras 16, 18; UNSC Res 2584 (2021) paras 17, 20; UNSC Res 2640 (2022) paras 15, 17. UNSC Res 2690 (2023) para 1 terminated MINUSMA at Mali's request.

[71] These missions take the form of protection forces, multidimensional integrated stabilisation missions, operations and stabilisation missions. Examples of these not mandated under Chapter VII or not including a protection of civilians mandate include: the United Nations Mission in the Central African Republic (MINURCA); the United Nations Assistance Mission for Iraq (UNAMI); the United Nations Integrated Mission in Timor-Leste (UNMIT); the United Nations Mission in Côte d'Ivoire (MINUCI); the United Nations Mission in Haiti (UNMIH); and the United Nations Support Mission in Haiti (UNSMIH). See also United Nations Interim Force in Lebanon (UNIFIL), although UNSC Res 1701 (2006) *authorised* UNIFIL to 'take the necessary action in areas of deployment of its forces and as it deems within its capabilities' to among others 'ensure that its area of operations is not utilized for hostile activities of any kind, to resist attempts by forceful means to prevent it from discharging its duties' and 'protect civilians under imminent threat of physical violence', it was not adopted under Chapter VII. See UN Doc S/PV.5511 (2006) 9 (Qatar).

[72] See also Sheeran (n 1) 367.

usual phrasing of take 'all necessary means [or] measures' or 'take the necessary action' is present. Instead, the authorisation to use force is derived from a peacekeeping mission's mandate.[73] Mandates authorising the use of force, therefore, usually include the 'protection of civilians language formulation'.[74] This formulation is often expressed as 'the protection of civilians under imminent threat' and 'within capabilities and areas of deployment'.[75]

A. Resolution 1509 (2003) | UNMIL

In 2003 the UNSC established the United Nations Mission in Liberia (UNMIL) under Resolution 1509 (2003). UNMIL's establishment was first called for under Resolution 1497 (2003) to take over from the Economic Community of West African States' ECOMIL deployment in Liberia. UNMIL was to consist of up to 15,000 UN military personnel and was to support peace agreements in Liberia following ECOMIL's enforcement action in the country. In Resolution 1509 (2003), the UNSC determined that the situation in Liberia continued to constitute a threat to peace and security and to the stability of the West African sub-region. UNMIL was established under Chapter VII and mandated to, among others, support the implementation of ceasefire agreements, carry out a Disarmament, Demobilisation, Reintegration and Reconciliation (DDRR) programme and protect civilians under imminent threat of physical violence.[76]

Several of the objectives outlined under UNMIL's mandate were of a particularly forceful nature.[77] Despite this and even though UNMIL was to assume several ECOMIL tasks, Resolution 1509 (2003) lacked any reference to 'all necessary means [or] measures'.[78]

It is worth noting here that when UNMIL was first deployed, it was far below that envisaged by Resolution 1509 (2003), with only a third of its initial

[73] As Blokker notes, '[w]hen examining these operations' authority to use force, it is noteworthy that two resolutions (1542 concerning MINUSTAH (Haiti) and 1561 concerning UNMIL (Liberia)) do not at all refer to such authority, even though they explicitly refer to Chapter VII and even though their mandates appear to require the possibility to use force' (footnote omitted). See Niels Blokker, 'The Security Council and the Use of Force: On Recent Practice' in Niels Blokker and Nico Schrijver (eds), *The Security Council and the Use of Force: Theory and Reality – A Need for Change?*' (Marinus Nijhoff Publishers 2005) 20. See, however, fn 64 in which Blokker acknowledges that both resolutions lack an (explicit) reference for the authorisation to use force. See also Willmot and Mamiya (n 46) 387–88.

[74] UNSC Res 1509 (2003) para 3(j); UNSC Res 1542 (2004) para 7(I)(f).

[75] See also Willmot and Mamiya (n 46) 387–88.

[76] UNSC Res 1509 (2003) paras 1, 3(j). See Blokker (n 73) 101 who notes that '[t]he growing complexity of the mandates of peacekeeping operations in recent years has meant that rules of engagement now need to reflect very accurately the circumstances under which force may be used beyond self-defence'.

[77] Sloan (n 1) 222.

[78] Sloan (n 1) 222.

size being deployed.[79] Moreover, UNMIL's mandate was interpreted narrowly to exclude the use of force beyond self-defence. This was a critical factor which compromised UNMIL's willingness to engage in forceful action even for purposes of protecting civilians.[80] Even though UNMIL did not make actual use of much force in implementing its mandate, a question remained whether Resolution 1509 (2003) authorised UNMIL's use of force (especially given it determined the situation a threat to peace and security and invoked Chapter VII in relation to UNMIL's mandate).

The position was well summarised by the UN Legal Counsel at the time. Pointing to the fact that the UNSC had both made an Article 39 determination and invoked Chapter VII in the resolution, the legal counsel indicated the UNSC was clearly exercising its powers under Chapter VII.[81] Acknowledging the fact that the resolution did not contain the usual phrasing of 'all necessary measures' or 'take the necessary measures', the legal counsel added that whether the UNSC authorised force depended on the content of the resolution as well as the actual intention of the UNSC.[82] Noteworthy is that the Counsel also expressed the opinion that the mere fact that the usual phrasing to authorise force was not employed did not mean that the UNSC in fact had not authorised force.[83] Interpreting the words of the resolution on an 'ordinary and natural meaning', in light of the object and purpose and in context of the resolution, including the history and adoption of the resolution, the legal counsel concluded that '[i]t is evident that the [UNSC] fully intended … to authorise UNMIL to use armed force, otherwise than in self-defence'.[84]

In explaining his interpretation, the legal counsel also indicated that UNMIL would not effectively have been able to discharge certain objectives without resorting to armed force – pointing specifically to paragraph 3(j) of the resolution concerning the protection of UN personnel and facilities, ensuring security and freedom of movement of personnel, and the protection of civilians under imminent threat of physical violence.[85] Moreover, the Counsel considered the UN Secretary-General's concept of operations for UNMIL preceding the adoption of Resolution 1509 (2003) as reasonably pointing towards UNMIL being able to resort to force under a robust mandate.[86] On the whole, Resolution 1509 (2003) can affirmatively be regarded as having authorised the use of force

[79] Sloan (n 1) 222–23.
[80] Sloan (n 1) 224.
[81] UN, 'Note to the Under-Secretary-General of the Department of Peacekeeping Operations, United Nations; (2003) United Nations Juridical Yearbook Part Two, Chapter VI (United Nations Publication Sales NO E.07.V1) 538–40 as quoted in Sloan (n 1) 225–26.
[82] Sloan (n 1) 225–26.
[83] Sloan (n 1) 225–26.
[84] Sloan (n 1) 226.
[85] Sloan (n 1) 226; UNSC Res 1509 (2003) para 3(j).
[86] Sloan (n 1) 226.

beyond self-defence given a holistic interpretation and that it contained both an Article 39 determination and Chapter VII invocation.[87]

What however remained uncertain was whether UNMIL's authorisation to use force was extended under subsequent resolutions. In Resolution 1561 (2004), the UNSC extended UNMIL's mandate until 19 September 2005.[88] Although its preamble recalled Resolution 1509 (2003), Resolution 1561 (2004) contained no Article 39 determination nor did it invoke Chapter VII. On this basis, it is unlikely subsequent resolutions not adopted under Chapter VII extended authorisation of force. However, when the UNSC extended UNMIL's mandate beyond 19 September 2005, it did so by explicitly invoking Chapter VII and consistently determining the situation in Liberia continued to constitute a threat to international peace and security. The UNSC therefore, extending UNMIL's mandate originally provided for in Resolution 1509 (2003), evidently also extended its authorisation to use force in 16 subsequent resolutions until its eventual termination in March 2018.[89]

B. Resolutions 1542 (2004) and 2350 (2017) | MINUSTAH and MINUJUSTH

In 2004, the UNSC adopted Resolution 1542 (2004) establishing and mandating the United Nations Stabilisation Mission in Haiti (MINUSTAH). MINUSTAH was established following the Multinational Interim Force (MIF) which was deployed to Haiti under Resolution 1529 (2004). Under Resolution 1542 (2004), authority was to be transferred from the MIF to MINUSTAH by June 2004.[90] The fact that Resolution 1542 (2004) mandated the use of force by MINUSTAH was evident in the way its mandate was laid out in the resolution. Paragraph 7, section I in particular set out a broad mandate under Chapter VII for, among others, protecting civilians under imminent threat of physical violence.[91]

What is important to note is that the invocation of Chapter VII was specifically for MINUSTAH's mandate under paragraph 7 section I, and not

[87] Blokker (n 73) 20; Sloan (n 1) 227–28.

[88] UNSC Res 1561 (2004).

[89] See UNSC Res 1626 (2005) para 1; UNSC Res 1667 (2006) para 1; UNSC Res 1712 (2006) para 1; UNSC Res 1750 (2007) para 1; UNSC Res 1777 (2007) para 1; UNSC Res 1836 (2008) para 1; UNSC Res 1885 (2009) para 1; UNSC Res 1938 (2010) para 1; UNSC Res 2008 (2011) para 1; UNSC Res 2066 (2012) para 1; UNSC Res 2116 (2013) para 1; UNSC Res 2176 (2014) para 1. From UNSC Res 2190 (2014) paras 9, 10, the UNSC explicitly outlined UNMIL's protection of civilians mandate, which it extended in UNSC Res 2239 (2015) paras 9, 10; UNSC Res 2308 (2016) para 1; UNSC Res 2333 (2016) paras 10, 11 (in which the UNSC did not explicitly determine a threat to peace and security but referred to its '*mindful* of its primary responsibilities' phrasing).

[90] UNSC Res 1542 (2004) para 1.

[91] UNSC Res 1542 (2004) para 7(I).

sections II and III.[92] Section I specifically mandated tasks relating to the establishment of a secure and stable environment, including restoring and maintaining the rule of law and public order, protecting UN personnel and facilities, and protecting civilians under imminent threat of physical violence. From this mandate, it was clear that MINUSTAH was authorised to perform certain objectives that may have required the use of force beyond self-defence, although the resolution did not contain the terms 'all necessary means [or] measures'.[93] That MINUSTAH indeed resorted to force was confirmed when it began implementing its mandate. MINUSTAH supported the Haitian National Police (HNP) and engaged in joint operations of a confrontational nature with it, including apprehension of gang members and disarmament operations.[94]

The fact that MINUSTAH was authorised to use force was therefore attributable to its explicit mandate, combined with the fact that it was explicitly given under Chapter VII.[95] Moreover, it is also reasonable to conclude that all resolutions extending MINUSTAH's mandate also extended its authorisation to use force. This is particularly evident since all resolutions extending its mandate referenced its authorisation under Resolution 1542 (2004), determined that the situation in Haiti continued to constitute a threat to peace and security, and invoked Chapter VII.[96]

From 2017 onwards and with the adoption of Resolution 2350 (2017), the UNSC established a follow-up mission, the United Nations Mission for Justice Support in Haiti (MINUJUSTH). Under Resolution 2350 (2017), MINUSTAH's authority was to be transferred to MINUJUSTH. MINUJUSTH was *authorised* to 'use all necessary means to carry out its mandate to support and develop the HNP' and *further authorised* to 'protect civilians under imminent threat of physical violence, within its capabilities and areas of deployment'.[97] This explicit authorisation of force was renewed under Resolution 2410 (2018) and Resolution 2466 (2019), with the exception that in the latter resolution the UNSC did not explicitly indicate a threat to peace and security but instead used the 'mindful of its primary responsibility for the maintenance of international peace and security' phrasing.[98]

[92] Sloan (n 1) 248.

[93] Sloan (n 1) 248, 254–55.

[94] Sloan (n 1) 249–52. See also UN Doc S/2004/908 (2004) paras 15–16; UN Doc S/2005/313 (2005) paras 14–17; UN Doc S/2005/631 (2005) paras 23–25.

[95] Sloan (n 1) 255. See also Blokker (n 73) 20.

[96] See in this regard UNSC Res 1576 (2004) para 1; UNSC Res 1601 (2005) para 1; UNSC Res 1608 (2005) para 1; UNSC Res 1658 (2006) para 1; UNSC Res 1702 (2006) para 1; UNSC Res 1743 (2007) para 1; UNSC Res 1780 (2007) para 1; UNSC Res 1840 (2008) para 1; UNSC Res 1892 (2009) para 1; UNSC Res 1944 (2010) para 1; UNSC Res 2012 (2011) para 1; UNSC Res 2070 (2012) para 1; UNSC Res 2119 (2013) para 1; UNSC Res 2180 (2014) para 1; UNSC Res 2243 (2015) para 1; UNSC Res 2313 (2016) para 1; UNSC Res 2350 (2017) para 1.

[97] UNSC Res 2350 (2017) paras 1, 12, 13.

[98] UNSC Res 2410 (2018) paras 1, 14–15; UNSC Res 2466 (2019), paras 1, 9–10.

C. The Nature of Mandated Authorisation

Given that mandated authorisation differs in so far as the UNSC does not use explicit language to authorise force, it is prudent to outline some of its limitations. First, mandated authorisation is attributable only to UN peacekeeping missions. A similar form of authorisation to Member States or regional organisations is difficult to reconcile in the absence of explicit temporal limitations to mandates and the requirement that the UNSC maintain some form of control over operations it authorises. Unlike authorisation to Member States or regional organisations, UN peacekeeping forces remain under the direct control of the UN.

Additionally, from the practice of the UNSC already analysed, it has yet not adopted a resolution that can be definitely regarded as having mandated the use of force any Member State or regional organisation in the same manner it has mandated force to peacekeeping missions. And second, mandated authorising resolutions have included a closed list of objectives that a peacekeeping mission undertakes. These always contain an element of civilian protection. Additionally, these mandates often include objectives such as guarding key installations, protecting UN personnel and facilities, and DDRR tasks. Although these objectives in themselves suggest that the use of force is envisaged, they can only be interpreted affirmatively authorising the use of force where resolutions setting out these mandates also include an Article 39 determination and a Chapter VII invocation.

V. CONCLUSION

The chapter has examined the explicit authorisation of force to UN peacekeeping missions across some 60 resolutions that have either established or extended such authorisation. Where peacekeeping missions are concerned, authorisation takes two forms. First, either the UNSC explicitly authorises the use of force by making an Article 39 determination, including a Chapter VII invocation and using explicit language in operative paragraphs. Alternatively, the UNSC, albeit only ever on two occasions, has authorised the use of force by peacekeeping missions through their mandates. This *mandated authorisation* authorises the use of force not by using the term ‘all necessary means’, but by specifying objectives to a peacekeeping mission that on a reasonable interpretation cannot preclude the use of force for the successful accomplishment of that peacekeeping mission’s tasks.

Where explicit authorisation concerns, UNSC practice shows two particular patterns. The first is authorisation through the ‘all necessary means [or] measures’ phrasing, a similar practice of how it authorises force to Member States and regional organisations. The second manner of authorisation employs the phrasing ‘take the necessary actions’. Moreover, where the UNSC employs this phrase, it always invokes Chapter VII in that paragraph, and not generally under its preamble. In addition, the mandate under which a peacekeeping mission is authorised to 'take the necessary actions' is almost always tied to the protection of civilians from imminent or physical violence.

The UNSC employed this practice when it established and authorised force to UNAMSIL (1999),[99] MONUC (2000),[100] UNMISET (2002),[101] UNMIS (2005),[102] UNAMID (2007)[103] and UNISFA (2011).[104] On a number of occasions, it extended such authorisation however under the take 'all necessary means [or] measures' phrasing. From 2009 with the establishment of MINURCAT, the UNSC has preferred to use the term 'all necessary means [or] measures' when establishing or extending authorisation of force. Hence, when it established MONUSCO (2010) UNMISS (2011), MINUSMA (2013), MINUSCA (2014) and MINUJUSTH (2017), it consistently authorised these missions to use 'all necessary means [or] measures'. Exceptionally, when it established UNISFA in 2011, the UNSC authorised it to 'take the necessary action'.

Where mandated authorisation concerns, only two examples have been noted. These concern UNMIL established in 2003 and MINUSTAH established in 2004. As noted above in relation to mandated authorisation, caution should always be employed when interpreting these resolutions. The only reason why they can definitively be interpreted to have authorised the use of force was not solely because it is reasonably foreseeable that their robust mandates required the use of force, but because these mandates were explicitly given under Chapter VII and after the UNSC had determined a situation to be a threat to peace and security.

When examining authorisation to UN peacekeeping missions generally, it may seem easier to deduce which missions in fact have not been authorised to use force, at least not beyond self-defence. These missions either do not invoke Chapter VII or do not have a robust mandate indicating objectives that may reasonably require the use of force. With that said, however, the fact that a UN peacekeeping mission is given a mandate under Chapter VII does not necessitate the conclusion that force is automatically authorised.[105] Only by interpreting the mandate of a UN peacekeeping mission, a resolution's provisions holistically, the context of its adoption, and on a case-by-case basis, can a more definitive answer be given.

Where UNSC practice of mandate extension concerns, the following should also be noted. Authorisation of force to UN peacekeeping missions can always be traced to one specific resolution (an initial authorising resolution).

[99] UNSC Res 1270 (1999) para 14.
[100] UNSC Res 1291 (2000) para 8.
[101] UNSC Res 1410 (2002) para 6.
[102] UNSC Res 1590 (2005) para 16.
[103] UNSC Res 1769 (2007) para 15.
[104] UNSC Res 1990 (2011) para 3.
[105] Sheeran, 'The Use of Force in Peacekeeping Operations' (n 1) 365.

On occasion, and depending on the respective situations, the UNSC has established UN peacekeeping missions without invoking Chapter VII. Thereafter, changing situations on the ground may motivate the UNSC to provide a more robust mandate under Chapter VII.

There are well over one hundred resolutions extending Chapter VII mandates to various UN peacekeeping missions. The UNSC has however not been as consistent in extending peacekeeping missions' authorisation of force as it has when extending authorisation of force to Member States and regional organisations. The UNSC has habitually extended authorisation in two different ways. It either adopts a resolution under Chapter VII and merely *decides* to extend the mandate of a mission without again referencing the use of 'all necessary means [or] measures' language as part of the mandate extension. Such an extension of the authorisation of force does not present problems since these resolutions invoke Chapter VII and contain an Article 39 determination.

However, a second manner in which the UNSC extends authorisation of force under a UN peacekeeping mission's mandate is more complicated. The UNSC has on occasion adopted a resolution extending a peacekeeping mission's mandate by solely referring to its mandate. Most problematic is when these resolutions do not contain an explicit Chapter VII invocation. Consequently, it remains uncertain as to whether the UNSC intended to, beyond extending the mission's mandate, also extend the authorisation for it to use force. Be that as it may, it would be difficult to reconcile the extension of a peacekeeping mission's mandate with an automatic extension of its authorisation to use force, particularly where there is no explicit Chapter VII invocation. In addition, situations within which UN peacekeeping mission function may change over time. While the continued presence of mission may be merited, the continued authorisation of force beyond self-defence should not be assumed.

6

The (In)admissibility of Implicit UN Security Council Authorisation

I. INTRODUCTION

THE CHARTER OF the United Nations (UN Charter) neither in Chapter VII nor VII indicates that authorisation of force by the United Nations Security Council (UNSC) should be explicit.[1] Nor does the UN Charter indicate any specific form that authorising resolutions should take. The four preceding chapters have shown extensive UNSC practice favouring explicit authorisation. Authorising resolutions usually determine or reaffirm a threat to international peace and security, invoke Chapter VII or VIII, and include specific authorising language in their operative paragraphs. Moreover, authorising resolutions usually include temporal limitations alongside (albeit limited) reporting requirements.

Be that as it may, there have been no less than four situations since 1990 in which either States or scholars have argued that one or several resolutions in combination have authorised force 'implicitly'.[2]

[1] Corten provides one of the most comprehensive treatments of implicit authorisation to date. See Olivier Corten, *The Law Against War: The Prohibition on the Use of Force in Contemporary International Law* (2nd edn, Hart Publishing 2021) 348–98.

[2] Implicit authorisation has been addressed widely in scholarship. See broadly Corten, *The Law Against War* (n 1) 348–98; Alexander Orakhelashvili, *Collective Security* (Oxford University Press 2011) 263–64; 299–300; Ugo Villani, 'The Security Council's Authorisation of Enforcement Action by Regional Organisations' (2002) 6 *Max Planck Yearbook of United Nations Law* 535; Erika de Wet, *The Chapter VII Powers of the United Nations Security Council* (Hart Publishing 2004) 294–308; Ian Johnstone, 'When the Security Council is Divided: Imprecise Authorisations, Implied Mandates, and the Unreasonable Veto' in Marc Weller (ed), *The Oxford Handbook of the Use of Force in International Law* (Oxford University Press 2015) 234–48; Jules Lobel and Michael Ratner, 'Bypassing the Security Council: Ambiguous Authorisations to Use Force, Cease-Fires and the Iraqi Inspection Regime' (1999) 93 *American Journal of International Law* 124; Michael Wood and Eran Sthoeger, *The UN Security Council and International Law* (Cambridge University Press 2022) 122–26, 143–45; Anthony Clark Arend and Robert J Beck, *International Law and the Use of Force* (Routledge 1993) 62; Ademola Abass, *Regional Organisations and the Development of Collective Security: Beyond Chapter VIII of the UN Charter* (Hart 2004) 52–57; Christine Gray, *International Law and the Use of Force* (Oxford University Press 2018) 361–77; Erika de Wet, 'Article 42' in Bruno Simma et al (eds), *The Charter of the United Nations: A Commentary* (4th edn, Vol II, Oxford University Press 2024) 1706–11; Patrice Ekomodi Totshingo, 'L'autorisation de recourir à la force accordée par le Conseil de sécurité des Nations Unies' (University of Montreal 2009) 85–148.

This chapter considers the nature of implicit authorisation. It departs by examining the very admissibility of implicit authorisation under the UN Charter and its system of collective security. In so doing, it outlines some doctrinal debates in scholarship. It then examines four situations and eight corresponding resolutions in which implicit authorisation has been argued. The chapter ultimately argues against such a form of authorisation.

II. THE NATURE OF IMPLICIT AUTHORISATION

Three terms are commonly used in literature to indicate the absence of explicit authorisation: 'implicit authorisation', 'implied authorisation' and 'presumed authorisation'. In context, all three terms are used to refer to a lack of explicit authorisation.[3] A key distinction is that in the case of implicit and implied authorisation, the existence of a UNSC resolution is a prerequisite. 'Implicit' and 'implied' authorisation therefore rely on the interpretation of a resolution to refer to a decision that may be suggested (or encouraged), but not directly articulated.[4] On the other hand, 'presumed' authorisation considers instances of the use of force to have been authorised not necessarily or directly by a formal decision taken by the UNSC but, rather, based on the behaviour of the UNSC itself.[5] The most notable instances favouring presumed authorisation concern situations where States or regional organisations act militarily and the UNSC remains silent as to whether such action should be supported or condemned.[6] While this form of authorisation is not based on a formal decision reflected in a resolution of the UNSC, it nonetheless informs and contributes to the debate at hand.[7] In the context of this chapter, all three forms of authorisation are considered collectively, given they all represent a lack of explicit authorisation of force.[8]

[3] Corten, *The Law Against War* (n 1) 353 refers to 'presumed authorisation'.

[4] The Oxford English Dictionary (OED) defines the word 'implicit' contextually as 'implied though not plainly expressed, naturally or necessarily involved in, or capable of being inferred from'. In contrast, the word 'presumed' is defined by the OED as 'assumed, esp. in advance or without proof … anticipated, expected'.

[5] Corten, *The Law Against War* (n 1) 353–54. See also the terminology used in Johnstone, 'When the Security Council is Divided' (n 2) 234, 238. See also Totshingo, 'L'autorisation de recourir à la force' (n 1) 85–86.

[6] Corten, *The Law Against War* (n 1) 354–55. See also Villani, 'The Security Council's Authorisation' (n 2) 549–551, while acknowledging the possibility of implicit authorisation, Villani however adds that '[i]t is both clear and unequivocal, such an authorization cannot be gleaned merely through the silence or inactivity of the Security Council'.

[7] The notion of silence as authorisation has similarly been rejected. See Corten, *The Law Against War* (n 1) 355; see also Villani, 'The Security Council's Authorisation' (n 2) 549–50.

[8] See however the point by Blokker that cases of implicit authorisation find legal debate in the weight attributable to Article 2(4) and the legitimacy of bypassing the UNSC for humanitarian or other reasons. See Niels Blokker, 'Is the Authorisation Authorised? Powers and Practice of the UN Security Council to Authorise the Use of Force by "Coalitions of the Able and Willing"' (2000) 11 (3) *European Journal of International Law* 546.

III. THE INCOMPATIBILITY AND INADMISSIBILITY OF IMPLICIT AUTHORISATION

As mentioned, the provisions of the UN Charter pertaining to UNSC authorisation do not expressly dictate the form and character such authorisation should take.[9] The need for explicit authorisation also did not arise during the Dumbarton Oaks proposal and the subsequent discussions surrounding the adoption of the UN Charter. Combined with the fact that implicit (and even retroactive) authorisation was argued on at least four occasions, the consequences have given rise to complex debates about the very compatibility and admissibility of such authorisation with both the UN Charter and broader State practice.

Corten points to five factors which argue in favour of explicit authorisation. Two of these should be noted here. The first regards the 'institutional logic' of the UNSC whereby a resolution requires the affirmative (explicit) votes of nine UNSC members, provided no veto is used.[10] This in itself suggests explicit action by the UNSC where decision making concerns, given that an affirmative vote is precluded in cases of an abstention or absence.[11] Taken further, the requirement of an explicit vote presupposes that at the time of voting, each UNSC Member State understands the nature and extent of a decision voted upon.[12] In this regard, it has also been submitted that authorisation itself must be established *at the time* the resolution is adopted, thereby precluding an implicit justification of authorisation after the fact.[13] In the same manner, it may be argued that the UN Charter, which requires an affirmative vote (may) also require explicit action where substantive decisions of the UNSC are concerned. It therefore remains questionable why some UNSC decisions (and the expression of these decisions) must be taken explicitly, and why the possibility would exist that other decisions may be taken implicitly.

Second, Corten highlights another factor against implicit authorisation in so far as delegated enforcement action requires oversight. It is well accepted that while the UNSC may delegate the use of force, the UN Charter's system of collective security requires the UNSC retain a degree of control over delegated enforcement action.[14] Moreover and as Corten notes, the limits to delegated

[9] Corten, *The Law Against War* (n 1) 353–54.

[10] Arts 27(2) and (3) explicitly require an 'affirmative vote' by UNSC members. Art 27(1) regards procedural matters, whereas art 27(3) refers to 'all other matters'; Corten, *The Law Against War* (n 1) 393.

[11] Corten, *The Law Against War* (n 1) 393; see also Rosalyn Higgins et al, *Oppenheim's International Law United Nations, Volume I* (Oxford University Press 2017) 375.

[12] Corten, *The Law Against War* (n 1) 393.

[13] Corten, *The Law Against War* (n 1) 393.

[14] Corten, *The Law Against War* (n 1) 393. De Wet, *The Chapter VII Powers* (n 2) 265 highlights the necessity of overall command and control by the UNSC by saying that despite the UNSC's power to delegate enforcement action, it does not mean that it could delegate ultimate control over a military operation. Danesh Sarooshi, *The United Nations and the Development of Collective Security: The*

enforcement action requiring UNSC control imply 'the existence of certain guarantee mechanisms', in particular, the reporting requirement of measures taken under such delegated enforcement action.[15] These guarantee mechanisms arguably become redundant if the UNSC has not clearly specified the scope of its authorisation and to what extent entities it has authorised may use force.[16] Naturally, arguments in which States base their actions on implicit authorisation (on occasion with little limitation) would arguably go against the UNSC's primary responsibility over international peace and security.[17]

Another line of argument supporting explicit authorisation derives its reasoning from the UN Charter's support for the peaceful settlement of disputes. Accordingly, the suggestion put forward is that the wording of Articles 33 and 42 support the notion of the need for explicit authorisation.[18] More specifically, the presumption of peaceful means of dispute settlement in the UN Charter's purposes and principles suggest that implicit authorisation of force should be disfavoured and explicit authorisation of force should be narrowly interpreted.[19] It has been submitted that when the UNSC authorises the use of force, it applies a two-staged judgment. The UNSC first determines the existence of a threat to international peace and security. It must then, at the least consider Article 41 measures before authorising force. This two-stage judgment suggests that UNSC decisions need to be explicit. Since force is to be used only as a last resort, the procedural requirements of Article 42 may require the UNSC to only authorise the use of force clearly and specifically.[20] Combined with Article 33's provisions seeking peaceful settlement of disputes, and the principle that force be used only as a last resort, explicit authorisation, therefore, would serve as a 'brake on the

Delegation by the UN Security Council of its Chapter VII Powers (Oxford University Press 1999) 209 who also notes that this 'implicit condition of the delegation of powers' by the UNSC was highlighted in Council debates on the adoption of UNSC Res 875 (1993) and subsequently recognised in UNSC Res 917 (1994).

[15] Corten, *The Law Against War* (n 1) 393. Blokker, 'Is the Authorisation Authorised?' (n 2) 561, 564–65; De Wet, *The Chapter VII Powers* (n 2) 272 who notes that reporting has become an overall established procedural practice for monitoring military operations under Chapter VII. Importantly, Blokker notes that reporting does not strictly speaking give the UNSC more control over operations but is meaningful for effective supervision. Blokker also notes in this regard, however, that it is unlikely that coalition states would report on their actions outside the mandate of the UNSC resolution. For this reason, Blokker indicates that it is important that the Secretary-General is also obliged to report on a matter.

[16] Corten, *The Law Against War* (n 1) 393; De Wet, *The Chapter VII Power* (n 2) 269; Sarooshi, *The United Nations and the Development of Collective Security* (n 14) 155.

[17] Corten, *The Law Against War* (n 1) 393; De Wet, *The Chapter VII Powers* (n 2) 268. As Corten notes, 'under such a hypothesis, states intervene militarily without limitation or constraint, which is plainly incompatible with the Charter requirements that confer on the Security Council itself the main responsibility for maintaining international peace and security'. In the same manner, De Wet notes that 'in order for the Security Council to remain in control of a military operation, the use of force must be explicitly recognised in a Security Council resolution'. See also Lobel and Ratner, 'Bypassing the Security Council' (n 2) 128; de Wet, 'Article 42' (n 2) 1707.

[18] Lobel and Ratner, 'Bypassing the Security Council' (n 2) 128.

[19] Lobel and Ratner, 'Bypassing the Security Council' (n 2) 128–29.

[20] Lobel and Ratner, 'Bypassing the Security Council' (n 2) 128.

use of force' ensuring that it is considered only when absolutely necessary, and only when explicitly expressed.[21]

In addition to arguments disfavouring implicit authorisation against the UN Charter, it is worth noting that States have, albeit on only a limited occasion either pronounced on the need for explicit authorisation or rejected assertions favouring implicit authorisation.

Corten points to three specific instances in which these pronouncements have been made. The most notable of these concerned the debates preceding the adoption of General Assembly Resolutions 2625 (XXV) and 3314 (XXIX). These discussions show that several Latin American States pronounced that the use of force under Article 53 required the 'express authorisation' of the UNSC.[22]

State practice rejecting implicit UNSC authorisation of force has, for obvious reasons, been far louder within the UNSC. Rejection of implicit UNSC authorisation has predominantly taken place in the context of existing situations where one or more States have claimed to be acting in pursuit of objectives laid down within previous UNSC resolutions. Four of these situations will be examined further below. It is however prudent to note here that in addition to those situations, the UNSC has in more recent times habitually adopted resolutions expressly excluding force. The reason for this is precisely to ensure that its resolutions cannot be interpreted in favour of any implicit authorisation of force. It would seem that such habit has in part arisen exactly because some of its previous resolutions had been argued as implicitly authorising force.[23]

One such example is that of Resolution 1696 (2006) concerning Iran's nuclear programme. The UNSC, expressing concern that the International Atomic Energy Agency was not satisfied that its nuclear programme was intended exclusively for peaceful purposes, specifically stated it was taking provisional measures explicitly under Article 40.[24] Moreover, in its eighth operative paragraph, the resolution explicitly added that in the event of non-compliance, the UNSC would adopt further measures but only under Article 41.[25] UNSC debates

[21] Lobel and Ratner, 'Bypassing the Security Council' (n 2) 129. See also de Wet, 'Article 42' (n 2) 1706–07.

[22] Corten, *The Law Against War* (n 1) 390, see also 391–94 in relation to the International Coalition for the Responsibility to Protect, 'Report on the General Assembly Plenary Debate on the Responsibility to Protect' (15 September 2009), and also Organisation Internationale de La Francophonie, 'Xe Conférence des chefs d'Etat et de gouvernement des pays ayant le français en partage – Déclaration de Ouagadougou' (27 November 2004) Ouagadougou, Burkina Faso 26–27 novembre 2004' para 80.

[23] See also Sir Nigel Rodley, 'The Future for International Law after Iraq' in Phil Shiner and Andrew Williams (eds), *The Iraq War and International Law* (Hart Publishing 2008) 315–16, 325.

[24] UNSC Res 1696 (2006). The careful constructed Chapter VII invocation reads: '*Acting* under article 40 of Chapter VII of the Charter of the United Nations in order to make mandatory the suspension required by the IAEA.'

[25] UNSC Res 1696 (2006) para 8.

preceding the adoption of the resolution confirm UNSC Members explicitly intended to exclude any interpretation in favour of military measures.[26] These provisions in particular have been observed as a safety net preventing 'implicit' UNSC authorisation of force similar to that which the United States argued justified its actions in Iraq in 2003.[27]

The UNSC regularly repeat this practice in subsequent resolutions addressing Iran and non-proliferation.[28] The UNSC has followed the same approach with the situation in North Korea. Expressing grave concern by North Korea's withdrawal from the Treaty on the Non-Proliferation of Nuclear Weapons, the UNSC in Resolution 1695 (2006) excluded determining the situation a threat to international peace and security and also did not invoke Chapter VII.[29] When North Korea later tested a nuclear device, the UNSC under Resolution 1718 (2006) again refrained from enabling any interpretation of implicit authorisation. Resolution 1718 (2006), although adopted under Chapter VII, explicitly stated that the UNSC was acting under Article 41 and indicated that should additional measures be necessary, 'further decisions will be required'.[30] Subsequently, every UNSC resolution adopted on the situation since has strictly expressed as having been taken under Article 41 when invoking Chapter VII.[31]

Similarly, UNSC Members States' reluctance, particularly that of China and Russia, to accept even the slightest indication of an implicit authorisation of force was evident when the UNSC considered the ongoing civil war in Syria.[32] Both China and Russia have consistently attributed the use of the veto power to a lack of express indication in draft resolutions that military measures were ruled out.[33] In so doing, Russia continues to argue that without such a safety measure of explicitly opting out of military measures, these resolutions may be abusively interpreted as having impliedly authorised force.[34] Such practice arguably only arose after a series of UNSC resolutions were interpreted in favour of implicitly authorising force. No less than four specific situations are regularly cited in this regard, toward which attention may now be directed.

[26] UN Doc S/PV.5500 (2006) 4 (United Kingdom), 5 (China, Russia), 6 (Tanzania), 7 (Argentina).

[27] Gray, *International Law and the Use of Force* (n 2) 384–85.

[28] See for example UNSC Res 1737 (2006); UNSC Res 1747 (2007); UNSC Res 1803 (2008); UNSC Res 1929 (2010); UNSC Res 1984 (2011).

[29] UNSC Res 1695 (2006). Instead, the UNSC merely stated it was 'acting under its special responsibility for the maintenance of international peace and security'.

[30] UNSC Res 1718 (2006). The same approach was taken in subsequent resolutions: UNSC Res 1847 (2009); UNSC Res 1928 (2010); UNSC Res 2087 (2013); UNSC Res 2094 (2013); UNSC Res 2270 (2016); UNSC Res 2321 (2016); UNSC Res 2356 (2017); Gray, *International Law and the Use of Force* (n 2) 383.

[31] See UNSC Res 2371 (2017); UNSC Res 2375 (2017); UNSC Res 2397 (2017); UNSC Res 2407 (2018).

[32] No less than 12 UNSC draft resolutions on the situation in Syria have been vetoed, most of which by Russia, but also a considerable number by China.

[33] See UN Doc S/PV.6627 (2011) 4. See also UN Doc S/PV.6810 (2012) 8.

[34] UN Doc S/PV.6810 (2012) 8.

IV. ALLEGED PRACTICE OF IMPLICIT AUTHORISATION

A. Implicit Authorisation on the Situation in Iraq

Previous chapters have examined the explicit authorisation given to Member States with the adoption of Resolution 678 (1990) to ensure Iraqi withdrawal from Kuwait. However, military operations against Iraq continued for some time, even after it withdrew from Kuwait and the UNSC mandated an inspection regime against it. While over a dozen resolutions were adopted on the situation after Resolution 678 (1990), three resolutions in particular were cited for subsequent military operations against Iraq. The first is that of Resolution 688 (1991), which was later referenced justifying military operations charged with protecting safe havens and patrolling no-fly zones in Iraq. While this resolution stood alone in its supposedly 'implicitly authorising' force, two later resolutions – Resolution 1154 and 1205 were argued as having 'revived' authorisation under Resolution 678 (1990).

i. Resolution 688 (1991) | Safe Havens and No-fly Zones in Iraq

Following Iraq's withdrawal from Kuwait, an internal uprising against the Hussein regime was met with considerable repression by the Iraqi government. The UNSC, albeit hesitant to involve itself in the domestic affairs of a State, adopted Resolution 688 (1991) condemning the Iraqi repression.[35] In response, the United States, United Kingdom and France set up safe havens first in the north of Iraq, and then later in the south, and used force to protect these safe havens. All three States, including others who were part of the campaign, referred to Resolution 688 (1991) as a justification for their actions at the time.[36] When they subsequently established a no-fly zone over Iraq, Gray highlights how these States indicated their actions were 'consistent with', 'in [the] implementation of', 'in support of' and 'pursuant to' Resolution 688 (1991).[37]

The provisions and drafting history of Resolution 688 (1991) however clearly demonstrate it did not authorise any force. Most notably, Resolution 688 (1991) did not invoke Chapter VII. Moreover, the language used in the resolution's operative paragraphs is difficult to reconcile with any authorisation of force. In operative paragraph six the UNSC *appeals* to Member States to *contribute* to humanitarian efforts. The UNSC has never in its operative paragraphs authorised force by *appealing* to Member States and especially not to *contribute* to

[35] UNSC Res 688 (1991).

[36] Phil Shiner, 'The Iraq War, International Law and the Search for Legal Accountability' in Shiner and Williams (n 23) 26.

[37] Gray, *International Law and the Use of Force* (n 2) 362; Gray, 'From Unity to Polarization: International Law and the Use of Force Against Iraq' (2002) 13(1) *European Journal of International Law* 9. See also Corten, *The Law Against War* (n 1) 356; UN Doc S/PV.4008 (1999) 3 and 'No-fly zones: The legal position' (19 February 2001) *BBC*.

humanitarian efforts. Instead, it uses the terms *authorises*, *calls upon*, *decides* or *reaffirms*.

It has also never resorted to equating the ordinary meaning of *contribute* to necessarily be understood as authorising force. Even if one takes the argument presented by the states that their actions had implicitly been authorised on humanitarian grounds, other resolutions that authorised force for such grounds bear remarkable differences. For example, when the UNSC authorised member states to use force for humanitarian purposes in Somalia the following year Resolution 688 (1991) was adopted, it *authorised* Member States to use 'all necessary means' to 'establish as soon as possible a secure environment for humanitarian relief operations'.[38] Similarly, its actions in Rwanda and the Great Lakes Region over the course of the decade used unequivocal language in which it *authorised all necessary means* to achieve specific *humanitarian objectives* which were always set out in the respective resolutions.[39]

The same may be said of all instances in which the UNSC authorised the use of force based on humanitarian grounds in the FRY in that it authorised member states and regional organisations to *facilitate*, *deliver* or *provide assistance* by using *all necessary means*. Resolution 688 (1991) makes no mention of establishing, facilitating, delivering or providing assistance, at least not directly, for humanitarian purposes.

Neither is there any mention in the resolution of safe havens or no-fly zones for the purposes of *contributing* to humanitarian efforts. Consequently, Resolution 688 (1991) contains no reporting obligations nor time frames the UNSC ordinarily imposes alongside its authorisation of force. In such light, it is difficult to maintain any suggestion that Resolution 688 (1991) implicitly authorised force.

UNSC debates at the time support this conclusion. In fact, the use of force was never mentioned during the UNSC meeting preceding the adoption of Resolution 688 (1990), presumably because UNSC members had never contemplated such a possibility.[40] On the contrary, several UNSC Members later expressly rejected the assertion that Resolution 688 (1991) had authorised subsequent military actions over Iraq or condemned the actions in question.[41] By 2001, the United Kingdom had seemingly accepted that Resolution 688 (1991) could not be a basis for resort to force, acknowledging that the 'legal justification for patrolling of the no-fly zones does not rest on Security Council Resolution 688'.[42] Instead, it justified its actions on humanitarian necessity and has

[38] UNSC Res 794 (1992) para 10.

[39] UNSC Res 929 (1994) para 3; UNSC Res 1080 (1996) para 5. See also Totshingo, 'L'autorisation de recourir à la force' (n 1) 91–92.

[40] UN Doc S/PV.2982 (1991); Corten, *The Law Against War* (n 1) 357.

[41] Gray, 'From Unity to Polarization' (n 37) 10. See also UN Doc S/PV.4008 (1999) at 2 (Russia), 4 (China).

[42] Gray, 'From Unit to Polarization' (n 37) 9–10; see also Corten, *The Law Against War* (n 1) 353; Totshingo, 'L'autorisation de recourir à la force' (n 1) 92.

since carved out an argument favouring unilateral humanitarian intervention.[43] Subsequently, commentators have overwhelmingly argued against any authorisation of force under Resolution 688 (1991).[44]

As will also be seen in several further situations examined below, even those States which had initially justified military actions on implicit UNSC authorisation often seek out alternative or further legal bases for their actions.

ii. Resolutions 1154 and 1205 (1998) | The Birth of 'Revived Authorisation'

While States had taken action against Iraq 'implicitly' in line with Resolution 688 (1991), in 1998 the United States and United Kingdom commenced *Operation Desert Fox* – for the first time expressly referring to implicit UNSC authorisation. *Operation Desert Fox* was taken in response to Iraq's suspension of cooperation with United Nations Special Commission (UNSCOM) and the International Atomic Energy Agency – conditions initially set out under Resolution 687 (1991) which imposed a ceasefire following authorisation of force granted in Resolution 678 (1991).[45]

The UNSC, in response to Iraq's move, first adopted Resolution 1154 (1998) warning it of 'severe consequences' of violations of Resolution 687 (1991).[46] Eight months later, the UNSC in Resolution 1205 (1998) *condemned* Iraq's suspension of cooperation and *demanded* it rescind its decision.[47] While both resolutions were adopted under Chapter VII, no explicit authorisation of force was to be found within their provisions.[48]

UNSC debates preceding the adoption of Resolution 1154 (1998) confirm that UNSC Members expressly excluded any interpretation favouring authorisation of force under the resolution. Specifically, an interpretation suggesting an 'automaticity' to use force given Iraq's violation of Resolution 687 (1991) was expressly rejected or its exclusion from the resolution welcomed. This sentiment was shared by Brazil, Kenya, France, The Gambia, China, Russia and even one of the resolution's co-sponsors, Japan.[49] That Resolution 1154 (1998) did not authorise force was the dominant view within the UNSC.

UNSC debates on Resolution 1205 (1998) repeated much of these sentiments. Russia noted the resolution sought a political solution and contained 'no language that could be arbitrarily interpreted as some kind of permission to use

[43] Gray, 'From Unity to Polarization' (n 37) 10–11; see also Corten, *The Law Against War* (n 1) 353.

[44] Corten, *The Law Against War* (n 1) 356–59; Gray, 'From Unity to Polarization' (n 37) 10; Gray, *International Law and the Use of Force* (n 2) 362–63; Totshingo, 'L'autorisation de recourir à la force' (n 1) 91–92.

[45] UNSC Res 687 (1991) paras 8–13.

[46] UNSC Res 1154 (1998) para 3.

[47] UNSC Res 1205 (1998) paras 1, 2.

[48] Gray, 'From Unity to Polarization' (n 37) 11.

[49] UN Doc S/PV.3858 (1998) 7. 10 (Kenya), 11 (Japan), 12 (China), 15 (France), 17 (Russia), 18 (The Gambia). See also the position of Sweden at 9.

force' and Kenya voted in favour of the resolution because it contained 'nothing that could open the door in any eventuality for any kind of action without the clear and precise authority of the Security Council'.[50]

It is not surprising that several UNSC member had approached both resolutions with caution, since by the time of its adoption it was clear that both the United States and United Kingdom were ready to take military action against Iraq. The UK's position during the UNSC debate on Resolution 1205 (1998) summarised a however contrary view:

> It is well established that the authorization to use force given by the Security Council in 1990 may be revived if the Council decides that there has been a sufficiently serious breach of the conditions laid down by the Council for the ceasefire.[51]

This position was again expressed when the UNSC met on 16 December 1998, the same day *Operation Desert Fox* commenced:

> There is a clear legal basis for military action in the resolutions adopted by the Security Council. Resolution 1154 (1998) made it clear that any violation by Iraq of its obligations … would have the severest consequences. That was three resolutions and nine months ago. Resolution 1205 (1998) established that Iraq's decision of 31 October 1998 to cease cooperation … was a flagrant violation of resolution 687 (1991), which laid down the conditions for the 1991 ceasefire. By that resolution, therefore, the Council implicitly revived the authorization to use force given in resolution 678 (1990).[52]

That subsequent resolutions may 'implicitly revive' authorisation under Resolution 678 (1990) has been broadly rejected by States and scholars alike. First, it neglects the fact that it is the UNSC which would determine the consequences of a violation of its resolutions (including the ceasefire in Resolution 687 (1991)), and not individual States.[53] Consequences of the breach of UNSC resolutions do not necessarily nor automatically mean a use of force is contemplated. Second, UNSC debates both during and after the adoption of these resolutions indicate that the majority of UNSC members expressly viewed the resolutions as not authorising force.[54] And third, comparing these resolutions to others adopted in the same period which authorised force shows without doubt the disparity between authorising and non-authorising resolutions.

Nonetheless, 'revived authorisation' would later be used to justify *Operation Iraqi Freedom*. As will be seen below, widespread rejection and condemnation of such authorisation would be of a far greater magnitude that that seen in 1998.

[50] UN Doc S/PV.3939 (1998) 4 (Russia), 7 (Kenya).
[51] UN Doc S/PV.3939 (1998) 10.
[52] UN Doc S/PV.3955 (1998) 6.
[53] Gray, 'From Unity to Polarization' (n 37) 12–13.
[54] See UN Doc S/PV.3955 (1998); UN Doc S/PV.3858 (1998); and UN Doc S/PV.3939 (1998).

B. Resolutions 1160, 1199 and 1203 (1998) | NATO Campaign in Yugoslavia

Only months after an implicit (revived) authorisation was argued in favour of *Operation Desert Storm*, it was subsequently argued in favour of NATO's campaign against Yugoslavia. On 24 March 1999, NATO began what was to be a 78-day air campaign against the Federal Republic of Yugoslavia after a political settlement to Kosovo's autonomy had failed. NATO's actions were justified in part by widespread reports of human rights violations and war crimes committed by Yugoslav armed forces and Serbian military and paramilitary forces. NATO's military campaign, *Operation Allied Force*, outlined five predominant objectives, including among others: ending civilian killings in Kosovo perpetrated by Yugoslav military and police forces and the withdrawal of those troops from the territory of Kosovo.[55] In addition to the justification of humanitarian objectives set out by NATO States, its use of force was also justified on an implicit authorisation derived from three resolutions the UNSC had adopted the year before.[56] These included Resolutions 1160, 1199 and 1203 (1998).

Resolution 1160 (1998) was the first resolution adopted on the situation under Chapter VII. Although not determining the situation a threat to peace and security, the UNSC principally called for political dialogue between Belgrade and Kosovar leaders in ensuring a peaceful solution to the unfolding crisis.[57] In addition, it *emphasised* that a failure to make constructive progress toward the peaceful resolution of the situation would lead to a consideration of additional measures.[58]

By Resolution 1199 (1998), the UNSC expressed somewhat firmer language. It expressed grave concern at all acts of violence, the mass displacement of persons and condemned all acts of violence by any party.[59] The UNSC also *affirmed* that the deteriorating situation in Kosovo constituted a threat to peace and security in the region. Acting under Chapter VII, it demanded that all parties cease hostilities to reduce what it viewed as a humanitarian catastrophe.[60] It further demanded that the FRY immediately implement concrete measures under the

[55] See also Jeffrey Morton, 'The Legality of NATO's Intervention in Yugoslavia in 1999: Implications for the Progressive Development of International Law' (2002) 9(75) *ILSA Journal of International and Comparative Law* 78.

[56] On several occasions, some States fell short of directly justifying the NATO action with UNSC resolutions. See UN Doc S/PV.3988 (1999) 4 (United States), 5 (France), 6 (Slovenia), 8 (The Netherlands). See also UN Doc. S/PV.3989 (1998) 4, position of The Netherlands that the 'NATO action, in which we are participating, follows directly from resolution 1203 (1998)'. But see also Peter van Walsum indicating that the Netherlands had considered but ultimately rejected the idea to secure a UNSC resolution before the NATO action. See Peter van Walsum, 'The Security Council and the Use of Force: The Cases of Kosovo, East Timor, and Iraq' in Niels Blokker and Nico Schrijver (eds), *The Security Council and the Use of Force: Theory and Reality – A Need for Change?*' (Martinus Nijhoff 2005) 67; Totshingo, 'L'autorisation de recourir à la force' (n 1) 94.

[57] UNSC Res 1160 (1998) paras 1–4.

[58] UNSC Res 1160 (1998) para 19.

[59] UNSC Res 1199 (1998) preamble paras 6, 7, 9.

[60] UNSC Res 1199 (1998) para 1.

resolution to achieve a political solution to the Kosovo crisis. Among these were the cessation of all activities by its military forces and the withdrawal of those units used for civilian repression, the enabling of international monitoring of the situation in Kosovo, and facilitation of the safe return of refugees and humanitarian organisations and supplies there.[61] Finally, the UNSC made clear its decision that if the provisions of its resolution were not adhered to, it would 'consider further action and additional measures to maintain or restore peace and stability in the region'.[62]

The UNSC then in Resolution 1203 (1998) *affirmed* that the 'unresolved situation in Kosovo' constituted a continuing threat to peace and security in the region. Acting under Chapter VII, it demanded full and swift compliance with its resolutions and stressed the need for as negotiated political solution.[63] Notably, in Resolution 1203 (1998) the UNSC did not repeat its position to consider further measures in case peaceful resolution failed.

None of the resolutions adopted on the situation explicitly authorised force: Resolution 1160 (1998) did not determine the situation a threat to peace and security and Resolutions 1199 and 1203 (1998) while invoking Chapter VII, contained to language indicating force was authorised. In addition, it has been pointed out that the UNSC's emphasis that it will consider 'additional measures' is in no way an implicit authorisation of force.[64] UNSC debates preceding the adoption of Resolution 1160 (1998) make no mention of the use of force. In UNSC debates surrounding Resolution 1199 (1998), Russia explicitly stated that 'no force and no sanctions' were being imposed at that stage.[65] This was reaffirmed in UNSC debates on Resolution 1203 (1998). Costa Rica pointed out that '[a]ny action which implies the use of force … requires clear authorization by the Security Council'.[66] Both China and Russia abstaining from voting, noting that any elements of enforcement action were removed from the draft resolution and that it in no way, directly or indirectly authorised force.[67]

That none of these resolutions authorised force, even implicitly so, was highlighted on several occasions after NATO commenced *Operation Allied Force*.[68] Instead, what followed was broad condemnation both within and beyond the UNSC.[69] On 26 March 1999, a draft resolution introduced by Belarus, India and Russia sought to condemn the operation by expressing deep concern that

[61] UNSC Res 1199 (1998) para 4.

[62] UNSC Res 1199 (1998) para 16.

[63] UNSC Res 1203 (1998) paras 3, 5.

[64] Daniel Franchini and Antonio Tzanakopoulos, 'The Kosovo Crisis – 1999' in Tom Ruys and Olivier Corten (eds), *The Use of Force in International Law: A Case-Based Approach* (Oxford University Press 2018) 611; Totshingo, 'L'autorisation de recourir à la force' (n 1) 95.

[65] UN Doc S/PV.3930 (1998) 3.

[66] UN Doc S/PV.3937 (1998) 6 (Costa Rica); see also 10–11 (Brazil).

[67] UN Doc S/PV.3937 (1998) 11 (Russia), 14 (China).

[68] See for example UN Doc S/PV.3988 (1999) 6–7, 8; UN Doc S/PV.3989 (1999) 4.

[69] Franchini and Tzanakopoulos, 'The Kosovo Crisis' (n 64) 603–05.

NATO 'used military force against the Federal Republic of Yugoslavia *without the authorisation by the Council*'.[70] Despite receiving support only from Russia, China and Namibia, it was a clear indication that at least two permanent members disagreed on the existence of any authorisation for the NATO operation.[71] Subsequently, Belarus called it an act of aggression;[72] Ukraine considered it an instance of use of force without UNSC authorisation and without a UNSC mandate;[73] China and Cuba called for an immediate end to the NATO military campaign;[74] and Iraq called it a flagrant violation of the UN Charter.[75] India labelled the NATO campaign 'unprovoked military aggression' and Namibia, Gabon and Argentina all opposed the operation in its entirety.[76] Several regional organisations also shared a negative view of the operation. The Inter-Parliamentary Assembly of States Members of the Commonwealth of Independent States adopted a declaration calling the NATO action 'without the authorisation of the United Nations Security Council' a threat to peace and stability in Europe.[77] The Rio Group expressed regret at the military action which it said was 'in contravention of the provisions of article 53, paragraph 1, and article 54' of the UN Charter.[78] Similarly, the Non-Aligned Movement called for an immediate cessation of hostilities and that Resolutions 1199 and 1203 (1998) constituted the only basis for a peaceful and equitable solution.[79]

A legal basis under implicit UNSC authorisation therefore not only proved controversial but has been widely rejected since.[80] As with *Operation Desert Storm*, some of the States involved went at great length to provide alternative legal basis, most notably that of humanitarian intervention.[81] As mentioned, that these States invoked additional legal bases suggested their own reliance on implicit authorisation was at the least not entirely convincing.

[70] Emphasis added. UN Doc S/1999/328 (1999).

[71] S/PV.3989 (1998) in which several members either acknowledged or condemned the lack of UNSC authorisation, 4 (Slovenia); 5 (Russia). De Wet, *The Chapter VII Powers* (n 2) 307.

[72] UN Doc S/1999/332 (1999); see also UN Doc S/PV.4000 (1999) 9.

[73] UN Doc S/1999/335 (1999) and UN Doc S/1999/336 (1999).

[74] UN Doc S/PV.4000 (1999) 11, convened at the request of China following the bombing of the Chinese embassy in Belgrade.

[75] UN Doc S/PV.4000 (n 1999) 9.

[76] UN Doc S/PV.3988 (1999) 16, 10–11.

[77] UN Doc A/53/920 (1999); see also UN Doc. S/1999/461 (1999). The organisation at the time was comprised of Armenia, Azerbaijan, Belarus, Georgia, Kazakhstan, Kyrgyzstan, Moldova, Russia, Tajikistan and Uzbekistan, as well as associate member Ukraine.

[78] UN Doc A/53/884 (1999). See also UN Doc S/1999/347. The Rio Group at the time was comprised of Argentina, Bolivia, Brazil, Chile, Colombia, Ecuador, Mexico, Paraguay, Peru, Panama, Uruguay and Venezuela.

[79] Statement by the NAM on the situation in Kosovo (9 April 1999) www.nam/gov.za/media/990409kos.htm.

[80] Franchini and Tzanakopoulos, 'The Kosovo Crisis' (n 64); Gray, *International Law and the Use of Force* (n 2) 366–67. See also Guillaume Le Floch, 'Le principe de l'interdiction du recours à la force a-t-il encore valeur positive?' (2009) 1 *Interdits* paras 23–24.

[81] Gray, 'From Unit to Polarization' (n 37) 14–15.

C. Resolutions 1368 and 1373 (2001) | Operation Enduring Freedom in Afghanistan

Following the 11 September 2001 terrorist attacks perpetrated by al-Qaeda, the United States began its 'War on Terror'. On 7 October of that year, the United States officially launched its *Operation Enduring Freedom* against Taliban and al-Qaeda positions in Afghanistan. The operation initially began as an air campaign but later also included ground forces operating in Afghanistan.[82] At the time, the United States and its allies put forward several legal justifications for their use of force, most notably, that of self-defence.[83] At the same time however, several States made direct reference to two specific resolutions adopted shortly after the terrorist attacks: Resolutions 1368 and 1373 (2001).[84] The adoption of these two resolutions raised several questions of legality: first, whether Resolutions 1368 and 1373 (2001) indeed authorised the use of force, even implicitly so; and second, what the implications were of the reference to self-defence, particularly in Resolution 1368 (2001).

i. No UNSC Authorisation

Resolution 1368 (2001) was adopted on 12 September 2001, a day after the terrorist attacks. *Determined* to 'combat by all means threats to international peace and security caused by terrorist acts', and *recognising* 'the inherent right of individual or collective self-defence', the UNSC *unequivocally condemned* the terrorist attacks against the United States.[85] While not invoking Chapter VII, operative paragraph five *expressed* the UNCS's readiness to 'take all necessary steps' to respond to the 11 September terrorist attacks.[86]

Resolution 1373 (2001) subsequently expressed firmer language; explicitly determining that acts of terrorism constituted a threat to international peace and security, invoking Chapter VII and *reaffirming* the inherent right of individual or collective self-defence recognised in Resolution 1368 (2001).[87] Under its operative paragraphs, the UNSC imposed broad and numerous obligations concerning domestic jurisdiction of States to prevent and suppress terrorist acts within their territories.[88]

[82] Gray, *International Law and the Use of Force* (n 2) 231.

[83] On the operation and the justification of self-defence, see Ryan Williams, 'Dangerous Precedent: America's Illegal War in Afghanistan' (2011) 33 *University of Pennsylvania Journal of International Law* 569; Mary O'Connell, 'Lawful Self-Defence to Terrorism' (2002) 63 *University of Pittsburgh Law Review* 897–98; Gray, *International Law and the Use of Force* (n 2) 231–232; Patrick Terry, 'The War in Afghanistan: Was the Use of Force Legal and/or Wise?' (2011) 9 *New Zealand Yearbook of International Law* 73. See also UN Doc S/2001/946 (2001) and UN Doc S/2001/947 (2001).

[84] See also Corten, *The Law Against War* (n 1) 363.

[85] UNSC Res 1368 (2001) para 1.

[86] UNSC Res 1386 (2001) para 5.

[87] UNSC Res 1373 (2001).

[88] UNSC Res 1373 (2001) paras 1–3.

Neither Resolution 1368 nor 1373 (2001), individually or collectively, contained any reference to the use of force. Indeed, Afghanistan was not mentioned on a single occasion in either resolution. The United States however seemed to have in part implicitly considered either one or both resolutions as constituting the legal basis for resort to force.[89] While these States did not offer any detailed arguments why these resolutions authorised force, several commentators have argued either in favour of such a conclusion or at least its admissibility.

As such, these arguments tend to point to the language used in these resolutions. Accordingly, the terms 'combat by all means' and 'suppress terrorist attacks and take action against perpetrators of such acts' is sufficiently broad to provide authorisation, despite the absence of explicit UNSC language of authorising 'all necessary means'.[90] While the terms 'combat by all means' is strikingly suggestive in favour of force (as it the term 'by all necessary means [or] measures'), its appearance is limited to the preamble of both resolutions. Suffice it to say that the UNSC has never rightfully authorised force in its preamble, opting to specify in its operative paragraphs any action taken under Chapter VII.[91] Consequently, authorisation in operative paragraphs ordinarily includes temporal limitations and reporting requirements, which appear in neither of the resolutions in question.

Moreover, it does not appear that Member States are directed to 'combat by all means' threats to international peace and security. Rather, this provision is an expression of the UNSC's determination it takes up itself, and to the end that it combats *threats to international peace and security*. In addition, the reference to 'take action against perpetrators of such acts' found in paragraph 3(c) of Resolution 1373 (2001) must be considered holistically and in context. That context likely considers that any 'action' contemplated is meant to address investigative aspects and criminal law issues related to terrorism, and not an implicit authorisation of force.[92] Given this, it is difficult to conclude that either of the resolutions authorised force.[93]

ii. The Invocation of Self-Defence in UNSC Resolutions

Whereas the UNSC did not implicitly authorise force in these resolutions, it did in fact 'invoke' the right of self-defence. It *recognised* this right in Resolution 1368

[89] But see Corten, *The Law Against War* (n 1) 364 who indicates that the legal basis was only self-defence and not UNSC authorization. See also Totshingo, 'L'autorisation de recourir à la force' (n 1) 100.

[90] Jordan Paust, 'Use of Armed Force against Terrorists in Afghanistan, Iraq and Beyond' (2002) 35(3) *Cornell International Law Journal* 544–45.

[91] Terry, 'The War in Afghanistan' (n 83) 71.

[92] Terry, 'The War in Afghanistan' (n 83) 70–71, fn 5.

[93] Gray, *International Law and the Use of Force* (n 2) 232; Corten, *The Law Against War* (n 1) 363; Williams, 'Dangerous Precedent' (n 83) 592.

(2001) and *reaffirmed* it in Resolution 1373 (2001). Both the United States and United Kingdom in letters to the UNSC declared that they were acting in self-defence under Article 51 when they launched operations against Afghanistan on 7 October 2001.[94] The question which subsequently arose was whether these resolutions may have (implicitly) authorised force by virtue of their recognition of the right of self-defence.[95] At the outset, this raises several legal problems that misconstrue the very nature of collective security under Chapter VII of the UN Charter. As has been detailed in both the Korean War and the Iraqi invasion of Kuwait, a divergence in opinion remains as to whether the Chapter VII legal basis of resolutions rests with Article 42 or Article 51.[96] Whereas the UNSC authorises force under Article 42 in maintaining international peace and security, Article 51 of the UN Charter merely affirms the right of individual or collective self-defence available to Member States.[97] Consequently, the UNSC need not recognise the right of self-defence for Member States to be able to act in the exercise of such right.[98]

The fact that the UNSC *recognises* and *reaffirms* the right can also not be equated to an implicit authorisation of force. In the case at hand, it is also worth noting that the right of self-defence was only referenced exclusively in the resolutions' preambles. Other than the Article 39 determination the UNSC ordinarily makes in a resolution's preamble, the UNSC has never authorised force outside of its operative paragraphs.[99] Rather, *Operation Enduring Freedom* was based strictly on self-defence, not merely because the UNSC recognised this right in its resolutions, but because it was available to the United States independently of the UNSC.[100] Neither Resolutions 1368 nor 1373 (2001) therefore introduced any shift in how the UNSC ordinarily authorises the use of force.

In addition, one may point to subsequent resolutions that in fact made reference to *Operation Enduring Freedom* after it had commenced. In particular, under Resolution 1386 (2001) the UNSC established the International Security Assistance Force (ISAF), and under Resolution 1510 (2003) it called upon ISAF to work in close consultation with *Operation Enduring Freedom*.[101] As has been discussed elsewhere, the authorisation provided for in Resolution 1510 (2003)

[94] UN Doc S/2001/946 (2001); UN Doc S/2001/947 (2001).

[95] Corten, *The Law Against War* (n 1) 363 states that the reference to self-defence may not readily be interpreted as an authorisation to use force and that the United States had not sought such an authorisation.

[96] See the discussions in ch 2 pertaining to UNSC Res 83 (1950) and Res 678 (1990).

[97] Derek Bowett, 'Collective Security and Collective Self-Defence' in Rama Montaldo (ed), *El derecho internacional* quoted in Michael Wood, 'Self-Defence and Collective Security: Key Distinctions' in Weller (n 2) 653.

[98] Terry, 'The War in Afghanistan' (n 83) 76.

[99] Terry, 'The War in Afghanistan' (n 83) 71.

[100] Corten, *The Law Against War* (n 1) 364; see broadly, John Quiqley, 'The Afghanistan War and Self-Defence' (2003) 37(2) *Valparaiso University Law Review Symposium on Operation Enduring Freedom and the War on Terrorism* 543. However, see also the view of Terry, 'The War in Afghanistan' (n 83) 74.

[101] UNSC Res 1386 (2001); UNSC Res 1510 (2003).

was specifically and distinctly accorded to ISAF.[102] The fact that the UNSC had acknowledged the United States operation in that and several additional resolutions did not mean that it had implicitly authorised its presence or mandate there.[103] Instead, Byers has noted that the acknowledgment of the operation in subsequent resolutions was likely to be a recognition of its presence on the ground and a fact that the UN and ISAF had to work with.[104] All resolutions authorising the use of force to ISAF did so explicitly and directly, and it suffices to say that there is no doubt that the UNSC did not intend to implicitly authorise *Operation Enduring Freedom* in any subsequent resolution.[105]

D. Resolutions 678 (1990), 687 (1991) and 1441 (2002) | Revived Authorisation

Up until the United States operation in Afghanistan, implicit UNSC authorisation was considered at most a secondary legal basis justifying the use of force by States. The most controversial argument for such a justification, however, only arose when in 2003, the United States together with the United Kingdom and Australia launched *Operation Iraqi Freedom.* The unprecedented military action was undertaken to 'disarm Iraq of weapons of mass destruction, to end Saddam Hussein's support for terrorism, and to free the Iraqi people'.[106]

The United States-led coalition commenced *Operation Iraqi Freedom* on 19 March, with some 177,000 troops deployed to Iraq. At that time, several justifications were raised in support of the operation, including the 'War on Terror' following the 11 September terrorist attacks against the United States. More prominent, however, were arguments forwarded by the coalition that their actions were based on implicit UNSC authorisation under Resolution 1441 (2002) and by virtue of Iraq's development of weapons of mass destruction (WMDs) in violation of Resolution 687 (1991).[107] The legality of *Operation Iraqi Freedom* as well as arguments considering revived authorisation are well

[102] See ch 4 at 120–124.

[103] See for example UNSC Res 1563 (2004); UNSC Res 1589 (2005); UNSC Res 1623 (2005); UNSC Res 1659 (2006); UNSC Res 1662 (2006); UNSC Res 1707 (2006); UNSC Res 1746 (2007); UNSC Res 1776 (2007). See more recently UNSC Res 2120 (2013) and UNSC Res 2145 (2014).

[104] Michael Byers, 'The Intervention in Afghanistan – 2001-' in Ruys and Corten (n 64) 637.

[105] See UNSC Res 1563 (2004); UNSC Res 1589 (2005); UNSC Res 1623 (2005). Similar recognition and commendation by the UNSC was present in a dozen further resolutions. However, none could be interpreted as having authorised its use of force in Afghanistan.

[106] The White House, Office of the Press Secretary, 'President Discusses Beginning of Operation Iraqi Freedom' (22 March 2003) https://georgewbush-whitehouse.archives.gov/news/releases/2003/03/20030322.html.

[107] UNSC Res 687 (1991). Paulus, however, notes that the terms of suspension of Resolution 678 (1990) were based on Iraq's acceptance of the provisions of Resolution 687 (1991) and not its compliance therewith. See Andreas Paulus, 'The War Against Iraq and the Future of International Law: Hegemony of Pluralism?' (2004) 25 *Michigan Journal of International Law* 699.

documented in literature.[108] Nevertheless, it represents one of the most notable situations questioning the need for explicit UNSC authorisation.

i. Implicit Authorisation under Resolution 1441 (2002)

Resolution 687 (1991) was adopted on 3 April 1991 and was one of the first resolutions to note concerns that Iraq was attempting to acquire materials for a nuclear weapons programme and weapons of mass destruction.[109] The resolution established a UN weapons inspectorate empowered to ensure Iraqi disarmament of WMDs.[110] At that time, Iraq accepted the provisions of the resolution and agreed to the complete disarmament of WMDs and other biological and chemical weapons. However, in 1998 the United States undertook *Operation Desert Fox*. UN weapons inspectors were withdrawn and Iraq never permitted them to return.[111] Iraq's continued refusal to allow the inspection team to return consequently aroused suspicion in both the United States and United Kingdom that it had forged ahead with its WMDs ambitions. In an attempt to give Iraq one final opportunity to comply with its obligations, the UNSC adopted Resolution 1441 (2002).[112]

Resolution 1441 (2002) was adopted unanimously on 8 November 2002. The UNSC recalled all previous relevant resolutions on the situation between Iraq and Kuwait. Among these were Resolution 678 (1990), which had authorised States to use force to ensure the Iraqi withdrawal from Kuwait, and Resolution 687 (1991), which contained the ceasefire and Iraqi inspection regime. The resolution specifically *recognised* that Iraq's violation of its obligations under previous resolutions and its proliferation of WMDs posed a threat to international peace and security. In addition, it deplored Iraq's failure to comply with, among others, Resolution 688 (1991) with regard to terrorism. Acting under Chapter VII, the UNSC then determined that Iraq had been and remained in 'material breach' of its obligations under relevant resolutions, specifically

[108] For the most part, such arguments have been broadly rejected. Thomas Franck, 'What Happens Now? The United Nations After Iraq' (2003) 97 *American Journal of International Law* 612–14; Corten, *The Law Against War* (n 1) 370–71; Paulus, 'The War Against Iraq' (n 107) 697–701; Nigel White and Eric Myjer, 'Editorial: The Use of Force Against Iraq' (2003) 8(1) *Journal of Conflict and Security Law* 2–4; Vaughan Lowe, 'The Iraq Crisis: What Now?' (2003) 52(4) *International and Comparative Law Quarterly* 866. See also Dino Kritsiotis, 'Arguments of Mass Confusion' (2004) 15(2) *European Journal of International Law* 267–69; Lindsay Moir, *Reappraising the Resort to Force: International Law, Jus ad Bellum and the War on Terror* (Hart Publishing 2010) 104–05. See however Christopher Greenwood, 'International Law and the Pre-Emptive Use of Force: Afghanistan, Al-Qaida, and Iraq' (2003) 4 *San Diego International Law Journal* 33–36.

[109] UNSC Res 687 (1991) preamble para 15 expressed concerns over reports by Member States that Iraq 'has attempted to acquire material for a nuclear-weapons programme contrary to its obligations under the Treaty on the Non-Proliferation of Nuclear Weapons'.

[110] UNSC Res 687 (1991) paras 7–8, 11–13. Gray, *International Law and the Use of Force* (n 2) 368.

[111] Gray, *International Law and the Use of Force* (n 2) 368.

[112] UNSC Res 1441 (2002).

those under paragraphs 8–13 of Resolution 687 (1991).[113] Paragraph two then afforded Iraq 'a final opportunity to comply with its disarmament obligations under relevant resolutions'.[114] This final opportunity took the form of a more comprehensive inspection regime to which Iraq was to adhere. The UNSC also requested that Member States give full support to the inspection regime. Finally, the UNSC decided that upon receipt of the report of the inspection regime, it would convene immediately to consider the situation and the need for full compliance to secure international peace and security.[115] In addition, it also *recalled* that Iraq would face 'serious consequences' if it continued to violate its obligations.[116]

The wording of Resolution 1441's (2002) preamble and operative paragraphs were without a doubt a stern warning to Iraq that the UNSC demanded it adhere to its obligations. The fact that the UNSC did not use the usual wording that it determines it to be a threat to peace and security, rather opting for the words *recognises* and *poses* a threat, was overcome by the fact that it recalled no less than eight previous resolutions that had made such a determination. In addition, it invoked Chapter VII in the entirety of the resolution's operative paragraphs. Yet, the Resolution 1441's (2002) wording clearly demonstrates it fell short of authorising force.[117] This position was evident in UNSC debates following its adoption.[118] The United Kingdom acknowledged that the resolution contained no automaticity to resort to military force against Iraq and that any further breaches would be reported to the UNSC for further consideration.[119] Mexico stressed the resolution eliminated the concept of automaticity in the use of force without the 'explicit agreement' of the UNSC.[120] It notably added: 'We reiterate the belief reflected in the agreed text that the possibility of the use of force is valid only as a last resort, with *prior explicit authorization* required from the Security Council.'[121]

[113] UNSC Res 1441 (2002) para 1.
[114] UNSC Res 1441 (2002) para 2.
[115] UNSC Res 1441 (2002) para 12.
[116] UNSC Res 1441 (2002) para 13.
[117] De Wet, *The Chapter VII Powers* (n 2) 289; Corten, *The Law Against War* (n 1) 369–70; Totshingo, 'L'autorisation de recourir à la force' (n 1) 106; Marc Weller, 'The Iraq War – 2003' in Ruys and Corten (n 64) 651, 654; Paulus, 'The War Against Iraq' (n 107) 697; White and Myjer, 'Editorial' (n 108) 1–3; Alex Conte, 'All Necessary Means to Maintain Peace and Security: Did the United Nations Authorise the Use of Force in Iraq?' (2003) 14(9) *Canterbury Law Review* 316; Lowe, 'The Iraq Crisis' (n 108) 865; Le Floch, 'Le principe de l'interdiction du recours à la force' (n 80) para 30.
[118] Previous UNSC debates show that Members were also not willing to accept an authorisation of force against Iraq at the time. See for example UN Doc S/PV.4625 (2002); UN Doc S/PV.4625 (Resumption 2); UN Doc S.PV.4625 (Resumption 3).
[119] UN Doc S/PV.4644 (2002) para 5.
[120] UN Doc S/PV.4644 (2002) 6.
[121] UN Doc S/PV.4644 (2002) 6.

Ireland welcomed the purpose of the resolution to ensure compliance and 'not to establish a basis for the use of military force',[122] Russia said that the resolution contained no provisions for the automatic use of force,[123] Bulgaria noted that the resolution was not a pretext for automatic recourse to use force[124] and China stated that the text no longer included automaticity for authorising the use of force.[125] Even the United States representative acknowledged that the resolution contained no 'hidden triggers' or 'automaticity' with respect to the use of force.[126] The representative added that any failure on Iraq's part would result in the matter being reconsidered by the UNSC. However, in the same vein, the representative added that the resolution did not constrain 'any Member States from acting to defend itself against the threat posed by Iraq or to enforce relevant [UNSC] resolutions and protect world peace and security'.[127] On the one hand, this suggested that the United States considered that it was entitled to 'enforce UNSC resolutions' perhaps despite no explicit authorisation to use force. On the other hand, what was clear from the discussion among Member States at the time was that only a new resolution could authorise force against Iraq.

This position, however, was contradicted by both the United States and United Kingdom once *Operation Iraqi Freedom* commenced. In particular, they argued that since Iraq was in material breach of its obligations and that Resolution 1441 (2002) did not explicitly require an additional resolution, they were entitled to act based on a revived authorisation.[128] Moreover, they argued that paragraph 12 of Resolution 1441 (2002) merely required the UNSC to consider the situation and not to take a formal decision on further action.[129] Despite their argument, further attempts were made to obtain a second UNSC resolution, although this was eventually withdrawn when it became clear it would not muster enough support to be adopted.[130] Initially introduced on 24 February and amended on 7 March, the draft resolution was submitted by the United States, the United Kingdom and Spain.[131] The draft resolution contained 11 preambular and three operative paragraphs. In its preamble, the draft resolution sought to once again

[122] UN Doc S/PV.4644 (2002) 7.

[123] UN Doc S/PV.4644 (2002) 8. See also The Legal Department of the Ministry of Foreign Affairs of the Russian Federation, 'Legal Assessment of the Use of Force Against Iraq' (2003) 52(4) *International and Comparative Law Quarterly* 1059.

[124] UN Doc S/PV.4644 (2002) 9.

[125] UN Doc S/PV.4644 (2002) 13.

[126] UN Doc S/PV.4644 (2002) 3.

[127] UN Doc S/PV.4644 (2002) 3.

[128] Corten, *The Law Against War* (n 1) 368–69; Gray, *International Law and the Use of Force* (n 2) 371–72; Weller, 'The Iraq War – 2003' (n 117) 644–50; see also the analysis of Di Carlo in Giuseppina di Carlo, 'The Language of the UN: Vagueness in Security Council Resolutions Relating to the Second Gulf War' (2013) 26(3) *International Journal for the Semiotics of Law* 696, 698.

[129] Gray, *International Law and the Use of Force* (n 2) 370.

[130] Gray, *International Law and the Use of Force* (n 2) 370.

[131] UN Doc S/2003/215 (2003).

condemn Iraq's non-compliance, to recall in particular Resolutions 678 (1990), 687 (1991) and 1441 (2002), and to determine that Iraq's non-compliance and proliferation of WMDs constituted a threat to international peace and security. It invoked Chapter VII and contained the UNSC's 'mindful of its primary responsibilities' phrasing. Operative paragraph one then merely sought to express that the UNSC had decided that 'Iraq has failed to take the final opportunity afforded to it in Resolution 1441 (2002)'.[132]

In addition to the fact that Resolution 1441 (2002) could not have been interpreted to have authorised the use of force, it is doubtful whether the proposed draft resolution could have had a different effect. The primary purpose of the draft resolution was to declare that Iraq had failed to take its final opportunity to comply with UNSC resolutions. However, even if this declaration had been made, it was not necessarily to be interpreted as an automatic authorisation of force.[133]

Despite containing an Article 39 determination and invoking Chapter VII, even in combination with Resolution 1441 (2002), that Iraq was in material breach of its obligations and that it would face 'serious consequences' did not automatically mean that force against Iraq was such a consequence.[134] In effect, this would suggest that Member States were given a discretion to determine what 'serious consequences' were; a statement which was originally made by the UNSC.[135]

Turning back to Resolution 1441 (2002), any suggestion that it authorised of force remains contrary to conventional UNSC practice.[136] First, no usual phrasing of 'all necessary means [or] measures' was included in the resolution.[137] It was precisely this crucial phrasing that was interpreted to authorise force on 21 prior occasions before November 2002 and on a broad range of situations,[138] without which Chapter VII resolutions were not interpreted in such a manner.[139] Second, the alleged authorisation was neither prescribed to Member States nor to a regional organisation as is the usual practice of the UNSC.[140] In addition, nothing in the

[132] UN Doc S/2003/215 (2003) 3.

[133] De Wet, *The Chapter VII Powers* (n 2) 289; White and Myjer, 'Editorial' (n 108) 6; Conte, 'All Necessary Means to Maintain Peace and Security' (n 117) 316.

[134] De Wet, *The Chapter VII Powers* (n 2) 289; Franck, 'What Happens Now' (n 108) 612; Paulus, 'The War Against Iraq' (n 107) 697; White and Myjer, 'Editorial' (n 108) 3; also Michael Byers, 'Agreeing to Disagree: Security Council Resolution 1441 and International Ambiguity' (2004) 10 *Global Governance* 172; Conte, 'All Necessary Means' (n 117) 316.

[135] Franck, 'What Happens Now' (n 108) 613, Lowe, 'The Iraq Crisis' (n 108) 865. Lowe points to UNSC Res 686 (1991) and UNSC Res 687 (1991) as having suggested that the authorisation to use force was only for the duration of the military operation to force Iraq out of Kuwait and that it was up to the UNSC to decide on further measures. Lowe, 'The Iraq Crisis' (n 108) 866.

[136] See also Byers, 'Agreeing to Disagree' (n 134) 171–72.

[137] Byers, 'Agreeing to Disagree' (n 134) 172.

[138] See the relevant resolutions analysed in chs 2, 3 and 4.

[139] See also the analysis by Conte, 'All Necessary Means' (n 117) 312.

[140] See the analysis of other resolutions in previous chapters where UNSC resolutions have always *authorised*, *called upon* or *decided* that 'all necessary means [or] measures' were to be used by Member States or regional organisations.

resolution suggests a mandate under which force was to be used. Consequently, the resolution imposed neither time limitations nor reporting obligations. Any suggestion pointing towards authorisation would therefore also suggest that the UNSC authorised states at their own discretion to determine what objectives were to be undertaken, how they were to be undertaken, and for how long such action may be undertaken. At most, Resolution 1441 (2002) could be considered an ultimatum given to Iraq to ensure its compliance with UNSC decisions.[141]

ii. Revived Authorisation

Despite arguments against any authorisation under Resolution 1441 (2002), the United States, United Kingdom and Australia justified their actions under the UNSC resolutions. More specifically, they claimed that Iraq's failure to comply with obligations undermining a ceasefire had led to the revival of the UNSC's previous authorisation to use force. This argument was summarised well on 20 March by the United States Permanent Representative to the UN:

> The actions being taken are authorized under existing Council resolutions, including its resolutions 678 (1990) and 687 (1991) … It has been long recognized and understood that a material breach of these obligations removes the basis of the ceasefire and *revives the authority to use force under resolution 678* (1990) … In view of Iraq's material breaches, the *basis for the ceasefire has been removed and use of force is authorized under resolution 678 (1990)*.[142]

The positions of the United Kingdom and Australia were similarly expressed.[143] In particular, the United Kingdom Attorney-General argued a stringent set of causality upon which its actions were based.[144] Specifically, it was noted that Resolution 687 (1991) suspended the authorisation to use force in Resolution 678 (1990) but did not terminate it.[145] Since under Resolution 1441 (2002) the UNSC determined that Iraq was in material breach of its obligations under Resolution 687 (1991) which established the ceasefire, the authority to use force under Resolution 678 (1990) was *revived* given the breach of such ceasefire.[146]

[141] See Paulus, 'The War Against Iraq' (n 107) 699–700 who argues against the connection between the ceasefire and authorisation for the use of force under Article 60 of the Vienna Convention on the Law of Treaties, stating that it was the UNSC that was to decide on a breach of the ceasefire it had imposed, and not Member States. See also Franck, 'What Happens Now' (n 108) 612; White and Myjer, 'Editorial' (n 108) 6.

[142] UN Doc S/2003/351 (2003).

[143] See also UN Doc S/2003/350 (2003) and UN Doc S/2003/352 (2003).

[144] See the well-detailed UK position in Gray, *International Law and the Use of Force* (n 2) 371–72; and 'III. Attorney General's Advice on the Iraq War Iraq: Resolution 1441' (2005) *International and Comparative Law Quarterly* 767.

[145] See the position of White and Myjer, 'Editorial' (n 108) 7 that the authority to use force under Resolution 678 (1990) was in fact revoked.

[146] See 'III. Attorney General's Advice on the Iraq War Iraq: Resolution 1441' (2005) *International and Comparative Law Quarterly* 769 in which the Attorney-General noted the controversy of revived authorisation.

In addition, constant emphasis was placed on the fact that Iraq had been given a *final opportunity* to comply with UNSC resolutions, that the UNSC had warned it of *serious consequences* and that under Resolution 1441 (2002) all that was further needed was for the UNSC to *consider* the matter, and not decide on authorisation.[147]

The argument of revived authorisation sought by the coalition was a strategic interpretation of UNSC resolutions adopted some 12 years apart. Under Resolution 687 (1991) the UNSC decided to impose a ceasefire on military measures undertaken under Resolution 678 (1990) upon notification of Iraq's acceptance of the resolution's provisions. It also expressed its readiness to consider further measures in securing peace and security in the region. First, the fact that Resolution 1441 (2002) determined a material breach by Iraq of, among others, its obligations under Resolution 687 (1991), does not necessarily mean that the UNSC automatically considered that such a breach effectively revived military measures under Resolution 678 (1990).[148] This was a conclusion reached by the respective Member States on a UNSC decision, and not the UNSC that decided as such. Even if one accepts this conclusion, it would mean that authorisation for the use of force was broken up into three separate UNSC decisions under three different UNSC resolutions adopted over a 10-year period.[149]

At the same time, the argument of causality also relies heavily on the intention of the UNSC when it adopted Resolution 687 (1991). The argument of revived authorisation thus assumed that the UNSC intended military measures to come into effect should the ceasefire be violated. This assumption, however, seems incorrect if one considers the context under which Resolution 687 (1991) was adopted. In fact, the exact purpose of suspending the use of force in the resolution was brought up by Yemen at the time, who raised the point that it was (although it should not have been) the coalition forces that would decide whether the ceasefire had been complied with.[150] The general sentiment expressed at the time however directed attention to a more permanent and peaceful resolution of the crisis, citing the need for a UN mission, the withdrawal of coalition forces and the need for border demarcations.[151] Additionally, it has been pointed out that Resolution 687 (1991) conditioned the ceasefire agreement on Iraq's 'acceptance' of the provisions of the resolution, and not its 'compliance' therewith.[152]

[147] See also the Australian position in 'Memorandum of Advice to the Commonwealth Government on the Use of Force Against Iraq' in Bill Campbell et al, 'Special Feature: Advice on the Use of Force Against Iraq' (2003) 4 *Melbourne Journal of International Law* 178.

[148] Byers, 'Agreeing to Disagree' (n 134) 171–72.

[149] White and Myjer, 'Editorial' (n 108) 7 describe it as an 'unconvincing attempt to unlock Resolution 678 of 1990, which was the only resolution in which the Council explicitly authorized necessary measures against Iraq'.

[150] UN Doc S/PV.2981 (1991) 46; Paulus, 'The War Against Iraq' (n 107) 699; Byers, 'Agreeing to Disagree' (n 134) 172.

[151] Franck, 'What Happens Now' (n 108) 613.

[152] Franck, 'What Happens Now' (n 108) 613; De Wet, *The Chapter VII Powers* (n 2) 289.

Hence, the UNSC's inclusion of the final provision that it decides to 'remain seized of the matter' and was ready to consider further steps to ensure peace and security.[153] It is of course unlikely that any UNSC Member States could have foreseen that force would be justified based in part on the wording of Resolution 687 (1991) almost a decade later.[154]

iii. Condemnation of Operation Iraqi Freedom

The strategic interpretation of UNSC resolutions to justify *Operation Iraqi Freedom* was met with widespread condemnation. It was clear both well before the operation and even after its commencement that states refused to accept implicit authorisation even with the existence of the resolutions used to justify it. Instead, what was strongly favour during several UNSC meetings was explicit authorisation. For example, some four months before the operation, several UNSC Members expressed their concern over potential military action taken without clear and explicit UNSC authorisation. South Africa reiterated that the UNSC should 'explicitly and clearly define the objectives of its resolutions';[155] Pakistan noted that grave consequences of UNSC decisions meant that there should be no doubt when the UNSC expressly authorised force, adding that Article 42 did not allow for States to unilaterally and independently decide on forceful measures without 'explicit approval' of the UNSC;[156] and Ecuador referred to setting the grounds of use of force in an explicit resolution that would set forward the conditions of the use of force.[157] In addition, France also made it clear that it was in any case not willing to allow the adoption of a resolution that allowed for the automatic use of force against Iraq.[158]

Widespread condemnation was evident immediately after the United States had launched its operation. Switzerland said that an intervention had been launched 'without the explicit authorisation' of the UNSC;[159] South Africa, Malaysia, Yemen, Libya, Brazil and Iran referred to it as a unilateral resort to

[153] Franck, 'What Happens Now' (n 108) 613; Paulus, 'The War Against Iraq' (n 107) 699; White and Myjer, 'Editorial' (n 108) 7; Byers, 'Agreeing to Disagree' (n 134) 171–72; Lowe, 'The Iraq Crisis' (n 108) 866; Tom Bingham, 'The Rule of Law in the International Legal Order' in Robert McCorquodale (ed), *The Rule of Law in International and Comparative Context* (British Institute of International and Comparative Law 2010) 14.

[154] See however the statement by Malaysia in UN Doc S/PV.4625 (Resumption 2) (2002): 'Therefore, the issue before the Council should not be one of authorizing use of force against Iraq on the presumption of Iraqi non-compliance with Resolution 1284 (1999), but one of allowing UNMOVIC to commence its work in Iraq as expeditiously as possible.'

[155] UN Doc S/PV.4625 (2002) 6.

[156] UN Doc S/PV.4625 (2002) 18.

[157] UN Doc S/PV.4709 (Resumption 1) (2003) 15.

[158] UN Doc S/PV.4714 (2003) 19. See also the statement by Lebanon in UN Doc S/PV.4717 (2003) 33 and the joint statement by China, France and Russia in UN Doc S/2002/1236 (2002).

[159] UN Doc S/PV.4726 (2003) 30. See also 'Switzerland aims for bigger role on world stage' *SwissInfo* (18 December 2003) and the condemnation by Sweden in 'War with Iraq is not inevitable', questions to Anna Lindh, Ministry for Foreign Affairs.

force taken without UNSC authorisation;[160] and Algeria called it an 'unauthorised' use of force.[161] These sentiments were also shared by the League of Arab States which condemned the invasion, calling it an act of aggression.[162]

Consequently, given the interpretation of the respective resolutions, the concerns shared by States before the operation, and the condemnation against it once it commenced, it was clear that the only acceptable use of force was that rightfully and explicitly authorised by the UNSC.[163] For this reason, the actions undertaken against Iraq under the pretext of implicit authorisation find very limited support. They remain inherently controversial and have been widely considered unlawful. As such, the arguments in favour of implicit and even revived authorisation under the relevant resolutions cannot hold precedential value for UNSC practice. More so, they may even be regarded as clear examples that exacerbated the consensus among States for the need for explicit UNSC authorisation.

V. CONCLUSION

The chapter has considered the nature of implicit authorisation and outlined doctrinal debates disfavouring such authorisation based on its incompatibility with the UN Charter. It also examined four situations in which implicit UNSC authorisation has been alleged. The following may be noted in relation to implicit authorisation.

First, the very nature of implicit authorisation presents legal challenges and ought to be rightfully considered incompatible with the UN Charter for several reasons. The fact that the UN Charter does not specify that authorisation needs to be explicit, nor does it specify any specific form, does not mean that implicit authorisation is legally acceptable. Under the principles and purposes embodied in the UN Charter, it is clear that the regulation of the use of force, and its reliance only in the last resort, is of crucial importance to the UN system of collective security. The power of the UNSC to authorise force is subject to both an Article 39 determination and a consideration of Article 41 non-military measures. This two-staged judgment suggests that UNSC decisions need to be explicit.[164] Similarly, the UN Charter's encapsulation of the use of force only as a last resort rightfully suggests that when it is indeed resorted to, it should do so only when necessary, and only when explicitly expressed.

[160] UN Doc S/PV.4726 (2003) 20, 7, 8, 13, 17, 28, 33. Liechtenstein acknowledged the same in UN Doc S/PV.4726 (Resumption 1) (2003) 2.

[161] UN Doc S/PV.4726 (2003) 11.

[162] UN Doc S/2003/365 (2003).

[163] De Wet, *The Chapter VII Powers* (n 2) 289; Franck, 'What Happens Now' (n 108) 614; Conte, 'All Necessary Means' (n 117) 316–17.

[164] Lobel and Ratner, 'Bypassing the Security Council' (n 2) 128. See also de Wet, 'Article 42' (n 2) 1706–07.

Similarly, implicit authorisation seems too incompatible with the institutional logic of the UN Charter where its voting procedure is concerned. When adopting a resolution, it has become clear that a positive (explicit) vote by Member States is required, thereby avoiding the possibility of an 'implicit vote'. This requirement evidently requires that all Members understand the nature and extent of the decision they are voting on at the time of voting.[165]

Doctrinal debates have also pointed out that implicit authorisation is likely incompatible with the UN Charter's requirement that the UNSC maintain (some) command of and control over its authorised operations. The fact that the UNSC has guarantee mechanisms to ensure some degree of control, most notably, the reporting requirement of measures undertaken by States when engaging in enforcement action, becomes redundant if the UNSC does not clearly and explicitly express objectives under its resolutions.

Finally, the argument that a lack of condemnation by the UNSC may present a case of implicit authorisation has also been dispensed with. The fact that any of the five permanent members may veto a UNSC decision means that it may be impossible for the UNSC to condemn certain uses of force. This was particularly the case when a Russian draft resolution seeking to condemn the NATO intervention against the FRY in 1999 was vetoed. To this end, it is inaccurate to suggest that the silence of the UNSC on the use of force may be equivalent to the authorisation thereof.[166]

Nonetheless, despite the general restrictions faced by implicit authorisation, it has been used to justify no less than five separate instances on four situations in which states have resorted to force: Iraq (1991, 1998, 2003), FRY (1999) and Afghanistan (2001). Insights into the above analysis may be summarised as follows: First, while implicit authorising resolutions usually determine a threat to international peace and security and invoke Chapter VII, they do not contain any language that can rightfully be interpreted as authorisation for the use of force. No typical authorising language such as 'all necessary means [or] measures' therefore appears in their provisions. Consequently, there is no specific entity that has been directed to act, nor do these resolutions impose the necessary restrictions on the use of force as the UNSC occasionally does. Hence, there are no reporting requirements imposed on Member States, nor time limits during which action may be taken.

Second, it is interesting to note that alleged cases of implicit authorising resolutions are occasionally preceded by draft resolutions attempting, at least to some degree, authorise force explicitly.[167] When the potential for prior draft resolutions failed or would not reasonably succeed for among others a lack of

[165] Corten, *The Law Against War* (n 1) 395.

[166] Lobel and Ratner, 'Bypassing the Security Council' (n 2) 130.

[167] In the case of Kosovo, an attempt to secure an UNSC authorisation was consider in the Netherlands. See Van Walsum, 'The Security Council and the Use of Force' (n 56) 67. In the case of Iraq in 2003, see UN Doc S/2003/215 (2003).

consensus among UNSC Members, then only did States rely on arguments in favour of implicit authorisation. This suggests that even those States which have occasionally argued in favour of implicit authorisation have conceded the need to obtain at least some more explicitly form of authorisation. Only once this was unattainable did they justify their actions on an implicit authorisation.

Third, an examination of State responses shows that resolutions which had in the past explicitly authorised force face little to no criticism. The exception is where only those States against which measures were authorised raise concern. The general attitude, however, suggests that when the UNSC explicitly authorises force, it does so based on widely accepted consensus that it has indeed authorised such force. In contrast, alleged UNSC practice of implicit authorisation have always faced the harshest of criticism across a diversity of Member States (and occasionally, regional organisations too).

Fourth, one can legitimately question whether the resolutions assessed above ought to at all be considered as cases of alleged implicit authorisation or whether they are much rather instances of abusive interpretation of UNSC resolutions. For reasons mentioned above, it is submitted that the ambitious attempt to justify the use of force through implicit UNSC authorisation is a practice in legal interpretive gymnastics and certainly not a genuine expression of the UNSC's intentions. The few instances of alleged implicit authorisation have limited, if any precedent at all, in relation to UNSC practice.

At the same time, these resolutions and the interpretation thereof have certainly had a long-term impact on the functioning of the UNSC. The UNSC has, for example, taken a much more cautious approach to ensure that further resolutions are not construed as implicitly authorising force.[168] This has particularly been the case with resolutions adopted on the situations in North Korea, Iran and Syria.[169] In contrast to the resolutions considered above, the overwhelming practice of explicit UNSC authorisation serves as a strong argument pointing towards an established practice. That practice strictly dictates against implicit authorisation.

[168] Security Council Report, 'Security Council Action Under Chapter VII: Myths and Realities (2008) I' *Security Council Report* 1 (Security Council Report) 4; see 17 on the non-necessity of invoking Chapter VII.

[169] Gray, *International Law and the Use of Force* (n 2) 383–84.

7

The (In)admissibility of Retroactive UN Security Council Authorisation

I. INTRODUCTION

THAT IMPLICIT UNITED Nations Security Council (UNSC) authorisation remains controversial under both the Charter of the United Nations (UN Charter) and through UNSC practice has been well detailed in the previous chapter. This chapter now directs its attention to an equally controversial form of authorisation: retroactive authorisation. Similar to that of implicit authorisation, retroactive authorisation has featured prominently in legal literature. Equally so, the very possibility and admissibility of such a form of authorisation has faced significant controversy. Nevertheless, there have been no fewer than three situations in which States and regional organisations have used force without explicit prior authorisation and where the UNSC has subsequently adopted resolutions suggesting a retroactive authorisation.

This has raised prominent questions in international law.[1] First, given the text of the UN Charter, is it legally possible for the UNSC to retroactively authorise force? Does UNSC practice of alleged retroactive authorisation support such a

[1] See Olivier Corten, *The Law Against War: The Prohibition on the Use of Force in Contemporary International Law* (2nd edn, Hart Publishing 2021) 370–90; Patrice Ekomodi Totshingo, 'L'autorisation de recourir à la force accordée par le Conseil de sécurité des Nations Unies' (University of Montreal 2009) 112–24; Inger Österdahl, 'Preach What you Practice: The Security Council and the Legislation *Ex Post Facto* of the Unilateral Use of Force' (2005) 74 *Nordic Journal of International Law* 231. See the view taken by in Jules Lobel and Michael Ratner, 'Bypassing the Security Council: Ambitious Authorisations to Use Force, Cease-Fires and the Iraqi Inspection Regime' (1999) 93(1) *American Journal of International Law* 125, who argue against implicit or unclear authorisations based on the UN Charter's resort to force as a last measure, presupposing that peaceful measures ought to first be entirely exhausted. See also Erika de Wet, *The Chapter VII Powers of the United Nations Security Council* (Hart Publishing 2004) who similarly supports the need for prior explicit UNSC authorisation. However, see on a contrary note Ben Kioko, 'The Right of Intervention Under the African Union's Constitutive Act: From Non-Interference to Non-Intervention' (2003) 85 *RICR* 821 on the drafting history and intention of the drafters of the AU Constitutive Act and intervention without UNSC authorisation. See also Thomas Franck, 'When, If Ever, May States Deploy Military Force Without Prior Security Council Authorisation?' (2001) 5 *Washington University Journal of Law and Policy* 56–57, 65 suggesting that the 1997 ECOWAS intervention in Liberia was retroactively authorised.

possibility? What is the effect of UNSC resolutions adopted after the use of force has commenced? Moreover, when assessing the respective UNSC resolutions, it becomes clear that in addition to being considered retroactive authorisation, they are also implicit in their authorisation. Nonetheless, as with the analysis in previous chapters, UNSC resolutions must be interpreted holistically, considering their provisions and the context surrounding their adoption.

This chapter will first consider some doctrinal debates concerned with retroactive authorisation and the provisions of the UN Charter. It will then examine the respective cases and corresponding resolutions in which retroactive authorisation has been argued. These include the resolutions adopted following the Economic Community of West African States' (ECOWAS) interventions into both Liberia in 1990 and Sierra Leone in 1997, and the North Atlantic Treaty Organisation's (NATO) intervention against the Federal Republic of Yugoslavia (FRY) in 1999.

II. DOCTRINAL DEBATES AND THE (IN)ADMISSIBILITY OF RETROACTIVE AUTHORISATION

The *travaux préparatoires* of the UN Charter does not provide sufficient clarity on whether UNSC authorisation needs to be prior to the enforcement action in question. Even so, discussions on the need for prior authorisation featured prominently. During the third commission on amendments to the Dumbarton Oaks Agreement, Venezuela indicated that prior UNSC authorisation may cause delays when a regional organisation was to 'neutralise the effects of measures of a peremptory character'.[2] It added that consideration should be given to the fact that such action may be taken but subject to 'revision by the [UNSC]', although it remains unclear what exactly is meant if the UNSC revises action.[3] Czechoslovakia proposed that measures taken may be submitted to the UNSC for its approval after the fact, but only in cases where the UNSC had authorised automatic action in advance.[4] This implies at least that some prior authorisation was given (perhaps an ex ante authorisation, that need not be approved on an ad hoc basis). France suggested that prior UNSC authorisation was not needed with measures of an urgent nature provided for in treaties of assistance of which the UNSC had been informed. It did insist that there was an obligation to report to the UNSC on the measures taken. Turkey similarly suggested that all regional organisations of a defensive nature would not need prior authorisation so long

[2] United Nations, 'United Nations Conference on International Organisation' San Francisco, 1945, Volume XII, Commission III Security Council (UNCIO) 784.

[3] United Nations, 'United Nations Conference on International Organisation' San Francisco, 1945, Volume XII, Commission III Security Council (UNCIO) 784.

[4] United Nations, 'United Nations Conference on International Organisation' San Francisco, 1945, Volume XII, Commission III Security Council (UNCIO) 837. See also Volume III 470.

as they reported their actions to the UNSC.[5] On one other occasion, Belgium expressed its stance that in matters where immediate action may be necessary, enforcement action should 'not be held in abeyance pending the Security Council's authorisation'.[6] However, it added that it was appropriate that the UNSC retained control over the action undertaken and that it would retain the right to suspend such action. In contrast, Bolivia submitted that States could only take enforcement action with prior UNSC approval.[7]

Neither Article 42 nor Article 53 refers to a need for authorisation prior to the enforcement action in question. This of course does not necessitate a conclusion that retroactive authorisation is legally acceptable under the UN Charter. A number of arguments have been put forward in literature arguing in favour of prior authorisation.

In particular, Corten has forwarded several arguments against 'presumed authorisation', both implicit and retroactive, that are worth noting. First, presumed (retroactive) authorisation is incompatible with the 'institutional logic' of the UNSC's powers in so far as authorisation needs to be established at the time UNSC Member States vote on such decision.[8] In other words, authorisation must be established at the time that Member States vote for it, thereby excluding the possibility that States could argue in favour of authorisation after a resolution is adopted (and where they had not done so during the adoption of such resolution).[9]

Second, UNSC authorisation is subject to limitations in so far as the UNSC is required to maintain some control over operations it authorises – including the obligation to report to the UNSC on authorisation made use of.[10] It is entirely debatable whether the UNSC is able to exercise control over operations it authorises where such authorisation has been given after the fact. Third, Corten rightly notes that the UNSC has in practice never formally authorised a prior use of force. Rather, resolutions adopted subsequent to the use of force have at most considered facts on the ground without a specific vote on authorisation of force itself.[11] Finally, retroactive authorisation of force seems to go against the 'logic of the intertemporal law of international responsibility'.[12] In other words,

[5] United Nations, 'United Nations Conference on International Organisation' San Francisco, 1945, Volume XII, Commission III Security Council (UNCIO) 837. See also Volume III at 387.

[6] United Nations, 'United Nations Conference on International Organisation' San Francisco, 1945, Volume III, Dumbarton Oaks Proposals: Comments and Proposed Amendments 334.

[7] United Nations, 'United Nations Conference on International Organisation' San Francisco, 1945, Volume III, Dumbarton Oaks Proposals: Comments and Proposed Amendments 836.

[8] Corten, *The Law Against War* (n 1) 393; Totshingo, *L'autorisation de recourir à la force* (n 1) 143–44.

[9] Corten, *The Law Against War* (n 1) 393; Totshingo, *L'autorisation de recourir à la force* (n 1) 143–44.

[10] Corten, *The Law Against War* (n 1) 393–94.

[11] Corten, *The Law Against War* (n 1) 393.

[12] Corten, *The Law Against War* (n 1) 392; Totshingo, *L'autorisation de recourir à la force* (n 1) 144.

an initial and unlawful use of force, if retroactively authorised, would legalise such use of force. This could create serious uncertainty where the role of parties to conflict, aggressor and victim State, could be entirely reversed.[13] As Corten points out, a State initially acting in self-defence could therefore find itself the aggressor.[14]

A further argument in favour of prior authorisation can also be deduced from the UN Charter system of collective security. Article 24 gives the UNSC primary responsibility over matters of international peace and security. It is arguable that where Member States or regional organisations engage in the use of force without prior authorisation, they violate the UNSC's competencies as the primary organ responsible for international peace and security.[15] Such violation could by extension also be contrary to Articles 39, 42 and 48, which empowers (only) the UNSC to determine the existence of a threat to international peace and security before authorising force. These provisions empower the UNSC with decision making authority (and not Member States). More so, if one reads Article 43 simply to ascertain the intention of the collective security system of the chapter, it is clear that Member States should make available to the UNSC armed forces 'on its call'. This not only reaffirms that it is the UNSC that takes decisions on enforcement action, but that Member States are to assist only once the UNSC has taken such a decision. This in turn implies a forward-looking situation in which Member States are to contribute *after* the UNSC has taken a decision. This is supported by the provisions of Article 48, under which it is the UNSC which may decide who and how many Member States are needed for 'action required to carry out the decisions of the Security Council'. Again, this provision implies a forward-looking approach where the UNSC has first taken a decision and thereafter has called on Member States to assist it in implementing such a decision. In turn, this implies that the UN Charter does not allow for action by Member States first to be taken, and afterwards for the UNSC to decide on its necessity and only then to authorise it.[16]

Despite these challenges, arguments in favour of retroactive authorisation have been raised on no less than three separate situations. For this reason, attention is directed at examining both the substantive resolutions adopted by the UNSC and the subsequent State reactions to these resolutions in determining whether they had in fact authorised the preceding interventions in question.

[13] Corten, *The Law Against War* (n 1) 394; Totshingo, *L'autorisation de recourir à la force* (n 1) 144.

[14] Corten, *The Law Against War* (n 1) 394.

[15] Corten, *The Law Against War* (n 1) 393; Lobel and Ratner, 'Bypassing the Security Council' (n 1) 135.

[16] Similar sentiment may be shared on the wording of Art 53, which states the UNSC 'shall', where appropriate, utilise regional organisations. See also Djamchid Momtaz, 'La Delegation par le Conseil de Sécurité de L'exécution de ses Actions Coercitives aux Organisations Régionales' (1997) 43 *Annuaire Français de Droit International* 113–14.

III. ALLEGED UNSC PRACTICE OF RETROACTIVE AUTHORISATION

A. Resolutions 788 (1992) and 866 (1993) | Liberia

In response to the escalation of violence during the Liberian civil war of 1989, on 27 August 1990, ECOWAS deployed its Cease-Fire Monitoring Group (ECOMOG). The ECOWAS operation raised notable questions as to its legal basis, with arguments ranging from intervention by invitation to humanitarian assistance. ECOWAS at the time possessed no legal instruments that would have allowed for the intervention,[17] neither had the UNSC adopted a resolution authorising the ECOWAS deployment, at least not before the deployment commenced.[18] Although there was no prior authorisation for the intervention, the UNSC subsequently adopted no less than 15 resolutions dealing with the situation in Liberia over the course of six years following the ECOWAS deployment. While most of these resolutions dealt with the follow-up UN Observer Mission in Liberia, several resolutions in particular made mention of the preceding ECOWAS actions. The principal issue raised was whether the UNSC had retroactively authorised the preceding ECOWAS enforcement action or whether it had merely endorsed a regional peacekeeping initiative.

Two resolutions are cited in scholarship as having 'authorised' or 'approved' of the ECOWAS operation: Resolutions 788 (1992) and Resolution 866 (1993).[19] In Resolution 788 (1992), the UNSC explicitly determined the deterioration of the situation in Liberia constituted a threat to international peace and security and recalled Chapter VIII of the UN Charter.[20] While it welcomed the continued ECOWAS 'efforts towards a peaceful resolution of the Liberian conflict', operative paragraph one commended ECOWAS for its 'efforts to restore peace,

[17] De Wet, *The Chapter VII Powers* (n 1) 289–99; Ugo Villani, 'The ECOWAS Intervention in Liberia – 1990–97' in Tom Ruys and Olivier Corten (eds), *The Use of Force in International Law: A Case-Based Approach* (Oxford University Press 2018) 448.

[18] De Wet, *The Chapter VII Powers* (n 1) 299.

[19] UNSC Res 788 (1992) para 1 and UNSC Res 813 (1993) para 1; De Wet, *The Chapter VII Powers* (n 1) 299. There is some disparity on whether the UNSC authorised these interventions, or merely approved of them. See Christopher Greenwood, 'International Law and the NATO Intervention in Kosovo' (2000) 49 *International and Comparative Law Quarterly* 929 who refers to approval of the Liberian intervention; Gary Wilson, *The United Nations and Collective Security* (Routledge 2014) 213 refers to it as commendation as per the wording of the relevant resolutions. Christine Gray, *International Law and the Use of Force* (Oxford University Press 2018) 429 similarly refrains from using the term 'authorisation', rather suggesting that the legality of the ECOWAS operations seemed to have been assumed by the UNSC. Villani, 'The ECOWAS Intervention in Liberia' (n 17) 453 raises the same distinction between 'authorisation' and 'approval' or 'ratification'. See also other terms used such as 'legalisation', 'commendation' and 'authorisation' in Vera Gowlland-Debbas, 'The Limits of Unilateral Enforcement of Community Objectives in the Framework of UN Peace Maintenance' (2000) 11(2) *European Journal of International Law* 375; Österdahl, 'Preach What you Practice' (n 1) 239, 246.

[20] UNSC Res 788 (1992) preamble paras 5, 6.

security and stability in Liberia'.[21] Other operative paragraphs made mention of ECOWAS peacekeeping forces and the implementation of ceasefire agreements.[22]

The question which subsequently arose was whether Resolution 788 (1992) was a case of retroactive authorisation or whether the UNSC was merely 'approving' a regional peacekeeping mission. Despite having determined the situation in Liberia as a threat to peace and security, there is little that points towards any real authorisation of the preceding ECOWAS operation. The resolution had only *recalled* Chapter VIII in the preamble, therefore not invoking it in the ordinary sense that the UNSC does. Chapter VII was only invoked from operative paragraph 8 onward and pertained to the enforcement of an arms embargo; a requested in fact made by ECOWAS itself.[23] The invocation of Chapter VII from operative paragraph 8 onwards would also exclude its application to operative paragraph one in which the UNSC 'commended' ECOWAS for its actions.[24] In addition, the UNSC has never authorised the use of force by 'commending' an entity, opting rather for terms such as 'authorises', 'calls upon' or 'decides'.[25] The use of such language in Resolution 788 (1992) can rightfully be called vague, and it seems unlikely to entail any proper authorisation.[26]

Equally as significant is the fact that in operative paragraph four, the UNSC referred to the ECOWAS deployment as a peacekeeping force. This suggests that at the time the resolution was adopted, the UNSC had taken into account that the ECOWAS deployment had been made at the request of the Liberian government and that the rebel forces themselves had consented to the ECOWAS peace proposal.[27] In effect, this may have granted the ECOWAS deployment a classic peacekeeping status.[28] Should this be the case, then UNSC authorisation of

[21] UNSC Res 788 (1992), preamble para 8, para 1.

[22] UNSC Res 788 (1992), paras 3, 4, 6, 9.

[23] Villani, 'The ECOWAS Intervention in Liberia' (n 17) 452.

[24] See also Simon Chesterman, *Just War or Just Peace? Humanitarian Intervention and International Law* (Oxford University Press 2000) 178.

[25] As Gowlland-Debbas, 'The Limits of Unilateral Enforcement' (n 19) 375 points out, it is also not clear as to whether the UNSC was endorsing ECOWAS diplomatic efforts or military actions. See also Österdahl, 'Preach What you Practice' (n 1) 241.

[26] See also Lobel and Ratner, 'Bypassing the Security Council' (n 1) 132. As Marten Zwananeburg, 'Regional Organisations and the Maintenance of International Peace and Security: Three Recent Regional African Peace Operations' (2006) 11(3) *Journal of Conflict and Security Law* 507 states, UNSC decisions to authorise force should be expressed in clear language. See also Corten, *The Law Against War* (n 1) 374–78 suggests that the only Chapter VII enforcement regards the arms embargo pursuant to Article 41 of the UN Charter, adding that ECOWAS in fact never requested authorisation.

[27] See also De Wet, *The Chapter VII Powers* (n 1) 300–01.

[28] Herbert Howe, 'Lessons of Liberia: ECOMOG and Regional Peacekeeping' (1996/1997) 21(3) *International Security* 151–52 acknowledges that the ECOWAS deployment in Liberia received a broad mandate which encompassed both peacekeeping and peace enforcement. See broadly also David Wippman, 'Pro-Democratic Intervention' in Marc Weller (ed), *The Oxford Handbook of the Use of Force in International Law* (Oxford University Press 2015) 804. Villani, 'The ECOWAS Intervention in Liberia' (n 17) 446 states that the ECOWAS deployment cannot be seen as a classic peacekeeping mission since it was established without the consent of Charles Taylor or the National

enforcement action would have been unnecessary.[29] In contrast to this, however, is the fact that at the time Resolution 788 (1992) was adopted, it was well detailed that the ECOWAS peace plans and ceasefire had been violated and the situation may not have represented a true mutual consensus to peacekeeping.[30] At the same time, however, Resolution 788 (1992) took this into account when it condemned the violation of ceasefire agreements by the parties to the conflict.[31]

Given the language adopted in Resolution 788 (1992) and the consent underpinning the ECOWAS deployment, it cannot reasonably be said that the UNSC properly authorised the ECOWAS actions in Liberia. Instead, what seems more logical is that the UNSC had approved of the ECOWAS initiative without formally authorising it.[32]

Some 10 months later the UNSC adopted Resolution 866 (1993) in which it established the United Nations Observer Mission in Liberia (UNOMIL).[33] Resolution 866 (1993) notably acknowledged that UNOMIL would be the first UN peacekeeping mission in Liberia and would cooperate with the ECOMOG. The preamble also acknowledged that peace agreements signed at the time assigned primary responsibility of implementing military provisions of the agreement with ECOWAS. UNOMIL was evidently tasked with a secondary responsibility of monitoring and verifying the process. It has been pointed out that the mere fact that UNOMIL was not tasked with enforcement action did not necessitate the conclusion that ECOWAS was.[34]

As significant is the fact that Resolution 866 (1993) deviates considerably from the manner in which the UNSC ordinarily authorises enforcement action. Resolution 866 (1993) did not itself determine the situation in Liberia a threat to peace and security, although recalling two previous resolutions that had made such a determination. There also was no invocation or mention of Chapters VII or VIII in the resolution.[35] In addition and similar to that of Resolution 788 (1992), there was no language in the resolution of which the UNSC ordinarily made use when authorising enforcement action.[36] When it chose to commend the ECOWAS actions, it did so on the basis of approving the peacekeeping engagement, rather than granting formal UNSC authorisation to the operation.

Patriotic Front of Liberia. See also Michelle Pitts, 'Sub-Regional Solutions for African Conflicts: The ECOMOG Experiment' (1999) 19(1) *Journal of Conflict Studies* 5.

[29] De Wet, *The Chapter VII Powers* (n 1) 301; Corten, *The Law Against War* (n 1) 372.

[30] Villani, 'The ECOWAS Intervention in Liberia' (n 17) 450.

[31] Corten, *The Law Against War* (n 1) 376. As Corten describes this, the resolution rather considers the ECOWAS action as a peacekeeping operation in the absence of state opposition.

[32] The general consensus suggests that the UNSC had tacitly approved the ECOWAS deployment although not formally authorising it. See also Villani, *The ECOWAS Intervention in Liberia* (n 17) 452–54.

[33] UNSC Res 866 (1993) para 2.

[34] De Wet, *The Chapter VII Powers* (n 3) 300–01; Corten, *The Law Against War* (n 1) 376.

[35] Corten, *The Law Against War* (n 1) 376–77.

[36] Corten, *The Law Against War* (n 1) 376.

It remains unconvincing that the UNSC intended to formally authorise the ECOWAS operations. No mention of authorisation or even the need therefore was made in UNSC debates on either resolution. Rather, there was continuous support for diplomatic and peaceful solutions to end the conflict in Liberia, with significant praise for the ECOWAS mediation efforts in the country.[37] Additionally, ECOWAS and its Member States received praise for attempting to resolve the situation among themselves.[38] Beyond the commendation it accorded to ECOWAS, the UNSC at no point set out a mandate for its deployment, neither did it impose any time limits on the supposed enforcement action. Consequently, no reporting obligations were imposed on ECOWAS either. This fact is understandable if one considers that the UNSC did not intend to authorise any enforcement action in Liberia.

In summary, the adoption of subsequent resolutions on Liberia following the ECOWAS deployment were meant to address the longer-term stability of the country. This was evident through its continued support for the relevant peace processes and the establishment of the follow-up UN peacekeeping mission. The UNSC could not reasonably have addressed the issues in Liberia without acknowledging the ECOWAS presence and its contribution to stability in the region. In so doing, it was clear that the UNSC had decided to not only acknowledge the ECOWAS actions, but to support it in so far as it had considered it a classic peacekeeping operation meant to assist in the implementation of peace agreements.[39] The resolutions subsequently adopted, while tacitly approving the operation, do not constitute implicit retroactive authorisation.[40]

Most importantly however and as Corten points out, arguments in favour of retroactive authorisation in the case of Liberia remain scholarly. Neither ECOWAS nor its Member States have claimed to have been retroactively authorised.[41]

B. Resolutions 1132 (1997) and 1181 (1998) | Sierra Leone

Six years after ECOWAS had deployed its ECOMOG forces in Liberia, a similar situation started to unfold in Sierra Leone when a military coup ousted President Kabbah. An increase in violence across Sierra Leone led ECOWAS to extend

[37] See UN Doc S.PV.3138 (1992).

[38] UN Doc S.PV.3138 (1992), see for example 62 (Zimbabwe), 71 (China), 74–76 (United States), 83 (Japan), 87 (India).

[39] See however Moritz Moelle, *The International Responsibility of International Organisations: Cooperation in Peacekeeping Operations* (Cambridge University Press 2017) 124, who notes that the commendation by the UNSC president of the ECOWAS operation in UN Doc S/22133 (1991) was akin to ex post facto authorisation.

[40] This conclusion is shared by many scholars. See Villani, *The ECOWAS Intervention in Liberia* (n 17) 452–54; Zwanenburg, 'Regional Organisations and the Maintenance of International Peace and Security' (n 26) 506–07; Corten, *The Law Against War* (n 1) 373.

[41] Corten, *The Law Against War* (n 1) 378.

ECOMOG's mandate to restore legitimate order there. Peaceful methods failed of resolve the conflict and by February 1998 ECOMOG intervened militarily. As with its Liberian intervention, neither ECOWAS legal instruments nor prior UNSC authorisation permitted the intervention. Unlike in Liberia however, the UNSC decided on an arms and oil embargo shortly after the ECOWAS deployment had commenced.

The UNSC adopted several additional resolutions over the course of two years, seemingly approving the ECOWAS intervention. Consequently, similar questions were raised as to whether the UNSC had retroactively authorised ECOWAS. Several additional issues of legality were also raised in this regard. As with Liberia, it was again unclear whether the ECOWAS intervention was based on a request by the ousted Sierra Leone President and whether UNSC authorisation was at all necessary. Some authors have also argued that the Sierra Leone intervention was an example of humanitarian intervention. Further, the ECOWAS action in Sierra Leone was continuously referred to as a peacekeeping mission, again questioning whether it was in fact enforcement action under the UN Charter and, consequently, whether UNSC authorisation was at all necessary.

The ECOWAS response to the situation in Sierra Leone first came when it adopted its own arms and oil embargo.[42] During its 20th session of the Authority of Heads of State and Government, ECOWAS decided that Member States were to use 'all necessary means' in implementing the embargo.[43] At that time, the UNSC gave support to the ECOWAS mediation efforts, and on several occasions presidential statements supported in particular the ECOWAS objective to restore the legitimate government of Sierra Leone.[44] On 8 October 1997 the UNSC adopted Resolution 1132 (1997), its first resolution at the time to authorise enforcement action. That resolution determined that the situation in Sierra Leone constituted a threat to peace and security and invoked Chapter VII in its operative paragraphs. While expressing full support for the ECOWAS mediation efforts, the UNSC's only decision on enforcement measures concerned the establishment and enforcement of an UN arms and petroleum embargo against Sierra Leone.[45]

The task of ensuring the implementation of the embargo was placed with ECOWAS. *Acting also* under Chapter VIII, the UNSC authorised ECOWAS to ensure strict implementation of the embargo by halting inward maritime shipping in order to verify and inspect cargo.[46] In addition, the UNSC had imposed a reporting requirement by ECOWAS on a 30-day cycle of measures it had taken pursuant to its authorisation.[47] Beyond this objective, there seemed to be no additional basis upon which the UNSC had authorised more broader ECOWAS

[42] UN Doc S/1997/695 (1997) para 25.
[43] See Arts 2, 7, Annex, UN Doc S/1997/695 (1997).
[44] See UN Doc S/PRST/1997/36 (1997) 1–2.
[45] UNSC Res 1132 (1997) para 7.
[46] UNSC Res 1132 (1997) para 8.
[47] UNSC Res 1132 (1997) para 9.

enforcement action. The exact purpose of Resolution 1132 (1997), therefore, was the imposition of the embargo which had aimed to ensure the return of Sierra Leone's legitimate government. To this end, it has been noted that Resolution 1132 (1997) therefore imposed certain restrictions on the authorisation granted to ECOWAS when it was to enforce the embargo. First, while the authorisation was not limited in time, it nonetheless contained a functional limitation, namely, that the authorisation persisted until the legitimate government's return to power.[48] Consequently, when President Kabbah returned to power, the UNSC terminated the oil embargo under Resolution 1156 (1998), and then the arms embargo under Resolution 1171 (1998).[49] Thus, as has been correctly suggested, upon the termination of these embargoes, the ECOWAS enforcement thereof was also terminated.[50]

Despite the fact that Resolution 1132 (1997) could not have been interpreted as authorisation for the ECOWAS operation (at least not beyond the task of enforcing the UN embargo), the UNSC passed several additional resolutions in which it commended ECOWAS for its role in Sierra Leone. It should also be noted that the ECOWAS operation subsisted well into the early 2000s and after the UNSC had terminated its arms and oil embargoes in 1998.[51] As with the ECOWAS operations in Liberia, these resolutions were adopted during a time when ECOAWS was still engaged in hostilities. As a result, they have also been interpreted as *retroactive* authorisation of the ECOWAS deployment. Among these was Resolution 1162 (1998) in which the UNSC commended ECOWAS for its support in restoring peace and security in Sierra Leone. Resolution 1162 (1998), although recalling previous resolutions, did not in itself determine the situation in Sierra Leone to be a threat to peace and security, nor was it adopted under Chapter VII.[52] Other resolutions adopted at the time that invoked Chapter VII either did not attribute it to the ECOWAS action or imposed embargoes on non-governmental officials and forces.[53] Under later resolutions, the UNSC commended ECOWAS for its contribution to security and stability, and specifically for the protection of civilians and the promotion of a peaceful settlement to the conflict.[54] These statements were made in resolutions adopted outside of Chapter VII and contained no language that could rightfully be construed as retroactive authorisation.[55]

As such, the resolutions adopted on the situation in Sierra Leone did not seem to authorise ECOWAS enforcement action beyond the UN arms and oil embargo. None of the resolutions commending its actions were adopted

[48] De Wet, *The Chapter VII Powers* (n 1) 302.
[49] De Wet, *The Chapter VII Powers* (n 1) 302–03.
[50] De Wet, *The Chapter VII Powers* (n 1) 303.
[51] De Wet, *The Chapter VII Powers* (n 1) 303; see also Chesterman, *Just War or Just Peace?* (n 24) 156.
[52] UNSC Res 1162 (1998).
[53] See for example UNSC Res 1171 (1998) para 5.
[54] UNSC Res 1260 (1999) para 3.
[55] De Wet, *The Chapter VII Powers* (n 1) 303.

under Chapter VII (or VIII) pursuant to an Article 39 determination, and none contained any language the UNSC has ordinarily come to use to authorise force. These resolutions are only comparable to the ones adopted on Liberia in that they, over and above acknowledging the ECOWAS presence, chose to express the UNSC's approval of its actions.

If one compares these resolutions to those adopted during the same time span which explicitly authorised the use of force, it becomes clear that it was not the intention of the UNSC to authorise any force. It must also be noted that when the UNSC in that same decade authorised force by Member States, other regional organisations, and peacekeeping missions, it consistently did so prior to the action in question, and explicitly so by *authorising* all necessary means or measures. More so, the UNSC always indicated to whom authorisation was granted, the objectives of such authorisation, and on occasion gave a time limit and reporting obligations on entities it authorised. No such characteristics were present in those resolution adopted on the situation in Sierra Leone. As such, its vague language of commending the ECOWAS actions were more notably a fact it considered present on the ground, rather than an intention to authorise the use of force in a situation in which it had itself only considered Article 41 measures.

Beyond what has been said above, as was the case with Liberia, the ECOWAS action in Sierra Leone faced questions similar to that of an alternative legal basis, namely, intervention by invitation. By the time the UNSC had adopted its first resolution on the situation, ECOWAS had already been engaged in what arguably was a request for assistance by President Kabbah. Again, that he longer was in effective control of Sierra Leone did not detract from the fact that he was widely recognised as the legitimate head of government. It has been rightfully suggested that for this reason, a UNSC resolution authorising ECOWAS enforcement action may have been unnecessary since ECOWAS was acting upon a request for intervention. This conclusion may be supported by the fact that the UNSC chose to address only the enforcement of an arms and oil embargo under Resolution 1132 (1997), since ECOWAS could not engage militarily in international waters based on a request for assistance. Resolution 1132 (1997) therefore gave ECOWAS this right which could, beyond its existing deployment, also broaden its enforcement action against the military junta in Sierra Leone.

The fact that the UNSC itself may have recognised this as a legal basis for ECOWAS finds some support in the expression of later resolutions. In particular, under Resolution 1181 (1998) the UNSC commended the positive efforts of ECOWAS in restoring peace, security and stability throughout Sierra Leone, adding that it was done so 'at the request of the [g]overnment of Sierra Leone'.[56] On the one hand, this may perhaps suggest that the UNSC had considered

[56] UNSC Res 1181 (1998) para 5. See also UNSC Res 1231 (1999) para 10 in which the UNSC again commended ECOWAS for its efforts at restoring peace, security and stability in Sierra Leone, calls upon member states to provide ECOMOG with financial and logistical support and 'to consider the provision of prompt bilateral assistance to the government of Sierra Leone'.

intervention by invitation as a legal basis for the ECOWAS action at the time, and in particular since the ECOWAS action was ongoing even after it had terminated its respective embargoes. Of course, on the other hand, it must be noted that at the time of the adoption of the resolutions, President Kabbah had been restored as the head of government for some four months, thereby giving legitimacy to any further request for assistance by ECOWAS.

A final consideration worth noting is whether the ECOWAS action could at all be considered enforcement action. It has been suggested that as with the Liberian engagement, the ECOWAS deployment may have been more of a peacekeeping mission than an enforcement action, thereby circumventing the need for formal UNSC authorisation. As has been noted, the ECOWAS action in Sierra Leone was from the outset presented as non-coercive.[57] ECOWAS itself refrained from any mention of its actions as being construed under Article 53 enforcement action.[58] On occasion, the ECOWAS engagement against the military junta was considered an act of self-defence in line with principles of peacekeeping.[59] The organisation was thus seemingly acting as a peacekeeping entity and did not seek UNSC authorisation for its actions. This sentiment was on several occasions supported even by the UNSC when it, for example, commended ECOWAS efforts and called on Member States to provide technical and logistical support so that ECOMOG might continue in its ability to 'carry out its peacekeeping role'.[60]

Finally, that the ECOWAS action was undertaken at the request of the government of Sierra Leone was also strongly shared among UNSC representatives in several Council meetings, suggesting the broader understanding of the ECOWAS action as falling beyond enforcement action requiring UNSC authorisation.[61] Rather than reflecting an instance of retroactive authorisation, the resolutions adopted on the situation in Sierra Leone were an ex post facto approval and acknowledgement of the situation on the ground.[62]

C. Resolution 1244 (1999) | Kosovo

The examination above considering retroactive UNSC authorisation of the ECOWAS operations was limited to three common characteristics: both

[57] Corten, *The Law Against War* (n 1) 378.

[58] See for example ECOWAS, 'Twentieth Ordinary Session' (Abuja, Nigeria, 28, 29 August 1997) para 25.

[59] Corten, *The Law Against War* (n 1) 379.

[60] UN Doc S/PRST/1998/13 (1998); see also UN Doc S/PRST/1998/5 (1998) and Corten, *The Law Against War* (n 1) 380.

[61] Corten, *The Law Against War* (n 1) 379. See also UN Doc S/PV.3882 (1998); UN Doc S/PV.3902 (1998) statements by Austria (3); United Kingdom (4); Slovenia (7); and Sweden (11). What also stands out is the reference of the complementarity between ECOMOG and the UN peacekeeping operation followed up to ECOMOG and UNOMSIL. See also UN Doc S/PV.3857 (1998). However, see UN Doc S/1997/499 (27 June 1997) para 9(iii) on a limited instance to the contrary.

[62] As concluded by De Wet, *The Chapter VII Powers* (n 1) 304. See Chesterman, *Just War or Just Peace?* (n 24) 156 who refers to it as 'retrospective validation' rather than authorisation.

operations were conducted by an Article 53 regional organisation, both operations faced similar ambivalence as to their legal basis (peacekeeping or enforcement action), and both operations faced plausible justifications based on intervention by invitation. In addition, not a single UNSC Member State condemned or disapproved of the operations and neither ECOWAS nor the UNSC had ever claimed any retroactive authorisation. As such, subsequent resolutions reflected more of an ex post facto stamp of approval rather than formal or substantive authorisation.

This position changed significantly when in 1999 NATO carried out a 78-day military campaign against the FRY. Despite no prior explicit UNSC authorisation, the NATO operation was justified on several grounds. Among these were that it was based on a right of humanitarian intervention and that it was also implicitly authorised by the UNSC based on three resolutions adopted prior to the operation.[63] While implicit authorisation was considered in the previous chapter, attention in now directed at one final justification, that the adoption of Resolution 1244 (1999) may have retroactively authorised the preceding NATO operation.

Arguments favouring retroactive authorisation under Resolution 1244 (1999) may be considered along two lines. The first is that the UNSC did not formally condemn the preceding NATO operation, therefore implicitly authorising it. This argument has already been addressed above and may be dispensed with in so far as the silence of the UNSC cannot be equated to an implicit authorisation. Additionally, to say that the NATO operation was not condemned is inaccurate, with a Russian draft resolution seeking to declare the operation unlawful.[64] More generally, the NATO operation faced considerable condemnation among UN Member States than most other non-UNSC authorised operations.

The second argument directly concerns the adoption of Resolution 1244 (1999) and that the establishment of a NATO presence in Kosovo may in itself be considered retroactive authorisation of the preceding NATO intervention.[65] An examination of Resolution 1244's (1999) provisions however suggest otherwise. First and foremost, unlike those resolutions adopted on the ECOWAS operations, Resolution 1244 (1999) makes no mention of the preceding NATO intervention. It therefore neither acknowledges nor commends those actions.[66] This of course does not suggest that the UNSC chose to ignore the operation. Rather, in light of

[63] See broadly Daniel Franschini and Antonios Tzanakopoulos, 'The Kosovo Crisis – 1999' in Ruys and Corten (n 17) 608–18. These include UNSC Res 1160 (1998), UNSC Res 1199 (1998) and UNSC Res 1203 (1998). See ch 6 at p 162–164.

[64] UN Doc S/1999/328 (1999). Corten, *The Law Against War* (n 1) 384; De Wet, *The Chapter VII Powers* (n 1) 307.

[65] However, Zsuzsanna Deen-Racsmany, 'A Redistribution of Authority Between the UN and Regional Organizations in the Field of the Maintenance of Peace and Security' (2000) 13(2) *Leiden Journal of International Law* 329, while acknowledging this as a possibility, suggests in light of the criticism to the NATO intervention in Kosovo, that there is no relaxation of obligations to seek explicit, prior UNSC authorisation; cf 330 regarding the position when an intervention is supported by the internationally recognised or legitimate government.

[66] Deen-Racsmany (n 65) 324; Corten, *The Law Against War* (n 1) 385.

the serious reservations against it, particularly by Russia, China and even India, it was politically unlikely that the resolution would have been passed if it in any way gave even the slightest approval to the NATO operation.[67]

In a similar vein, the intervention faced strong resistance from several UNSC permanent members both before and after its occurrence. Again, both Russia and China had in clear terms stated, preceding the adoption of Resolutions 1160 (1998) and 1199 (1998), that they would veto any resolution that sought to authorise NATO intervention in the FRY. Therefore, the adoption of Resolution 1244 (1999) was unlikely should it have given any approval to the NATO operation. Consequently, it was apparent at the time that there was no clear consensus among the UNSC over the operation. UNSC debates preceding the adoption of Resolution 1244 (1999) clearly showed the difference in opinion among Member States, suggesting that they were not prepared to adopt any resolution that could have potentially been interpreted as approval of the NATO operation.

Recognising what it called 'an attempt ... at legalising *post festum*' the NATO military campaign, the FRY wanted the resolution to explicitly condemn the attacks against it.[68] China shared similar concerns that the resolution had failed to acknowledge the consequences of the NATO operation, and that limitations to the resolution's invocation of Chapter VII had not been imposed.[69] Russia, however, stated that the invocation of Chapter VII did not at all relate to the use of force but that it was rather intended for the safety and security of international personnel in relation to their assigned tasks under the resolution.[70]

The provisions of Resolution 1244 (1999) likewise disfavour the possibility of any retroactive authorisation. Rather, the authorisation in the resolution can only be interpreted prospectively.[71] The resolution authorised Member States and 'relevant international organisations' to establish an international security presence in Kosovo as set out in annex II of the resolution.[72] The fact of establishment implies a subsequent action, suggesting its prospective nature. Acting under Chapter VII, the UNSC authorised Member States and international organisations to use 'all necessary means' to fulfil the mandate of the international security presence.[73] It must be noted that this mandate by its very nature was a forward-looking one, aimed at creating stable conditions in future. Although some objectives were similar to those towards which the preceding NATO operation seemingly aimed at, they were attributable to the tasks of the International Security Force (KFOR), and not to the preceding NATO operation.

[67] See also Corten, *The Law Against War* (n 1) 386.
[68] UN Doc S/PV.4011 (1999) para 6.
[69] UN Doc S/PV.4011 (1999) 9.
[70] UN Doc S/PV.4011 (1999) 8.
[71] De Wet, *The Chapter VII Powers* (n 1) 307.
[72] UNSC Res 1244 (1999) para 7. The resolution also established an international civil presence for the administration of the territory of Kosovo (UNMIK). See further De Wet, *The Chapter VII Powers* (n 1) 311–12.
[73] UNSC Res 1244 (1999) paras 9(a)–(h).

The adoption of Resolution 1244 (1999) was an attempt by the UNSC to remedy the situation in Kosovo with a longer-term approach. Despite the fact that it did not formally acknowledge the preceding NATO campaign, the UNSC under Resolution 1244 (1999) chose to rather accept the *fait accompli* when it established KFOR.[74] It has been well pointed out that the lack of commendation combined with the very text of the resolution leaves no room for an interpretation favouring retroactive authorisation.[75] On the contrary, should the UNSC have actually intended to authorise any action (even *retroactively*), it ought to have done so explicitly and under clear terms. For this reason, one may even consider that unlike the ECOWAS operations which received retroactive approval, the UNSC did not repeat its actions on Kosovo. This in turn suggests a certain degree of tacit disapproval – a drastic departure from the positive sentiment given on the ECOWAS interventions.

IV. COMPARISON OF CASES AND THE INABILITY TO DEDUCE AN ESTABLISHED PRACTICE

The three cases examined above remain the primary examples cited in favour of retroactive UNSC authorisation. In this light, it is worth noting several issues which these cases have brought up. First is the nexus between retroactive authorisation and additional or alternative (or complimentary) legal basis for the operations in question. It is worth recalling that the operations addressed above arose out of somewhat different contexts. In the case of the ECOWAS actions in Liberia and again in Sierra Leone, the interventions were predominantly aimed at restoring the internationally recognised governments of those states. In contrast, both States and scholars argue that a humanitarian basis underlined the NATO actions against the FRY.

The implications of this specifically pertain to the alternative legal bases present at the time the UNSC had adopted what was argued to be retroactive authorisation. The ECOWAS interventions were arguably taken at the request of the ousted internationally recognised governments. To this end, some scholars maintain that the interventions were consensual, given that they were undertaken pursuant to a request by the internationally recognised governments at the time.[76] In contrast, no parallel may be drawn to that of the NATO intervention, conducted entirely against the consent of the FRY. This reasoning may perhaps lend support to why the UNSC chose to retroactively approve

[74] Corten, *The Law Against War* (n 1) 387; De Wet, *The Chapter VII Powers* (n 1) 297; Franschini and Tzanakopoulos, 'The Kosovo Crisis' (n 17) 612.

[75] Corten, *The Law Against War* (n 1) 386; De Wet, *The Chapter VII Powers* (n 1) 307; Franschini and Tzanakopoulos (n 17) 612.

[76] See broadly Erika de Wet, 'The Modern Practice of Intervention by Invitation in Africa and its Implications for the Prohibition of the Use of Force' (2015) 26 *European Journal of International Law* 983–85, 990–91. See also Gregory Fox, 'Intervention by Invitation' in Weller (n 28) 834–37.

the ECOWAS intervention, and not so the NATO action. On the other hand, however, the actions against the FRY were also seen as humanitarian-based and, thus, received no consent from the government.[77]

On this basis, the relationship between peacekeeping and peace enforcement also requires consideration. Whereas the ECOWAS actions were consistently argued as being of a peacekeeping nature, the NATO intervention was clearly a case of enforcement action.[78] To this end, the opposing spectrums of criticism these operations faced suggest that interventions to restore the legitimate head of a state (at the request of that head of state) may not necessarily be considered enforcement action, even where such an intervention is also not necessarily a peacekeeping force.[79] After all, the status of the ECOWAS deployments in Liberia and Sierra Leone remains disputed, and to classify them as a peacekeeping engagement does not take sufficient account of their actions against the coup instigators. Consequently, the ECOWAS interventions may suggest that, in fact, in such engagements UNSC authorisation is unnecessary. This argument is supported if one also considers that those resolutions commending the ECOWAS actions are nothing more than UNSC approval of what may be regarded as otherwise consensual interventions.

The NATO actions in the FRY differ significantly. Specifically, when one considers the strong condemnation against the operation, one suggestion is that the refusal by states (most notably, Russia and China) to retroactively authorise the NATO action was aimed at breaking any inference of a potential precedent arising from the ECOWAS operations.[80] This may also explain the positions taken up by several States which insisted that NATO required prior, explicit authorisation in conformity with the UN Charter.[81] At the same time, however, the UNSC consistently referred to the ECOWAS actions as 'efforts' toward a 'peaceful resolution' of the crisis. This implies that in the case of Liberia and Sierra Leone, the UNSC was careful not to equate the ECOWAS operation with enforcement action, thereby preventing the interpretation of subsequent resolutions as retroactive authorisation.[82] This was most certainly not the case with the NATO intervention, during which time its actions were consistently referred to as acts of aggression and contrary to Article 2(4) of the UN Charter, even by several permanent UNSC Member States.[83]

Moreover, the divergent contexts under which these resolutions were adopted puts their precedential value into question. It becomes difficult to systematically highlight each resolution and to build an argument that suggests any consistent

[77] The United Kingdom consistently referred to the NATO intervention in Kosovo as based on humanitarian intervention. See also UN Doc S/PV.3988 (1999) 12 and UN Doc S/PV.3989 (1999) 7.

[78] See the full analysis of UNSC Res 1244 (1999) in ch 4 at 117–120.

[79] De Wet, 'The Modern Practice of Intervention' (n 76) 998.

[80] Deen-Racsmany (n 65) 327.

[81] See statements made in the relevant UNSC debates.

[82] Deen-Racsmany (n 65) 327.

[83] See for example UN Doc S/PV.4011 (1999); UN Doc S/1999/328.

or repeated practice. For example, one cannot merely state that the first instance of retroactive authorisation occurred in Liberia and thereafter in Sierra Leone, culminating in a further occurrence in Kosovo. Such an argument does not sufficiently consider the relevant contexts in which these resolutions were adopted nor the weight attributable to potential alterative legal bases of these operations. Notwithstanding arguments contrary to the very permissibility of retroactive authorisation, even if one accepts its practice in the above cases, it is clear that such a practice remains a rare occurrence. To that end, the limited instances in which such a right has been raised disproves any established UNSC practice in this regard.[84]

V. CONCLUSION

The chapter has examined the notion of retroactive authorisation; considering the provisions of the UN Charter, doctrinal debates against such a notion and comparing three instances of alleged UNSC practice. As Österdahl has noted, accepting the possibility of retroactive authorisation is like accepting a unilateral use of force with the possibility of future approval thereof.[85] Such notation would indeed serve to reverse the presumption against the use of force under Article 2(4) of the UN Charter, a well-established rule under international law.[86] Arguments suggesting an exception to this rule based on a possibility that the UNSC may subsequently approve the use of force remain unconvincing. To this end, they do not take due account of the holistic framework of collective security under the UN Charter in which it is the UNSC that is vested with the primary responsibility of regulating the use of force in so far as it seeks to maintain or restore international peace and security.

At the same time, the debate surrounding this form of authorisation emerged already during the drafting of the UN Charter. The *travaux préparatoires* serves as testament to the complex debates and the lack of consensus when the question of prior authorisation first arose. One must concede, however, that States already then realised the potential consequences of limiting enforcement action to take place after an explicit authorisation by the UNSC. Yet, the outcome of these negotiations resulted in a text that arguably maintained a need for prior UNSC authorisation. One reaches this conclusion when examining the very provisions of the UN Charter that restrict the use of force and that enable the UNSC to regulate it as a measure of last resort. As has been pointed out in particular by Corten, it remains difficult to reconcile the UN Charter's provisions with anything but a prior authorisation from the UNSC.[87]

[84] As concluded by Corten, *The Law Against War* (n 1) 388.
[85] Österdahl, 'Preach What you Practice' (n 1) 234.
[86] Österdahl, 'Preach What you Practice' (n 1) 234.
[87] Corten, *The Law Against War* (n 1) 396.

It is only once the UNSC has considered a situation and determined the existence of a threat to international peace and security that it may authorise force, a call to which States and regional organisations alike may heed. Those that act on a situation before the UNSC has considered or decided upon the necessary action required to restore international peace and security deprive it of its primary responsibilities under Article 24 of the UN Charter. More so, they usurp the UNSC's competencies to decide on the necessary actions, be they military or non-military measures. In addition, it remains debatable as to how much control the UNSC would have over operations it has not initiated and has purportedly retroactively 'authorised'.

Considering the alleged UNSC practice argued as supporting retroactive authorisation, it becomes clear that these instances are rarities among a long-standing consistent practice of prior explicit authorisation. In fact, only three such instances have been credited to a retroactive authorisation: the situations in Liberia, in Sierra Leone and in Kosovo. In the case of the ECOWAS interventions in Liberia and Sierra Leone, it was clear that the UNSC may perhaps not have opposed these actions, having on several occasions expressed commendation. It is true in these two situations, both instances may represent a unique UNSC retroactive 'approval', 'legalisation', 'ratification' or 'acceptance' of the ECOWAS operations. Authorisations, however, they are not. Rather, the reference to ECOWAS in the respective UNSC resolutions was a modest approach by the UNSC in acknowledging facts on the ground when it decided on a longer-term solution to the situations.

The resolution adopted following the NATO enforcement action, however, stood in contrast to the ECOWAS experience. The overwhelming criticism voiced by States and regional organisations against the NATO operation, combined with the fact that the UNSC made no mention of its preceding actions, seem to be a clear break from any parallel that may be drawn to that of the ECOWAS interventions. As a result, it was also shown above why any comparison between these three situations would be arbitrary, neglecting the inherently different circumstances, the responses by the organisations in question and in turn the response by the UNSC. Not only have all three cases examined above argued in favour of retroactive authorisation, but they have also evidently fallen into the category of implicit authorisation. As was seen in the previous chapter, arguments in favour of implicit authorisation should be presumed against. A conclusion reasonably reached is that cases of (implicit) retroactive authorisation stand in contrast to an overwhelming practice of prior explicit UNSC authorisation.

8

Contemporary Developments Challenging the Need for Prior Explicit Authorisation

I. INTRODUCTION

UNTIL NOW IT has been argued (and shown) that prior explicit United Nations Security Council (UNSC) authorisation of force is a well-established practice. The analysis has focused on the very form and character of prior explicit authorisation, arguing against instances of implicit and retroactive authorisation. Nevertheless, two contemporary developments need further consideration where UNSC authorisation concerns. Both developments may be summarised collectively as a perceived bypassing of the UNSC and the need for authorisation. The first concerns the development of African regional and sub-regional treaty law frameworks suggesting force may be used without the need for UNSC authorisation. The second concerns the (repeated) resort to individual and collective self-defence by some Member States which itself requires no UNSC authorisation.

The former concerns the Constitutive Act of the African Union, replacing the Organisation of African Unity with that of the African Union (AU). Article 4(h) of the Constitutive Act seemingly empowers the AU to intervene militarily in its Member States in situations of war crimes, genocide and crimes against humanity. Notably, the Constitutive Act makes no mention of the need for UNSC authorisation. In a similar manner, the 1999 Protocol Mechanism of the Economic Community of West African States (ECOWAS) established its own right of intervention without the need for UNSC authorisation. Both the ECOWAS and AU treaty law frameworks have led to much debate about whether UNSC authorisation is at all required. Put differently, can the need for prior explicit UNSC authorisation be avoided by sidestepping the Council completely?

The latter circumstance concerns the reliance on individual and collective self-defence whereby Member States may use force without UNSC authorisation. Several situations, such as the United States intervention in Afghanistan and its broader war on terror, have already been considered in previous chapters. What complicates the matter however, and forms part of the present analysis, is when the UNSC has attempted to address certain situations by itself invoking the provisions of Article 51 within its resolutions. Can the recognition of self-defence in UNSC resolutions render UNSC authorisation unnecessary in certain situations? These considerations concern more the weight attributable to the prohibition of force and its exceptions in the UN Charter, rather than the precise form and character UNSC resolutions take. Nevertheless, they raise equally significant questions as to whether the UNSC's own recognition of an alternative legal basis (such as self-defence) render prior explicit authorisation unnecessary? This ultimately leads to the question whether the recognition of an alternative basis for the use of force is akin to the UNSC authorising force itself?

II. DECENTRALISED COLLECTIVE SECURITY: AFRICAN REGIONAL AND SUB-REGIONAL SECURITY FRAMEWORKS

A. The African Union and Article 4(h)

The AU's Constitutive Act remains the principal instrument driving the AU's approach to continental peace and security.[1] Its most influential provision rests with Article 4(h), which empowers the AU to intervene militarily in its Member States under circumstances of war crimes, genocide and crimes against humanity. The UN Charter is mentioned only incidentally and nowhere is AU intervention conditioned on UNSC authorisation. Consequently, questions have arisen as to its compatibility with Article 53(1) of the UN Charter, which states that no enforcement action may be undertaken without UNSC authorisation. Corresponding literature has approached this question from several perspectives.[2] Some have interpreted Article 4(h) as a treaty-based consent to potential future

[1] Constitutive Act of the African Union (adopted 11 July 2000, entered into force 26 May 2001) 2158 UNTS 3 (Constitutive Act).

[2] See broadly Martin Kunschak, 'The African Union and the Right of Intervention: Is There a Need for UN Security Council Authorisation?' (2006) 31 *South African Yearbook of International Law* 195. See also Dan Kuwali, *Persuasive Prevention: Towards a Principle for Implementing Article 4(h) and R2P by the African Union* (Nordiska Afrikainstitutet 2009); Erika de Wet, 'Regional Organisations and Arrangements: Authorisation, Ratification, or Independent Action' in Marc Weller (ed), *The Oxford Handbook of the Use of Force in International Law* (Oxford University Press 2015) 314; Kithure Kindiki, 'The Normative and Institutional Frameworks of the African Union Relating to the Protection of Human Rights and the Maintenance of International Peace and Security: A Critical Appraisal' (2003) 3 *African Human Rights Law Journal* 108–09; Gabriel Amvane, 'Intervention Pursuant to Article 4(h) of the Constitutive Act of the African Union Without United Nations Security Council Authorisation' (2015) 15 *African Human Rights Law Journal* 283; Suyash Paliwal, 'The Primacy of Regional Organisations in International Peacekeeping: The African Example' (2010) 51 (1) *Virginia Journal of International Law* 185; Ademola Abass and Mashood Baderin, 'Towards Effective Collective Security and Human Rights Protection in Africa: An Assessment of the Constitutive Act of the New African Union' (2002) 49(1) *Netherlands International Law Review* 17; Alemu Aneme, *A Study of the African Union Right of Intervention Against Genocide, War Crimes and Crimes against Humanity* (Wolf Legal Publishers 2011) 184 points out that such consent must, however, be valid.

AU intervention (if the grounds for such intervention arise). Such an interpretation argues that Article 4(h) represents ex ante consent to future intervention (thereby rendering UNSC authorisation unnecessary).[3] These arguments rely on the validity of consent similar to as if it had been given on an ad hoc basis.[4] Not everyone agrees. Some argue that such 'forward-looking' consent is illegal and that ad hoc consent is required for each individual intervention.[5] Nonetheless, if one views Article 4(h) intervention on the basis of consent, it is true that Article 53(1) may be entirely bypassed and the need for UNSC authorisation would not arise.[6]

Another interpretation of Article 4(h) considers it a regional codification of the Responsibility to Protect (R2P) doctrine. Coined in the 2005 World Summit Outcome, the R2P doctrine declares that States have the primary obligation to protect their populations from mass atrocities. That responsibility falls on the international community in cases where States are unable or unwilling to protect their populations. In this light, Article 4(h) is seen as a regional right of humanitarian intervention.[7] That said, whether a right of humanitarian intervention exists in international law is highly controversial. The UN Charter makes no exception for such a right. In addition, the need for UNSC authorisation in all cases was explicitly brought up both in the 2005 World Summit Outcome and the Report of the International Commission on Intervention and State Sovereignty (ICISS).[8]

A final and more novel interpretation of Article 4(h) considers it a manifestation of collective self-defence. Wyse argues that when the UNSC fails in its primary responsibility to maintain international peace and security, the terms of Article 51 ought to be construed broadly.[9] A broad construction of Article 51 in turn ensures the maintenance of international peace and security, including the protection of human rights.[10] Taken further, AU Member States may empower the AU to exercise collective self-defence which does not in fact require

[3] Kunschak, 'The African Union and the Right of Intervention' (n 2) 207; Kuwali, *Persuasive Prevention* (n 2) 19.

[4] Amvane, 'Intervention Pursuant to Article 4(h)' (n 2) 296–97; Kunschak, 'The African Union and the Right of Intervention' (n 2) 207; Gregory Fox, 'Intervention by Invitation' in Weller (n 2) 832.

[5] Eliav Lieblich, 'Intervention and Consent: Consensual Forcible Interventions in Internal Armed Conflicts as International Agreements' (2011) 29 *Boston University International Law Journal* 371–73.

[6] David Wippman, 'Military Intervention, Regional Organizations, and Host-State Consent' (1996) 7 *Duke Journal of Comparative and International Law* 209, but see also 231.

[7] Jeremy Sarkin, 'The Responsibility to Protect and Humanitarian Intervention in Africa, Global Responsibility to Protect' (2010) 2(4) *Global Responsibility to Protect* 378–80; Paliwal, 'The Primacy of Regional Organisations' (n 2) 225–26.

[8] UN Doc A/RES/60/1 (2005); Report of the International Commission on Intervention and State Sovereignty, The Responsibility to Protect (2001) International Development Research Centre (ICISS R2P Report), para 139.

[9] Christian Wyse, 'The African Union's Right of Humanitarian Intervention as Collective Self-Defence' (2018) 19 (1) *Chicago Journal of International Law* 324–25.

[10] Wyse, 'The African Union's Right' (n 9) 325–26.

UNSC authorisation.[11] Such interpretation also stresses that it is Article 51 which strikes a balance between the prohibition of the use of force in Article 2(4) and the maintenance of international peace and security.[12] In theory therefore, a threat to collective African security could be found in the circumstances listed in Article 4(h), thereby giving rise to a right of collective self-defence.[13] Such an interpretation of Article 4(h) represents a novel approach to reconciling the tensions between consensual treaty-based intervention and that of a regional R2P codification. Nevertheless, it would in turn present a serious broadening of the understanding of self-defence.

Whichever interpretation one adopts, two aspects are worth noting. First, various interpretations of Article 4(h) are rooted more in exceptions to the Article 2(4) prohibition of force, thereby alleviating the requirement of UNSC authorisation. Second, it is worth noting that the AU's own subsequent practice suggests a very different view. Despite numerous conflicts, many of which are marred by allegations of human rights violations including war crimes and crimes against humanity, the AU has yet to invoke Article 4(h) some two decades since the Constitutive Act was adopted. Its subsequent practice of military engagements instead shows it has consistently relied on UNSC authorisation or military assistance on request.

In 2003, the AU deployed its first ever peacekeeping mission, the African Mission in Burundi (AMIB) following the Burundian Civil War. AMIB's deployment was based on a ceasefire agreement signed in December 2002 between the Transitional Government and the Conseil national pour la défense de la démocratie-Forces pour la défense de la démocratie.[14] The ceasefire agreement explicitly requested the deployment of an 'African mission', to which the AU responded with the deployment of AMIB. The deployment was therefore based on the consent of the parties, requiring no UNSC authorisation.[15]

One year later, the AU deployed the African Union Mission in Sudan (AMIS) in response to the civil war there. The AMIS deployment was primarily based on the consent of the Sudanese government which was also a member of the AU Peace and Security Council at the time. In addition, the UNSC continuously supported the AU's proposal for the AMIS deployment. By Resolution 1556 (2004), the UNSC welcomed the envisioned protection force, by Resolution 1574 (2004) it supported the AU's decision to increase the mission size, and by Resolution 1590 (2005), the UNSC established the UN Mission in Sudan, requesting it to coordinate with AMIS.[16] In 2008 the UNSC by Resolution 1769 (2008) established the AU-UN Hybrid Operation in Darfur (UNAMID), the legal successor to both

[11] Wyse, 'The African Union's Right' (n 9) 326.
[12] Wyse, 'The African Union's Right' (n 9) 326.
[13] Wyse, 'The African Union's Right' (n 9) 327.
[14] UN Doc S/2002/1329 (2002).
[15] AMIB was succeeded by the United Nations Operation in Burundi.
[16] UNSC Res 1556 (2004) para 2; UNSC Res 1574 (2004) para 13; UNSC Res 1590 (2005) paras 1, 2. But see the view of Paliwal, 'The Primacy of Regional Organisations' (n 2) 199–201.

AMIS and UNMIS.[17] Given that AMIS was a peacekeeping operation, no UNSC authorisation was necessary.

In 2006, the AU became involved in Somalia. First, the AU endorsed the Intergovernmental Authority on Development's (IGAD) deployment, authorised under Resolution 1725 (2006).[18] Then in 2007, the UNSC authorised under Resolution 1744 (2007) the AU Mission in Somalia (AMISOM). AMISOM was explicitly authorised under Chapter VII to 'take all necessary measures as appropriate' to carry out its mandate.[19] The AU's actions in Somalia have therefore consistently been based on UNSC authorisation and that authorisation has always been explicit.[20]

In 2007, following contested election results, the AU deployed its Electoral and Security Assistance Mission to the Comoros (MAES) when former President Mohammed Bacar refused to relinquish power. This AU mission was arguably based on the request for assistance issued by incoming President Abdallah Sambi, largely perceived as the legitimate head of state at the time. Consequently, it has also been argued that this intervention was based on Article 4(j) – codifying military assistance on request at the level of the AU.[21]

Mention should also be made of the AU's Regional Cooperative Initiative for the Elimination of the Lord's Resistance Army (RCI-LRA). Established in 2012, the RCI-LRA was deployed across central Africa. Although it had never received formal UNSC endorsement, presidential statements consistently commended the operation.[22] It is also worth noting that the RCI-LRA's operations were undertaken within the affected states' territories in combination with military personnel from those territories (and with the consent of those states). The consensual nature of the operation therefore did not require UNSC authorisation.

In 2013, the African Union deployed the African-Led International Support Mission in the CAR (MISCA). As with AMISOM, the UNSC established and authorised MISCA when it adopted Resolution 2127 (2013). Under that same resolution, the UNSC explicitly authorised MISCA to 'take all necessary measures' in carrying out its mandate.[23]

These operations aside, the AU attempted to invoke Article 4(h) only once, during the 2015 crisis in Burundi.[24] It authorised a 5,000 troop African Prevention and Protection Mission in Burundi (MAPROBU) and gave the

[17] UNSC Res 1769 (2008) para 1.

[18] UNSC Res 1725 (2006) para 3.

[19] UNSC Res 1744 (2007) para 4.

[20] See ch 3 at p 69–70. See also De Wet, 'Regional Organisations and Arrangements' (n 2); Paliwal, 'The Primacy of Regional Organisations' (n 2) 203–04.

[21] De Wet, 'Regional Organisations and Arrangements' (n 2) 327.

[22] UN Doc S/PRST/2012/18 (2012) 2; UN Doc S/PRST/2015/12 (2015) 3; UN Doc S/PRST/2012/28 (2012) 1–2; UN Doc S/PRST/2013/18 (2013) 2; UN Doc S/PRST/2014/8 (2014) 2; UN Doc S/PRST/2014/25 (2014) 2. See also UN Doc S/PV.6796 (2012) 3–4, 6, 8, 12–13, 15, 18–19.

[23] UNSC Res 2127 (2013) para 28.

[24] AU Doc PSC/PR/COMM.(DLXV) (PSC Communiqué of 17 December 2015).

Burundi government 96 hours to approve the deployment. In addition, even while attempting to invoke Article 4(h), the AU appealed to the UNSC to adopt a resolution under Chapter VII supporting its decision.[25] Burundi never approved the deployment, the UNSC never adopted the resolution so requested, and the AU never followed through with the deployment. Moreover, the AU's attempt to invoke Article 4(h) was met with harsh criticism from its own Member States.[26] The failed invocation of Article 4(h) was therefore indicative that even under the AU's own treaty law framework, it would not move forward with intervention, at least not without UNSC authorisation.

Considering the subsequent practice of the AU, it is clear that its operations have historically been undertaken on a consensual basis (request for assistance; ceasefire agreements) or with the prior explicit authorisation of the UNSC. The fact that the AU has in practice never formally based an operation on Article 4(h) suggests it considers UNSC authorisation a prerequisite before intervening into its Member States.

B. ECOWAS and the 1999 Protocol Mechanism

Much like the AU, ECOWAS too has carved out a prominent role in matters of regional peace and security. The 1993 Revised Treaty of ECOWAS formally established a regional peace and security observation system and provides for the deployment of peacekeeping forces when necessary.[27] Then, in 1999 ECOWAS adopted its Protocol Relating to the Mechanism for Conflict Prevention, Management, Resolution, Peace-Keeping and Security (Protocol Mechanism).[28] The objectives of the Protocol Mechanism include the maintenance and consolidation of peace, security and stability and the creation and deployment of a civilian and military force.[29] ECOMOG, the organisation's monitoring group, is to serve as a multi-purpose (civilian and military) standby unit ready for immediate deployment charged with peacekeeping, the restoration of peace and humanitarian intervention.[30]

Article 25 of the Protocol Mechanism is arguable its most notable provision. It allows ECOWAS to intervene into its Member States when inter-State

[25] PSC Communiqué 17 December 2015, para 15.

[26] See also International Crisis Group, 'The African Union and the Burundi Crisis: Ambition Versus Reality' (Briefing No 122, 28 September 2016) 7–8, 10; Institute for Security Studies, 'The AU's Challenged Responsibility to Protect in Burundi' (Peace and Security Council Report, 18 January 2016).

[27] Art 58(2)(f), Revised Treaty of the Economic Community of West African States (ECOWAS) (adopted 24 July 1993, entered into force 23 August 1995) 2373 UNTS 233 (Revised Treaty).

[28] ECOWAS Protocol Relating to the Mechanism for Conflict Prevention, Management, Resolution, Peacekeeping and Security (adopted 10 December 1999, entered into force 20 January 2000) (Protocol Mechanism).

[29] Art 3(e), (h), Protocol Mechanism.

[30] Arts 21, 22, Protocol Mechanism.

and internal State conflicts arise. Article 25 lists six such situations: cases of aggression or conflict or threat thereof in any Member State, cases of conflict between Member States, in the event of serious and massive violations of human rights and the rule of law and in the event of the overthrowal or attempted overthrowal of a democratically elected government. In addition, purely internal conflicts that threaten to trigger a humanitarian disaster or that pose a serious threat to peace and security in the sub-region may also trigger intervention.[31]

Much like the AU, neither the Revised ECOWAS Treaty nor the Protocol Mechanism condition ECOWAS intervention on UNSC authorisation.[32] Although the Mechanism may be initiated at the request of the UN, arguably embodying the provisions of Article 53 of the UN Charter, the Protocol suggests that UNSC authorisation is not required. It would therefore seem that ECOWAS has too carved out its own right of intervention without the need for UNSC authorisation. Similar to that of the AU however, ECOWAS subsequent practice of interventions suggests this is not entirely the case.

Notwithstanding its interventions in Liberia and Sierra Leone already discussed in the context of retroactive authorisation, ECOWAS has yet to rely on its unilateral right of intervention. In 1998 it intervened in Guinea-Bissau. This intervention took place before the 1999 Protocol Mechanism and was based on the Abuja Accords signed between the Guinea-Bissau government and the self-proclaimed military junta.[33] The subsequent ECOMOG deployment was therefore a peacekeeping operation, swiftly commended and mandated by the UNSC in Resolution 1216 (1998).[34]

Between 2002 and 2011 ECOWAS intervened twice in Cote d'Ivoire. In 2002, a coup against President Laurent Gbagbo prompted ECOWAS action. Although not authorised by the UNSC, it was likely based on the request for assistance by President Gbagbo. In addition, by Resolution 1464 (2004), the UNSC authorised ECOWAS, 'in accordance with Chapter VIII … to take the necessary steps to guarantee the security and freedom of movement of their personnel and to ensure … the protection of civilians'.[35] Ironically, in 2011 ECOWAS intervened again, this time to remove President Gbagbo who had refused to relinquish power to President-Elect Alassane Ouattara. The subsequent ECOWAS intervention was therefore based on the request of the incoming president, seen as

[31] Art 25, Protocol Mechanism.

[32] See the remarks by John-Mark Iyi, *Humanitarian Intervention and the AU-ECOWAS Intervention Treaties Under International Law: Towards a Theory of Regional Responsibility to Protect* (Springer 2016) 165.

[33] UN Doc S/1998/1028 (1998).

[34] UNSC Res 1216 (1998) paras 2–3; De Wet, 'Regional Organisations and Arrangements' (n 2) 363; Paliwal, 'The Primacy of Regional Organisations' (n 2) 211 who notes it was the 'first explicit ex ante authorisation of an ECOWAS peacekeeping operation'.

[35] UNSC Res 1464 (2003) para 9; De Wet, 'Regional Organisations and Arrangements' (n 2) 364; Paliwal, 'The Primacy of Regional Organisations' (n 2) 212.

the legitimate head of state.[36] In addition, the UNSC in Resolution 1975 (2011) recalled authorisation given to the United Nations Operation in Cote d'Ivoire (UNOCI) – a hybrid force composed of ECOWAS as well as UNOCI's predecessor, MINUCI – to 'use all necessary means to carry out its mandate'.[37]

The following year ECOWAS intervened in Mali following a coup against President Amadou Toumani Toure. This time, the intervention was based on both the request of the ousted president and Resolution 2085 (2012), authorising the deployment of an African-led International Support Mission to Mali (AFISMA). AFISMA, discussed in chapter three in relation to explicit authorisation to regional peacekeeping initiatives, was authorised to 'take all necessary measures' to carry out its tasks.[38]

It is therefore reasonable to conclude that despite the Revised ECOWAS Treaty and its Protocol Mechanism, ECOWAS has yet to challenge the provisions of Article 53 of the UN Charter in practice. Instead, its interventions have historically been based on either prior explicit UNSC authorisation or at the request of the legitimate head of state. That said, its recent intervention in The Gambia in 2017 needs brief consideration, in so far it has raised questions as to whether its actions were indeed authorised by the UNSC.

i. Resolution 2337 (2017) | ECOWAS Intervention in The Gambia

Following a presidential election in December 2016, outgoing President Yahya Jammeh refused to relinquish power to President-Elect Adama Barrow. Political pressure from ECOWAS and the broader international community, including the UNSC, failed to convince Jammeh.[39] On 19 January 2017 Barrow was sworn in as President of The Gambia in the Gambian embassy in Dakar, Senegal. During his inaugural speech, Barrow immediately and explicitly 'appeal[ed] to ECOWAS, [the] AU and the UN, particularly the Security Council, to support the government and the people of [T]he Gambia in enforcing their will'.[40] On the same day, Senegal submitted a draft resolution on the situation to the UNSC. The draft resolution was unanimously adopted by the UNSC as Resolution 2337 (2017).

[36] See however Julie Dube Gagnon, 'ECOWAS's Right to Intervene in Côte d'Ivoire to Install Alassane Outtara as President-Elect' (2013) 3(1) *Notre Dame Journal of International and Comparative Law* 65–68.

[37] UNSC Res 1975 (20181) paras 4, 6.

[38] UNSC Res 2085 (2012) para 9; see also ch 3 at p 90–91.

[39] Emma Farge and Lisa Shumaker, 'US Condemns Gambian President Jammeh's Rejection of Election Results' (10 December 2016) *Reuters*. See also European Parliament Resolution of 12 May 2016 on The Gambia (2016/2693(RSP)) which had urged The Gambia to ratify the African Charter on Democracy, Elections and Governance in advance of the 1 December 2016 elections; Emma Farge and Matthew Bigg, 'Senegal Calls for UN Security Council Meeting Over Gambia' (10 December 2016) *Reuters*; United Nations, 'Statement Attributable to the Spokesman for the Secretary-General on the Presidential Election in The Gambia' (10 December 2016) https://shorturl.at/Nt3eN; UN Doc S/PRST/2016/19 (2016).

[40] Ruth Maclean, 'Troops Enter The Gambia After Adama Barrow is Inaugurated in Senegal' (19 January 2017) *The Guardian*.

By the time Resolution 2337 (2017) was adopted, both the AU and ECOWAS had taken steps to pressure Jammeh to step down.[41] For its part, ECOWAS declared that it would 'take all necessary measures to strictly enforce the results of the 1st December 2016 elections'.[42]

Following President Barrow's appeal for help, Senegalese forces, assisted by forces from Ghana and Nigeria, entered The Gambia and placed it under a naval blockade.[43] On 21 January Jammeh conceded defeated in a statement on state television, saying that 'I have decided today in good conscience to relinquish the mantle of leadership of this great nation with infinite gratitude to all Gambians'.[44] While the ECOWAS intervention was widely praised as a success, its legality was questioned. Notwithstanding that ECOWAS may have legally acted under Article 25 of the Protocol Mechanism and that President Barrow had explicitly requested assistance, a specific question which arose was whether the UNSC had (albeit) implicitly authorised ECOWAS under Resolution 2337 (2017).

It should first and foremost be noted that neither the structure nor language of Resolution 2337 (2017) suggest force was authorised. The initial draft resolution submitted by Senegal expressed the UNSC's support to ECOWAS' commitment 'to take all necessary measures' to ensure respect of the will of the The Gambian people.[45] This language was removed in an amended version, citing concerns from some UNSC Members, which was adopted as Resolution 2337 (2017). The UNSC debates confirm unambiguously that the resolution adopted did not authorise force.[46] However, it is true that at the time the resolution was adopted, the UNSC was aware that ECOWAS intended to intervene. Indeed, paragraph 6 of the resolution notably *expressed* the UNSC's 'full support to the ECOWAS in its commitment to ensure by political means *first*, the respect of the will of the people of The Gambia'. This curious choice in phrasing of 'by political means *first*' in combination with formal recognition of President Barrow suggests the UNSC, although supporting peaceful means, had at the least formally acknowledged that the use of force may have been an eventuality.[47]

That eventuality, however, was not a direct consequence of Resolution 2337 (2017). The fact that the UNSC may have acknowledged an alternative legal basis for any subsequent use of force cannot be akin to an implicit authorisation

[41] AU Doc PSC/PR/COMM (DCXLIV) (2016) 1. See also AU Doc PSC/PR/BR (CDXLII) (2016).

[42] ECOWAS Final Communiqué, 50th Ordinary Session of the ECOWAS Authority of Heads of State and Government (17 December 2016) 7. See also AU Doc PSC/PR/COMM (DCXLVII) (2017) 2.

[43] 'Gambia Crisis: Senegal Sends in Troops to Back Elected Leader' (19 January 2017) *BBC News*.

[44] 'Gambia's Yahya Jammeh Confirms He Will Step Down' (21 January 2017) *Al Jazeera*.

[45] 'Resolution on The Gambia: Insights on the Work of the UN Security Council' *What's In The Blue* (19 January 2017) www.whatsinblue.org/2017/01/resolution-on-the-gambia-php.

[46] UN Doc S/PV.7866 (2017), see specifically 3 (Uruguay, Russia, Bolivia), 5 (France), 6 (Egypt) pointing to no authorised enforcement action under the resolution.

[47] Benjamin Nuβberger, 'The Post-Election Crisis in The Gambia: An Interplay of a Security Council's "Non-Authorisation" and Intervention by Invitation' (8 February 2017) *Opinio Juris*.

for that use of force. Its recognition of Barrow as the legitimate head of state was more of a recognition of the *fait accompli* and possible further action that Barrow may have requested, rather than an attempt at authorising enforcement action.

Resolution 2337 (2017) is however notable in that it represents a situation where the UNSC potentially albeit implicitly acknowledged an alternative legal basis for the use of force without itself authorising force. One question which follows is whether in so doing, the UNSC marginalises itself when it is either unable or unwilling to authorise force but nonetheless recognises situations where force may be used.[48] As will be seen below, the UNSC has repeated this 'non-prohibitive non-authorisation' practice particularly where concerns self-defence.[49]

C. The Southern African Development Community

In contrast to both the AU and ECOWAS treaty law frameworks permitting unilateral intervention into Member States, it should briefly be noted that the Southern African Development Community's (SADC) framework expressly requires UNSC authorisation. In 2004 SADC adopted its Protocol on Politics, Defence and Security Co-operation (Protocol).[50] Notably, the Protocol established the SADC Organ, with the overall responsibility for regional peace and security. The Protocol explicitly charges the Organ with responsibility in ensuring SADC Member States adhere and enforce UNSC sanctions and that conflicts are resolved by peaceful means.[51]

In carrying out its obligations, the Organ may employ among others, preventive diplomacy, negotiation and arbitration. Where peaceful means of resolving a conflict fail, the Organ may recommend enforcement action which may be decided upon by the SADC Summit, the highest decision-making body within SADC. Most notably, the Summit shall resort to enforcement action 'only as a matter of last resort and, in accordance with Article 53 of the United Nations Charter, only with the authorisation of the United Nations Security Council'.[52] The explicit requirement of UNSC authorisation is a notable break from that of the AU and ECOWAS. In principle, SADC therefore requires UNSC authorisation in cases where it seeks to intervene militarily within its Member States. It should be noted in this regard that SADC has never intervened militarily into its Member States without the consent of such State. Its interventions in the

[48] See also Nuβberger, 'The Post-Election Crisis' (n 47).
[49] As noted by Nuβberger, 'The Post-Election Crisis' (n 47).
[50] SADC Protocol on Politics, Defence and Security Co-Operation (adopted 14 August 2001, entered into force 2 March 2004) (SADC Protocol).
[51] Art 11(1)(c), (d), SADC Protocol.
[52] Art 11(3)(d), SADC Protocol.

Democratic Republic of the Congo in 1998 and again in 2023, in Lesotho in 1998 and 2017, and in Mozambique in 2021 were all undertaken either at the request of the internationally recognised governments of the State in question or with their consent.[53] As such, both the SADC treaty law framework and its subsequent practice entirely adhere to the UN Charter system of collective security requiring prior explicit UNSC authorisation.[54]

III. THE RIGHT OF SELF-DEFENCE AND ITS INTERSECTION WITH UN SECURITY COUNCIL AUTHORISATION

Whereas the development of African regional treaty law frameworks seems to have challenged the very need for UNSC authorisation, the right of individual and collective self-defence is a clear exception to the prohibition of force requiring no UNSC authorisation. Article 51 speaks of self-defence as an 'inherent right', only requiring that once Member States exercise this right, they report it to the UNSC.

One intersection between self-defence and UNSC authorisation is of course the fact that the UNSC can determine an armed attack giving rise to self-defence as a breach of the peace or threat to international peace and security. The UNSC did as much in Resolution 83 (1950), determining that the 'armed attack' against South Korea by North Korean forces constitutes a 'breach of the peace'.[55] It similarly determined the existence of a 'breach of international peace and security' when Iraq invaded Kuwait in 1990.[56] Where the UNSC has authorised force subsequently to its Article 39 determination, it has done so in clear terms. However, what is far less clear is when the UNSC has seemingly acknowledged the right of self-defence in its resolutions without necessarily authorising military measures. One question which arises is whether the UNSC has implicitly acknowledged a right to use force without itself authorising that force?

Several situations and corresponding resolutions stand out. Most notable of these include Resolutions 1368 and 1373 (2001), adopted following the 11 September terrorist attacks against the United States. In Resolution 1368 (2001) the UNSC 'recognis[ed] the inherent right of individual or collective self-defence in accordance with the Charter' and in Resolution 1373 (2001) it

[53] Marko Svicevic, 'The SADC Mission in Mozambique: Contextualising the Historical Role of SADC Military Operations under International Law' in Marko Svicevic and Martha Bradley, *Mozambique's Cabo Delgado Conflict: International Humanitarian Law and Regional Security* (Routledge 2024) 237–43.

[54] Marko Svicevic, 'Collective Self-Defence or Regional Enforcement Action: The Legality of a SADC Intervention in Cabo Delgado and the Question of Mozambican Consent' (2022) 9(1) *Journal on the Use of Force and International Law* 165.

[55] UNSC Res 82 (1950) preamble paras 3, 4. See also ch 2 at p 18.

[56] UNSC Res 660 (1990) preamble para 2. See also ch 2 at p 31.

reaffirmed this recognition.[57] Chapter six has already addressed these resolutions, arguing that the invocation of self-defence is not akin to an authorisation of force.[58] In addition, neither the United States nor United Kingdom referenced these resolutions in their Article 51 communiques when they commenced operations against Afghanistan.[59]

Nevertheless, the UNSC has repeated its practice of, albeit sometimes implicitly invoking or allegedly supporting a right of self-defence in its resolutions. Two particular resolutions merit attention here: Resolution 2249 (2015) adopted following several terrorist attacks by the Islamic State (ISIS), and Resolution 2722 (2023) adopted following a series of attacks by the Houthis against maritime vessels in the Red Sea.

A. Resolution 2249 (2015) | Threats to International Peace and Security Caused by Terrorist Acts

Resolution 2249 (2015) was adopted on 20 November 2015 shortly after a spate of terrorist attacks by ISIS in, most notably, Paris, Ankara and Beirut.[60] In its preamble, Resolution 2249 (2015) determined that ISIS constituted a 'global and unprecedented threat to international peace and security'. In the seventh preambular paragraph the UNSC states it is *determined* to combat 'by all means' this unprecedented threat. While the UNSC *unequivocally condemned* the terrorist attacks and expressed *sympathy* for the victims of these attacks, most significant were the provisions of operative paragraph 5. In it, the UNSC *calls upon* Member States that have the capacity to take 'all necessary measures', in compliance with international law and the UN Charter, to 'redouble and coordinate their efforts to prevent and suppress terrorist acts' on the territory under control by ISIS in Syria and Iraq.[61]

It is precisely because of this wording that the provisions of Resolution 2249 (2015) have been described as unprecedented.[62] On the one hand, a legitimate

[57] UNSC Res 1368 (2001) preamble para 3; UNSC Res 1373 (2001) preamble para 4.

[58] See ch 6 at p 166–168.

[59] UN Doc S/2001/946 (2011); UN Doc S/2001/947 (2011). See also ch 6 at p 167.

[60] UNSC Res 2249 (2015). See also 'Three Hours of Terror in Paris, Moment by Moment' (9 November 2016) *The New York Times* and Megan Alpert, 'It's Not Just Paris: From Nigeria to Egypt, 10 of 2015's Worst Terrorist Attacks' (16 November 2015) *Foreign Policy*.

[61] UNSC Res 2249 (2015) para 5. See the excellent analysis on operative paragraph 5 in Dapo Akande and Marko Milanovic, 'The Constructive Ambiguity of the Security Council's ISIS Resolution' (21 November 2015) *EJIL:Talk!*; see also Ashley Deeks, 'Threading the Needle in Security Council Resolution 2249' (23 November 2015) *Lawfare*.

[62] See Akande and Milanovic, 'The Constructive Ambiguity' (n 61); Deeks, 'Threading the Needle' (n 61). See also Marc Weller, 'Pertinent Imminence of Armed Attacks: Resolution 2249 (2015) and the Right to Self Defence Against Designated Terrorist Groups *EJIL: Talk!* (25 November 2015). See also broadly Peter Hilpold, 'The Fight Against Terrorism and SC Resolution 2249 (2015): Towards a More Hobbesian or a More Kantian International Society?' (2015) 55(4) *Indian Journal of International Law* 535.

question concerns whether Resolution 2249 (2015) authorised force in any way. On the other hand, the question also arises as to whether Resolution 2249 (2015) authorises force by implication in so far as it seems to endorse military measures already undertaken against ISIS.

Where UNSC authorisation concerns, it should be noted that Resolution 2249 (2015), although recalling 14 previous resolutions (of which seven were explicitly adopted under Chapter VII),[63] is not itself a Chapter VII resolution.[64] Nevertheless, paragraph five of the resolution goes on to express the infamous use of 'all necessary measures'. Be that as it may, interpreted in context and within the paragraph as a whole, no force is authorised. Some authors point to the paragraph's wording that the UNSC 'calls upon' Member States and does not *decide* or *authorise* them, as indicating force is not authorised.[65] It should be mentioned though that the UNSC has in fact authorised force by *calling upon* Member States on more than a dozen occasions.[66] UNSC practice shows it has opted for a combination of language, operative verbs such as *authorises*, *decides*, *calls upon*, *recalls* or *reiterates*, together with the notorious 'all necessary means [or] measures' phrasing.[67] It has however been well noted that the combination of 'calls upon' *without* a Chapter VII invocation suggests no force is authorised.

In addition, these authors also note that the overall language of the resolution, particularly the term 'calls upon' Member States to use all necessary measures 'in compliance with international law, and in particular the United Nations Charter' suggests that although force is not authorised, it may be contemplated or even welcomed under an alternative basis or by the fact that it recognises States may rely on self-defence.[68]

If one accepts that Resolution 2249 (2015) does not authorise force under the UN Charter,[69] the question arises as to implications of recognising the existence

[63] See UNSC Res 1267 (1999); UNSC Res 1373 (2001); UNSC Res 2083 (2012); UNSC Res 2161 (2014); UNSC Res 2170 (2014); UNSC Res 2178 (2014); UNSC Res 2199 (2015).

[64] Akande and Milanovic, 'The Constructive Ambiguity' (n 61); Deeks, 'Threading the Needle' (n 61).

[65] Akande and Milanovic, 'The Constructive Ambiguity' (n 61). See also Deeks, 'Threading the Needle' (n 61).

[66] Hilpold, 'The Fight Against Terrorism and SC Resolution 2249 (2015)' (n 62) 542 who notes that there more of an imperative to act when 'called upon' then when 'authorised'.

[67] See conclusions of chapters two, three and four. Hilpold, 'The Fight Against Terrorism and SC Resolution 2249 (2015)' (n 62) 542 states that 'calls upon' can be argued as an even broader gate for the use of force. However, see also the analysis by Dan Joyner of the binding nature of Chapter VII and the use of certain operative verbs to indicate such. Dan Joyner, 'Legal Blindness of Security Council Resolutions Generally, and Resolution 2334 on the Israeli Settlements in Particular' (9 January 2017) *EJIL: Talk!*.

[68] Akande and Milanovic, 'The Constructive Ambiguity' (n 61) para 6; UNSC Res 2249 (2015) was adopted seven days after an ISIS attack claimed 130 lives in Paris, with a further 600 people injured. UNSC Res 2249 (2015) was a French draft in response to these events; Weller, 'Pertinent Imminence' (n 62) para 4 states that '[a] resolution [adopted outside of Chapter VII] cannot authorize the use of force beyond that which is already permitted by virtue of general international law'.

[69] As concluded by Akande and Milanovic, 'The Constructive Ambiguity' (n 61) para 10; Deeks, 'Threading the Needle' (n 61) para 3. See also Christine Gray, *International Law and the Use of*

of an alternative legal basis for the use of force. It certainly may be one way in which the UNSC legitimises States' resort to force. It may also be indicative of a developing practice where the UNSC avoids authorising force given the ever-growing division of the Council's permanent Members and the threat of the veto.

The potential emergence of such a practice remains dubious; its implications yet unclear. Or should such a practice rather be considered an abdication of the UNSC's primary responsibility over matters of international peace and security? Additionally, does such a practice present a paradox where the UNSC marginalises its central position in collective security by encouraging states and regional organisations to decide on their own prerogative to use force based on an alternative legal basis?[70] Nonetheless, such a rationale is supported by the fact that no Member State engaged in the fight against ISIS has directly invoked Resolution 2249 (2015) as a legal basis for their actions. Instead, Member States have consistently justified their actions either on individual or collective self-defence, or based on the consent of either the Iraqi or Syrian governments.[71]

Their reliance on self-defence is consistent with Article 51 communiqués issued to the UNSC both before and after the adoption of Resolution 2249 (2015).[72] The only difference is that subsequent to the resolution's adoption, they occasionally cited the resolution's recognition of this right rather than

Force (Oxford University Press 2018) 386; Weller, 'Pertinent Imminence of Armed Attacks' (n 62) para 4; and Patrick Terry, 'Germany Joins the Campaign against ISIS in Syria: A Case of Collective Self-Defence or Rather the Unlawful Use of Force?' (2016) 4(1) *Russian Law Journal* 29. Hilpold, 'The Fight Against Terrorism and SC Resolution 2249 (2015)' (n 62) 553 reaches a similar conclusion.

[70] Erika de Wet and Marko Svicevic, *The Military Clauses in the Treaty of Versailles and the Birth of a Collective Security System* (Pedone 2020) 10; Paulina Starski, '"Legitimized Self-Defence" – Quo Vadis Security Council' (10 December 2015) *EJIL:Talk!*.

[71] Gray, *International Law and the Use of Force* (n 69) 386. See for example the United Kingdom Prime Minister David Cameron's report to Parliament in which he, relying on UNSC Res 2249 (2015), suggested a legal basis for offensive action, but only by referencing self-defence in terms of the resolution. See 'Memorandum to the Foreign Affairs Select Committee Prime Minister's Response to the Foreign Affairs Select Committee's Second Report of Session 2015–16: The Extension of Offensive British Military Operations to Syria' (November 2015) 15, 17 https://shorturl.at/kA6uU. Terry, 'Germany Joins the Campaign against ISIS in Syria' (n 69) 29 indicates that neither the United Kingdom nor Germany is basing their actions on explicit UNSC authorisation under UNSC Res 2249 (2015). See also Anne Peters, 'German Parliament Decides to Send Troops to Combat ISIS – Based on Collective Self-Defence "in Conjunction With" SC Res 2249' (8 December 2015) *EJIL: Talk!*. See the comprehensive annexes of UN Member States communications to the UNSC of the purported exercise of the right of individual or collective self-defence in Dustin A Lewis, Naz K Modirzadeh and Gabriella Blum, 'Quantum of Silence: Inaction and *Jus ad Bellum*' (2019) *Harvard Law School Program on International Law and Armed Conflict*, Annex: HLS PILAC Catalogue of Communications to the Security Council of Measures Taken by United Nations Member States in Purported Exercise of the Right of Self-Defence: October 24, 1945 Through December 31, 2018 (*Quantum of Silence*).

[72] *Quantum of Silence* (n 71) 176–85. See in this regard the following Communiqués: the United States in UN Doc S/2014/695 (2014); the United Kingdom in UN Doc S/2014/851 (2014) and UN Doc S/2015/688 (2015); Turkey in UN Doc S/2015/127 (2015) and UN Doc S/2015/563 (2015); Canada in UN Doc S/2015/221 (2015); France in UN Doc S/2015/745 (2015); Australia in UN Doc S/2015/693 (2015).

considering it as a separate legal basis.[73] At the time the resolution was adopted, four of the five permanent members of the UNSC were militarily engaged in the fight against ISIS either in Iraq or Syria. Russia began airstrikes against ISIS in Syria in October of that year citing consent by the Syrian government for its actions.[74] The United States had been engaged in fighting terrorist militants in Iraq since 2014 basing its actions on self-defence. Similarly, both France and the United Kingdom were engaged in air strikes against ISIS positions in Iraq and Syria at the time.[75] From the subsequent practice of these States, it seems that a reasonable interpretation of Resolution 2249 (2015) is that, rather than authorising the use of force, it has simply recognised existing exceptions under which force may be used.

B. Resolution 2722 (2024) | Houthi Strikes in the Red Sea

From October 2023, the Houthi movement commenced strikes against merchant vessels sailing in the Red Sea, including attacks against military vessels. In response to these attacks, the UNSC adopted Resolution 2722 (2024) on 10 January 2024. While Resolution 2722 (2024) does not authorise force against the Houthis (there is no Chapter VII invocation nor any authorising language), in operative paragraph 3 the UNSC:

> *Affirms* the exercise of navigational rights and freedoms by merchant and commercial vessels, in accordance with international law, must be respected, and takes note of the right of Member States, in accordance with international law, to *defend their vessels from attacks*, including those that undermine navigational rights and freedoms.[76]

The UNSC's choice of wording in paragraph 3 is somewhat puzzling and has been open to interpretation. Unlike its resolutions following the 11 September attacks, Resolution 2722 (2024) does not seem to explicitly recognise a right

[73] *Quantum of Silence* (n 71) 187 onward. See the following Communiqués from: the United Kingdom in UN Doc S/2015/928 (2015); Germany in UN Doc S/2015/946 (2015); Denmark in UN Doc S/2016/34 (2016); The Netherlands in UN Doc S/2016/132 (2016); Norway in UN Doc S/2016/513 (2016); Belgium in UN Doc S/2016/523 (2016). See however Anne Peters, 'German Parliament Decides to Send Troops to Combat ISIS – Based on Collective Self-Defence "in conjunction with" SC Res. 2249' (8 December 2015) *EJIL:Talk!*.

[74] Ed Payne, Barbara Starr and Susannah Cullinane, 'Russia Launches First Airstrikes in Syria' (1 October 2015) *CNN*.

[75] The French airstrikes began in September 2014 under *Operation Chammal*. See 'France Launches First Air Strikes on IS in Iraq' (19 September 2014) *BBC*. See also 'Assessing the Legal Basis for UK Military Action in Syria' (26 November 2015) *Chatham House, The Royal Institute of International Affairs*. See also Marko Milanovic, 'How the Ambiguity of Resolution 2249 Does Its Work' (3 December 2015) *EJIL:Talk!*.

[76] Emphasis added. UNSC Res 2722 (2024) para 3. See broadly Christian Henderson, 'US and UK Military Strikes in Yemen and the *Jus ad Bellum*' (2024) 73 *International and Comparative Law Quarterly* 771.

of self-defence.[77] Instead, it merely 'takes note of the right' of Member States to 'defend their vessels from attack'. UNSC debates preceding the resolution's adoption evidence contradictory interpretations of the provision.

Initially, Russia unsuccessfully attempted to remove any mention of defence of vessels, arguing such right 'does not exist in international law'.[78] The United States voted against the Russian move, arguing 'it is long accepted that States have a right to defend merchant and commercial vessels from attacks'.[79] Switzerland seemed to distinguish between the right of self-defence and the defence of vessels which was 'strictly limited to military measures to intercept attacks against merchant vessels and warships to protect said vessels and the persons on board'.[80] Slovenia on the other hand interpreted the resolution in line with the right of self-defence. '[O]ur interpretation of operative paragraph 3 provides that any response to attacks in the Red Sea must be in line with international law, in particular international humanitarian and human rights law, and within the strict conditions of the exercise of self-defence'.[81] For its part, the United States repeated its interpretation favouring a right of self-defence when it noted paragraph three 'referenced the inherent right of Member States to defend, in accordance with international law, their vessels from attacks'.[82] Such mention of 'inherent right' was no doubt a refence to Article 51 of the UN Charter.[83]

Be that as it may, no State engaged militarily against the Houthis has relied on the wording of Resolution 2722 (2024) directly. Article 51 communiques from both the United States and United Kingdom underline that Resolution 2722 (2024) took note of the right of Member States to defend their vessels from attack.[84] They however primarily base their actions on the exercise of the right of self-defence 'as reflected in' and 'in accordance with' Article 51 of the UN Charter. Subsequent statements and legal positions by both States indeed make no mention of paragraph three of Resolution 2722 (2024) and further Article 51 communiques relying on self-defence no longer reference it either.[85]

[77] Marko Svicevic, 'Strikes Against the Houthis: The Relationship between Resolution 2722 (2024) and the Right of Self-Defence' (6 February 2024) *Articles of War*.

[78] UN Doc S/PV.9527 (2024) 2.

[79] United States Mission to the United Nations, 'Explanation of Vote Delivered by Ambassador Thomas-Greenfield on Russia's Amendments to a UNSC Resolution Condemning Houthi Attacks in the Red Sea' (10 January 2024).

[80] UN Doc S/PV. 9527 (2024) 8.

[81] UN Doc S/PV. 9527 (2024) 8; see also UN Doc S/PV.9532 (2024) 6.

[82] UN Doc S.PV/9532 (2024) 5.

[83] Svicevic, 'Strikes Against the Houthis' (n 77).

[84] See UN Doc S/2024/56 (2024); UN Doc S/2024/55 (2024).

[85] United Kingdom Government, 'PM Statement on Strikes Against Houthi Military Targets: 12 January 2024' (12 January 2024); United Kingdom Government, 'Summary of the UK Government Legal Position: The Legality of UK Military Action to Target Houthi Facilities in Yemen on 12 January 2024' (12 January 2024); United Kingdom Government, 'Summary of the UK Government Legal Position: The Legality of UK Military Action to Target Houthi Facilities in Yemen on 22 January 2024' (23 January 2024); The White House, 'Joint Statement from the

Albeit limited ambiguity surrounded the adoption of Resolution 2772 (2024) and its reference to 'defence of vessels' in paragraph three, subsequent State practice suggests limited significance in so far as States directly relied on Article 51.[86] Resolution 2722 (2024) therefore holds limited precedent when considering the UNSC's reference to alternative legal bases in the absence of prior explicit UNSC authorisation.

IV. BETWEEN AMBIGUITY FOR UNANIMITY AND ABDICATION OF RESPONSIBILITY

It is no understatement that the UNSC's functioning has faced significant constraint in the last two decades, particularly because of divisions between its permanent Members. The result thereof is that the UNSC has been unable to act substantively on several situations, including those of Gaza, Syria and Ukraine.[87] Much of the UNSC's current paralysis may in fact be traced back to controversial uses of force without prior explicit UNSC authorisation. In place of specific and comprehensive action, including Chapter VII authorisation of the use of force, the UNSC has increasingly relied on indirect means to maintain or restore international peace and security. Instead of itself authorising force, it has increasingly recognised (and sometimes encouraged) lawful resort to force without the need for UNSC authorisation.

On the one hand, in adopting such an approach, the UNSC is able to overcome its perceived paralysis in authorising force and remedy a situation without its direct intervention. It also seems to alleviate the problem of the veto – while not authorising force, yet still being able to take some decisions on a matter. On the other hand, it is a dangerous situation where the UNSC acknowledges a right to use force while having no control over its exercise. Even where a State or regional organisation initially makes use of a lawful resort to force, the UNSC may be paralysed to act should such resort to force be abused. Equally as significant are the implications of this approach in which the UNSC seemingly abdicates its primary responsibility over matters of international peace and security – by acknowledging or even encouraging the use of force based on alternative basis.[88]

Governments of Australia, Bahrain, Canada, Denmark, Germany, Netherlands, New Zealand, Republic of Korea, United Kingdom, and the United States' (11 January 2024). See also UN Doc S/2024/103 (2024); UN Doc S/2024/106 (2024).

[86] Henderson, 'US and UK Military Strikes' (n 76) 773.

[87] Scott Sheeran, 'UN Security Council Veto is Killing People' *The Conversation* (11 August 2014). See broadly Oona A Hathaway and Stewart Patrick, 'Can the UN Security Council Still Help Keep the Peace? Reassessing its Role, Relevance, and Potential for Reform' (2 July 2024) *Carnegie Endowment for International Peace*.

[88] Jules Lobel and Michael Ratner, 'Bypassing the Security Council: Ambiguous Authorisations to Use Force, Cease-Fires and the Iraqi Inspection Regime' (1999) 93 (1) *American Journal of International Law* 135; Starski, 'Legitimized Self-Defence' (n 70).

V. CONCLUSION

The chapter has considered two recent developments arguably challenging not only that UNSC authorisation should be prior and explicit, but whether it is at all required. While these developments ultimately attribute greater weight to the Article 2(4) prohibition of force and lawful exceptions to it, the very (albeit occasionally limited) involvement of the UNSC has at times caused ambiguity.

In the African regional and sub-regional context, it is arguable that organisations such as the AU and ECOWAS have developed their security frameworks allowing them to intervene in their Member States without UNSC authorisation. Article 4(h) of the Constitutive Act and Article 25 of the Protocol Mechanism are such examples. The SADC treaty law framework however stands in contrast to the AU and ECOWAS, explicitly conditioning intervention on UNSC authorisation.

At the same time, these organisations have not yet exercised their right to unilateral intervention. Based on the subsequent practice of both the AU and ECOWAS, it is arguable that they have not yet usurped the need for UNSC authorisation. That the UNSC has on more than one occasion acknowledged ECOWAS' prior use of force or acknowledged an alternative basis to use force (without authorising such force) remains notable. Resolution 2337 (2017) is the most recent such example, giving rise to considerable debate.

In the context of the right of individual and collective self-defence, that no UNSC authorisation is required does not mean no UNSC involvement is merited. Armed attacks giving rise to a right of self-defence may also qualify as threats to international peace and security, clearly bringing them into the purview of UNSC action. The resolutions adopted following the 11 September 2001 terrorist attacks against the United States remain significant. Both Resolution 1368 and 1373 (2001) are clear examples where the UNSC has acknowledged the right of self-defence, but without itself authorising force. The most recent such example would seem to be Resolution 2249 (2015).

The UNSC's recognition of certain situations giving rise to a right of self-defence is entirely understandable. It would be difficult to imagine situations where the UNSC acknowledges an armed attack without also recognising a corresponding right of self-defence. At the same time, the recognition of an alternative legal basis upon which States (or regional organisations) may resort to force may be open to abusive interpretations. It is worth recalling that the ongoing tension within the UNSC itself may be traced back to abusive interpretations of UNSC resolutions, often those which have themselves given rise to questions on whether force has been authorised.

Acknowledging an alternative legal basis for force without itself authoring force seems to have proven useful to the UNSC, particularly when any authorisation of force faces potential veto. Overcoming the threat of veto in such a manner however ultimately displaces the UNSC of its primary responsibility for the maintenance of international peace and security. At least for now, recent situations where the UNSC has acknowledged a right to use force without itself authorising such force has had limited effect. Subsequent State practice following the adoption of Resolutions 2249 (2015) and 2722 (2024), although giving rise to significant debates both among States and scholars, suggests restrained interpretations of these resolutions when States chose to base their actions strictly on self-defence. Nevertheless, considering that previous UNSC resolutions with far less indication of any UNSC authorisation of force or any implied recognition of an alternative basis for force have been abused, the UNSC should tread cautiously. Even in situations where the UNSC is politically unlikely to authorise force, implying an alternative basis for force entrenches an ambiguity already often far too present in its resolutions.

9

Conclusion

I. INTRODUCTION

THE BOOK'S CENTRAL examination concerned the necessity and character of United Nations Security Council (UNSC) authorisation of force. Three forms of authorisation were considered: prior explicit authorisation, implicit authorisation and retroactive authorisation. Considering some 300 resolutions adopted since 1945, it is arguable that the UN Security Council has a well-established practice of prior explicit authorisation. The more direct consideration surrounding explicit authorisation concerned the form and language developed by the UNSC when authorising force.

An analysis of UNSC practice of explicit authorisation was conducted across four chapters considering authorisation to different entities. These included explicit authorisation to Member States, regional organisations and regional peacekeeping initiatives, NATO and UN peacekeeping missions. Across these chapters, the well-established practice of the UNSC was ascertained. Attention was then directed to cases of alleged implicit and retroactive authorisation; a form of authorisation ultimately argued against.

II. EXPLICIT AUTHORISATION AS A WELL-ESTABLISHED PRACTICE

Early UNSC practice shows that it did not follow a routine when authorising force. Whether the UNSC in fact authorised force was ascertainable only by examining the specific wording of resolutions and the context of their adoption – an approach that nonetheless ought to be followed today too.[1] Nevertheless, the UNSC has particularly from the 1990s onward developed a routine approach when authorising force. This routine may be summarised as constituting a number of core characteristics, and several accompanying traits.

First, the UNSC makes an Article 39 determination – today broadly considered a threshold requirement before Chapter VII measures are employed. Second, it invokes Chapter VII (it has also invoked, albeit rarely, Chapter VIII). Third,

[1] Security Council Report, 'Security Council Action Under Chapter VII: Myths and Realities' (23 June 2008) 3 (*Security Council Report*).

it uses specific verbs either recommending or instructing Member States in operative paragraphs whereby it *authorises, decides, calls upon, or recommends* certain actions. Fourth, the UNSC explicitly *authorises, decides, calls upon or recommends* the use of 'all necessary measures' or 'all necessary means'. Rarely has it authorised the 'use of force'. Fifth, the authorisation of force is frequently accompanied by time limits or functional limits after which authorisation of force terminates. Sixth, the authorisation of force is frequently accompanied by reporting obligations imposed on those making use of the authorisation in question. Finally, it should be noted that authorising resolutions are usually a 'last resort', whereby the UNSC has previously taken action under Articles 40 and 41, before eventually resorting to Article 42 authorisation.

A. Article 39 Determination

Where the determination of a threat to international peace and security concerns, early UNSC practice referred to a 'breach of the peace',[2] 'threat to the peace'[3] or on occasion simply a 'threat to peace and security'.[4] More frequently however, UNSC practice has formulated the Article 39 determination as a 'threat to international peace and security'[5] or a threat to (international) peace and security 'in the region'.[6] The UNSC has on occasion also expanded this formulation to include certain qualifications to the threat, such as including in this determination a threat to the stability of a region or sub-region,[7] or the peace-process in a State.[8] UNSC practice in this regard suggests that an Article 39 determination remains one of the most consistent practices to date where authorisation

[2] UNSC Res 83 (1950).
[3] UNSC Res 221 (1966); UNSC Res 787 (1992).
[4] UNSC Res 1272 (1999).
[5] UNSC Res 161 (1961); UNSC Res 770 (1992); UNSC Res 743 (1992); UNSC Res 1511 (2003); UNSC Res 816 (1993); UNSC Res 836 (1993); UNSC Res 1031 (1994); UNSC Res 1037 (1996); UNSC Res 1088 (1996); UNSC Res 1120 (1997); UNSC Res 1244 (1999); UNSC Res 1386 (2001); UNSC Res 1575 (2004); UNSC Res 1590 (2005); UNSC Res 1701 (2006); UNSC Res 1706 (2006); UNSC Res 1769 (2007); UNSC Res 1861 (2009); UNSC Res 1973 (2011); UNSC Res 1990 (2011); UNSC Res 2085 (2012); UNSC Res 2100 (2013); UNSC Res 2127 (2013); UNSC Res 2181 (2014).
[6] UNSC Res 875 (1993); UNSC Res 917 (1994); UNSC Res 940 (1994); UNSC Res 929 (1994); UNSC Res 1080 (1996); UNSC Res 1101 (1997); UNSC Res 1114 (1997); UNSC Res 1270 (1999); UNSC Res 1289 (1999); UNSC Res 1291 (2000); UNSC Res 1464 (2003); UNSC Res 1484 (2003); UNSC Res 1493 (2003); UNSC Res 1527 (2004); UNSC Res 1528 (2004); UNSC Res 1542 (2004); UNSC Res 1545 (2004); UNSC Res 1562 (2004); UNSC Res 1565 (2004); UNSC Res 1572 (2004); UNSC Res 1584 (2005); UNSC Res 1671 (2006); UNSC Res 1739 (2007); UNSC Res 1744 (2007); UNSC Res 1778 (2007); UNSC Res 1816 (2008); UNSC Res 1838 (2008); UNSC Res 1846 (2008); UNSC Res 1851 (2008); UNSC Res 1856 (2008); UNSC Res 1897 (2009); UNSC Res 1925 (2010); UNSC Res 1933 (2010); UNSC Res 1996 (2011); UNSC Res 2098 (2013); UNSC Res 2134 (2014); UNSC Res 2147 (2014); UNSC Res 2149 (2014); UNSC Res 2211 (2015); UNSC Res 2217 (2015); UNSC Res 2277 (2016); UNSC Res 2301 (2017); UNSC Res 2348 (2017); UNSC Res 2387 (2017); UNSC Res 2448 (2018); UNSC Res 2699 (2023).
[7] UNSC Res 1529 (2004).
[8] UNSC Res 1497 (2003).

of force concerns. Even its early resolutions that did not invoke Chapter VII nevertheless included an Article 39 determination.[9]

B. Chapter VII (or VIII) Invocation

The UNSC's earlier practice did not explicitly invoke Chapter VII when it made use of its powers under that chapter. Whether it was acting under Chapter VII was ascertained based on the wording and context of its resolutions.[10] Resolutions 83 and 84 (1950) on North Korea, Resolution 221 (1966) on Southern Rhodesia and Resolution 665 (1990) on Iraq did not expressly invoke Chapter VII, but were nonetheless interpreted as authorising force.[11]

The UNSC's invocation of Chapter VII (sometimes Chapter VIII) in authorising resolutions have taken two predominant forms. The first is where Chapter VII is invoked at the end of the preamble in which a resolution states that the UNSC is 'acting under Chapter VII'.[12] The invocation of Chapter VII therefore encompasses the entirety of the resolution's operative paragraphs. The second form of invocation is where the UNSC invokes Chapter VII under a specific section or operative paragraph(s).[13] In so doing, Chapter VII applies only to that section or paragraph(s) of the resolution.[14]

It should however be stressed in this regard that the mere invocation of Chapter VII is insufficient to authorise force alone.[15] Over seven hundred UNSC resolutions have explicitly invoked Chapter VII on various situations. Of these, only a handful of these may be rightfully considered as having authorised force.

[9] UNSC Res 83 (1950); UNSC Res 221 (1966); UNSC Res 695 (1990).

[10] *Security Council Report* (n 1) 3.

[11] UNSC Res 83 (1950); UNSC Res 221 (1966); UNSC Res 665 (1990).

[12] UNSC Res 678 (1990); UNSC Res 770 (1992); UNSC Res 816 (1993); UNSC Res 836 (1993); UNSC Res 875 (1993); UNSC Res 908 (1994); UNSC Res 958 (1994); UNSC Res 981 (1995); UNSC Res 1031 (1995); UNSC Res 1037 (1996) UNSC Res 1080 (1996); UNSC Res 1088 (1996); UNSC Res 1101 (1997); UNSC Res 1114 (1997); UNSC Res 1120 (1997); UNSC Res 1244 (1999); UNSC Res 1264 (1999); UNSC Res 1386 (2001); UNSC Res 1484 (2003); UNSC Res 1497 (2003); UNSC Res 1511 (2003); UNSC Res 1527 (2004); UNSC Res 1528 (2004); UNSC Res 1529 (2004); UNSC Res 1575 (2004); UNSC Res 1671 (2006); UNSC Res 1744 (2007); UNSC Res 1816 (2008); UNSC Res 1846 (2008); UNSC Res 1973 (2011); UNSC Res 2085 (2012); UNSC Res 2127 (2013); UNSC Res 2149 (2014); UNSC Res 2181 (2014); UNSC Res 2240 (2015).

[13] UNSC Res 787 (1992) paras 9–12; UNSC Res 794 (1992) paras 10, 16; UNSC Res 917 (1994) paras 1–19; UNSC Res 929 (1994) para 3; UNSC Res 940 (1994) para 4; UNSC Res 1464 (2003) para 9; UNSC Res 1778 (2007) para 6; UNSC Res 2134 (2014) para 29.

[14] Niels Blokker, 'Outsourcing the Use of Force: Towards More Security Council Control of Authorised Operations' in Marc Weller (ed), *The Oxford Handbook of the Use of Force in International Law* (Oxford University Press 2015) 209–10.

[15] Blokker, 'Outsourcing the Use of Force' (n 14) 210. Similarly, that a UN peacekeeping mission is given a mandate under Chapter VII does not automatically indicate force is authorised. See Scott Sheeran, 'The Use of Force in United Nations Peacekeeping Operations' in Weller (n 14) 365; Christine Gray, *International Law and the Use of Force* (Oxford University Press 2018) 313.

It is also worth noting that in so far as Chapter VIII concerns, the UNSC has rarely ever invoked it in authorising resolutions. Despite authorising what are arguably Chapter VIII 'regional arrangements and agencies', the UNSC in practice authorises these entities under Chapter VII. It has been noted that when the UNSC authorises these organisations (either regional organisations or collective defence alliance such as NATO) to act against a Member State or within its geographical area, the UNSC could legally rely on Chapter VIII or Article 53.[16] Where these entities are authorised to engage militarily outside of their geographical areas or against non-Member States of their organisations, the UNSC's authorisation of NATO in the Federal Republic of Yugoslavia (FRY) is a strong example of UNSC practice relying on Chapter VII (rather than Chapter VIII).

C. Authorising Language

A third observation noted is the language employed by the UNSC in its operative paragraphs when it authorises the use of force by Member States. It has employed a number of verbs in its operative paragraphs: the UNSC *recommends*, *calls upon*, *decides* or *authorises* entities to take action. On occasion, the UNSC also *reaffirms* or *reiterates* authorisation to an entity, but these resolutions usually extend the authorisation in question and do not establish it.[17]

These verbs are used in combination with explicit authorisation for Member States to use 'all necessary means' or 'all necessary measures'. On one occasion, the UNSC even expressly referred to the 'use of force, if necessary' when authorising a Member State to use force.[18] The combination of such explicit phrasing, in particular the terms 'all necessary means [or] measures' is today widely accepted as a declaration permitting the use of force.

Beyond this phrasing, the UNSC has also habitually referred to the 'use such measures commensurate to the specific circumstances as may be necessary' phrasing. UNSC practice in this regard has shown that this is one variation that has also become known as a clear authorisation of force and usually one involving more limited force (such as embargo enforcement).[19]

[16] See, extensively, Ademola Abass, *Regional Organisations and the Development of Collective Security* (Hart Publishing 2004) 66–69, 71–78. See also Danesh Sarooshi, *The United Nations and the Development of Collective Security: The Delegation by the UN Security Council of its Chapter VII Powers* (Oxford University Press 1999) 247–53; Mary O'Connell, 'The UN, NATO, and International Law after Kosovo' (2000) 22(1) *Human Rights Quarterly* 65–67, 69.

[17] See for example UNSC Res 1120 (1997).

[18] UNSC Res 221 (1966).

[19] UNSC Res 665 (1990) para 5; UNSC Res 787 (1992) para 12; UNSC Res 875 (1993) para 1; UNSC Res 917 (1994) para 10; UNSC Res 1973 (2011) para 13; UNSC Res 2240 (2015) para 10 (on a slight deviation).

Where explicit authorisation to UN peacekeeping missions' concerns, UNSC practice shows two particular patterns. The first is authorisation through the 'all necessary means [or] measures' phrasing, a similar practice of how it authorises force to Member States and regional organisations. The second manner of authorisation employs the phrasing 'take the necessary actions'. Moreover, where the UNSC employs this phrase, it always invokes Chapter VII in that paragraph. In addition, the mandate under which a peacekeeping mission is authorised to 'take the necessary actions' is almost always tied to the protection of civilians from imminent or physical violence. UNSC practice in this regard includes its authorisation to UNAMSIL (1999),[20] MONUC (2000),[21] UNMISET (2002),[22] UNMIS (2005),[23] UNAMID (2007)[24] and UNISFA (2011).[25] From 2009 and with the establishment of MINURCAT, the UNSC has preferred to use the term 'all necessary means [or] measures' when establishing or extending authorisation of force. Such explicit authorising language is evident in resolutions authorising MONUSCO (2010), UNMISS (2011), MINUSMA (2013), MINUSCA (2014) and MINUJUSTH (2017).[26]

Two exceptions should be noted here where regards authorisation to UN peacekeeping missions. These concern UNMIL established in 2003 and MINUSTAH established in 2004. Both peacekeeping missions arguably authorised force in so far as the mission's robust mandates required the use of force and were explicitly given under Chapter VII. Exceptionally, the UNSC did not employ its usual authorising language of 'all necessary means [or] measures' or 'take the necessary actions'.

D. Limitations to Authorisation: Duration and Function

A fourth observation on UNSC practice is that authorising resolutions usually also include limitations to how long force may be used. To this end, the UNSC has occasionally imposed time limitations on its authorisations. These time limitations are usually frequently given for six to 12 months at a time, after which the UNSC may decide to extend such authorisation. On occasion, the UNSC has also imposed functional limitations – suggesting that its authorisation terminates after a specific outcome or goal is achieved. This kind of limitation has sometimes been criticised since it presents difficulty in practice to determine when such functional limitation terminates the authorisation to use force.

[20] UNSC Res 1270 (1999) para 14.
[21] UNSC Res 1291 (2000) para 8.
[22] UNSC Res 1410 (2002) para 6.
[23] UNSC Res 1590 (2005) para 16.
[24] UNSC Res 1769 (2007) para 15.
[25] UNSC Res 1990 (2011) para 3.
[26] The exception to this remains the authorisation given to UNISFA.

In addition, it has been well pointed out that there exists an inherent danger when the UNSC authorises force in the absence of particular time limitations. In cases where a subsequent resolution will be required in order to terminate the authorisation, the adoption of the resolution may be frustrated by the veto power. In turn this would imply that without strict limits to its authorisation, such authorisation may be perpetual in nature. Resolution 1244 (1999) remains the most notable example, where the UNSC did not impose time limits to its authorisation.

Where extension of authorisation of force concerns, the UNSC has occasionally initially authorised the use of force but subsequently only extended a mandate without extending authorisation for the use of force. In effect, these instances meant that the initial authorisation was limited in time, and that subsequent resolutions merely extended operations without any use of force. This was evident in Resolution 1861 (2009) which extended the EU operation in the Central African Republic. Although Chapter VII was invoked in the resolution, it was only attributable to the mandate of MINURCAT. The same may be said of the UNSC authorisation for the use of force by the multinational force in Haiti in 2004 under Resolution 1529 (2004). Resolution 1542 (2009) adopted thereafter explicitly extended the force's mandate but without extending its authorisation to use force. Similarly, the invocation of Chapter VII was attributable to the mandate of MINUSTAH and not to the multinational force.[27]

Similar sentiment may be shared on the extension of UN peacekeeping missions. These resolutions usually extend the authorisation of force in explicit terms. The resolution contains an Article 39 determination, invokes Chapter VII and explicitly references the use of all necessary measures in the mandating operative paragraphs. This is certainly the more consistent practice. However, the UNSC has on occasion renewed authorisation in two divergent ways. It either adopts a resolution under Chapter VII and *decides* to extend the mandate of a mission without referencing the use of all necessary measures. This form of extension does not present problems since these resolutions invoke Chapter VII and contain an Article 39 determination. Some resolutions refer to the initial resolution that authorised the use of force and contained the reference to 'all necessary measures'.

The second manner of extension has referred solely to a peacekeeping mission's mandate. These extensions are complicated by the fact that the resolutions extending the mandate do not invoke Chapter VII. It therefore remains uncertain as to whether the UNSC intended to, beyond extending the mission's mandate, also extend the authorisation of force. The matter is given some clarity if such a resolution also contains an Article 39 determination or at the least recalls a previous authorising resolution. Beyond this, these resolutions should be treated cautiously. In particular, there should be no assumption

[27] UNSC Res 1542 (2004) para 7. See also Ch 5 at 147–148.

that when the UNSC extends a mission's mandate, it automatically also extends its authorisation to use force. In some instances, the situation on the ground may have improved significantly where the presence of a peacekeeping mission is still merited, but not its authorisation to use force. One example in this regard concerns Resolutions 1913 (2010) and 1922 (2010), which extended MINURCAT's mandate. The only reason they could be interpreted as having extended the authorisation for the use of force was their reference to MINURCAT's mandate under Resolution 1861 (2009). Resolution 1861 (2009) explicitly referred to the use of force. Even so, where such authorisation concerns, the UNSC should as a matter of certainty explicitly extend a mission's authorisation to use force.

E. Reporting Obligations

In combination with limits to its authorisation, it has been observed that one way in which the UNSC maintains overall command and control of operations it authorises is by imposing reporting obligations on entities it authorises. While these reporting obligations vary in nature, they usually involve the submission of reports to the UNSC or reporting through the UN Secretary-General.

F. Authorisation as a Last Resort

A final observation is the UNSC's consistency in adopting authorising resolutions as a 'last resort'. When authorising the use of force, authorising resolutions usually invoke a previous resolution that either already determined a situation to be a threat to peace and security or invoked Chapter VII. This implies that authorising resolutions are usually preceded by previous resolutions in which the UNSC has taken some other form of action or decision, usually non-coercive in nature. In turn, this implies that the UNSC very rarely, if ever, authorises military measures under the first resolution it adopts on a situation.

III. EXCEPTIONS TO PRIOR EXPLICIT AUTHORISATION?

Having examined the nature and character of prior explicit authorisation, subsequent chapters considered controversial cases of alleged implicit and retroactive authorisation. These cases are occasionally argued in literature and have only exceptionally been raised by States. In addition to a critical examination of these forms of authorisation, a final examination concerned some developments and practice. Chapter eight focused on two specific developments and practice. First, the very need for UNSC authorisation challenged by the development of

African regional and sub-regional organisations' security frameworks. Second, the increasing reliance placed on individual and collective self-defence, including the UNSC's own invocation of this right, suggesting formal UNSC authorisation is not required. The following sections outline some observations.

A. The Inadmissibility of Implicit Authorisation

Despite the arguably well-established practice of prior explicit UNSC authorisation, no fewer than five situations have been argued in literature (and exceptionally relied upon by States) in favour of implicit authorisation. Scholars have rightfully pointed out that the very nature of implicit authorisation presents complex legal challenges and is arguably incompatible with the UN Charter. These inconsistencies strike at the very centre of the UN Charter system of collective security. The UN Charter envisages that force be used as a last resort and that the UNSC bears primary responsibility over matters of international peace and security. In so doing, given the broad competencies bestowed upon the UNSC particularly in Chapter VII, it is no wonder that when exercising such powers, the UNSC should do so clearly and explicitly.

Nevertheless, there have been no less than five separate instances in which an implicit authorisation has arisen: Iraq (1991, 1998, 2003), FRY (1999) and Afghanistan (2001). Considering the corresponding resolutions however, the analysis has shown some interesting trends. First, while implicit authorising resolutions usually contain an Article 39 determination and invoke Chapter VII, they contain no language that can rightfully be interpreted as authorising force.[28] In other words, these resolutions lack any reference to 'all necessary means [or] measures'. Consequently, they do not direct any specific entity to take any specified action, contain no time limits to the supposed authorisation of force, and impose no reporting requirements the UNSC ordinarily includes in its authorising resolutions. Instances of resort to force based on resolutions which have allegedly implicitly authorised force also face condemnation by States. An examination of State acquiescence versus States protest shows that resolutions that have in the past explicitly authorised force face little to no criticism – the exception being those States against which measures are being taken.[29] The general sentiment, however, suggests that when the UNSC explicitly authorises the use of force, it does so based on widely accepted consensus that it has indeed authorised such force. Based on this, the incidences of supposed implicit authorisation do not necessarily set precedents in relation

[28] In the case of UNSC Res 688 (1991), it neither determined a threat to the peace nor invoked Chapter VII. See ch 6 at p 158–160.

[29] See for example the protest of North Korean against UNSC Res 83 and UNSC Res 84 (1950), and the Iraqi protests against UNSC Res 678 (1990).

to UNSC practice, nor can they be regarded as having contributed to the development of any exception to the need for explicit UNSC authorisation.[30]

Even so, the reliance placed with these resolutions as allegedly authorising force has not gone unnoticed. As has been seen, in response to justifications based on implicit authorisation, the UNSC has become more cautious to ensure that future resolutions are not construed as implicitly authorising force.[31] The resolutions adopted more recently on the situations in North Korea, Iran and Syria serve as testament to this reserved approach.[32] In conclusion and in contrast to the cases of implicit authorisation analysed, the overwhelming practice of explicit UNSC authorisation only serves to build a stronger case of an established practice, a practice that strictly dictates against implicit authorisation.

B. The Inadmissibility of Retroactive Authorisation

The analysis of instances of alleged retroactive authorisation has similarly led to several notable conclusions. It has been reasonably and correctly suggested that to accept the possibility of retroactive UNSC authorisation would be akin to accepting the unilateral use of force, subject to the mere possibility of retroactive approval of such action.[33] It is further suggested that this would in effect reverse the presumption against the use of force under Article 2(4) of the UN Charter, a well-established rule of international law.[34] Arguments suggesting an exception to this rule based on a possibility that the UNSC may subsequently approve the use of force remain unconvincing. To this end, they do not take due account of the inherently centralised collective security system under the UN Charter in which it is the UNSC that is vested with the primary responsibility of maintaining and restoring international peace and security. Alleged cases of retroactive authorisation not only displace the UNSC of this primary responsibility, but they arguably cannot account how the UNSC maintains overall control of operations it did not authorise beforehand.

To date, only three instances have been credited to a retroactive authorisation, namely, following the situations that arose in Liberia, Sierra Leone and Kosovo. In the case of the ECOWAS actions in Liberia and Sierra Leone, it was clear that the UNSC was not opposed to these actions, having on several occasions

[30] As concluded by Olivier Corten, *The Law Against War: The Prohibition on the Use of Force in Contemporary International Law* (2nd edn, Hart Publishing 2021) 354–80; Gray, *International Law and the Use of Force* (n 15) 382–83.

[31] Security Council Report, 'Security Council Action Under Chapter VII: Myths and Realities (2008) I' *Security Council Report* (Security Council Report I (2008)) 4; cf 17 on the non-necessity of invoking Chapter VII.

[32] Gray, *International Law and the Use of Force* (n 15) 383–86.

[33] Inger Österdahl, 'Preach What You Practice: The Security Council and the Legislation *Ex Post Facto* of the Unilateral Use of Force' (2005) 74(2) *Nordic Journal of International Law* 234.

[34] See also Österdahl (n 33) 234; Corten (30) 394.

commended them. However, scholars have rightfully considered this as retroactive 'approval' or 'ratification' rather than formal authorisation. Accepting such retroactive approach as authorisation would be a far stretch, especially considering that before the situation in Liberia, the UNSC had never in its existence attempted such a practice. Rather, the reference to ECOWAS in the respective UNSC resolutions was a modest approach in acknowledging facts on the ground when it decided on a longer-term peace plan in those states.

The resolution adopted following the NATO enforcement action, however, stood in contrast to the ECOWAS experience. The overwhelming criticism voiced by States against the NATO operation, combined with the fact that the UNSC made no mention of its preceding actions, seems a clear break from any parallel that may be drawn to that of the ECOWAS interventions. As a result, any comparison between these three instances would be arbitrary, neglecting the inherently different circumstances on the ground, the responses by the organisations and, in turn, the response by the UNSC.[35] Not only are all three cases examined argued in favour of retroactive authorisation, but they also represent examples of supposed implicit authorisation. As has been seen in the analysis in previous chapters, arguments in favour of implicit authorisation should be presumed against. The conclusion reasonably drawn is that cases of (implicit) retroactive authorisation stand in contrast to an overwhelming practice of prior explicit UNSC authorisation.

IV. CONTEMPORARY DEVELOPMENTS AND PRACTICE CHALLENGING THE NEED FOR UNSC AUTHORISATION?

A. The Continued Need for Authorisation in the African Regional Context

It is well established today that the UNSC may utilise regional organisations in matters of peace and security. Article 52 of the UN Charter recognises the important role that regional organisations play in matters of peace and security, and empowers the UNSC under Article 53 to authorise regional enforcement action.[36] The inclusion of the second sentence in Article 53 served to limit unilateral regional enforcement action to the extent that only action authorised by the UNSC was acceptable. The debate surrounding regional enforcement action has in recent years gained traction in the African context for several reasons. Principally because both the AU and ECOWAS have developed their security frameworks in a manner suggesting that they no longer require UNSC authorisation. This approach was first adopted by ECOWAS when it revised its founding treaty in 1993, paving the way for the 1999 ECOWAS Protocol Relating to the

[35] See ch 7 at p 193–195.

[36] Arts 52, 53, United Nations, Charter of the United Nations (adopted 26 June 1945, entered into force 24 October 1945) UNCIO XV, 335 (UN Charter).

Mechanism for Conflict Prevention, Management, Resolution, Peacekeeping and Security (Protocol Mechanism).[37] Through it, ECOWAS adopted the right to unilaterally intervene in its Member States should certain listed grounds arise. These include both external and internal situations that the Protocol Mechanism encompasses as grounds for intervention. In turn, ECOWAS developed a mechanism to ensure a capacity to intervene through ECOMOG, and proposed interventions were taken based on a two-thirds majority vote of the Authority of Heads of State and Government.

For its part, the AU followed a similar approach with its transformation from the Organisation of African Unity (OAU) and the adoption of the Constitutive Act of the African Union (Constitutive Act) in 2000.[38] Article 4(h) of the Constitutive Act remains the most controversial treaty-based attempt at unilateral enforcement action without the need for UNSC authorisation. As with ECOWAS, the AU developed a mechanism to ensure its capacity to timeously intervene in matters that threatened its Member States. To this end, African regional and sub-regional organisations have undoubtedly created mechanisms to ensure their own security. The extent to which these security frameworks have resulted in any exceptions to the need for UNSC authorisation however remains uncertain. Neither the AU nor ECOWAS have undertaken unilateral interventions in the true sense. Moreover, the AU has never applied Article 4(h) in practice, and ECOWAS has never invoked Article 25. Their subsequent practice shows that all their interventions have been based on either Chapter VII UNSC authorisation or, in the alternative, on an invitation from the internationally recognised government or head of state. This suggests that the AU has not yet realised its own security frameworks and, consequently, its practice remains in conformity with the UN Charter system of collective security. A similar sentiment may be shared on that of ECOWAS practice.

While its earlier interventions in Liberia and Sierra Leone in the 1990s suggest unilateral action, they face plausible arguments in favour of grounding these interventions based on an invitation by the legitimate head of state. All of its other interventions were based either on Chapter VII UNSC authorisation, or intervention by invitation. As such, it also seems that ECOWAS has as yet not realised its own security instruments, and it is reasonable to conclude that it has also remained in conformity with the UN Charter system of collective security. The result thereof is that even in the African context where regional organisations have evidently developed a right to unilateral intervention, their

[37] Revised Treaty of the Economic Community of West African States (ECOWAS) (adopted 24 July 1993, entered into force 23 August 1995) (Revised ECOWAS Treaty); ECOWAS, Protocol Relating to the Mechanism for Conflict Prevention, Management, Resolution, Peacekeeping and Security (adopted 10 December 1999, entered 1 January 2000).

[38] African Union, Constitutive Act of the African Union (adopted 11 July 2000, entered into force 26 May 2001) 2158 UNTS 3 (AU Constitutive Act).

subsequent practice suggests that they continue to interpret Article 53(1) UNSC authorisation as a requirement.

B. The Invocation of Self-Defence in UNSC Resolutions

Whereas the development of African regional security frameworks prima facie seems to have challenged the very need for UNSC authorisation, the right of individual and collective self-defence is a clear exception to the prohibition of force requiring no UNSC authorisation. There is a history of UN Member States relying on the right of individual or collective self-defence as a basis for their resort to force. In principle, they concern inherently different considerations, as self-defence stands as a separate exception to Article 2(4).

Be that as it may, States have at times based their actions not only (nor strictly) on a right of self-defence, but also on the recognition of such a right in UNSC resolutions. The clearest examples remain Resolutions 1368 and 1373 (2001), adopted following the 11 September terrorist attacks against the United States, in which the UNSC *recognised* and subsequently *reaffirmed* the right.[39] The invocation of Article 51 (or generally the right of self-defence) in UNSC resolutions has rightfully raised a number of questions. Most notable of these is whether the UNSC authorises force (implicitly) by virtue of the recognition of the right of self-defence. Chapter six considered this very question, ultimately concluding that the invocation of self-defence in UNSC resolutions is not akin to an authorisation. Least of which because the right of self-defence requires no UNSC authorisation and that the right stands separately to such authorisation, at the disposal of States and not the UNSC itself.

The UNSC's acknowledgement of an alternative legal basis for resort to force is not limited to the right of self-defence. It is worth recalling Resolution 2337 (2017), in which the UNSC formally recognised incoming President Adama Barrow as president of The Gambia. In addition, it *expressed* its support for ECOWAS efforts to ensure, *by political means first*, the respect of the will of the people of The Gambia. This resolution, together with others seemingly recognising or even encouraging a right of self-defence such as Resolution 2449 (2015), suggests an emerging practice whereby the UNSC acknowledges a right to use force without itself authorising force. This practice has been rightfully described as a self-marginalisation by the UNSC of its primary responsibility in matters of international peace and security.[40]

[39] UNSC Res 1368 (2001) preamble para 3; UNSC Res 1373 (2001) preamble para 4.

[40] See the important remarks by Jules Lobel and Michael Ratner, 'Bypassing the Security Council: Ambiguous Authorizations to Use Force, Cease-Fires and the Iraqi Inspection Regime' (1999) 93 (1) *American Journal of International Law* 124, specifically at 135.

V. CONCLUDING OBSERVATIONS

There can be little doubt today that prior explicit UNSC authorisation of force is a well-established practice. That practice undoubtedly entails a combination of characteristics in authorising resolutions. These include explicit determinations of threats to international peace and security (which UNSC practice suggests is broadly construed), the invocation of Chapter VII (or VIII) as instrumental for interpreting a resolution as authorising force, and operative paragraphs explicitly in which the UNSC *authorises, decides* or *calls upon* entities to 'use all necessary means' or 'measures'. The entity authorised may be specific Member States, or Member States acting nationally or through regional organisations, specified regional organisations, collective defence alliances, UN peacekeeping missions or regional peacekeeping initiatives.

In combination with the above, authorising resolutions usually also have additional characteristics that are imposed as a matter of procedure under the UN Charter. For example, they contain a certain objective or set of objectives sufficiently detailed. They impose a certain time period during which such action may be taken. Subsequent resolutions may extend such authorisation, provided they do so explicitly. Moreover, authorising resolutions also tend to impose a certain degree of reporting requirements on the entities they authorise. On several occasions, Member States have been directed to report directly to the UN Secretary-General on measures taken pursuant to a resolution. Time frames for reporting differ between several weeks to several months. UNSC resolutions that do not contain the above elements or purport to implicitly or retroactive authorise the use of force are to be presumed against.

When all is said and done, caution must be underlined. First, resolutions that do not impose some form of time limit to entities they authorise could in effect render such authorisation perpetual. Because authorisation for the use of force is granted under Chapter VII, a new resolution also under that chapter is needed to terminate a mandate. This presents a dangerous situation in which the UNSC could authorise the use of force without a time limit, and then later be unable to terminate such authorisation because of the veto.[41] In addition, the mere invocation of Chapter VII is insufficient to authorise force.

The analysis has also raised two final considerations. The first concerns the legal basis of UNSC-authorised enforcement action. It is submitted that such a basis can only be that of Article 42 read together with Article 48(1) or, in the alternative, Article 53 of the UN Charter. As has been mentioned, when the UNSC authorises the use of force, it does so under its Chapter VII and VIII powers. Arguments suggesting Article 51 as a legal basis for UNSC

[41] Karine Bannelier and Théodore Christakis, 'Between Flexibility and Accountability: How Can the Security Council Strengthen Oversight of Use-of-Force Mandates?' in Jeremy Farrall and Hilary Charlesworth (eds), *Strengthening the Rule of Law Through the UN Security Council* (Routledge 2016) 211–12.

enforcement action seemingly convolute key distinctions between self-defence and collective security.[42]

Finally, concerning UNSC practice whereby it acknowledges or recognises a legal basis to use force but without itself authorising force, the following should be noted. The fact that the UNSC recognises an alternative legal basis for resort to force without itself authorising force is not tantamount to an implicit authorisation. The potential for the UNSC to adopt such a habit of recognition rather than authorisation does not impede the existence of the alternative legal basis nor the right of Member States or regional organisations to resort to it. While this emerging practice may perhaps be one way in which the UNSC could overcome the threat of the veto, it may too be representative of a tacit abdication. Such a conclusion points all the more reason as to why the UNSC should be more explicit. Recognising a right to resort to force cannot usurp its power of authorising force. Such a power remains in the hands of the UNSC, which inherently holds primary responsibility over matters of international peace and security.

[42] See broadly Michael Wood, 'Self-Defence and Collective Security: Key Distinctions' in Weller (n 14) 650–54.

Index

www.ingramcontent.com/pod-product-compliance
Ingram Content Group UK Ltd.
Pitfield, Milton Keynes, MK11 3LW, UK
UKHW021029041026
15470UKWH00013B/948

9 781509 971251